DETOUR

DETOUR

Grace H. Kaiser

Good Books

Intercourse, Pennsylvania 17534

Published by Good Books, Intercourse, PA 17534

Design by Dawn J. Ranck

Cover design and illustration by Cheryl A. Benner

DETOUR

Copyright © 1990 by Grace H. Kaiser

International Standard Book Number: 0-934672-87-3

Library of Congress Card Catalog Number: 90-3361

Library of Congress Cataloging-in-Publication Data

Kaiser, Grace H.
    Detour / Grace H. Kaiser.
        p.   cm.
    ISBN 0-934672-87-3 : $15.95
    1. Kaiser, Grace H. — Health.   2. Obstetricians — Pennsylvania — Lancaster County —
Biography.   3. Gynecologists — Pennsylvania — Lancaster County — Biography.   4. Osteopaths —
Pennsylvania — Lancaster County — Biography.   5. Physically handicapped — Pennsylvania —
Lancaster County — Biography.   6. Amish — Pennsylvania — Lancaster County — Social life and
Customs.   I. Title.
RG76.K34A3   1990
618.2′0092 — dc20
[B]
                                                                                    90-3361
                                                                                    CIP

This book is dedicated to my husband, to Peter who has picked me from the floor more times than I wish to remember, held my arm to guide me over places my legs could not walk alone. He prodded me when I became discouraged and remained by my side when many marriages would have been shattered by the sudden addition of a disabled mate.

These stories are true. Most names and places have been changed and relocated. In several chapters experiences have been combined to create a continuous story. The excerpts from Peter's journal are printed as he wrote them.

Table of Contents

"In the middle of the journey of our life I
came to myself within a dark wood where the
straight way was lost."

Dante
The Divine Comedy

1
Blizzard

People die in blizzards. Sometimes they get lost in the whirling frenzy and their frozen bodies lie in an isolated furrow or among corn stubble and are not found until the snow melts.

Growing up in eastern Pennsylvania, I had watched blizzards from behind window panes, in the comfort of warm rooms but had never seen a winter snowstorm unleashed on Lancaster County. Never had it been my responsibility to clash with this adversary. It would happen some day, and the knowledge that my rural patients expected their doctor to meet any villainous weather chilled me as snowflakes sifted into the barren pear tree and blew against mounded rose bushes. I dreaded snowstorms.

Blizzards hold awesome terror and beauty in their majestic power. Stories of people lost in drifts, frozen stiff, fingers and toes turning black and falling off, were among Grandfather's retold legends. Until his death, he relived the blizzard of 1888 in vivid detail at each winter's first flakes.

In the gray dusk Pete and I watched snowflakes of a predicted blizzard pirouette across our brown barn in fairy dances. They swirled against the faded wooden garage and dropped exhausted into an infant drift fingering its way across the drive.

My husband put an arm around me. "I'm sure glad it's Friday and

I don't have to think about leaving the house until Monday," he said, shivering at the thought.

By bedtime only a little muffled traffic traveled New Holland's streets. The night was occasionally punctuated by a broken tire chain thumping a fender in sharp rhythm as some adventuresome soul braved the snowy night. The streetlight across Main Street was a milky blur. Icy blasts churned drifted snow with the falling flakes. It blew down the fireplace chimney, sending ashes into the living room. The storm wailed through the naked elm trees like sirens.

"Hope all my pregnant women stay quiet," I said at bedtime, pulling my nightgown over my head. "I've stocked up on bread and milk like everybody else. If the storm doesn't take down the electric lines, we'll be warm and fed. I got out the campstove and some candles, just in case." The quilts pulled around my neck gave a warm safe feeling.

Pallid morning showed no letup. Spruce trees behind the house sagged with vanilla frosting. Our driveway was closed. An occasional truck drove the street. It was a day to crawl into a warm hole, curl up and watch others flounder in the drifts.

As positive as an engraved invitation, the telephone rang, requesting my presence at a birthing. No R.S.V.P. possible.

"Emma'll be needin' ya after while," Marvin Weaver said. "No hurry but in this weather ya better start out. Her labor ain't too strong yet."

Emma, why Emma, far out in the country? Why Emma, tenth pregnancy, twins the last time, maybe trouble at this birthing? Could I even get to her? She would need a doctor, not a neighbor or husband substitute. It would be better for me to reach her for the planned home birth than try to get her out and end up in a snowbank. "Your road open?" I asked.

"I think so, but not our lane. I'll meet ya at the highway with the tractor in an hour and bring you into the house. Okay?"

"Okay." But it was not okay. Neither my husband nor I owned a four-wheel drive. Even traveling in New Holland without it would be risky. The Weaver's serpentine lane followed along a tree-edged creek that caught wind and snow for nearly a mile. No other road in. I must have a 4×4. Last summer George Hoover, a block down Main Street, had offered his Jeep if I ever needed transportation in a storm. I had to use it.

Pete threw a shovel into the Jeep and sat beside George. I took my office nurse Anna Good with us. She would be an extra pair of hands, dressing the baby and enjoying the emotional high that birthing a baby gives the participants. Wrapped in blue wool hat, heavy red coat and swathed in a green plaid muffler, Anna squeezed in beside me on the back seat. Every time we opened the Jeep's door or met an icy blast, cold wind stung our faces and squinted our eyes. I was glad that I did not have to fight the blizzard alone.

Certain that the shortcut back roads through the farmlands would be drifted shut, we drove to Blue Ball and west. The blowing snow mingled with the new flakes obscuring roads, fences and ditches. The landscape melted together in an opaque distorted haze.

George knew that the road lay between telephone poles on one roadbank and electric poles on the other. He steered down the middle hoping we met no other cars navigating the same course. Our tire chains grabbed the snow sending us through drifts we could not see until they flew over us like hurricane waves crashing the bow of a ship. At times we moved ahead in a straight line; sometimes we slid drunkenly along the crown of the road.

Passing through crossroad villages, houses stood out in blurred silhouettes, their gloomy windows dark sunken eyes. "Looks like we're coming into Hinkletown," George called from within the wrappings of a gray muffler. The vapor of his words rose in a steamy cloud.

Staring intently into the storm, we nearly missed Marvin waiting at the roadside. He jumped from his caterpillar tractor like a huge black bear charging from its winter den, shook snow from his coat and exhaled mist like a smokestack. "Glad you made it. Emma's fine yet. We'll hafta go through the fields. I'll break the way with the tractor." Snow dusted Marvin's long lashes and stubbled cheeks, closely framed by a black leather hat that fit over his ears and neck. He squinted through our open door. "Okay?"

"Yes," George agreed, slim shoulders shrinking deeper into his red mackinaw as a gust of cold wind rattled the Jeep's canvas roof. He pulled his brown wool cap over his ears, revved the engine and nodded to the bear.

"Follow me." Marvin kicked the tractor to loosen snow from his knee-high gum boots and heaved himself onto the caterpillar seat, grasping its control levers with hands clothed in bulky black gloves.

Off across the field. Sometimes stuck, backing up to churn forward, grinding in low gear, rushing forward, always the clanking tractor ahead, always snow in the wind and under our spinning, sliding wheels.

Halfway to the house we stopped, the Jeep engine roared, wheels whirling. "The transmission. Guess we tore the rear out." George moaned, rubbing his reddened beakish nose. "We're as far as we'll go."

Pete and George got out, tromping around in snow to their boot tops. We watched them mutter and gesture.

Marvin backed the tractor to the Jeep. "I'll take the women into the house on the tractor then we can see about your Jeep. It'll take two trips."

Powdery snow filled my boots as I stepped out of the Jeep to stand on the tractor hitch that last summer had coupled Marvin's plow. With one hand I clutched the black bag needed for Emma's delivery, the other gripped the tractor seat. We crept over the fields, the clanking caterpillar tracks braiding wide bands in the snow. Wind-driven flakes knifed my cheeks and blinded me. The only protection was behind Marvin. I was disoriented in the bland landscape, but Marvin knew his geography. Finally his snow-smudged red barn emerged through the white curtain. At the wire yard fence I dismounted onto a shoveled walk to the house. Marvin returned to fetch Anna.

The old stuccoed stone farmhouse took on a fresh clean face in its plaster of snow. Its dark shuttered windows looked like the black openings into ancient cliff dwellings.

At the kitchen door I shook snow from my corduroy slacks, took off my boots, knocked out the snow and entered stocking-footed. I warmed myself at the hot space heater. It felt like the best thing that had happened to me that day.

The room seemed filled with children. Mary and Barbara put dishes away into the cupboard. Their brother John, in a lounge chair, read a book. Three little boys played quietly with wooden cows and horses on the couch near the space heater that crackled with fresh coal. Twin brother and sister, the youngest children at four, crayoned a Sears catalogue at a long linoleum-covered table. All the boys wore work pants and blue shirts. Elva, the eldest, wore a white net cap, covering over hair combed into a bun at the nape of her neck. The little girls wore gingham dresses. Two older girls wore a cape and apron in the style of Old Order Mennonites.

Marvin Weaver's family belonged to a group of Mennonites that allowed tractors in the field but no modern conveniences in the house. A bucket of water pumped from the well sat with a long-handled dipper in the lead-lined dry sink.

For transportation Marvin and Emma rode in a horse-drawn black buggy on errands to Ephrata or New Holland. Every other Sunday they drove their horse to the frame church enclosed by wagon sheds, the cemetery and the highway. An iron pump poked through the scuffed grass of the gravel churchyard like a periscope.

Unmarried boys and girls rode bicycles everywhere. On Sunday afternoons they clustered on country roads like swarming bees. Men often biked on errands, but older women usually walked or harnessed a horse to wagon or buggy.

Elva, sixteen, was in charge of the Weaver kitchen. She poured hot cornmeal mush into pans at the brown enameled coal range. Several kettles whispered gentle steam, salivating bubbles that danced across the hot iron plates until they disappeared. She asked Eva, thirteen, to hang my snowy hooded coat behind the stove and Barbara to carry the mush into the washhouse. "Mom's in the bedroom." Her voice was soft. She nodded toward a closed door and blushed.

I pulled my boots back on and entered the bedroom. Its combed varnished trim was scuffed from years of habitation. Glare from the snow pierced white lace curtains and reflected on bare walls and peeling paper once bright with roses. Marvin's Sunday suit and several dresses hung from hangers and metal hooks on a board nailed against one wall. An antique bed, with high headboard and sleigh footboard, was spread with a plastic sheet and covered with a newspaper pad according to instructions. A wash basin sat on the matching oak dresser.

Emma paced the worn linoleum floor; her long muslin nightgown swayed around brown felt slippers as she moved toward the square brown space heater to turn warming baby clothes. "I stay in here to be away from the children," she said. The smile that wrinkled her jowled face assured me that she was in control of her labor. During a contraction she held her pendent abdomen, smiled again and pushed loose gray hair under her cap. "Not right away," she said. "But with this blizzard we thought you oughta start out in plentya time."

Anna came into the room, her face apple-red from the whipping snow of her tractor ride. "The men are out in the field digging and pulling the Jeep out." She laid a towel-wrapped pack of sterile clamps and scissors on a plank bottom chair, drew Pitocin into a syringe and checked the warming baby blankets.

Anna and I rocked in cushioned parlor chairs two hours, past noon dinner, while Emma labored. After one hour the men came into the kitchen, glad to be warm and out of the frigid relentless wind. Marvin checked on the bedroom progress frequently until time to stay with his wife during the birthing. George and Pete shed boots and coats and waited on the kitchen couch.

Over all my years of practice, if there was anything that impressed Pete about any of my patients, it was the quiet obedience and behavior of those ten Weaver children. Elva, with the help of her sisters, dished out a meal of mashed potatoes, fried sausage with gravy, home-canned string beans, fresh baked bread, applesauce, jars of peaches and chocolate cake. Marvin ate with them but the men on the couch declined. The meal finished, the boys went to feed the steers and open the lane with tractor and shovel. The girls cleaned the kitchen.

My concerns for Emma's birthing, our isolation should she hemorrhage or be unable to deliver, were unnecessary. When the patient finally stopped walking and agreed to lie down, birth was ten minutes away. With Emma's final push came a wet black-haired head, corrugated by pressure as it crowned the perineum, next a fat-cheeked face. I wiped away the flood of fluid and mucus from the baby's nose as it tumbled onto the bed. It coughed and cried but stopped when she felt the warmed blankets. Until the baby girl gave her first lusty cry, no one in the kitchen knew Emma's labor was over.

Anna and I cleaned up and packed up. The children in the kitchen filed into the bedroom to see their new sister. Each one held her a moment before we laid the baby beside Emma. Anna and I talked about the tedious trip home, wondering if the highway had been completely closed in the past hours.

"The boys opened the lane. The Jeep's okay," Pete said. "We were hung up on a drift with all the wheels spinning in the snow." He pulled on boots, hat and a bulky brown corduroy coat. He looked like an overstuffed chair. I interpreted the grin that spread over his round face as happiness in heading home.

"Son John says there's a snowplow waiting for ya at the end of the lane to help ya home," Marvin announced as we layered ourselves into the Jeep.

Before the birth we had seen through the bedroom windows that the snow had stopped and the sun come out. But I was not prepared for the dazzling, blinding brilliance. A breathless silence claimed the land. Snow drifts cast no shadows. Height and depth indistinguishable, the rolling fields and fence rows appeared level from one distant tree line to the next. The land was as unblemished as the newborn cuddled in Emma's arms. Until we reached the highway, the only sound was the winding churning creek and the Jeep engine, muted by the snow.

The snowplow driver hailed us, "Glad to see ya. Waited here in case ya had any emergency."

"Thank you," I said. The possibility always made me uneasy. "How long have you waited?"

"'Bout an hour. According to the radio, New Holland is completely isolated, declared a state of emergency." The driver climbed into the cinder-loaded dump truck. "Follow me. I'll take ya home." He gunned his engine, lowered the great V-blade and plowed east into the drifts of Route 322.

All the side roads were bank full with blizzard. As the plow sliced drift after drift, crimping white margins like the crinkled edge of a pie crust, we marveled that we had traveled this road four hours ago.

Nothing moved around us. Not even a crow skimmed the turquoise sky. Smug behind the carving plow, we debated how many days before farms on the horizon could travel their roads again, how many gallons of milk would be poured onto the ground before silver beetle milk trucks could suck out bulk tanks. A few herdsmen would haul milk cans by sleigh or wagon out to a plowed main road for pickup. By evening fences would be cut open and newly rutted field lanes packed by wagons and tractors on their way to the outside world. Tomorrow, Sunday services would be cancelled; Monday, the schools closed until buses could travel safely.

During blizzards snowplow drivers worked around the clock, exhausted but grateful for time-and-a-half and double-time tax money. Winters with too many snows depleted appropriations and made unhappy commissioners juggle funds.

Several miles west of Blue Ball, we met a black car hopelessly stuck in the ditch. When the plow stopped, two young men and two girls, clothed only in sweaters, nothing on their shoes, stepped out into hip-deep snow chattering that they had driven from Philadelphia to see what the blizzard on the radio was like. Philadelphia and Downingtown had had only a dusting of snow. Pete and George, aided by the plow, pulled them from the drift and turned them back toward Downingtown. They followed our Jeep. Amazed at city people's foolishness, we shook our heads. No native would go without chains or snow tires scantily dressed into a snowstorm.

Through Blue Ball and along Route 23 into New Holland, heavily coated and gloved snow shovelers stopped digging out driveways to watch our parade behind the plow. Several pickups and cars followed us to our house, then to George's edge of town where the plow turned back to Blue Ball and eastward.

The tourists from Philadelphia may have considered the blizzard a winter picnic, but I was thankful that I had been able to reach Emma without freezing to death in a snowbank, that her delivery was uneventful, that the plow had waited and brought us home.

The fireplace at 561 West Main Street felt as warm and friendly as the people helping each other through the snow. Life was good and would go on forever. I would retire when I was too old and feeble to practice. In my declining years I saw myself visiting former patients, rocking and chatting in their cozy farm kitchens. But fantasies are not truth.

2
Pizzicato

Even today I cannot believe that it all happened, that life without warning can dogleg so rapidly into an unpredictable direction.

"Never in a thousand years," I kept saying to friends who came to gaze over my hospital bedrails and offer condolences. "Never could I imagine myself disabled." Me, two-steps-at-a-time mother and doctor, vigorous and indefatigable.

Pete and I, with another couple, had chosen Starlight Campground to manage a square dance weekend reminiscent of the many we had conducted when we owned Spring Gulch Campground.

One final pizzicato and it was over. I was alive, but I could not move. Death had swooped down in a streak of orange light. Its searing talons had seized me, let go. Paralysis was immediate. I fell like a soggy scrub rag. The tent camper shook on impact. The floor was dark, cold against my cheek.

Only a second before I had looked over my shoulder to see what trapped my left leg as I slid along a bench behind the table. I reached for a sleeping bag on the far bunk. The light cord wrapped my left ankle, released.

Then the blow between the eyes. A fiery blaze. My legs and hips seemed to rise to an impossible right angle above my body before they drifted in phantom slow motion to a contorted tangle on the floor.

Pete's steps crunched gravel between the shower house and our campsite.

"Come in, Pete," I called. "I fell and really hurt myself."

My husband opened the camper door. "What happened?" He shone his flashlight over my limp body. "I heard the thump outside."

"Run your hands over my legs." I waited a moment. "Did you do it?"

"Yes, pinched them too."

"I didn't feel anything."

"Shine your light on my face. What is trickling from my nose?"

"Blood." Pete answered.

"Good." At impact my body had hurled against the edge of the bunk like a discus at full speed. My head felt as if it had been split open from the inside. I was sure that I had fractured my skull. If it were possible for clear fluid around the brain to leak through the nose after an injury, I was in bad trouble. I was a doctor. My diagnoses ran wild journeys. Where was my injury? What had happened?

"Don't let anyone touch me or move me," I told Pete. Survival could depend upon the way I was moved. We had driven Pete's van. No car phone. "Go down to the campground office and call the special ambulance from Community Hospital in Lancaster."

It was an ambulance equipped for trauma, heart attacks or other catastrophic emergencies. Specially trained paramedics stood by around the clock, ready to speed away in the ambulance parked outside the emergency room door. I wanted to be moved by experts.

"Okay. I'll get somebody to be with you until I get back." I heard Pete run to the campsite across the driveway and ask Mary Stoner to stay with me.

"Let's cover you with a blanket," Mary said. She stood outside the camper at my head while Pete hurried down the mountain. "Do you hurt anywhere?"

"No."

"Anything I can do for you?"

"No," I answered.

We did not speak much but I heard her breathing in the doorway.

Her feet grated on the gravel.

"Can they come? Were they out on a call?" I asked Pete when he returned. I pulled myself into consciousness.

"They're on the way. Twenty miles will take awhile, even for an ambulance," he said.

"Don't move me," I repeated to the volunteer ambulance crew from Brickerville who came to strap a collar around my neck by request of Lancaster's emergency room. They fastened the thick collar and stayed, with their ambulance, to assist if needed. Time hung in black limbo on the cold air. We waited. Hushed voices mumbled outside the camper. Shoes crunched stones as people shifted feet or came and went.

"Where's that ambulance?" I asked several times. Lost? No siren cut night's silent curtain. How long did I lie under the blanket in my underwear drifting in and out of consciousness? Even the beeper I wore in my bra was silent. I thought about the happy weekend we had planned.

Our first childless weekend in many years. Pete and I had driven twenty-five miles west into the Furnace Hills area. The velvet October air was heavy with the odor of dank earth, speckled with gold and amber falling leaves. The narrow road twisted beneath the forest canopy. At the campground we spiraled hairpin turns to a campsite overlooking miles of wrinkled calico hills, red and yellow maples, green pine and spruce and brown fall oaks.

We had opened our camper and searched for firewood that I used to cook steaks. Inside the camper Pete clamped an overhead light to a strut that supported the camper's top. He ran a cord down the side and over the bench to a socket.

Accustomed to several decades of child watching, there seemed little to say in the void of watchful discipline. In two years our last child would leave for college. I wondered what couples talked about after their children left home. What common bond held them together. Nothing broke the awkward silence as we prepared our campsite and dressed for the square dance.

Friday the thirteenth was nearly over when Pete and I drove up the hill after the dance in the recreation hall. We would lie in our sleeping bags, smell the moist woods, listen to leaves sift onto the canvas roof, perhaps hear an owl hoot through the trees.

Pete walked to the shower house. I took off my dress and crinoline petticoat. It would be nice to sleep with my husband on one bed instead of alone, separated by the table and benches. I slid along the bench behind the table, stretched to reach a sleeping bag on the far bunk when my foot caught in the light cord. It released, hurling me forward. I lay on the floor, waiting.

"Isn't the ambulance here yet?" I asked several times, rousing to consciousness. "Can you hear it coming?" Often I had waited beside a patient for the welcome cry of a siren.

At last a pale lament, like the night yowl of distant dogs, then the modulating whine until it became a scream. Finally, blinking red lights reflected into my dark corner.

"What a trip up this mountain. Couldn't make good time, even with the state police escorting us as far as the campground," the ambulance crew complained. They conferred, deciding on the best way to apply a backboard to a woman scrunched in a heap, wedged between a table leg and the back wall of the camper. "Relax," they reassured me. "We'll soon have you out."

A tent camper is no more than a cube on wheels. Floor space is scarce. Ours had two beds that unfolded over the ground when in use. Lying with my face against one metal corner, it was impossible to see anything. The bleeding from my nose had stopped. Muffled voices seemed far away. Most of the time I felt drowsy but responded "no" when asked if I was cold, felt any pain or had a headache.

Strong arms pushed straps under my body, securing me to the backboard. The ambulance attendants spoke to me as they worked, explaining each step. Later Pete told me that the canvas top of the camper was unsnapped and the table removed. The night air revived me like a splash of cold water as I was lifted over the edge of the trailer, turned on my back and carried to the ambulance. Its familiar medicinal odors, the green oxygen tank against the bulkhead, the blood pressure cuff on my arm were comforting. I felt safe.

The ride out of the campground was a trip down a corkscrew. No wonder the men on the ambulance complained about the curves. I conversed with the attendants, spoke over the intercom to Terri, emergency care specialist. "No, I can breathe fine," I answered when she asked about respirations in order to determine if my injury was high enough in the neck to affect the nerves that control breathing. She laughed at a patient who answered instead of the crew. During Terri's days as a medical student, she had been a guest in my home, traveled night's country roads and sped down bleak farm lanes with me as we raced to home births.

Lying in the camper, I had felt no pain. It began in the bouncing, vibrating, boxy ambulance. Every sensory nerve fiber seemed over-stimulated, stood on end, scoured raw with sandpaper. Each crack and seam in the road felt like a pothole, accentuating and intensifying my agony. Would we never reach the hospital? I was crying with agitation and pain when we backed up to the emergency room doors.

The emergency room was warm and comforting. I was surrounded by familiar walls and faces. Often I had passed through these doors with patients on a rush trip to surgery or the delivery room.

At 2:00 a.m. I wondered if the orthopedic surgeon, whom I knew, and the strange neurosurgeon from General Hospital across town were called from bed or dragged away from a party . It was good to see them, but their presence prior to tests or X rays confirmed my conviction that this injury was serious, even life threatening. I was carefully undressed and gowned for x-ray.

The nurse handed Pete my beeper before she scissored my bra up the front. Men wore beepers on their belts, but I had no belt or pockets. Once at a banquet I had carried it in my purse and did not hear its signal. My answering service had been frantic, trying to locate me for a patient in labor. Mid-bra against the skin was the best place.

Strangers stared the first time they heard the beep, watching me dive and grope to find the "off" button. I pretended that mine was accepted procedure and the gawker unconventional. One Sunday morning during the sermon our minister mistook my beeper for the signal to turn his cassette over as he taped his sermon for shut-ins. I wore it at the Starlight weekend in case a woman began labor.

Except for the ride on the litter, taking the X rays remains hazy. Back in the emergency room both physicians examined, pinched, squeezed, pricked my legs and body up to my head. I could not move my arms or lift a finger. My legs did not respond when I tried to bend the knees or flex a foot.

"Nothing fractured or dislocated," the doctors said. "Wiggle your toes." On the left foot nothing happened. The big toe on the right foot answered with the slightest movement, a banner too heavy for the air. I lifted my head to watch its feeble attempt.

"Good, wonderful," the orthopedist said. "She doesn't need me. I might as well go home."

"You'll get it back again," the neurosurgeon said, meaning mobility. He smiled. "We'll send you upstairs. I'll write orders and keep tabs on you."

"How long before I can get back to the office?" I asked, seeing in my mind the long list of women who would need me the next months. Who would care for Emma Hoover confined to bed in Vogansville, threatening to deliver a seven-month baby? Annie Stoltzfus from White Horse would soon birth twins. I thought of Martha Martin and all the other women who depended on me to drop whatever I was doing and go to their bedsides when their husbands phoned. Many patients had never had another doctor deliver them. Next week's appointments must be cancelled. But how? Some people used public telephones or their neighbor's. It would require careful planning, and someone to cover my practice until I could work again. With all the farm accidents in twenty-eight years of practice, I had seen no spinal-cord-injured patients, but remembering medical school classes, I knew it would require weeks to recover.

"Nine months to a year," the doctor answered.

I hung my hope and future on his promise. Life without a list of women due to deliver babies, without office appointments, away from telephone or beeper was inconceivable. From that moment the days, weeks, months, were a countdown toward nine.

Nine months. A long time. Occasional summer camping trips of four weeks always seemed endless.

A medical practice is necessarily a business. While the emergency room nurse prepared me for bed, I gave Pete instructions. Office nurse Edie would not be needed. Betts could continue to answer the phone, keep records and reroute patients to other doctors until I returned to the office next summer.

"No use paying for a car phone," I said. "Might as well take it out.

Return the beeper to Ephrata too. Tell Patsy at the answering service who will cover my practice."

The treatment and prognosis of spinal cord injuries were as foreign to me as the fevers and cures of deepest Africa. My longest hospital stay had been a routine five postpartum days. Nine months was not the rest of my life. I resolved to do whatever was needed to hammer down that time. I would accept the verdict, be a model patient, focusing on the promise and filled with hope.

"You'll get it back. Nine months to a year." I tatooed these words into my brain, read and reread them through winter and spring into summer. I had asked an honest question. Deception was unbelievable.

I was comforted by the thought that nine months was not forever. Our children were grown and did not need me. The next months would not be easy, but I could resume my practice and continue life as before. Resigned to accept my injury, I resolved to shorten the nine months. Sleep came easily.

3

Hospital Daze

Saturday, first hospital day after the accident, was distorted. Like Alice in Wonderland, I had passed through the mirror. The world appeared mangled. Instead of standing beside the bed giving orders, I was in it, even basic self-care impossible. The rigid handle on the door had more motion than I as it swung open and shut all day with nurses recording vital signs, giving cortisone, turning me every two hours. They checked IVs and the Foley catheter that drained my bladder.

While the last twelve years of my twenty-eight-year rural practice had been limited to obstetrics, the rest of medicine had jetted into new territory. The procedures on this hospital wing were a trip into a foreign land. The landscape and its people cast strange shadows. New phrases, letters and abbreviations rolled off tongues as rapidly as the nurses moving room to room.

My hands seemed alien when the nurse lifted them at my morning bath. They were like the clawed ones that grope the edges of caskets in horror movies. Without nerve supply, the muscles had collapsed against the bones like wilted flowers hugging their stems. Even the tortuous blue veins had disappeared. The palms were flat, cupless, as the nurse stretched out spastic fingers to wipe hands insensitive and numb. The hand resumed fist position when released.

The hands, wrists and arms that had delivered several thousand babies, changed flat tires along country roads, thrown my children over one shoulder and down the other looked as if I had been on a six-week fast.

Only last week I had jogged New Holland streets on crisp October evenings. Now my legs seemed lifeless, vericosities sunken into collapsed muscles. "My legs feel ice cold," I said.

"Your legs are toasty warm," the nurse assured me. "Just yell if you want anything. We're right across the hall." Pressing a call button was impossible. Screaming "nurse" until one heard me was demeaning. It reminded me of withered, toothless, disoriented elderly patients restrained in bed and chair calling pitifully for nurse and family.

My husband hung a clay windchime above my head. I lifted my head and grasped the leather thong in my teeth, but it had to hang inches above my face. On the second day I pulled too hard. The chime fell, hit me on the head, bounced to the floor and broke. I resigned myself to shouting.

"What name do you want us to call you?" the nurse asked the routine question on admission.

Immobility was new, but inside lived a member of the medical staff. I had always been addressed as Doctor Kaiser. Why should I demand less respect than when I walked the halls and wrote orders? Little remained other than my name. "Doctor Kaiser," I answered.

When I requested a mirror, I saw a swollen nose between puffy black-and-blue eyes. "Who won the fight?" the nurse asked. Laughing hurt my head. A small towel rolled under my neck relieved pain where the vertebrae hyper-extended as I fell.

Saturday afternoon my wedding band felt tight as my fingers began to swell. A nurse soaped, wiggled and pulled to work it over the thickened knuckle.

A nurse checking vital signs Saturday evening aroused me from heavy sleep. "What is your normal pulse?" Stuporous,I told her that it was usually about eighty. Within minutes she returned with Doctor Jack, the house physician. I had known him as he traveled through medical school, internship and residency. Now he was in charge of me.

"What is it?" I asked, too groggy to open my eyes.

"Thirty-five," he said.

"It's never been that low before." After two atropine injections my heart rate improved and I became alert.

That first weekend the muscle spasms began. Leg muscles contracted in knots like those that had made me pace the floor when calcium levels fell during pregnancies. This time I could not walk or rub them. My calcium was normal. I did not know that the uncontrollable jerks were due to interruption of cord impulses caused by my injury. The spasms were not painful but my jumping legs shook my body. Antispasmotics had little effect.

Intermittent impulses, charges of electricity, began to fly down my arms and legs. They zipped to the tips of fingers and toes in bursts of burning sparks, like exploding sky rockets on July Fourth.

If only someone had explained that spasms were a part of spinal cord injuries, that I would be a spastic the rest of my life, I would have understood and known what to expect. I thought of chickens beheaded for Sunday dinner on my childhood farm. They had twitched and jumped after Grandfather's axe chopped off their heads. Little of my symptoms or recovery was discussed with me. Time unraveled the story of my accident and what it meant.

If I as a physician did not know what to expect, I have often wondered how other patients survive tragic accidents. My medical background was often an asset in recovery, but the experience was new to me.

The spinal cord is like a cable of kite strings running downward inside the vertebral column, from a multitude of kite nuclei in the brain. At various levels between the vertebrae, dendrite fibers, the kite strings, leave the cord to end in muscles and organs. The purpose of the cord, protected by the vertebrae and wrapped in a myelin sheath, is conduction of impulses between fiber endings and the nuclei in the brain. If cut, these fibers of the central nervous system never regenerate, nor can they be reconnected. Research has shown where and how given impulses travel but has not been able to discover how to repair cut pathways. Even a bruise of the cord can damage delicate tracts forever.

Mine was a bruise of the cord. There was no way to determine the amount of residual destruction or how much recovery to expect. Physical examination determined the level of injury to be at the seventh cervical vertebra.

The quadriplegic effect of my incomplete cord injury was the same as a complete one in which the spinal cord is severed — paralysis from neck to toes. The amount of possible recovery was unknown. Circulation to the cord is poor, healing slowly.

Slowly. Lying in bed, nine months sounded endless. I put myself in limbo until recovered, determined to be a model patient, do everything possible to return to practice sooner, make this detour as short as possible.

I had always regarded the handicapped with curiosity, pity and misunderstanding, distanced myself from them. No one in our family had been disabled or admitted to anything other than the discomforts of arthritis and old age. We prided good health, stamina and an invulnerability passed from generation to generation.

"Never in a thousand years could I have imagined myself disabled." I repeated this over and over to physicians and hospital staff who stopped to visit.

A physician friend planted the seed, "Now you can write a book. Your country experiences would make interesting reading."

"Me. Write a book! Don't be foolish, Hal." I laughed. "I can't even hold a pencil. Besides I don't know how to write." How could he be serious?

"Use a tape recorder," he said, as if covering the germ with earth and tamping it down.

Germination and harvest would be several years away but the words remained. I agonized over my fate. So much had been plundered. Write a book! Ridiculous. Never. Where was justice if fate had plucked me from essential work among my patients in order to write a book? The idea was ludicrous. Every day's total effort lay in recovery, in one shaft of light, therapy.

Therapy began the first Monday morning when the hospital cranked into full motion after the weekend. Cynthia, head of Occupational Therapy, came to my room to mold and rivet fleece-lined splints that held my hands in a semi-flexed position. Lamb's wool lined the splints fitting my calves, behind the heels and under the feet. Arms and legs fastened into the splints with velcro, I felt like a turkey dressed for an oven. The splints were part of me for more than six months, except during baths or therapy.

And then Joe came, slipping into view on crepe-soled shoes. "I'm from physiotherapy," he said. "Let's see what you can do." He poked, tapped and tested muscles. When he flexed my legs, I could kick them straight. They felt like sodden cold logs, but it was wonderful to know that some motion remained. Joe assured me that my legs were warm, but they had no feeling and seemed as frigid and hard as glacial ice.

My therapist was a clean shaven, apple cheeked, freckled, hammered-down, red headed, rotund Santa, built like a wrestler. His marble facade hid a temper that forged more conflicts than he often bargained for. He dressed neatly in tee shirt and creased pants. When supervising a patient's therapy, he pushed to the limit. He knew when to cajole, scold or compliment, to make a patient take one more step with crutches or walker, to raise an arm a bit higher. Joe demanded the most effort I could give. He became kind and understanding when I exhausted. If I felt down, he bragged about badgering his mother into washing his car or laundry. He boasted about girl friends. I enjoyed the entertainment which contained only a whiff of distorted truth.

Joe came to my room twice each day to make me use muscles I could not feel move. He felt minuscule responses when I attempted to use fingers, feet and limbs. "He's my ticket out of this hospital," I told Hal one day. I cooperated and tried to do everything asked of me. Each week muscles strengthened until mobility was perceptible.

Misery arrived the second week with a custom-fitted Philadelphia collar. It put pressure against my jaw making conversation difficult. The contraption was torture. At first I wore the collar all day, later only when upright. It allowed me to sit up and be removed from the bed. After ten days it was discontinued.

The collar did permit me to go to the gym for therapy. The porter moved me by litter to the only unfamiliar room in the hospital. Enroute between X ray and laboratory I had never taken time to see the mass of tubs, bars and exercise equipment. When we had enlarged the hospital, the physiatrist, physician in charge of physiotherapy, had risen in committee meetings to fight for space and equipment, but I never thought of the gym except for the valuable amount of hospital space it utilized. Now it was my life.

After two weeks in bed I was strapped to the tilt table to determine tolerance to erect posture. When I no longer became light-headed or had blood pressure changes, I graduated to a wheelchair.

One day Joe and several assistants braced my legs, locked the wheelchair before parallel bars and cinched a heavy webbed belt around my waist. "Stand up."

I rebelled. "No, I can't. My knees will buckle. My legs. I'll fall." Cold spindly tree-limb legs could not support me. The tile floor looked far below and hard. "Don't make me stand. No. No."

"If your knees buckle, you'll be on the floor. Let's go." Joe took a deep breath, grabbed the belt, watching my legs. He pulled me to my feet. "Keep your knees stiff."

My arms dangled, unable to hold the bars and prevent falling. I looked down. My knees had not collapsed. How long would Joe make me stand? He gripped the strap that balanced me. I felt like the Tower of Pisa, forgot to breathe.

"Now, take a step," Joe commanded.

"A what?" One step. Slowly I raised the right foot and slid it forward a few inches. Walking was not as I remembered. Concentrate. Remember to breathe. The left foot slid gingerly beside the right, then the right again. Three steps. Joe let me sink slowly into the chair an assistant had moved behind us. I was exhausted but ecstatic. I had walked.

Joe shrugged his shoulders. "It was okay." But I knew by his crooked smile and the spark in his eyes that he was pleased.

Within a week I walked ten then fifteen steps, watching my feet move between the parallel bars without feeling the floor. It was like walking on the stilts Father made when I was twelve. My feet had clumped everywhere that summer, rarely touching the ground.

It was only mid-November. I knew that July would find me fully recovered, back in my office and chasing storks again. "I'll walk by Thanksgiving, run by Christmas," I bragged to the neurosurgeon at his next visit. His response was a look I could not interpret. Did he doubt me?

Learning to walk was a small part of therapy. Pushing my limp body into a bathing suit for water exercise in the Hubbard Tank was like stuffing a rag doll into a dress shrunken three sizes too small. I could help by lifting my hips from the mattress but despite the loss of several pounds there seemed to be too much of me. Tugging off the wet suit was as difficult. Everytime I went to the gym, the retention catheter had to be connected and disconnected from the leg bag.

The Hubbard Tank rested in the gym floor. Therapy in its warmed water was worth the bathing suit struggle. Joe in swim trunks waited in the tank as I was lowered by hydraulic crane on a special litter. The buoyancy of water increased the range of motion when I flexed and extended fingers, arms, feet and legs. I could walk better in the tank. Joe wore a crazy plastic hat the day the photographer took pictures for the hospital newsletter.

I had worked at a swimming pool during medical school days, taught swimming and was not afraid of the water despite Joe's frequent threats to dunk me. The sessions in the water were a welcome break in routine, but I returned to bed fatigued and slept until supper.

The gym was a fascinating place, full of varied activity. Out-patients and in-patients learned to walk after strokes or amputations. Patients came for burn therapy. Men and women lined up in wheelchairs for whirlpools or practiced using crutches. Every day was new and busy.

Monday through Friday were scheduled morning and afternoon visits to physiotherapy. Each day I spent one hour after lunch in Occupational Therapy, strengthening hands and fingers by placing pegs in holes, stacking cones as high as I could reach. Twice a day I was lifted into a wheelchair, and Doris the porter wheeled me to the gym. On Saturday one therapist worked with urgent cases, and I went to the gym only once.

Everywhere someone had to pick me up, set me down. I was balanced with pillows, turned, dressed and fed. "I feel like a sack of potatoes," I told Joe, remembering how Father shook 100-pound bags to settle knobby spuds, how he lugged and dragged them from corner to corner. They stayed wherever he put them. "I'm worthless," I complained.

The day I looked into the gym's full-length mirror, I saw a bulky sack. Gym patients wore a front-tied billowing hospital gown over the gown worn in bed. I wore no bra or underwear. The gowns dangled from my shoulders like windless sails flapping the yardarms of an ancient ship. A woman's hospital hair style, arranged by her pillow, is "bird nest." The mirror reflected a sagging lumpy gunnysack, voluminous beyond my 150 pounds and older than 54 years. Slumped into the wheelchair, I looked like a pathetic bag lady dragged from the streets and dressed in her shroud.

I could not believe the reflection. After three weeks only traces of the black eyes remained, but could I look that unkempt and dowdy? Back in my room, the nurse dialed the phone and held it while I called home. Pete brought slacks, bras, blouses, socks and shoes to the hospital. I wore them every day. Before I left my room a nurse combed my hair. I became a new person.

The nurses were caring and conscientious, but I required special attention. They tried to feed me before the food cooled, but there were other patients to feed. Morning bath and dressing had to be completed before Doris came to push me to the gym. Morning and evening a nurse gave range-of-motion exercises to fingers, hands, arms, toes and legs. When in bed nurses used a draw sheet to turn me every two hours, buttressing my back with pillows. Despite concerned nursing care, the skin over my sacrum broke down and would not heal. Every nursing shift had its own remedy. Having no sensory perception, I was the worst enemy by lying on my back, the only position which relieved the relentless leg spasms.

Particularly until the dried blood from my nose was gone, having a nurse hold a tissue for nose blowing was a most uncomfortable part of care. I remembered my toddlers rolling their heads and squirming out of grasp. Teeth brushing was another annoying event. The toothbrush always seemed too hard, the paste too much, the pressure too light. It was more like a peppermint fist in my mouth.

Many nurses were familiar for their care to Mother two years before, Father last spring when each of them had been on this floor. The familiar faces and visitors relieved my trips into chasms of uselessness and depression that seemed bottomless. Often I felt as empty as Monday's church.

Nurse friends from the obstetrical floor stopped frequently. They brought gifts of perfume, lotion, kitchen crafts or crocheted bed socks. Best of all they carried departmental chitchat and news of my patients delivered by substitute doctors. They carried back my best wishes to the new mothers.

"Remember Mary and Emory?" Donna from obstetrics asked.

"How could I forget them?" I laughed remembering the couple.

"She delivered a boy during the night."

"Did she come in by ambulance this time?" I asked. "She sure caused a commotion when she came in for her last baby. Remember how surprised I was about the ambulance, how happy it made her?"

4

An Ambulance for Mary

"Ambulance?" I said, taking a step backward. "What ambulance?" Mary had called about 2:00 a.m. from a neighbor's phone. Hers had been disconnected because of unpaid bills. "She said she was in a hurry to have this baby and her husband would drive her in." Obstetricians have a knack for half-awake conversations. Had I missed something?

The scrub-suited nurse behind the labor room desk took a sip of black coffee and a deep breath, laid her pen on a page of nurse's notes and handed me Mary Jensen's chart. "Where did you find this patient? She's polished her nails and fixed her hair all morning. She's not in labor."

"Lives in a trailer court on Narvon Hill."

I thought about the hill between Blue Ball and Honeybrook and the trailer court on the edge of the Welsh Mountains. Big or little trailers, new and junky ones were poked between trees like fingers in a glove. I leafed Mary's chart.

"She seems like a poor soul." Nurse Cameron smiled, waiting to hear more.

"She is poor. Mousy and half afraid of her husband. Wouldn't be surprised if he knocks her around sometimes. She comes to me because I'm a woman and have had babies."

The nurse lifted another chart from the rack. "Mary's on welfare."

"Most families on that hill are. I get a lot of grief for the $35.00 Pennsylvania pays me for each baby delivered."

The nurse sipped again, swallowed, scratched her permed auburn head. "Night shift said Mary was a mess when the ambulance brought her in, hair hanging in strings, face dirty."

"But I still don't understand the ambulance. What happened? How is she now?"

Nurse Cameron insisted on completing her story, running a slim finger around the edge of her cup. "Night shift said she puffed and groaned when the ambulance crew brought her in, hugging a scruffy cardboard suitcase."

"They made her shower?"

The nurse nodded emphatically. "Then she got combed, put on makeup, quieted down."

"Guess Mary's never had much. She's from a family of twelve kids on the south side of the mountain. Father was a junk man. When he could find junk or felt like working. Between babies her mother cleaned houses for valley people."

The nurse added more coffee to her cup from an electric urn. "Looks like she's following her mother."

"Pregnant and married Emory at fifteen. A baby almost every year or so, except the time Emory was jailed for stealing chickens from a farm near Churchtown. Never saw her in my office wearing anything but a faded cotton dress and old sneakers. Always a kid hanging on her skirt."

"Not bad looking now she's fixed up. Doesn't talk much," Nurse Cameron said.

I nodded. "Answers when spoken to but doesn't look at you. Except for other trailer women, her social life is going to the store or the Methodist Sunday School on the other side of the mountain, when Emory takes her, which isn't often."

"The nurses on eleven to seven shift said her husband is no prize."

"He fits the lazy mountaineer picture. It's hard for welfare to dispute a bad back. Doesn't keep him from shuffling cards or rolling dice."

I opened the wide wooden door to Mary's labor room.

"Doctor, wait'ill you hear what happened to us on the way to the hospital." Mary sat up in bed. Vivid lipstick and large brown eyes accentuated a thin white face, lined by thirty years of hard times and children. She smiled, excited.

I warmed my stethoscope in my palm.

"We'd just started down the hill when our old car lost a wheel, rolled off in a clump of briers and elderberry bushes near the railroad bridge. And me with hard pains too." She pouted her lower lip, put on a mournful face.

"But an ambulance?" I placed a hand on her mounded abdomen and awaited a contraction.

"Get an ambulance," I told Emory. "I need an ambulance. But he grumbled that I didn't need none mor'an he did and told me to stop my beller'n. I told him iff'in he didn't get it I'd go sit in the middle of the road 'til somebody got one." Even in the shapeless faded hospital gown that hung everywhere and nowhere Mary looked fresh, hair neatly combed and held by a blue ribbon. She was better groomed than I had ever seen her.

I smothered a grin, imagined Mary swaying onto the double lines and dropping like a stone onto the middle of Route 322, loose skirts wrapped around cornstalk legs and bulging abdomen and clasping the scuffed cardboard suitcase. "That was a dangerous place to sit," I said. "What next?"

"Me rockin' an moanin' and Emory fussin' that all the houses on the hill was black as coal. No place to call. He just leaned against the hood of that rickety green Chevy hangin' on three wheels along the road. He was suckin' air through his teeth and spittin' on the black top so hard it splashed. Stubborn mule." She waved a hand in disgust.

The only movement under my hand was an occasional baby kick. The uterus remained relaxed. This new Mary interested me. She glowed with an "I'm as good as anybody" look. I thought of the timid woman I had just discussed with Nurse Cameron.

"Told him I'd have the baby there on Narvon Hill if he didn't get the ambulance. I had the last one fast. You recollect me birthin' Betsy?" Mary leaned forward awaiting my answer, her face as flushed as a ripe peach. She sensed my amusement.

I slid my stethoscope along Mary's chest trying to maintain a rock-rigid face. How could I forget the commotion she had caused at the hospital at her last delivery when she arrived ready to birth, all delivery rooms full and labor patients overflowing into hall alcoves?

The charge nurse had told me how Emory stomped down the hall as if the entire affair was too much disgraceful bother. Baby Betsy had arrived on a litter in the hall before Mary had time to remove dress or underwear. It happened so fast that she was lucky to even have an intern and nurse's aide with her. No wonder Mary panicked at the first twinge of labor.

"Did Emory call the ambulance last night?" I paused to listen to the unborn's steady heartbeat through the stethoscope.

"Him? No way. Said he'd go home and borrow Will Bosley's pickup but I knowed Will had the engine all apart and spread around yesterday, so it weren't runnin'. Emory just rubbed his greasy chin what needed shavin' and started home; said no ambulance would come without no doctor's say-so cause too many people used 'em fer hospital trips."

Mary stopped to watch me press my thumb against her ankle, testing it for fluid retention. She closed her eyes concentrating on her tale.

"He called me a cow and said he'd drag me off the road hisself iff'in his back weren't so bad. He wanted me to walk back home. He oughta have a baby. Him and his back." She opened mascaraed lids.

My nod fueled Mary's report. I thought of the many assistance checks paid due to back pain. "So Emory finally called the ambulance?" I motioned Mary to lift her gown so I could examine her abdomen. The acrid odor of violet cologne rose to hang between us.

"No. He said somebody drivin' the hill'd think me plastered or hit me like some cat warmin' its feet on the road. Finally when he seen I wouldn't get up, he said he'd call the ambulance, but a car come up the hill and a man stopped to ask if we needed help or if we was hurt."

Mary brushed away an imaginary tear with a fire-red finger. "The man could see me in pain and cryin' so he went back down the hill to a pay phone in Beartown and called Honeybrook ambulance. I told him to hurry. After that Emory sulked against a dented fender, said you'd think I never had no baby before. He lit a cigarette and snorted smoke outa his nose like a wild bull."

I shook my head, not insulting her with a smile, pictured Mary delivering on the middle of the road with only Emory and an unfortunate stranger.

Mary lifted broom-handle arms and pointed to several scratches from the macadam on her knotty elbows. "Then I rolled over on my hands and knees, got up and waited by the car."

I imagined a crew of Honeybrook's ambulance volunteers, a garage attendant and perhaps a farmer and the school nurse routed from their beds to pick up Mary below the crest of Narvon Hill. The ambulance had stood winking and blinking like a marquee on Times Square. The men unfolded a stretcher and rolled it to the derelict car to strap Mary, with her moans and groans, between clean blankets.

I pulled the sheet over Mary's chest and patted her arm, listening to her story.

"Coupla other cars stopped after that, but Emory jabbed his old blue flannel shirt into his saggy jeans and said help was comin', like he'd gone fer it. When the ambulance was stopped, he hiked his belt under his big belly and waved his fat arms around directin' traffic like he was a cop. Then he sat on the front seat while we come them twenty miles to Lancaster, siren splittin' cars off the road like firewood."

"You had quite a night," I said, finishing her examination. "You were lucky this baby was not as speedy as the last one. The ambulance ride was okay then?"

"Yeah." She smiled, pleased as a child at a birthday party. "Always wanted to ride in an ambulance, lights flashin' and siren screamin', people gettin' out of the way, lookin'." Mary became somber. "When's this baby comin'?"

"Not for awhile. False labor last night."

"I'm hungry. Can I have somethin' to eat? Can I go home? I oughta go home."

"Who is watching your children?" I asked.

"Emory. That's why I gotta get home. Emory! He jest lets the kids run over the neighborhood while he sets drinkin' beer. Hollers at them all day. Ain't good for kids. I'm wonderin' how he's doin' with Betsy, diapers, feedin' and all. I told him to take her to Janet in the next trailer, iff'in she's home. Baby's only eighteen months ya know. Men!" She threw up bony hands and fell against the pillow.

"Mary, you may go home as soon as you find a way to get there."

"Thank you doctor, thank ya. I wonder what my next trip'ill be like?"

"So do I, Mary," I said, closing the labor room door behind me, not knowing that it would be two weeks before her next admission. "So do I."

5

The Flipside

"The good part of a bad problem is on its other side. Turn it over," Velma Wenger said, catching up on a pile of mending after a cow stepped on her bare foot and restricted her to chair and bed for a week.

How that elf of a woman accomplished so much work in a day I never understood. No more than shoulder high to the snappy sorrel she harnessed and drove to town, she steered pigtailed daughters and tousle-headed mischievous sons through lawn mowing, garden planting, weeding and household chores. I never passed the Wenger house on a clear day that bedding did not air from upstairs windows, sheets and blankets lapping the shingled gray house like thirsty tongues.

In the area of the Wenger home, few people other than local farmers and a sprinkling of trailer residents traveled the isolated byways chopped into nubbins of dead-end side roads when farmland and forest were wolfed up by the Pennsylvania Turnpike. Over the more traveled routes, the turnpike spit out occasional bridges, loose irregular sutures in the wide gash across the state.

Sumac, wild blackberry and sassafras edged summer's narrow macadam backroads blending into unrestrained woods of maple, oak and poplar trees. Small stony farms wrangled from barbarous hills by former generations and an occasional one-room school or a trailer home interrupted the wilderness. The dank odor of underbrush and overgrowth clung to the air like the tenacled poison ivy groping fencerails and consuming telephone poles.

The language chatted over kitchen telephones of most Narvon RD#2 homes was Pennsylvania Dutch. Old Order Mennonite folks east of Bowmansville drove to church with horse and carriage. Some homes used electricity. Most families lit lanterns and kerosene lamps for light.

Velma and David Wenger could not support a growing family on their meager acres. Every morning a trailer neighbor took David to work with him on the assembly line of New Holland Machine Company. Evenings and weekends David tilled and battled his earth for corn, potatoes and hay.

Five miles back in the boondocks from the main highway, a roadside vegetable stand would have been as useful to Velma as a load of hay delivered to Lancaster City Hall. She shared her excesses with friends and neighbors.

When Velma drove her horse and carriage fourteen miles to my office, it was part of a journey to hunt clothing at Rubinson's and Trimmer's Department Stores, to have her horse shod, to buy tools or seed at Kauffman's Hardware. New Holland provided abundant horse sheds and hitching rails.

Velma never learned to walk. Her gait was a permanent trot. In my office she propelled her pre-schoolers onto waiting room chairs, distributed children's books from the table and laid out rules of good behavior.

"Can you use some cheese again?" Velma asked as she sat beside my desk. She extracted a plastic-wrapped pale full moon from a crinkled paper bag and laid it on the desk. "Cow's fresh, have to use up the milk." She pushed the cool cylinder toward me with small slim fingers, knowing my family hungered for her cheese. Her rennin came by mail order from the Midwest. David had made cheese presses the size of cereal bowls. Nothing bad could come from Velma's immaculate kitchen.

"Thank you," I said, already imagining the cheese's soft texture on a cracker, incisor marks in its pliant anatomy, soft curd nestled on my tongue. "I'll have to hide this in the refrigerator if I want any of it."

"Will you come to my house in January?" Velma asked, removing her small black bonnet. She wrinkled her petite face in smiles, azure eyes bright as a child's. I never refused her.

"Promise no snowstorms?" I thought of the miles between us wrapped in blizzard solitude, roads impassible, snow-blocked.

"No guarantees," she laughed, remembering the times I had straddled one-track ice ruts to reach her. Backroads could be closed a week. Winter roadsides became a fairyland, naked bush and tree clothed in ice and snow. Snowbanks lured careless drivers to entrapment.

By late November my patient appeared to have a beach ball beneath her apron. Our suspicions were confirmed by two definite and different heartbeats ticked out by the Doppler I pressed against her abdomen to magnify its noises. Velma was exuberant at the prospect of twins. David waited impatiently for the birthing.

"It's a hospital birth this time," I insisted. "We'll not risk a baby for the lack of modern facilities."

The Wengers chose Ephrata Community Hospital located at the hub of Mennonite country. The distance from the Wenger home to the hospital was too inconvenient for David to attend the prenatal classes required for privileged admission to the delivery room. Velma said he moped like a sick kitten when he learned that he could not see the twins birthed.

Hospital rules must be obeyed, but to a husband present at six uneventful births the statute seemed illogical and unfair. Husbands were allowed to stay in the labor rooms with their wives until time to move to the delivery room. I could only smile, shrug and insist that laws are made for the good of someone but I was not sure whom.

January had weeks of unrelenting freezing temperatures. Where the sun melted snow on patches of earth and road, night and shadow snatched them back to glib ice.

Velma was a balloon with fence post legs, hustling about her work as usual. It may have been the overloaded basket of wet wash, or the clumsy package she carried beneath her apron that caused her to slip on an ice patch as she stepped from the cellar door. She fell forward fracturing her left kneecap.

Near due date the Ephrata orthopedist put Velma's injured limb in a straight full-length leg cast until he could operate after the twins' birth. She struggled several days between bed and chair, losing patience, hunting for the good side of her enforced immobility. Finally, labor began.

Velma's face flushed with anticipation. Between panting contractions she smiled and chatted with David, dressed in Sunday white shirt, black bow tie and black pants under the loose cover gowns required for the labor and delivery suite. His lean close-shaven face showed only furrowed concern for his wife as he fed her ice chips, comforted and guided her through contractions. When she changed position, he lifted and pillowed the awkward cast that weighted her leg.

"Is there no way I can go into the delivery room?" David pleaded. The black hair he brushed from his face was salted with white streaks.

"Can't do it," I said. "Rules are rules."

From the Wenger's labor room I could see traffic passing on the concrete strip of the old highway to Reading. Below, at the rear of the hospital lawn, horse-driving Mennonites had built a small stable for the convenience of visiting members. They cleaned and maintained it. I chuckled, wondering how many modern hospitals could claim a stable and hitching rail.

As I waited with Velma, the evening light cast a cold glow on snow patches from last week's blizzard. The sun descended in a blast of orange along the horizon.

Delivery was not far away. The delivery of twins both excited and concerned me. David repillowed Velma's cast, bemoaning the rule about to deprive him of the delivery room. Velma panted with her pressing babies. It was my move.

I spoke to nurse Lucy Burkholder. "Velma's cast looks more like a barn timber than a leg. How will the two of us manage that thing in the delivery room? We'll be busy enough with Velma and the babies. Even moving the patient at this time of labor will not be easy."

Lucy laughed and rolled the sterile instrument table into the labor room while I scrubbed for delivery. Even David's mask could not hide a victorious grin. Velma's eyes were moist with happiness and the final stages of labor.

While David supported the cast, covered by sterile drapes, the first Wenger boy came with the ease of a pin falling through a water pipe.

Before I could finish with him and reach for a leg to bring down the second baby, its head descended into the mother's pelvis. Six minutes after the first baby a second boy lay on the bed. Two vigorous babies lay in heated cribs. No rules had been violated.

"Ike and Mike," I said, examining a placenta that appeared to be the one of identical twins.

Velma laughed and lifted her head to watch the nurse snap wristbands on her sons. "Oh no, Mahlon and Galen." She laughed. "You know, breaking my knee wasn't all bad. David got to be with me and see the babies born."

6
Visitors And Thoughts

My hospital room contained more plants and flowers than a florist shop. When Pete returned from a week's business trip to Phoenix, he measured forty-two feet of floral gifts. People stopped by the room to admire them. Lying motionless in bed with a room full of greenery and blooms, the world seemed unreal. Surely I would awaken from this nightmare.

Word of my accident spread rapidly among my patients. Within days they began coming to admire my flowers and gaze over my bedrail. If an Amish family had a hospitalized friend or family member, I rated a visit. I recognized most of them but could not always put name and face together.

One evening a white-haired, stooped Amish woman limped to my bedside. I struggled to identify my spindly guest but did not recognize the shrunken face. "You'll have to tell me who you are. I'm afraid I don't recognize you," I said.

She pushed rimless glasses up the ridge of her peaked nose, creased a broad smile. "Oh, you never met me. I'm Priscilla Zook. I heard about you and wanted to see what you looked like." Bony fingers caressed a pink rose bud. "What beautiful flowers. So many." She spent several minutes in my flower shop before returning to her husband's bedside down the hall.

Amish woman, Lydia Glick, and her daughter Mary from Gordonville RD#1 were also strangers. "But you know my brother Amos and his wife Emma along the Strasburg Pike near Vintage," Lydia explained, laying their black bonnets on a chair. She smoothed gray-streaked black hair from a dumpling face, leaned over the bedrail and explained how Mary had slipped in the barn and fallen down a hayshoot when fifteen, injuring her neck. "Doctor said she hurt her spinal nerve."

Mary smiled, resting against the foot of my bed. She showed me her contracted index fingers. They moved stiffly when she opened her hand.

"We thought," Lydia took a deep breath and hesitated. "We thought, if it isn't too much trouble, maybe you could give us some advice." She looked at her daughter.

I wondered what I was to tell this pleasant woman, towering above me in Sunday black dress and apron. Of course. Mary must have a menstrual problem, I guessed to myself. I waited.

"Mary's been goin' with the young folks six years now," Lydia continued, shifting from one foot to the other. "She'll be twenty-one come January. She wants to marry this November. Problem is, she has trouble with her bladder. Can't always control it. Not bad if she goes often. Just sometimes she forgets herself. She can work good." Lydia exhaled a slow deep breath. Her brown eyes, fixed to my face, did not blink. "What do you think?"

Mary's shocking-pink cape, apron and dress added a rosy glow to her full cheeks. She was as still as a manikin. Black eyes traveled my splinted arms and hands. She waited.

Above all else I valued family. What would my past have been like without husband and children? I could not imagine the void. Life without the cares or gratifications of babies and adolescents. No husband to share goals and adversities.

I thought of patient Peggy Woods, confined to a wheelchair since eighteen. Three times I had seen her uneventfully through pregnancies and the delivery room. Should Mary's hopes be splattered on my hospital floor because of incontinence?

Slowly, as if pondering the answer, I smiled. "No," I said. "I see no reason why Mary should not marry and have a family."

"Thank you," Mary said. Her grim countenance changed to a grin.

She released a long breath. "Thank you."

Before they left, each woman opened a homesewn tapestry bag and brought out a gift. Mary's was a small pillow covered with a bright blue and green washcloth. Lydia laid a blue and white striped towel and a cake of Camay soap on the bed.

Gideon Petersheim's older daughter Susie came to visit. "Last winter I was driving home with a young horse from New Holland in the open wagon. A piece of white plastic rattled on the roadbank, then the wind picked it up and whirled it around the horse's head. He bolted and ran into the ditch. I bounced out and hit my head on a rock." Susie lifted both hands toward me so that I could see that the index and middle fingers on both hands were partially flexed. She could straighten them only by using the opposite hand. "I work three days a week cleaning houses in New Holland." She leaned forward, squinting through rimless glasses as if inspecting me for flaws, awaiting the answer for a question she had not asked. "The fingers don't stop me, but I wondered if something could be done."

I suggested she exercise them and consult her doctor. When we finished chatting about family and neighbors, she encased her thin face with a black bonnet and left a can of crushed pineapple on the bedside table.

Tall lanky Simon Riehl and his short dumpy wife stopped to see me when Sara's sister was a patient on the maternity wing. I had delivered four babies at home for Sara, but they were half-grown now and I had not heard of Simon and Sara for several years. Simon unhooked his coat and laid it with his big black hat on a chair with Sara's shawl before walking to my bed, leaning heavily on a brown cane.

He stroked his shaggy brown beard. "I had to give up farmin' and go to buildin' furniture." He leaned toward me, waved both hands to demonstrate fingers stiff and slow moving. "Slipped on wet grass playin' badminton. Hurt my neck the doctor said. I'm better now than at first but not sure of my feet sometimes." He waved the cane. "This is better than lying in bed. Bet you'll walk out of here too."

Before they went down the hall to visit neighbor John King and all the other Amish patients, Sara spread open the brown plastic handles of a voluminous green bag made of upholstery fabric and withdrew a square of white tissue paper, "Here, I'll open it for you."

She unwrapped the neat bundle, smiled. "Made these pot holders for you. Put 'em away until you can use 'em." She laid the two pink and blue flowered squares on the bed.

Another afternoon Meriam Miller visited. She hung her small black bonnet over a chair and settled her spare frame into it, bringing me up-to-date on the last fifteen years of family life. Her brown eyes were beacons in a sharply chiseled face. "We've been living in South America, then Texas," Meriam said, thin lips smiling. "We're living near Five Points now, still tending market stands." She removed a pillow case from a tote bag. I watched slim brown fingers deftly embroider red roses along its edge. The white organdy Amish cap that I had known years ago was now a smaller Mennonite one. "All the children are gone from home but Benny." She raised her gray head from the needlework, picked a stray red thread from the green cape that matched dress and apron. "We won't forget the day he was born, will we?"

"No." I laughed out loud, remembering. That day had begun with the usual breakfast rush. I had pushed daughter Elsa off to school, dressed a son for play in the November sunshine. The baby was diapered when the housekeeper arrived and the phone rang.

"Can you come take me to the hospital?" Meriam asked, "Better hurry."

It was time for her to deliver, but I transported patients to the hospital only in emergency situations. "Where's your husband?" I asked.

"John's not home."

Peculiar I thought, but she sounded desperate for help. "I'll leave now."

The Miller farm rode the margin of Lancaster City with Lancaster County along the Old Philadelphia Pike. The Miller barn leaned south, its unpainted siding weathered gray and eroded. The empty corn cribs were as bleak as the brown fallow fields, wild with tangled grass and stalks of last season's goldenrod. Next year a housing development, bedrooms for workers at RCA, High Steel or Skee Craft Boat Works, would erase all marks of the farm.

Meriam met me at the kettlehouse door, a black cardboard suitcase in one hand, her shawl over the other arm. "We'd better get going. I thought John would never get off to market. If he'd known I was in labor, he'd have stayed home. No use for that." She locked the door and lumbered to my station wagon, pausing during a contraction. "I felt like pushing with that one. Let's hurry. Wait till John gets home and finds out what I pulled on him." The slamming car door sliced her chuckle.

I laughed now, remembering the wild ride to the hospital, headlights on, horn blaring at every cross street and red light as we tore through them. Another scare but no baby in the station wagon that time.

Twenty years later Meriam still enjoyed recalling the day. Then she admired my rows of chrysanthemums, daisies and planters, laid a new towel and washcloth on the bedside table. Before leaving she leaned over the bedrail, patted my cheek, bent over and kissed it. The grief and sympathy in her face and the kiss by a patient was unexpected. It was a hot searing arrow piercing my facade.

As Grandmother lay in her casket, family and friends had leaned into it and kissed her paper-cold cheek. Immobile between rails, the room full of flowers, the kiss, the pity in the faces of visitors hurt more than the spasms in my legs. I felt like a corpse laid out for viewing.

***

The second hospital Sunday I fell apart. My head throbbed with forty drums pounding off-beat rhythms behind my eyes. The chief of the obstetrical department was in the room. "What will you do with your practice?" he asked.

"Dick, if you can find anybody to cover it, go ahead." The loss of an active practice is a loss to a hospital. "I can't talk about it today. I feel like a dice shaking in a cup. Can't anyone give me something?" I thrashed my head over the pillow. For the first time in my life I felt out of control. In my practice, nothing had unnerved me. I could talk about the weather, tobacco prices or naming the new baby while furiously fighting a maternal hemorrhage, but I could not stop the jarring in my head. It frightened me. Where had discipline and fortitude gone?

My friend left. A crowd of visitors waited in the hall, a sea of faces looking into the room. No one. I could not cope with one more guest or decision. When Pete called from Arizona, I could not speak with him. The room would not stand still. A **NO VISITORS** sign gave me the rest I needed.

Dick understood. Until a new physician came to take my practice in July, his obstetrical group generously covered my office and delivered the hospital cases. They saved a valuable practice and removed my major concern. I could focus on recovery.

Each step in recovery led to the next one. "Let's see if you can sit by yourself," Joe said several weeks after therapy began. He pulled me to the edge of the bed, then upright, my feet dangling over the mattress.

I clenched my teeth, determined not to fall over. Across the court of the U-shaped building stood the wing of the original hospital, utilized now for offices and maintenance. I had walked its halls as an intern, birthed our first baby there one steamy August. Now with breathless concentration, my eyes gripped its old bricks, white window frames and did not move.

"Breathe," Joe commanded, holding his arms out to catch me if I fell.

I sat without support several minutes. It was wonderful. "How was that?" I asked, happy with achievement.

Joe laid me down, shrugged his shoulders, half-smiled as he pulled up the sheet. He laughed. "Okay for today."

Gradually strength and mobility improved. One day as Joe exercised my legs, I felt a sudden tug and pull on my left shoulder. "Did my arm fall off the bed?" I asked.

Joe nodded. "Pick it up. Put it back on the bed."

I concentrated, tried. Too soon. My only arm motion was from the shoulder. Several weeks later when I became able to bend my elbows, Joe and Cynthia, from independent living, devised a feeding apparatus that clamped to the back of a chair. Its joints and springs fastened to my right arm with velcro. More velcro secured a fork in my hand.

"Let's see you feed yourself," Cynthia said.

Joe cut a toasted cheese sandwich into small pieces. "How could she miss that mouth?" He grinned.

The springs held my arms half-flexed and away from my body. Flapping like a crow, I rolled my shoulder forward, bent the elbow, then dive-bombed the plate to spear a bite. Often I missed the target, or the food dropped before it reached my mouth. I never ordered peas or gravy for lunch. The contraption made eating hard work. It was easier to have a nurse feed me. Besides, I would be fully recovered soon and not need the hassle.

Joe pushed and insisted. He gave much time and energy to my recovery. I tried to please him. Every noon he came to harness me into the feeding machine and tease me about the hospital fare. "How can you eat that? It's garbage can special. It's from last week's trays."

The kitchen made a special effort to send attractive food for my general diet, but we laughed at his descriptions. He was sure it was wormy or from the cattle sheds at the auction barns along the railroad.

I became more adept at spearing toasted cheese sandwiches. After the first day, I never ordered jello again. The cubes slithered away from the fork, fractured a few inches from the plate or avalanched strawberry down the front of my blouse.

Liquids, through a straw, were an easy trip to the mouth. The catheter I wore allowed luxurious amounts of fluid. After the accident I developed an intolerance to cold drinks and salt. The crab cakes I formerly enjoyed in the cafeteria burned my mouth with their salt.

When the nurses fed me breakfast and supper, I enjoyed not having to bounce my arm or spear my food to eat. Joe supervised at noon. "Be sure to eat enough. Build your strength." The longer I knew him the more he became like a mother hen.

When Joe began stopping to chat, evenings after playing basketball, I felt special. Joe had helped to organize the physiotherapy department and was its head therapist. He directed aides, secretaries, porters and kept records. He knew most of the medical staff. Having held offices and headed committees, I was hungry for news and savored every juicy detail of gossip from kitchen to surgery. He slouched into an armchair and relaxed, propped his sneakers on a stool, knowing our conversation was safe with me.

I listened to burn treatments, complaints about patients and physicians. I learned to know Joe's family and his problems. He made me feel like a whole person, like the one I had been, not a plastic manikin wheeled from bed to gym. We laughed at anecdotes, chewed over the same words week after week. I looked forward to his visits and worked harder to please him. My reward was a half-smile, half-a-compliment.

From Joe I learned that most of my recovery would occur the first year. I was not to be discouraged by plateaus in progress. "You must retrain in one year what a baby learns in several," he said. "After a year your progress will be slower." A year! In a year I would be back in practice, therapy finished.

Therapy, nursing care, naps, visitors kept the days busy. Nights. Bedtime drew the bare walls around me like a purse string. By dim lights the rows of flowers cast spectral shapes and ragged shadows on the walls. Nurses made swishing noises as they hurried down empty halls. The nurses mumbled at the desk. Bedpans rattled in the utility room. The aroma of fresh coffee drifted in from the kitchen.

Nights. In solitude my thoughts turned inward. Why did I have to lose one useless year from my life? When could I return to my office? What good could come from my tragedy? I needed someone to blame for the accident, but no one had thrown me against the edge of the bunk or wrapped the electric cord around my ankle. I had been alone. There was no one to blame, no one to sue for liability, no scapegoat. Frustration brewed and boiled until tears wet the pillow. I believed the nurses did not suspect a doctor would resort to tears until months later when I read their notes in my chart.

So many unknowns and I wanted answers. I looked forward to a discussion with my pastor. I mentally dialogued with him. As a trained counselor he would know what to say, ease the pain.

He came at the end of the first week, sat beside my bed in a black business suit, leaning against the bedrail. Initial greetings, congregational news, then a pause. "I'm a quad," I wailed. I had not even thought the word, now I spoke it. First tears burned my cheeks. Finally I could tell someone how bruised I felt inside and discuss the real me behind the false front I tried to maintain.

The pastor reached for a tissue to wipe away what I had saved for him. He had not understood. "No, no. The nurses can do that," I said. The moment had passed. Maintaining his Sunday pulpit face, he rendered a short prayer and left. Comfort and acceptance were still months in the future. I resolved to save tears for bedtime.

Nighttime thoughts searched for solid ground to moor my sanity. There must be some unseen purpose in the loss of a year. Everything seemed black. I was in the bottom of the darkest valley between steep cliffs. No way out for one used to walking the mountain tops.

Snatches of hymns played through my head. I extracted favorite phrases to repeat and dwell on. Scraps of psalms came to support me. The liturgy of morning church service, choir anthems all offered comfort in the dismal dark. I began to realize my parent's greatest gift was not the college education they had sacrificed to provide. I had always valued it for the happiness and for the comfortable life it gave me, but now in this time of enormous need the gift I drew out and depended upon was the one labeled Religious Background and Teaching.

Sleep and dreams. In dreams I again jogged my evening route through New Holland Machine Company grounds. Cold air whipped tears onto my cheeks. I felt the exhilarating thrust of the earth under my feet, the surge of blood to my head as I labored for breath. Our yellow dog ran with me, chasing a cloud of screeching killdeer from the grass between rows of red farm machinery that cast spectral shadows in the night lights.

Summer returned for a week in October. Nights were sultry. Air conditioning had been turned off until next year. It was too hot to cover with even a sheet. The window and door were open to catch any puff of air.

At bedtime the nurse gave me Talwin to relieve pain and spasms, to induce rest. I had used it successfully with my patients and asked for the shot each bedtime. One hot night before sleep came, I was aware of slowly rising off the bed, rising higher than the ceiling. Below, my body still lay propped on its left side, lower leg straight, the upper one flexed over it. Pillows wedged my back as the evening nurse had left them. The blue flowers on my gown stood out like ink blots. Slowly, I rose higher but was not aware of passing through the ceiling. I saw clearly my limp body, brown hair, the splinted arms and legs. Was I dead? Why? I had not been critical. Panic. Fear. I wanted to get down. Fighting a strong upward surge of energy like powerful magnetic rays, I willed my spirit back into my body.

The experience lasted only seconds, but it convinced me that I did not want to die as I often believed. The fear that I might leave my body again lingered. I was afraid that next time I would not get back. Details remain as clear as if it happened last night. I never again asked for bedtime medication.

As I lay in bed like a corpse, connected to bottles by a network of incoming and outflowing tubes, injected regularly with syringes of medication, it was easy to reflect how far medicine had come in twenty-eight years of practice.

During my 1950-1951 internship at Community Hospital only the A building had existed. Dressed in heavy gowns, standing for hours holding retractors during steamy July and August, had been a muggy job. Nurses patched and repatched the rubber gloves worn in obstetrics and surgery. Disposable supplies had not been introduced. Nurses cleansed, sterilized, reused IV tubing, syringes, gloves and surgical drapes. I shivered, thinking of the risks. It had required constant care to keep supplies in usable condition.

Groups of women traveled regularly from farm and village to repair or sew new doctor gowns and drapes. The hospital sewing room with its rows of sewing machines was supervised by a woman who directed the work of brown-bagging volunteers. Sometimes when passing the room, I recognized a group of Amish women and stopped to chat.

The idea of reusing a syringe or IV tubing, the risks and possibilities for contamination, the transfer of infection from patient to patient was unthinkable in present medicine. I had used only disposable equipment for years. However, when I began practice in 1951, I had a special stone to sharpen and remove the barbs from reusable needles and syringes before placing them into rubber-capped stainless tubes, 5cc and 10cc sizes. I sterilized them in my small autoclave and carried them to house calls. Individual dosage vials required a tiny saw to score the neck before breaking them open. It was embarrassing for a patient to see my occasional bloody fingers, even when using a gauze pad to snap vial necks.

Having moved into the big farm house in New Holland, Pete and I settled down to worry about meeting our $70.40 a month mortgage and paying the bill to remodel three front rooms into an office for me. Using time payments at Van Sciver's in the former umbrella factory at West King and Mulberry Streets in Lancaster, we bought the maple waiting room furniture sold at our sale when we left New Holland thirty years later. I stocked my dispensing shelves with medications, pill envelopes and boxes, ointment tins and bottles on credit from pharmaceutical salesmen anxious to open new accounts. There had been a multitude of salesmen who called every two to four weeks with new untested combinations of medications.

I placed notices of my September office opening in the local papers and with apprehension began my vigil, hoping that rumors at the hospital predicting that a woman doctor in the country would not be successful were untrue. Would anyone walk into my waiting room? Would they like me, be satisfied with my treatment, return? What would the first brave patients report to their friends? Would I fail? What if no one came?

Canasta was popular. Evening after evening Pete and I played cards in our bare kitchen at an old table given to us by his mother. I did not use appointments or have an office nurse. It was a great evening if the office bell rang three times to announce patients. Walking through the empty cubicle planned for living room furniture when we could afford it, I would leave our game and enter the office. Were my pounding footsteps hollow promises?

In December, with great joy, I scheduled my first obstetrical case. The practice was still not a sure success, but it was promising. In a year I was too busy for card games.

Many first patients were those who had already visited all other doctors in the community and were incurable hypochondriacs, but I welcomed anyone who entered my front door.

Thirty-five years after opening my practice my husband gave me a journal he had kept intermittently from July 1, 1951 until June 1961. After ten years I was no longer a young wife beginning housekeeping and a practice. By then we were halfway through our mortgage, had enlarged our house and had three children at the dinner table.

Included with Pete's journal were letters written by patients during the early years. The most prolific correspondent was unmarried Annie Burkholder. Annie was a short shy woman, pale, wispy, mousy. She wore the net cap, apron and dress of a conservative Mennonite group. Her black Chevrolet sedan, ten years old, was seldom driven further than Lancaster or more than forty miles per hour. In my office she timidly complained of chronic back pain but preferred to pour out and mail her weekly thoughts on tablet paper. She was determined to make me the perfect doctor by combining my efforts with those of the wonderful machine found in the office of her Lancaster chiropractor. In one letter she enclosed a clipping about Old Quaker Blood Tonic Capsules to help the blood. According to a Mrs. Martin quoted in the newspaper, "When I go without them, I break out in boils and my feet hurt . . . I advise anyone with diabetes to take these capsules, because they help the blood." In another letter Annie sent the contents of a horse liniment, Kendall's Veterinary Liniment Formula, she had used over several years and wrote, "And I think that the horse liniment that I rub on my hips makes me limp because my right heel is too high for me." Again, "I started to take one of Russel James Hyssop Tablets every day and I rub my left hip with liniment every day. I had some liniment that the Amish doctor had told me to rub on my back."

During my years in Lancaster County there were several Amish men, as well as women, who promoted themselves as healers and sold vitamins and advice for donations, thus not illegally practicing without a license. In one four-page letter Annie worried about her liniment because an aunt told her about a woman who had used the concoction. It made her bones brittle, and she broke a hip. Annie wrote, "They use this liniment for horses. The Amish doctor said if it is good for horses then it is good for the people also."

In the absence of hot water bottles many country people used corn bags and kept several on their space heater. Annie tells me how she made hers. "A bean bag is handier for me to use. I made a muslin bag about 14 inches square then filled it with soybeans. I put this bag in an old loaf cake pan and heat it in the oven. On the 8th of May I tried out the horse liniment alone. I did not use the bean bag at all and then I had to limp again." With Annie, as all patients, I listened to their home remedies and tales of visits to other healing establishments. I never criticized and learned much about my patients.

One scrawny emaciated young woman with pimply face and stringy blond hair used to spend her time in my waiting room selling vitamins. Jane supplemented her husband's income by urging everyone she met to try her marvelous formulas. I never felt threatened by her competition.

One woman who had called me to her house in false labor, wrote, "Sorry I spoiled your weekend. Here I am plugging away yet. I've been trying to help matters along by housecleaning. My forgetter is so busy again."

A Mrs. King sent a letter.

Dear Friend,

"A few lines this cloudy morning. I suppose you saw that I was there last nite. I guess you had just left, but it was my fault, we should have called, but I thought you were in the hospital all day. I didn't know if I should try to come again or not, but mother & I decided, since you have my urine it would not be necessary if you would give or send a bottle of pills [she means prenatal vitamins] to dads or send them down here. I have gained a few pounds but it has been six weeks since I was down there. I have about quit eating potatoes, bread, cake & pies etc. I have little to complain of, have the usual movements. Hope I need not come again and you will come here first, ha.

Sincerely,

Mary Ann King

The letter that amused me most was one in which a young husband begged for an exception to my rule that I would deliver no first babies at home. He complained about the high cost of food, coal and horse feed, writing, "I'm in the money saving business." It was at Amos and Mary's house several babies later that the pressure lantern flared, dimmed, flared and went out as the baby's head crowned. By the time Amos's mother finished fumbling about in the black kitchen for a flashlight, the crying newborn lay on the bed. When the lantern was refilled, we laughed, delivered the placenta and finished our work.

We were married two years, and separated during that second year by my internship, when Pete began his journal in a loose-leaf notebook. Many pages are yellow and brittle. I immerse myself in it, remembering those first ten years, loving the memories. Reading how he felt about our lives, I laugh and wonder how he weathered and endured. It is a great gift.

7

Excerpts from Pete's Journal

Dedicated to all suffering husbands who happen to love and marry a Woman Doctor — thereby joining that exclusive group of "Doctors' Husbands."

July 1, 1951

Today is, for all practical purposes, the day that Grace can open her office. [My internship was completed June 30th, but the office area was not ready. Official office opening was set for September 5th.] The past year has been a hard one for the husband. Since February 1st [the date he moved to New Holland] he has cooked his own meals and performed the menial chores — not to mention all the painting, scraping and high financing it takes to set up a practice before a single patient comes to the front door. We are expecting a maternity call. We have propped open the stairway door and placed the phone in the stairway so that it can be heard all the better. The joke of the story is that the bell is in the box on the wall which has nothing to do with where the phone is placed. Ah well! It is only the doctor's first case — so all anxiety is forgiven.

July 6, 1951

Grace was ironing and I had just tackled changing tapes on the old blinds in the office when in walks Jimmy Holler [Pete's schoolmate], Cookie [small daughter] and his expectant wife. Before I knew it I was appointed baby-sitter. Me, who never even had a baby-sitter of his own, to sit with a baby, a female one at that. Cookie was comfortable in her crib; I was chilled on the couch. However at 4 a.m. WHAM Cookie sounds off wanting Daddy and potty. By 8 a.m. Jimmy was father of a boy, I was the possessor of a pair of red eyes. For the Daddy and potty Jimmy promised me a bottle of wine. He bought the bottle, liked it, drank it and thanked me cordially for giving him the idea to buy the wine. Me — I still have red eyes.

Sept. 5, 1951

Today was the big day! The day Grace has been looking to for over nine long years, a day I've been looking forward to for about five years. The first day was a bust financially, morally or otherwise. Very few people knew that she was open for business. The ads in the paper won't be out until this coming Friday. She did have a non-paying customer; Mrs. Donahue needed a certificate of vaccination for Patty Ann. This waiting for the first paying customer is harder than the whole nine years put into a nutshell. In fact it can be most demoralizing. Funny thing, when the first one shows up you feel like slamming the door behind you and scooting out the back door.

Sept. 6, 1951

Believe it or not! A patient finally came into our trap and was deposited in the waiting room. He was a perfect stranger but had the two-fifty for the treatment of the foot. So the ice is broken, self-confidence restored in the heart and soul of the doctor. When the bell rang we weren't sure if the bell was ringing because a patient had entered or if I hadn't closed the door properly. When it rang the second time we were certain the trap was sprung and Grace was in practice.

Sept. 21, 1951

Our first night call was just about what we expected it to be, with of course a twist or two not in the manual. It seems that Friday [our police dog] was obtained to go along on night calls, but no, the lucky stiff slept while I took the dog's place. This being the first time the phone rang in the middle of the night, it sounded anything but like a phone. It dawned on us that it was ringing and we should answer it. I commenced by hunting the light switch on the far wall. Next time we'll have a night light. She commenced by groping over the floor for the phone. By next time we'll have a nightstand. I had better luck—hers was miserable. In fact she gave up and just hung out of bed and said, "How do you work this darn thing?" After awhile the dawn swept into our brains; we did take care of things in a professional manner. Got a complete description of what road to take, where to turn; all of which we missed when we looked for it. The patient proved to be on Bulltown Road, one of those Amish farms set off away from the road in a little dip so that it cannot be seen by the users of the road. With the moon shining and the stars twinkling in this warm fall air, the house was really beautiful. The shadows hid all the faults and the moonshine brought out all the highlights. On the hill I could hear cows grazing. This Amishman was of the old stock, no shoes and a beard, with no gas powered engines to defile his property. I believe that I could have spent the night there, just sitting under one of the trees and watching the slow and quiet movements of that which surrounded me.

Sept. 1951

One of the worst stomach turning feelings I've had is just sitting here across from Grace and doing nothing but watching and listening for that bell to go. I guess there are a number of ways you can kill this time between patients. One is to get your husband to play "cutthroat canasta." Another is to sneak into the waiting room and read the magazines that should be read by the patients, or to write a letter home telling them that you are doing better than expected, not to worry over you. It does help to bolster your morale a little too. But there is nothing that will rid you of that feeling in the stomach unless a patient walks in.

Now I guess Grace and I have played cards for two to three hours at a stretch with not the sound of that bell. By nine we would both be just playing and trying to juggle the "patient per day" average of two so that it would cover the blank evening and also give us the excuse for a brighter tomorrow. Believe me, those nights are the pathetic ones in our young life. You'd like to go to bed by nine as soon as hours are over, but you wait around until ten so that they will see the sign [electric on the lawn] and perhaps remember to come in the next day. In fact, you don't care if they come during hours or not — just as long as they come in.

Oct. 1, 1951

Today is the big day for Grace's step into New Holland's society. She was off to a covered dish supper and a chance to meet some of the private citizens in this town. Things don't always go as planned. In fact she had two patients come by 6:15 and I had to rush her back just as they were starting to eat. I couldn't tell who drooled more, her or Friday. It is now 8:25 and she has had naught but a bowl of peaches and a bowl of milk. I know she is starved. I guess the doctor's husband will get clipped for his last buck and take his ever-loving wife out to the local hamburger stand for her supper.

This chalks up her biggest day for her. She should have at least seven paying patients so it will do much to alleviate the flopping of the stomach.

Tis funny, last week her stomach flopped, growled and rolled because of no patients. This week it is because of too many patients.

The buggy rail has been put up. In fact, after a buggy parked itself in our garage it seemed that a rail was needed imminently. I spent a miserable Saturday outside digging the post holes, etc. In fact, the winds almost froze a few parts from my anatomy. One of the most fascinating pastimes a young doctor can have while waiting for patients is to play the averages. The hard part is to figure out and convince your wife that she has reached the average for the day by adding to lean days, patients who have presented themselves on fat ones. Brother, with Grace it takes some doing!

Dec. 1951

. . . take the gent, a quiet individual, it seemed, who came in with a bad back. When asked to take off his clothes to the waist he must have slipped his waist down to near his ankles. He compromised and settled for at least his shorts on.

Jan. 1952

I guess one of the things that will vex a husband more than

anything is to have a cold supper, or no supper at all. So the guy on my number one hate list is an egotistical servant of the Machine Company who cannot go to a doctor during hours. In fact, it can only be done to suit his convenience. "He" likes to have his supper on time and if he gets to the doctor by 5:45 he can be at his dinner table by 6:15. Consequently, on the nights he comes for his treatment we don't eat. In fact it is 8:30 and the poor kid hasn't had her supper yet. Just because of this one pompous so-and-so. So we could refuse him, but who is turning down four bucks at this time of the game? Heh!

Feb. 1952

I think one of the things that will always gripe me is that patient called a "Dead Beat." Of course doctors are supposed to be tolerant, but you can't live on that. Worse than that are the "Dead Beats" that tell you they only pay their bills once a month — but forget to tell you which one of the twelve. Other offensive "Dead Beats" don't pay, make more than I do [Pete worked in the office of New Holland Machine Co.] and then come for everything under the sun. Not once a day but twice or thrice is nothing unusual. But pay — what a laugh.

April 1952

Honestly, if all doctors are as my good wife, I just pity the other side of the team. Here we are, rolling along nicely, not coining it at a rapid clip, but neither are we losing out, and I think that is all breezy, when she gets a day with only one patient. So there she is, nose down, spirit down, starting to save money again by making me dig a ditch for the new water main. When just last week she was out spending it as fast as she was making it. I guess it is like all doctors. Money in their pockets sure burns like ethyl chloride on the skin. When she has it she spends it, when she doesn't have it she saves the stuff. Her latest hiding place is a daily calendar where she accumulated fifty dollars toward a new washer for Xmas. She was fooled though. The washer burned out and she had to produce the fifty dollars way ahead of time much to her embarrassment.

April 1952

Lately a maternity has been giving us a few sleepless hours. It's a house delivery and up to now the apple has refused to fall, but threatened twice. I tried to go to bed again. Sam Sagner was just coming home from work. I called him in and we both just sat around and chinned. By then it was almost four and the night was shot for both of us. Mrs. Fisher? She didn't deliver after three hours. She decided to do the wash and hang it up.

May 1952

Much has been said about the Amishman and his beard. He came in one day with a few cracked ribs. The moment of payoff came when in a moment of curiosity he looked down just as she was about to tape a strip rather high up. Temptation was great and it was all she could do to stop from laughing. But she kindly refrained from taping the beard to his chest.

Aug. 20, 1952

One of the first requirements of a doctor's husband is just like that of a doctor's wife—be ready for anything. Personnel Manager called me to give blood, said patient was in dire straights. Grace told me it was her patient, just to replace what was given.

Nov. 1952

Being a doctor's husband has taught me more tolerance toward my wife than I ever imagined I would have. Our waking hours revolve about her and only her. Best laid plans by us are changed by a phone call, something I am or was not used to. For me it was not uncommon to plan ahead three or four weeks, know what I would be doing at a certain hour on a certain day. Not now—a maternity is the most unpredictable event in the way of life. The birth makes liars out of experts, and so we confine ourselves to New Holland and vicinity.

Getting back to a tolerant husband, at heart I try to be, but sometimes, when I come home and find this scattered here, the mail all over, and shoes and stockings all over the bedroom I have to blow my top.

Nov. 1952

There are times when I'm sure Grace must have a feeling of complete helplessness. She never will say, but I can see it on her when she comes home after something has gone wrong. Usually after a birth she comes head up, chest out, swinging her bag, pets the dog, etc. But the opposite shows when all goes completely wrong, even when it is hopeless. She is depressed in spirit, listless, and the old vitality is out of her eyes. Recently two cases—a six months premature where the aid of the hospital, doctors and drugs could not bring the baby to breathe. The other—to a farm where an acetylene torch exploded, throwing splinters through a man's head. If things arc low I slack off also. It takes only a case of two like these to really make you realize how small and helpless man is when the hand of the reaper claims his soul.

Mar. 1953

The urge to kill was never greater. It was a cold night, storming, visibility zero and it was 2:30 a.m. We had been at friends in Lancaster for the evening, were just ready to eat when the call came. The main road was bad enough but the dirt lane of a mile was murder and bumpy. Only with luck we didn't get stuck. Grace had to carry her light and gear from the drive to the house. Brother, what did she find, everyone in bed. Forgot about the doctor coming, plus no pain at all.

Mar. & April 1953

Grace is pregnant! We were sure of it some time ago, but having hysterics. She is having considerable nausea, and I never saw a doctor who could take care of herself. Putting up a front to the patients has been a very hard thing also. Many a time she would beat a path to the bathroom as the patient left the front door. On house calls she would stop the car to disgorge, then go on her merry way. Of course it is going to help her in her practice. The maternity cases will get more sympathetic help from now on.

Late Summer 1953

Hiding that expanding belly was quite a problem, but she gradually discarded each garment for a looser one. One night she tried on a loose-fitting dress, black, and darned if she didn't look like a street walker on Arch and Race [Philadelphia]. Gradually it became known that she was pregnant and the clientele reacted very favorably towards it.

A most fitting climax was presented to this 9 months rage when Grace delivered somewhat in a hurry and the 14 mile dash to the hospital proved to be a necessity. A baby girl, 8 lbs. of crying dynamite [Aug. 31st]. She will and has changed our habits a great deal. No longer do we pick up and leave. Her patients have reacted very nicely. I hope they will come back to her when she starts again September 8th.

[There are no further entries until January 1961, after which the entries are mostly about blizzards, obstetrical deliveries and conflicts or interruptions of care of the three children.]

Chosen at random:
Our Amish friends keep amazing us. Grace was out on calls when one called wanting to know how his wife was. I didn't know so I told him to call back in 1/2 hour or so. His answer was, "Well, I guess I don't have to know."

Thursday night Grace left for the hospital right after hours; didn't get back until 7:30 a.m. It was a night for the rascals [children] to act up. They had been to a basketball game and just a little excited. So naturally Elsa had to go to the bathroom, and also had some bad dreams. Keith had a nosebleed about 5:30 a.m. and needed comforting. Poor kid, he was so upset that his sheet had blood on it. And Lorelei, every time the others stirred, she woke up. In fact, when Keith woke up at 5:30 a.m. she took it as a sign to get up and was put out that I insisted on her going back to sleep. She wanted no part of it.

Time after time the phone rings for the ambulance to go to the Welsh Mountains to take a girl to the hospital. All sorts of reasons are given as to why she can't go by regular car—too sick, no car available, no gas for the car, etc. All the reasons Grace has to turn down. It's rough. They're nasty, call her names, etc. One accused her of wanting the mother-to-be delivered like an animal in a stable. The fact is, that no matter how impossible it is for the girl to get to the hospital, she always manages very nicely and in plenty of time.

Started to teach Keith how to tie shoelaces; what a job; I didn't get far. He is still all boy. He was dressed for Bible School when I noticed a wet spot on his pants. He had his water pistol filled in his pocket, only it leaked. He owes me 39 cents for the pistol. It is going to be a riot getting the 39 cents out of him. He claims he doesn't have a 39 cent piece and that is that.

8
Amanda's Death

During my fifteen years of general practice, births challenged me the most; each small miracle a future to be molded by choices. It was death that I disliked most.

"Hello. This is Abram S. Stoltzfus near Paradise. Can you hurry over?" the husky voice panted over the telephone. "It's my wife Amanda. Can't get her air right. We think she's dying, won't let us call an ambulance."

Bed was comfort. I wanted to roll over, pull the quilt above my ears and pretend the phone had not rung. Deep in sleep after an early night birthing with a woman in Vogansville, another house call seemed a punishment for choosing to be a country doctor.

"Right away," I answered, groping the phone into its cradle. Careful not to disturb my snoring husband, I grabbed clothes from the rocking chair beside the bed, thinking of Amanda's long fight with cancer. Her death would be the first one in a home since I began practice, and it would leave a jagged hole in my life. The past three months a bond had developed between us as we chatted in her homey kitchen, often rich with the odor of drying apple snitz, sliced apples or fresh chocolate cake cooling on her drainboard.

Often as I wrapped Amanda's fleshy arm to check her blood pressure, she spoke of past generations—how her shriveled great-grandmother rocked beside the kitchen range after supper and smoked her pipe, knocking ashes into the coal scuttle. I never saw an Amish woman smoke and was surprised to hear that any Amish woman ever smoked.

While I counted Amanda's pills and capsules, she told of her great-grandfather's story about the first Stoltzfus cousins distant enough in kinship that they could marry. Amanda acknowledged that Abram was her second cousin.

Thinking of Amanda, I plunged my feet into scuffed brown boots and hoped I could drive to Paradise in time to ease her last hours if she needed me.

The night smelled of freshly plowed fields and spring's dankness of new growth. It was as obsidian as the bottom of my black bag. I eased the station wagon onto Main Street and drove south on roads that followed fence line and cow path. My headlights shown on roadbanks wild with new grass and old brambles. Holsteins grazed pastures white with dew. Cottontails dove into bushes, and cats scrambled from warming their paws on the macadam.

Amanda's face, thin and weary from weeks of pain and cancer, occupied my thoughts. I mourned her, worried about proper bedside manner. Hospital deaths in their clinical situation had an impersonal businesslike atmosphere. Could I maintain a professional stance and emotional isolation? Delivering babies at home were joyous occasions but a home death—I was uneasy about this first death outside the hospital.

The roads were empty. The first light was the searchlight on Beacon Hill near the sleeping village of Intercourse. The signal swiveled its powerful beam, helping to guide airplanes across country by a network of such beacons.

Newport Road seemed the most pock-marked, narrow, twisted road in our end of Lancaster County. The red reflector and dim taillights of a carriage shone ahead. I passed three Amish market wagons, gray-canvased matchboxes on wheels, thumping pothole and blacktop. I imagined the joggle and jar felt by the passengers. As if whipped, the lathered horses clopped south surrounded in their own mist.

Where were these carriages rushing, 3:30 a.m., midweek? Amish farmers rarely traveled the road so close to milking time. Herdsmen should be lighting lanterns to begin feeding cows. What emergency had aroused folks?

One brown horse or vibrating wagon was indistinguishable from another to me. But the Amish often recognized neighbor and family by their carriages.

I remembered the story Amanda told on herself. Driving home from a quilting bee at a sister's home, she could not understand why her horse jerked its head with a peculiar twist. She climbed from the wagon, inspected bridle and harness for broken straps, found nothing wrong and drove home. When Abram unharnessed the horse, he asked Amanda why she had driven brother-in-law Henry King's mare home instead of their Bud. A young nephew had hitched horses to the wagons after the quilting. Henry's mare had a habit of throwing her head, especially when headed away from home. Poor Amanda was teased at every family gathering. When Amanda told me about it, I laughed and bragged that my ignition key fit only my own gray station wagon.

Maneuvering curves and cavities, I remembered how Amanda had found a small lump in her breast last summer but did not tell anyone because Naomi, the last daughter at home, planned a November wedding. Wedding season was too busy a time to think of hospitals and surgery. By December the cancer had metastasized beyond cure.

As I drove, I imagined that Amanda would lie in her back bedroom when I arrived, green window shades pulled to the windowsills. She would rest in her old mahogany, high headboard bed where she birthed fourteen children and had spent most of the past several weeks. Abram and several children would gather around her. I steeled myself to be the professional efficient doctor they expected.

Abram Stoltzfus lived along a long lane that ran between two hardtopped roads. Large farms with rambling brick houses hunkered over each end. Abram's unmarried daughters, Lizzie and Mary, lived in a small frame house at mid-lane. They earned a living sewing summer straw hats for Amish men and boys.

When Abram and Amanda retired, son Joel moved onto one farm. Abram cut off an acre and built a small white frame house along the lane. Like most Amish homes it had the traditional two front doors, a glassed sunporch along the side and at the back door a kettlehouse for washday and storage. Amanda continued gardening and canning. Evenings Amanda said she could rock on the front porch and listen to the corn grow in the field across the lane. When needed, she grannied for daughters at their birthing times. In winter she quilted for a tourist shop in Bird-in-Hand. Abram made wooden toy animals and lawn ornaments in his shop. He rarely missed a day's work at the weekly cattle auction in Vintage.

Joel's home was dark except for a pale light in a kitchen window as I entered the gravel lane. Four weeks ago I had spent half a night talking cows and tobacco growing with Joel, while Salome labored with her fourth baby.

It had been the first birth at Joel's house that Amanda had not grannied for us. She usually bustled about, sorting out the proper baby clothes, hunting old rags or fanning Salome with a folded newspaper on hot summer nights. I had missed her constant smile, her large shadow playing along the wall and over my work as she waited to receive the newborn in warm blankets and dress the latest grandchild.

I slowed to a crawl behind a carriage, its iron-clad wheels crunching lane gravel, lights off to save the battery. The horse pulled to Abram's hitching rail beside a small barn and shop. Three tethered bays stomped their feet and whinnied as the new arrival took the last rail space. I parked before the white barn.

Clutching my bag, I hurried up the narrow walk toward the kettlehouse, family entrance of many Amish homes. A bobbing flashlight searched the dark from the enclosed porch.

"This way. Mom's in the kitchen. Use this door," daughter Annie from Black Horse Road called in a hushed voice. She shown light on the concrete steps.

I would rather have returned home, but followed the silhouette into the sunporch and wondered if the shadows made her plumper than usual or if I would soon add her name to my maternity list.

Windows and doors between the kitchen and porch had been removed to heat the glassed room. By light from the Coleman lantern above the kitchen table, I could see Amanda's hopes for another season growing in plum box seedlings. There were Campbell's Tomato Soup cans of cabbage, marigold and tomato plants lining the shelves under the porch windows.

Amanda's labored breathing filled the kitchen. In terminal heart failure, she sat on the green studio couch propped by bolsters and rose-embroidered cushions from parlor chairs. She pulled each wheezed breath in waves that heaved her large bosom with gasping exertion. When she saw me, her half-open eyes lit faintly with recognition. Fluid-logged lungs were unrelieved by her rattling cough.

"Doctor—don't make me—go to the hospital—please," Amanda panted through blue lips. "I wanta—die here—with the family." Her body, thin from cancer, had doubled its size with retained fluid since my last visit.

I accepted a kitchen chair and pulled it to her couch, warmed the stethoscope in my palm a moment before laying it against her clammy chest. Soggy lung rales, air bursting through moisture, rattled in my ears.

"You would be more comfortable in the hospital. Oxygen would ease your breathing," I said.

"No—please," Amanda choked. She coughed, sucking air through dry parted lips. Her eyes were puffy, her face bloated, ironing out the usual sagging jowls and wrinkles.

"How long has she been this bad?" I asked Abram.

"The girls have been taking turns staying with us overnight for several weeks, but this began yesterday. Much worse since this noon." He dropped his unhappy gaze. "We gave in to her, but the girls thought we oughta call you now."

Dressed in Sunday black broadfalls, vest and coat, Abram had eyes that were dark sad circles. He scarcely looked away from Amanda. Standing beside his wife's death bed, Abram wore a lined face, haggard above an untrimmed wiry beard that mingled white with red in the lamplight. Gray hair, cut to ear-lobe length, ringed a nearly bald head. What Abram lost in height, he compensated for in girth. He cleared his throat and stepped into the shadows, allowed me to take his place.

Abram continued, "Said she wanted the Lord to take her from her home, with family near." Craggy lines and hollow cheeks showed the strain of sleepless nights and worried days.

"No ambulance—no hospital," Amanda gasped. Black-ringed

eyes searched the room. "Sylvia — Isaac — Benuel — Naomi — not here yet?"

Salome rubbed her mother-in-law's wrists. Sarah fanned her mother violently with a newspaper folded in quarters. They lifted tree-trunk legs onto the couch. "Let her here if that's what she wants," they agreed.

"Let her be," Abram said. He looked toward the kitchen table for confirmation.

On benches and chairs around the linoleum-covered table a ring of black-coated sons and sons-in-law hunched quietly or murmured in Pennsylvania Dutch. They nodded glum agreement. From an iron hook above the table, the Coleman lantern with its milkglass globe hissed a monotone dirge adding heat to the stuffy room. Even at night, the polished birch cupboards reflected Amanda's meticulous care. The brown pebbled linoleum shone streaks of light. A coal snapped in the stove, splitting the rhythm of the mantle clock like an off-beat cymbal.

"Good-bye children — Abram," Amanda panted, closing her eyes.

Amanda's strident breathing dominated the room until a carriage ground stones on the lane and a stubby, black-shawled woman rushed through the kettlehouse doorway, breaking the room's tension.

Sylvia smiled recognition to her solemn brothers at the table. Amanda's struggling breaths sobered her chubby face. She kissed her mother's cheek, "Hello, Mam." She shook Abram's hand. "Glad I got here in time," she whispered. Tears wet her eyes as she turned to take bonnet and shawl into the parlor. She shook hands with everyone before relieving Sarah at the fanning.

"Good-bye," Amanda repeated, gave a deep gasp and stopped breathing.

Clock and lantern intruded like a gong in the silent room. I caught Amanda's last irregular heartbeats in my stethoscope. I nodded to Abram. The months of waiting for cancer to claim its victim were over. Our grief lay in the void of Amanda's struggle for breath. Lizzie and Mary began to remove pillows from the couch and lay their mother flat.

"No, no." Abram stepped forward, arm outstretched. "No. I want the other children to see her like she died," he commanded. "They will be here soon. I want them to see her sitting up, like she passed away. God is good. We wouldn't wish her back again. The way she suffered these last days—." He lifted silver-rimmed glasses and wiped his eyes, blew loudly into a white handkerchief.

The funeral director would remove Amanda's body long enough for embalmment, then return it, clothed in a white dress and lying in a plain, pine-box coffin. I had been to Amish homes after a death. The coffin would sit on trestles in the parlor, all furniture and carpet removed.

Flowers never embellish Amish funerals or decorate their cemeteries. Stark floor boards would add solemnity to the cold room, its green window shades pulled to polished pine sills during the two or three days of vigil before the funeral. Black-clad Amish neighbors and *freundschaft* (kinfolk) would come to embrace and shake hands with the grieving family, offer condolences, food and assistance at the funeral. After services a serpentine procession of chalk-numbered carriages would drive to the graveyard, then return to Joel's larger house for a meal.

With no telephone closer than a non-Amish neighbor two miles away or the pay phone at Paradise, my promise to telephone Mr. Brown, the funeral director at Christiana, and ask him to come for Amanda was an opportunity for the family to keep Amanda until the remaining children arrived. It would be forty-five minutes before I reached home and the telephone.

Abram's family spoke in whispers, grateful that Amanda had not been forced to go to the hospital, that her death had not been postponed by medical intervention. The men were glum. The women shed silent tears into white handkerchiefs, spoke of their mother's freedom from this life and from the pain of cancer suffered the past sleepless weeks.

Sorrow was contagious. I looked at Amanda, scarcely realizing that a friend was gone. My pleasant routine visits were finished. Should I have insisted on hospitalization? But why, when cancer consumed her? I could have done nothing more for her.

It was still the black of early morning when I packed my bag and shook hands around the room, took a last look at Amanda surrounded by pillows and loving grief. I started through the sunporch,

Annie beside me. I tugged her sleeve gently and whispered, "Do your people usually keep their dead in the position in which they die?"

She shook her head. "No," she murmered. "It's just because Dad wants it that way."

"Oh yes," Abram called to me. "You'll be passing preacher Elmer Zooks on the way home. His wife Mina is sister to Amanda. Could you stop and tell them? There's no close neighbor with a phone. Thank you."

Two carriages waited on the hard road to enter the lane as I drove out. A third still hurried south several miles away near Elmer's lane. I drove between whitewashed board fences beside grassy ditches and parked along the Zook's wire yard fence. In the dark I stumbled up the irregular flagstone walk under a leafing grape arbor. Spidery vines interlaced overhead in rambling roadmap designs and cast erratic webbed shadows at my feet.

Elmer's house and its inhabitants were familiar. Flu, measles and farm accidents had taken me to their home. I remembered the day Elmer amputated the end of two fingers in a V-belt. On postpartum leave from the office, I had driven him to the hospital.

I had frequently aroused Mina at night from her back bedroom to travel with me as granny for a daughter in labor. This morning, knocks on the sunporch door accomplished no more than shudders along its flimsy wooden wall and trembles in the glass panes. The porch and kitchen doors were unlocked. I groped around table and chairs hoping none stood out of place waiting for my shins. Heat from the range guided me around the stove toward the bedroom.

"Anybody home?" I called. "It's Doctor Kaiser. Anybody home? I hate to get you up." Did Elmer keep a loaded gun for intruders? I wished I had not been so quick to agree to stop here.

Grunts and grumbles beyond the door. "Who's there? What's wrong? Old Harry get out on the road again?" Elmer shouted, remembering the night I led his driving horse off the road and knocked on the bedroom window to wake him. Elmer appeared barefooted in the sleeping room doorway, silhouetted by a dim kerosene lamp on the bedside stand. He pulled suspendered broad-fall pants over an unbleached muslin nightshirt, rubbed squinting eyes with the back of a broad calloused hand.

"Somebody having a baby?" Mina called, sitting in a pile of quilts. "I don't know who it'd be." She straightened her muslin nightcap and pulled a blue flannel gown to her neck.

"No. It's Amanda. She died this morning," I answered.

"Well, Mom. You know what must be done. We'll go over right away," Elmer said. "A blessing for Amanda that she could go. Abram will need us."

Pondering my first home death, I drove home slowly. I was not sure what I had expected. Life and death had assumed new aspects. Amanda's family had not wailed or complained. Death for them seemed an extension of life. Lines of Bryant's poem *Thanatopsis* came to me like a hymn.

> *So live, that when thy summons comes to join*
> *The innumerable caravan which moves*
> *To that mysterious realm, where each shall take*
> *His chamber in the silent halls of death,*
> *Thou go not, like the quarry-slave at night,*
> *Scourged to his dungeon, but, sustained and soothed*
> *By an unfaltering trust . . .*

9
Your Baby or Mine

There are myths and fears about babies being mixed up in hospital nurseries, but I never thought it could happen to me, happen at a home delivery. One minute you hold your baby in your arms, the next moment someone else sees it as theirs.

Stevie Smucker called from his neighbor's telephone at 3:30 a.m., "Can you come now? It's Sallie's fifth you know."

I hated to slide out of warm sheets into a cold night. I tired of balancing cooking, babies and husband with patients and office hours. Too often blind justice tipped the scales away from family. In fantasy I quit practice many times, but I was entangled in a web of commitment, monthly lists of women who expected me to come when they called. Our relationships, repeated year after year, nourished me. I was an addict who did not want to recognize my affliction.

Winter nights husbands hated to leave warm houses for more than one telephone call so they often waited until the last minute. Sometimes they waited too long. Groping for clothes laid out on a chair at bedtime, I telephoned my office nurse, five houses down Main Street. "Anna, I'll pick you up in ten minutes."

"Ten minutes bed to street," I often bragged to Pete. Before running from the bedroom, I nudged my husband awake. He shook his pile of covers like a spaniel after a swim. "The Smuckers live at Mount Tabor, three miles south of New Holland," I said. "I'll be back in time to nurse the baby."

"You'd better be." Pete rolled over without missing a snoring beat.

He was right. At five months Lorelei slept all night, but she indisputably believed that milk came exclusively from breasts, never a hard rubber nipple. I expected her to sleep until seven before waking, hungry and screaming if not fed. I hated to disturb her, take her with me as I had always done my newborns, carrying black bag in one hand and a baby on the other arm. My infants had slept in nurses' lounges, on Amish couches or on spare beds. Returning before Lorelei's breakfast time seemed a safe gamble.

Stevie had reminded me, "Remember how fast Sallie was the last time? You didn't get your coat off before the baby came."

I hurried down our hall, not worried about Elsa, age seven, or Keith the kindergartner. Pete could get them breakfast and off to school. I looked at the baby, not even squirming in sleep.

The stars were out. Frost crunched under our boots as Anna and I went up Smucker's concrete walk and through their cold kettlehouse into the kitchen heated by a monstrous brown space heater crackling with fresh coal. Heat felt good. The stale odor of last night's supper mingled with that of cow stable, clinging to a row of shoes beneath the stove. Anna hung her red coat with my corduroy on hooks behind the stove with a row of black garb. We went into the adjoining bedroom to see Sallie.

She lay on a bed prepared according to printed instructions. On top of a clean sheet she had laid a square of protective plastic, then a cloth-covered newspaper pad. Her bed and dresser were a matching waterfall pattern, popular several decades ago.

"Guess I have everything you need," Sallie said, motioning toward a gray enamel washbasin, a pile of clean white rags and neat stacks of baby clothes on the bureau.

I crossed the flowered tan linoleum, opened my bag and laid out a box of plastic gloves and a sterile instrument pack on a bedside chair. "You won't be as fast this time," I said, after the examination.

"Then I might as well get up and work," Sallie said. "Maybe it'll help move things along. It would be good to have this baby before the kids get up." She slid a blue seersucker housecoat over the ragged nightgown worn for her birthing. She fumbled under the bed for tattered gray slippers.

"The milk truck gets here 'bout eight o'clock. Guess I'll go to the barn, get an early start on feedin' and milkin' case you want me later," Stevie said. His voice became demanding. "I sure wanta be in here when Sallie needs me. Be sure to come call me or set a kerosene lamp in the kitchen window if things get serious." His tone changed to doubtful. "Remember, I can't leave a milker on a cow and run. Gotta give me plentya time. I'll watch for a light."

He sat in his pine swivel chair at the head of the blue linoleum-covered kitchen table and laced up ankle-high work shoes cracked by mud and muck. A worn and dusty old coat taken from behind the stove had seen many hours in the barn. His blacktop hat wore ragged stain margins along its band.

In a culture of similar names, repeated like a stutter, the Amish are fond of nicknames. It was no wonder that Stevie was known in the community as Shorty Smucker. Dressed in wide-brimmed hat and bulky coat, he would have looked more like a smiling, half-grown adolescent, not a father of four and master of his farm, if it had not been for his bushy black beard. He was as round as a tree stump. His short arms ended in hands like soup plates. Ruddy cheeks were set in a face as round as the full moon, his nose a pointy afterthought. Boyish brown eyes and Amish ear-lobe length, bowl-cut hair with bangs might cause a stranger to ask him if his father was at home.

Satisfied that his wife was not alone, Stevie went down the walk to the barn, swinging a pressure lantern in each hand. I daydreamed, imagined him hurrying into the stable, closing the door quickly to keep the body heat of the cows from escaping into the crisp night. The cows would stretch out their black and white Holstein necks to lick up every last grain of feed, rough tongues scraping the concrete trough like sandpaper. Neck chains would rattle, cows yet unfed bawling with impatience. Their sweet breaths would mingle with the dust and odor of fresh-forked hay and warm milk streaming into buckets from the pumping milkers. Quiet would settle over the herd as loaded udders were drained. I reminisced the barn of my youth, thought of my own breasts soon in need of emptying and searched my dress for telltale wet circles.

While we waited for Sallie's labor to progress, Anna sat on the kitchen couch beside the closed sewing machine. I took a chair near the hissing Coleman lantern hung from a hook above the table. We talked winter weather, babies and cooking with Sallie while she swept the leaf-figured linoleum with a broom, then stacked last evening's supper dishes, a mishmash of size and pattern, into brown cupboards. The lantern cast a honey glow onto the cream-painted walls and varnished cupboards, worn smooth along the edges of doors by the busy hands of housewives.

During contractions Sallie stopped working to hold her abdomen. I could tell by her even panting that birthing was not imminent. Occasionally she drew more snugly the ends of an unbleached muslin kerchief covering her light brown hair, combed tightly from brow to bun at the nape of her neck. Shuffling around the room, she turned the baby blankets warming on a clothes rack at the stove, glanced at the mantle clock metering time behind the kitchen table. Five-thirty. The ticking beat out time toward seven.

At home Lorelei would soon be stirring for breakfast. I could feel the need for her in my breasts and remembered the painful mastitis and 104° fever I had suffered when Keith was a baby. I had been gone from him too long while waiting with Alta Sensenig in the hospital labor room. Then I had scrubbed for her delivery before going home to my own baby.

"Guess I'm not so fast this time," Sallie said. An apologetic smile crossed her oval face. "Sorry to keep you waiting so long."

We heard a cough and huffing in the barn as Stevie started the diesel engine to begin milking. The kitchen's green window shades were pulled to the deep varnished sills, in case a neighbor might see lights and guess that Sallie's birthing was in the wind. I raised a shade. Outside all was dark except for boxes of light marking the stable windows and larger distorted blocks reflecting onto the gravel lane. I stood at the window wishing the night to stand still or Sallie to deliver within minutes. Neither was likely.

If I went home, my patient's anxiety would probably speed up her labor, and she would deliver without my help. If I did not go home, Lorelei would soon be a squalling hungry baby and Pete an angry frustrated husband.

Anna drove my red station wagon back to Main Street and returned a half hour later with clean diapers and Lorelei in her car bed, a collapsible affair that rested on the rear seat and hooked over the back of the front seat. The baby slept until I lifted her from the bed.

Sallie was concerned about her family too. Soon her children would awaken and want to come downstairs where they were not wanted during their mother's labor and delivery. Amish children are not included in birthing events.

While I changed my baby across my spread knees, then nursed her, Sallie began breakfast. She brought from the pantry an enormous box of saltines, butter in a small crock, a basket of eggs and an iron frying pan. She carried a pail of milk in from the cold kettlehouse.

"Can you eat some eggs for breakfast?" Sallie lit the black propane gas stove under a pan of milk. Her deft thin fingers cracked eggs into a bowl without breaking a golden yolk. The odor and sputter of frying eggs spread through the kitchen. She filled soup plates with saltines.

I sat by the window burping my blanket-swathed baby against a shoulder. The sun's first light separated night from day along the horizon. As the minutes passed grotesque shapes took form; Smucker's grape arbor, the plastic-wrapped martin house on its pole, the skeletal windmill rising like an airport tower above the well in the yard.

The stable lanterns went out. Stevie's bundled apparition sauntered between the gateposts and started up the walk. Suddenly, as if stung by a bee, his silhouette ran for the kettlehouse door.

We heard his boots stomp the cement floor in pounding steps. He tore through the doorway into the kitchen like a summer gale. He could not see Sallie pouring hot milk over butter-dolloped crackers. She slid eggs over the saltines, two lidless orbs in each dish.

"Why? Why didn't you call me?" Stevie panted, throwing his coat over a chair, hat on top. His face was red, eyes flashing anger. The thick beard did not hide his indignation. He looked like a policeman catching a man at a crime.

Stepping farther into the kitchen, he saw Sallie as she started toward the table, a dish in each hand. He saw her still large protuberance hanging like over-ripe fruit, then Lorelei bobbing against my shoulder, and he began to laugh. Stevie aimed a long stretch of Pennsylvania Dutch, his native tongue, at his wife. She grasped her pendulous pear, spatula in hand, and joined the hilarity.

Confessing that all the Dutch I needed to know were *esse* and *gelt*—that "eat" and "money" would carry me through any requirements—I rediapered my baby and wondered at their secret.

"Stevie saw you at the window holding your baby and was upset because he thought it was our baby," Sallie finally explained. "He thought I had a baby, and you didn't call him in. He sure wants to be here when ours is born."

Sallie set three plates of breakfast on the white cotton tablecloth. I have never eaten at an Amish table without a tablecloth, even if it was stained or perforated with holes from hard use. Stevie, Anna and I bowed our heads for silent grace, ate our stewed crackers and finished with sweet crumbly shoofly pie washed down with coffee. Before we rose, another silent grace ended the meal. Sallie, not permitted breakfast until after she delivered, walked around the kitchen wishing that her baby would come soon.

Laughter must have helped. Her labor intensified, fortunately, because the children upstairs had dressed and were impatient to come down. They became louder and more boisterous. Stevie took a box of crackers, a handful of pretzels and slices of cheese up to them to satisfy their hunger and keep them occupied.

At seven Sallie went to bed. Several contractions later a wailing baby lay on the sheet. Anna covered the newborn with warm blankets, then carried her off to weigh and dress her while I delivered the placenta. Stevie hacked a hole in the half-frozen garden to bury the placenta from the dogs and the children.

The chattering children came down the stairway, nine-year-old Mary toting soggy Aarie on one hip. Melvin, seven, and Amos, four, slid along the wall behind Mary. Silence captured them when they spied Anna and me. They were even more astonished to see my baby in her car bed.

Sallie gave directions. "Melvin can go to school. I'll keep Mary home to tend Aarie and fetch things for me. That's the advantage of goin' to Amish school. The teacher will understand. My mom lives near Quarryville. Stevie and Mary can manage until we send a driver down for her."

Lorelei had gone to sleep. Her stomach satisfied, the rest of the world was of no concern to her. I picked up *MY* baby and went home.

10
Rehabilitation Center

This was the day. I did not want it, had not ordered it, but it had arrived. I had reluctantly agreed. This was the day to leave the friendly care of the hospital that had been a part of my life since the first day of internship and go for rehabilitation among strangers. I chose City Rehabilitation Center near Reading because it was closest to New Holland, about thirty-five miles away.

Joe had been the first to warn me. "They think you should enter a regular rehabilitation center," he said.

"Who's they, and why?" I asked. After seven weeks I could walk through the gym if a therapist held the back of my slacks for balance. Every evening I sat in a chair a few minutes longer to increase the time out of bed until my body ached to lie down. I fed myself lunch each day, fork fastened to my hand with velcro, the arm supported by springs. My swollen hands were useless; I carried a Foley catheter and its bag everywhere. A newborn had more mobility and as much dependence on others.

"You'll get special care and retraining," Joe said. "They have a large warm swimming pool as well as a psychiatrist. Most patients like you go through depression."

Joe received a turned-up nose, two inches of my tongue and a laugh. "I won't need a psychiatrist," I vowed. No one in my family had ever had an emotional problem. "That's a joke."

The "they" were the physician head of physiotherapy and my friend the neurosurgeon, whose name headed my chart and orders. The neurosurgeon was kind, generous and thoughtful. At his next visit he confirmed Joe's statements. "They'll get rid of your catheter at the rehab center. Urinary tract infections can be a problem in spinal cord patients," he said, smiling. "I remember a case during my residency. The man kept his catheter inside his hatband. He built up a resistance to any bacteria it carried." The doctor grinned, shook his head, remembering.

I imagined the man in a restroom unwinding his red rubber catheter from inside his hatband. Ingenious.

"You'll do fine at the rehabilitation center," the neurosurgeon continued. "We'll send you by ambulance."

On moving day the New Holland ambulance waited at the emergency room exit. A screaming ambulance chills me. The hair on my arms stands out straight, despite the times I gratefully watched one drive down a farm lane. My request to ride by car to the rehabilitation center was lost in the scuffle of "doing what was best."

There is nothing wonderful about an ambulance trip, even when anticipated. The atmosphere of this ride was calmer than the one seven weeks previous when admission for quadriplegia cut the night air with anxiety.

Wrapped in sheets and blankets, arms buckled straight to the body, a patient's view from a rolling litter is restricted to monotonous ceiling tiles passing overhead in hypnotizing repetitious squares. The gurney wheels corners, thrusts and bumps into elevators. Attendants mutter polite but unimportant phrases like "here we go," or "almost there, keep your elbows in."

The stretcher slips into an ambulance like a letter through a slot. The overhead view is white ceiling. The odor is hospital. The ride is a hybrid mating of dump truck and an Amish carriage. An open radio crackles messages to the county emergency units. Through side windows the world passes in the blur of a fast forward movie.

In seven weeks the snappy fall days of October had changed to cold December. A soft drizzle closed in the day and curtained the east coast from the sun. Leaves, once red and gold, clung to the ground in brown patches and soggy wads under naked maples and elms.

A chill air carried rain and the odor of moldering summer. It cooled my cheeks as I was unloaded at the brick rehabilitation hospital. Tied and wrapped I seemed more like a delivery of beef to the kitchen. The thought was both funny and depressing.

More acoustical tiles, reeling corners, the smell of disinfectants, the rattle of pills at the nurses' station. Pete signed admission papers. A "one, two, three," count slid me onto a bed, sheeted taut as an ironing board cover.

I said good-bye to my friends of the ambulance crew and lifted my head to view the large room. "Wrong room," I whispered. "There are men in those two beds."

"No," Pete said. "We were afraid if you knew this was a mixed ward you wouldn't come."

A nurse smiled and pulled the sheet to my shoulders. "Two men and two women. New experiment. You're all quads."

Right. I could not have imagined nor would I have consented to sharing a room with men. Gripped without choice in the jagged teeth of a decision made by some unknown authority, I decided to be open-minded and give it a try. One thing for certain, no hanky-panky possible with four quads.

Large institutional windows brightened the room. Jimmy's bed was beside the window. Mike's across from mine near the door. Cindy also had a window bed. In the aisle shared by Jimmy and Cindy a life-sized teddy bear straddled a commode chair. One of my pet peeves was the gift of stuffed animals to adult hospitalized patients, sending the message that for some reason their brain had also become disabled. Mine was the only bed not surrounded by greeting cards, stuffed animals or medical paraphernalia.

Mike and I were foot-to-foot across an aisle. "A big wave knocked me down at Atlantic City last July," Mike told me later. "When my wife didn't see my bald head come out of the water, she hunted around and dragged me to the beach. Thought I'd drown before she found me. Had an operation for a broken neck before I came here, in another hospital."

Mike was short, bony and mid-fifties. Nature had covered his skeleton with the barest necessity of skin and flesh, giving his face the phantasmal gaunt appearance of a man in the shadows. His smiles were pleasant but fleeting. Uncontrolled tremors, like aspen leaves quivering in a breeze, shook his feet. Depressed about being a quadriplegic and losing his ability to manage the family electrical business, he was quiet and polite. His wife visited every evening, his grown children several nights each week. Conversations were short except when he argued sporting heroes and baseball scores with Jimmy.

Jimmy had become adept at turning his *Popular Mechanics* and baseball magazines with a mouth stick, pecking page over page. Watching with repugnant awe, I shuddered wondering if I would be expected to use one. I had only heard of the rod used by quads to draw pen-and-ink designs on greeting cards. Jimmy clamped the top of the T-shaped stick between his lips and teeth directing the free end like a pencil.

"I should'na dived off that dock," Jimmy said. He laughed, dimpling smooth cheeks, "That old bay got me. Too shallow. I laid on the bottom 'til I thought I'd die. Couldn't figure what had happened to me. My cousin came in and pulled me out." Barely twenty, brown-eyed Jimmy was a mixture of youthful sunshine and moments of black clouds. His many friends visited several nights each week or took him out barhopping and to ball games by wheelchair. I tried to imagine him drinking beer through a straw. Or, did his pals lift his glass for each swallow? Jimmy's parents anticipated his eventual discharge by remodeling their house for wheelchair access, adding a room and special shower. They accepted their son's need for dependent care the rest of his life.

"How do we transfer you?" the nurse asked me at admission. "What can you do for yourself?"

"I sit unassisted, walk a few steps with help." I had been proud of my accomplishments. "My hands are swollen and useless. I can bend my right elbow enough to touch my face, move my shoulders the most." Now it sounded like so little progress. "I stand and pivot to transfer."

Stand-pivot is the toe of the patient's shoes against the nurse's toes. Knee bracing knee, the nurse lifts the patient under the arms, pivots on the balls of the feet and transfers the patient onto a bed or into a chair. It is safe as well as easy on the attendant's back.

The nurse examined the sore over my tail bone. "Have your

husband bring in a hair dryer to dry it. We'll put medication on your coccyx. Have to watch all quads and paras for sores. Between occupational and physical therapy schedules you won't have time to lie in bed."

The sore healed, but with no sensory perception below the shoulder level, I could easily burn myself with the hot packs we could request for spastic painful shoulders. My roommates were complete quads and had more skin problems than I did. Since small hemorrhages in my spinal cord had caused my injury and the cord was not severed, I knew that my full recovery was only months and intense therapy away. It had been promised.

Until rehabilitation was complete, I accepted the assigned wheelchair. "Look out behind," I called down the halls and out of elevators. My arms never became strong enough to push a wheelchair forward. Hoping unwary victims saw me in time to escape, I pushed backward with my feet, like a grasshopper in reverse.

At City Rehabilitation Center, Occupational Therapy fit a plywood lapboard, like a highchair tray, over the wheelchair arms. It helped secure me and was a way to transport things. I could also read a book or magazine from the surface.

"Will you bring me a *Woman's Day?*" I asked Pete. "And a rubber thumb like money counters use so I can turn pages." A nurse pushed the adhesive cot over my middle finger. Squeezing the magazine between the heels of both fists, I dragged it onto my lapboard. Pushing page over page, leafing recipes, I fumbled from slimming exercises to home remodeling. Cookies, pies and casseroles were not interesting without a kitchen or the ability to hold a mixing spoon. Homemaking articles and child rearing were worlds I could not relate to from a hospital. Cover to cover took an entire exhausting evening, but I accomplished it without a mouth stick. They were for the permanently disabled. My disaster was temporary.

The third day the porter pushed me to the psychiatrist for my appointment. Behind the mahogany desk a balding man in gold-rimmed glasses began asking questions about my accident.

"I'm fine," I said. "Having no problem adjusting. Everything is going well. I don't think I need any help."

"Good," he said, folding small white hands across my chart. "Would you be willing to participate in the group sessions twice a week? They might benefit you."

"Yes," I agreed. I might learn how my roommates felt about their disabilities if I could relate to them in a group. What thoughts and anxieties lay unspoken behind their easy banter? If only the doctor had asked me why I felt so sure about myself, if only he had pursued deeper into my thoughts. Often I have wondered if it would have eased later adjustments.

Most evenings Pete and friends visited. One night Pete brought a jar of peanuts. I chased the capricious nuts up and down my blouse several times before getting them into my mouth but was exalted to have regained enough motion in my right hand to press a nut between thumb and first finger. I bent the elbow and lifted my shoulder. If the peanut did not fall, I could lean forward and catch it between my lips. I had conquered the world. What happy satisfaction a baby must feel as it learns to finger morsels into its mouth.

"I think I could feed myself if you taped a fork into my hand," I told a nurse as she fed me the day after admission.

Occupational Therapy brought a spoon and fork, the handles pushed into four-inch lengths of round rubber, like garden hose. My semi-clenched fingers had no grasping power. An ace bandage bound the fork into my hand. I ordered food from the menu that I could spear easily. This was happiness, one step above the springs that suspended my arms during meals at the hospital.

The first day I struggled to harpoon three forkfuls, using shoulder and elbow muscles. Concentrating on arm position brought the food to my lips. I fought to remember how to coordinate feeding. For several days three trips per meal exhausted my arm. Volunteers from the community who came at mealtime to feed patients forked the remaining carrots and potatoes into my mouth. Slowly the number of self-fed trips increased, but someone had to uncover the plate, cut meat and vegetables, wrap the fork into my hand and finish the meal when I tired.

Then a wonderful thing happened. Marty came from New Holland one noon meal each week. We were friends at church; our children shared activities there and at school. In addition to beets and beans she fed me news of shared acquaintances, church events and hometown doings. I will be forever grateful for her kindness. Her visits were as refreshing as an arctic breeze in mid-July, satisfying a thirst for home and familiar things that I had not recognized as missing.

One evening Barbara, head nurse in obstetrics at Community Hospital, carried a heavy stack of charts to my bedside. As my friend reviewed cases, I dictated progress notes, case summaries and final diagnoses. I was tying off and snipping the loose ends of my life as a physician. Only the present mattered.

"Tomorrow's shower day," a nurse announced. After seven weeks of bed baths, even the word "shower" sounded wonderful. Twice a week we were swathed in towels, seated on the ring of a bottomless shower chair. Its contrary casters each chose to roll in diverse directions. The unfortunate nurse then shoved and pulled the wrapped mummy into a tiled shower alley which connected our ward with four women in the adjoining room.

At last a shampoo. It was like rain after a long drought. Warm water and suds cascaded through my hair and over my shoulders. The nurse was only slightly splashed and barely wet-footed. I felt renewed and clean for the first time in weeks.

Alone — the first weekend at the rehabilitation center. After therapy Friday afternoon my roommates were gathered like chicks under the wings of a brood hen and taken home to their families. Evening hung over the empty beds in a dark silence that seemed to accuse me of some unnamed crime or unanswerable fault that found me too guilty to be released into the world. In the void of catheter-wielding nurses working and chatting behind drawn curtains during bedtime undressing and teeth brushing, I missed my new friends. It had been eight weeks since I had seen New Holland.

Sunday night Cindy, Jimmy and Mike returned from furlough and routine resumed. When would I be allowed home visits?

"You can go home weekends," the doctor told me several days later. "And the week between Christmas and New Year if someone in your family will learn to catheterize you every four hours."

After admission my continuous catheter had been removed and intermittent bladder catheterization instituted every four hours. "Soon you will be able to void again," the nurse told me as she removed the Foley. I had lost bladder function when I lost everything else. The little red tubes became an important part of my routine.

Home. I could not wait until Pete returned from business in Arizona. Both daughters lived in Colorado. Certainly our two sons at home were not candidates for the procedure. Pete could do it.

"No! No," Pete shouted, pacing the foot of my bed. Panic froze his round face. He blanched from stubbled chin to the Arizona tan on his bald head. "You know I've never gotten involved with any part of medicine. No, I won't do it." Skittish as a big fish in shallow water, he grabbed his coat and left.

I had forgotten how he had broken into a sweat when he crushed his finger, fainted the night my aunt fell down the steps and I stitched her torn ear as she sat at the dining room table. When the children were small, Pete had mopped their upset stomachs off furniture and rug when the job nauseated me. He had cleaned up puppy messes and changed diapers. No doctor could have wanted a better phone answering service than Pete, but he could not help in medical situations. In my self-centered world of recovery, I had remembered only my own struggles and the word "home."

Pete's "no!" wet my pillow with tears. All night I felt defeated, boxed in by insurmountable rock cliffs. Home so close, within sight, impossible. I vowed to catheterize myself every four hours. Good, but I could not grasp the stiff slippery tube between my unresponsive fingers, could never guide it into the urethral passage to the bladder. Had the story of the catheter in the hatband been a fore-warning?

By morning I was tired and depressed. Ann, the seven-to-three nursing supervisor, took time from her busy day to stand at my bedside. She held my hand. "Is there anything I can do to help?"

"No," I answered. Fresh uncontrolled tears rolled across my cheeks. My hurt tumbled out in an icy avalanche of words.

"Men!" Ann was recently divorced.

In our heart-to-heart we shared views on the obstinate, egotistical, self-centered, domineering, inconsiderate male sex. I felt better.

"Maybe your husband will change his mind," Ann said, wiping my face with a tissue.

"Okay, what do I have to do?" Pete said that afternoon. Grim with resignation, he sighed, opened the sterile catheter kit, awkwardly pulled on plastic gloves and under supervision catheterized me the first time.

Home. What would it be like? Would my family be able to move me around? I felt vulnerable and afraid.

Mid-December was cold. I needed a coat but could not move my shoulders and arms backward to push the second limb into its sleeve. I was a stiff, uncoordinated, gigantic baby. We remembered an old Logan cape. The wool cloak slipped easily over spastic shoulders as stiff as curtain rods. A thick knitted hat and heavy scarf made me an overwrapped package as the front door of the hospital opened and my warm breath floated before my face in a white frosty mist.

Stand-pivot moved me onto the car seat. Out of the supportive wheelchair for the first time, I felt as unbalanced as a round-bottomed toy clown swaying side to side. Pete swung my feet into the car and tightened the seat belt. Stability returned. I was sure that I would fall over at road curves and stop signs. I pressed my shoes against the floor mat and fought to remain upright until we drove into the garage at New Holland.

I was sure that the dog would be glad to see me. Formerly my shadow, Lady circled living room chairs and hid under the dining room table. Was she afraid of the wheelchair or punishing me for deserting her? I had anticipated tongue licking and wild tail wagging. Disappointed, I waited until she decided to renew our friendship. The next Friday Pete helped me walk into the house. He brought the wheelchair in later. Lady slowly renewed our friendship.

Pete's mother, age seventy-six, had walked across our backyards every day since my accident to cook dinner for my husband and the boys. Oma prepared a good homecoming supper. Keith and Paul forked mashed potatoes, pork chop and peas into my mouth. It seemed funny, unreal. We laughed a lot.

The boys became as adept as Pete at transfers. Paul, a high school junior, chatted about his car and its problems. Keith had finished college and talked about poinsettia Christmas sales for the troop of Boy Scouts he served as leader. The big house seemed cold and drafty. I huddled like a hibernating bear beside the living room fire. Wrapped in a blanket, I watched family activity whirl around me. I felt useless and detached, a guest in the home I had managed, directed and served.

Pete unfolded the twin-size studio couches in the living room, easier than attempting the stairs. He undressed me at night, clothed me in the morning. "I'm no nurse," he said often. I waited under the covers until he built a living room fire and prepared breakfast. Accepting this dependency came because I knew that this new pattern was temporary. Independence would be restored in several months.

In two weeks the girls would be home from Denver for Christmas and routines would be easier.

Elsa had graduated from college; Lorelei was a freshman. When they arrived they made light of my dependency, bought duck-headed pins for "Mom's birdseyes" and laughed. The cutesy pins embarrassed Pete. He hated them, saw nothing funny in his wife's diapering.

Ever since the girls had attended elementary school, we had spent one pre-Christmas day shopping and eating in a restaurant. One afternoon following therapy, they came to the hospital for the annual spree. Elsa pulled a wool hat to my eyes. Lorelei scarfed and wrapped me to the ears. We sallied into Christmas.

"I can't see things down here in this wheelchair," I complained, wanting to choose items on store counters.

"How's this?" Elsa asked. She lifted a pair of men's socks from a stack. But I wanted to see everything, not only the front items on counters. I became impatient if I saw something to my right and my chair pusher steered left. Lorelei carried an assortment of flannel shirts to me because the racks were hanging too full of Christmas sweaters and jackets for my chair to pass through the narrow aisles. It was difficult to get a sales girl's attention from a wheelchair. People talked above my head. Eye contact at my level seemed an effort. I labored all evening in the agony of frustration and birthed a loathing for wheelchairs.

My daughters easily managed the stand-pivot-sit maneuver, loaded and unloaded me from the car at shopping center and restaurant. We decided on a seafood shanty.

"Stop acting silly," Lorelei cried, sprinting behind Elsa and me. "Stop! People will think we're crazy." Our joviality and the speeding wheelchair humiliated her.

Elsa ran me around the building twice, pushing and giggling, looking for the entrance. A cold wind knifed our cheeks and teared our eyes. We laughed too much.

The restaurant was crowded, its aisles barely wide enough to admit the wheelchair. The girls tugged off my wraps as I had pulled off theirs during awkward toddler years. To be fed in the hospital was acceptable but to be forked each mouthful in a restaurant, arms hanging like Raggedy Ann's, was conspicuous. I wondered how Cindy and Jimmy felt when their buddies carted them around. Between their bites, Elsa and Lorelei took turns popping a french fry or shrimp into my mouth. People stopped eating to watch.

"Take me back to the hospital," I said. Enough was enough.

Christmas season moved at a snail's pace. The holidays seemed a commercial mockery without gift buying and wrapping, baking and decorating. The tree at the nurses' station, the children who caroled the halls were as flavorless as flat ginger ale.

Each evening I watched black and white TV from a toaster-size box suspended like a dentist's drill over my bed. Most programs were Christmas specials. Rudolph, the Grinch, Perry Como, "Amahl and the Night Visitors" were a mockery, a world across a cold void I did not want to cross. I wondered if Christmas would ever be merry again, wished Christmas would go away so TV would show other programs.

"Change my channel, please," we quads frequently asked the evening nurses. "Scratch my chin. My nose itches."

The inalienable right to rub and scratch had been pirated the moment of spinal cord injury. I remembered how cows rub great trees barkless with their scouring. On television politicians and newscasters, the President, snatched a rub at ear or nose, unable to resist a polite scratch, even before the camera. In our ward, nurses scratched an itching nose or ear, rubbed an eye, changed a TV channel. The need for a good hard scratch began as an unconscious desire. Neglected, it built to a burning pain. If ignored long enough the need went away, but it took perseverance and distraction.

But Christmas did not go away. "Merry Christmas" was everywhere with tinsel, packages and the countdown of days. I remembered holidays past—annual cookie baking with the children, always the Friday after Thanksgiving. I remembered every one from the first year Elsa was old enough to spill flour on the floor and eat more raisins than decorated eyes and mouths of the gingerbread men. I smiled, recalled Christmas pines that appeared to be molting because small hands dropped the tree balls. I thought of packages scantily clad in red paper and bound with yards of Scotch tape, surprise socks or blouses too wonderful to keep secret.

I remembered Christmas Eves with slow-birthing women. Pete, Oma and the children waiting impatiently to eat our special German supper — potato salad, herring, *gehactus*, balognas, hard rolls ready for the table as soon as I drove into the garage. On frequent trips from the Amish house to my car phone I gave hope and often false promises to my hungry family who did not want Christmas food and packages without Mother. There had been no choice. Duty and obligation had stolen my time, over husband and children. Every year I anticipated a Christmas uninterrupted. Somehow we had always muddled through. Some years we were lucky and holiday babies arrived at night or early in the morning.

I remembered Christmas mornings when Pete kept the restless, tussling children in the stairway until I came home. For them it was unthinkable to rush into the living room to unload Santa's stockings before Mother returned from delivering a Christmas baby. They never waited long. I was just as anxious to begin the day's activities.

"A few more minutes. She's here now," Peter told the four. They lined up on the steps, youngest on the lowest step, the eldest highest. "Now," he called when I had thrown my coat over a chair. He poised his camera and, stepping aside, allowed the stampede to rush toward bulging stockings hung at the fireplace.

We were a half-inch from delusion and tragedy the year Santa nearly did not get to our house, the year Mary Beiler birthed a Christmas baby.

11
Christmas

Every Christmas I worried about the collision of patient and family, knew tragedy would strike eventually. I wretched at the possibility, torn jaggedly by loyalty to both.

Christmas Eve snow dropped around the station wagon like soggy feathers. It clotted against the windshield wipers, falling to the ground in long chunks, too heavy to drift. Bush and tree swayed humpbacked under their white burdens.

Pines and yews beside porches and on lawns nested gemstones of colored lights and brilliant Caribbean birds feeding on kilowatts set out by generous householders. The veil of snow along Route 23 reflected spectrumed light into the dark palm of night. It seemed I drove this routine road to Lancaster the first time.

"If Mary Beiler has her usual short labor, I will soon be home in bed," I thought, still humming "Silent Night." It had been the last hymn at Christmas Eve church service.

I had pushed baby Paul, limp as wilted lettuce, into his snowsuit and argued Lorelei into jacket and quilted pants. Elsa and Keith had tussled over the ownership of a red scarf.

Now as the big station wagon splashed through slippery slush, I reviewed our Christmas Eve. My husband's parents celebrated German style. Dessert had been Christmas cakes and cookies brought from secret places. Finally we had opened long awaited gifts.

I dimmed the headlights, slowed as a passing car splashed dirty mush over the windshield. Tomorrow the holiday would continue when my parents arrived for a roast beef dinner and more gifts. Everything was completed except four limp stockings dangling over the fireplace. Plenty of time for them after Mary had her baby. The stocking stuffings lay hidden in my closet behind shoes and skirts. Only I knew about them.

Amos Beiler had warned the answering service, "Tell Grace to come right away. I don't think she'll have to stay here long."

I took Peter and the children home from the church, called Patsy the town's phone answering service, then continued to Mary and Amos, an Amish couple halfway to Lancaster. The Christmas service still whirled through my head.

The old brick church had been lit only by fluttering candles and white bulbs on a tree hung with chrismons, Christian symbols cut from styrofoam and decorated with silver spangles. They flashed tinseled celebration into the nave. Banks of poinsettias surrounded the lectern and pulpit. Red-bowed pungent pine garlands draped the white walls. The energy of carols attacked even the weary with infectious holiday spirit.

"Merry Christmas" greetings mingled with fresh snowflakes as we tightened scarves and snuggled deeper into our coats when we left the church and met the cold midnight air.

An usher had tapped me on a shoulder. "Call your answering service. Patsy called the church trying to reach you."

I continued toward Lancaster through clinging flakes. At Bard's Crossing I turned south onto an untracked sideroad, the snow muting engine noise as I steered between fence rows and roadbanks onto a ridge. AMOS K. BEILER lettered a dented mailbox. His shadowy farm lay a long field's length below the road. Like a gap-toothed first grader, a blurry opening in the barn wall pointed out the far end of a lane, deep-furrowed on each side by soft demonic ditches. Beside the dim gloomy barn, the old brick farmhouse slept in a stand of bald and silent snow-clad maples. Spouses bedded for a long winter night.

From former visits I knew the lane was a straight line from mailbox to barn wall gate. If my car slid into the muddy gullies, it would take a team of Amos's mules to pull it out.

The station wagon eased onto the lane and slowly followed the headlights to the opening in the wall and through it. I turned the car around and headed downhill toward the road in case the weather turned worse and tried to trap me beside the barn. My car phone would pick up a signal here, but in this gully, behind the barn, calls out would be impossible.

I picked up my bag, hunted the concrete walk to the kettlehouse and stepped into Beiler's warm kitchen.

"A blessed Christmas to you," Mary greeted me.

"A blessed Christmas to you," I answered, shaking snow from my brown corduroy coat and hood. I noticed the Bible on the kitchen table lay open to the Christmas story in Luke.

"It's different tonight than with the last baby," Mary said. "Amos can be with us tonight and you're not in a family way too this time."

At her last delivery Amos had been hospitalized after mutilating his hand in the corn picker. With her husband away from home and his mother too disabled with arthritis to assist with a new baby, Mary had opted to deliver her baby in the hospital. Only two weeks from delivery myself, I had stopped at Beiler's farm to transport laboring Mary. Mommy Beiler, who lived in the nearby *Dawdy house*, had wondered which of us expected to deliver first.

"How is Amos these days?" I asked Mary, a petite woman no taller than my chin. Much of the family's managing fell on her slim shoulders—the farm bookkeeping, directing and disciplining the children and most important, discreetly allowing Amos the impression that he directed affairs.

"Amos does pretty good if he gets his rest and takes his medicine. I see to that. His nerves have been bad since the corn field accident."

"He's upstairs sleeping?" Before examining Mary in the bedroom, I warmed my hands over the square space heater between kitchen cupboards and a green couch. Coal glowed red through transparent oval windows in its door.

"Yes. We'll call him down near baby time. Things go better around here since Sammy's turned fourteen and is out of school."

"One day a week school?" I accepted the bright cushioned rocking chair Mary pulled from the unheated parlor.

"Yes. Josiah Beiler teaches Saturday school in our district for

children fourteen and past eighth grade. Have to obey the law."
Mary's thin face was grave acceptance. Moving around the kitchen
on slim quick legs, she was a chippy sparrow.

"A new baby will be a great Christmas gift," I said.

"Little Mary is two. She doesn't seem like a baby. We'll all enjoy a
new one. The children won't want to leave it to go to Christmas
church with Amos at John S. Stoltzfus's near Witmer."

"Do you expect guests today?"

"Not on first Christmas. Second Christmas, December 26, is
visiting day for our people. When folks hear in church that we have a
new baby, we'll have to put heat in the parlor stove, have plenty of
visitors."

"What will you cook for Christmas dinner?"

"We killed three chickens yesterday. Sarah will be thirteen next
month. She can stay with me and keep house two days until nurse
Annie Petersheim comes after the holiday. We'll probably keep her
from school this week to help at home."

Amish homes showed little holiday decoration in comparison to
my house, wreathed and garlanded from front to rear. An overladen
Christmas tree blinked in our living room. In Mary's kitchen
crayoned paper chains draped the wall under the mantle clock.
Three construction paper, school-made cards with "to Mom and
Dad" scrawled in uncertain letters dominated a dozen commercial
greeting cards taped to cupboard doors. Eight plump naval oranges
filled a bowl on the table.

"Mother and Dad Smucker bought a crate of oranges and gave
every child and grandchild one for Christmas, also a nice handkerchief," Mary said. She paused to breathe long and slow during a
contraction. "Mommy and Dawdy Beiler gave each one a candy cane
and a silver dollar."

"Christmas gifts are over for you?" I looked at the mantle clock on
the wall behind the table. 2:00 a.m. At five centimeters dilation Mary
could be hours from delivery or five minutes from precipitation. I
hoped for five minutes, or at least within an hour.

"The children couldn't wait for their gifts. I made Sammy a new
coat and pants for Sunday; Sylvia and Sarah, good dresses and white
Sunday aprons plus handbags; Amanda, a dress and school shoes.
Mary got a blue dress and I sewed a dress, apron and a little cap for a

new doll. We bought Christy a wooden barn with cows, horses and sheep from old Jake Beiler's shop on Brethren Church Road. They all got a new pair of stockings too."

The clock ticked the night away. 2:45 a.m. I had to get home, play Santa before going to bed.

From her lounge chair Mary continued in her quiet monotone. "We still have a Christmas dinner at Mary and Kore Smuckers near Meadville with my brothers and sisters as soon as I can travel with the baby. We'll exchange gifts with the names we drew at our picnic last summer at brother Seth Smucker's place."

By 3:15 a.m. Mary was six centimeters. Four more to go. She caught me watching the clock.

"Don't worry, I'll have this baby before milking time." She raised a green window shade and looked toward the barn. "The snow's stopped. It's good to have you here. Amos couldn't take losing sleep all night."

No need to reply. I lay on the kitchen couch and drew my coat over tired shoulders.

Mary paced the kitchen stopping to pant during contractions. "It's a good thing the Beiler Christmas dinner is over. We had it here early December. I drew Mom's name. Sister Elsie Riehl drew mine. I gave Mom canned goods for her pantry. I got sewing needles and material for a summer dress. I'll get it made soon as I'm allowed to treadle the sewing machine again after this baby."

At 5:00 a.m. Mary woke me when she called Amos downstairs. The clock clawed time slowly. The vision of empty stockings and four tearful faces stabbed my imagination in vivid apparition. I rubbed my eyes. Every year I had worried about missing Christmas.

"Looks like you had a good sleep too," Amos said, combing red beard and tousled black hair at the hand sink beside the kettlehouse door. "Time to think about the milkin'." The crow's feet disappeared from his coarse face as he squinted at the clock and reached for silver-rimmed glasses.

"Amos, Grace and I will go into the bedroom," Mary said. "You call Sammy down to do the feedin' and start milkin'." She stopped to pant. "I'll have this baby soon now."

Amos grinned a reply and shuffled stocking-footed to the stair door. I watched and tried to imagine Pete bearded, in black broadfall pants with leather suspenders.

At 5:23 a.m. Mary birthed a baby boy with scarcely more than a puffy contortion of her narrow face and the squeezing shut of her brown eyes. The placenta delivered within minutes. There were no sutures. "We already have a Christian. We might name him Joseph. The children can decide. Maybe this one should be Amos."

The husband chuckled, "We'll let you know when you come again."

A few minutes past six I stepped from the kettlehouse onto frozen snow. Quieter than the crunch under my boots, wind whispered in the maples. Silence blanketed the folded white hills along the horizon. Stars punctured the black sky. I would get home barely before my children awoke to raid Santa's stockings. If no one else had a baby today, Christmas could still be a great day.

12

After Christmas

When I returned to City Rehabilitation Center after Christmas, the idea of leaving it was barely a germ. But once nourished, it grew beyond containment. Not that the fire had anything to do with my decision.

"Fire! A fire!" Jimmy called one night. We were all asleep.

Whirling red and white lights streaked across our yellow ceiling. They reflected on the snowy pines along the rear driveway lighting them like Christmas trees. No siren, but the heavy truck idling under our windows sounded like a fire engine. It could not be an ambulance. They loaded and unloaded at the front door.

We lay in the dark like forgotten statues in a warehouse. Where were the nurses? Why didn't they come? The halls beyond our closed door were silent. Would we be pushed in our beds out into the winter night? Men's garbled staccato voices, muffled by windows and space, mingled with our fears. We sniffed for smoke. None. Why didn't someone come?

I was the only one in the room who could stand. But getting out of bed without help was impossible. Trussed hands and feet, I was helpless. My hard plastic foot splints would have hit the polished tile floor like roller skates. Newspaper stories about patients in nursing homes dying in their beds during a fire rose vividly in my imagination. Was this our end?

We waited. The sound of racing motors. The flashing lights slid over the walls and disappeared between the pines.

"A little fire in a hamper in the laundry," the night nurse reported when she opened our door. "Nothing like a little excitement."

I was happy to resume exercises after Christmas vacation. Skilled nursing care and hot showers were a luxury. The holiday at home had been good, but after a week I was an eagle in a robin's nest, pushed, pulled and fed. Most of the time I sat blanketed before the fireplace depending upon the family for action. Frustration wore claws as I watched others doing the Christmasy things that other seasons had been my responsibility and pleasure.

The phrase, "you did it enough years, now it is our turn," held no solace. The laughter, the teasing seemed contrived. My wheelchair was an ugly intrusion into our holidays. The kitchen was too small for Oma, the girls and my chair. My giving advice on a recipe or locating a utensil constituted a highlight.

Back at City Rehabilitation, I could lie on a bed not remade daily into a couch. Personal care was a business, not a game played by a family painfully aware of reversed roles. It was good to return, also to know that I was not forgotten by my community.

While at City, Lancaster's morning newspaper requested an article about my progress. It was an opportunity to communicate with Amish friends too far away to visit. Most Amish homes subscribed to the morning paper. I had heard a rumor that the Amish community was considering a collection of funds to help defray my hospital expenses. Thinking of my many patients who struggled day to week to pay their own bills, I was embarrassed, touched by their willingness to sacrifice for me. I could tell them that I had hospital insurance.

Eugene Kraybill interviewed me in the visitors' lounge. I did not want to appear disabled. Before the photographer took pictures, I carefully pulled both hands across my lap and away from the chair's arms to hide my wrist drop. Later an Amish friend said that she noticed the swollen fingers. I noticed that my hair had a plastered-down, uncombed look.

The journalist wrote that I missed delivering babies. "Happiness used to be a warm wet baby in my arms. I don't know how to do anything else but be a doctor," he quoted. True, plus home and family. While other doctors played golf, my hobby had been a vegetable garden, freezing and canning. Four children and Peter consumed any time not spent with patients. The article ended with my belief that I would be back on my feet. "And those squirming squealing babies will once again be warming the cockles of her heart."

The rooms and halls of the rehabilitation center were full of heartrending patients. Four ladies recovering from strokes occupied beds in the room next to ours. Stroke patients, often one arm in a sling, limping on a braced leg and frustrated by speech difficulties, seemed the unhappiest people. Sometimes they sobbed during therapy. Several of these patients, like Herbert, had had repeated strokes.

I met Herbert from Lancaster County in the gym. "All I want to do is get out of here and find work." He pulled the words from his mouth like taffy.

"I'll talk to my husband, see what he can do," I said.

He grimaced a crooked smile that wrinkled a sallow face, tapped his four-legged cane on the floor and laughed. "Don't forget. I'll count on it." His bald head reflected light from the long windows as he emphasized his words with a nod.

Whenever I met Herbert, we confirmed his job, but I speculated that he would be fortunate when he could drag himself from his chair to the table. "Don't forget that job," he would call across the gym, face contorted, pale eyes lit with the hope in our game. I felt lucky that my problem was not a stroke.

Leg amputees, mostly diabetics, came to the gym twice a day to practice walking on their new prostheses, as welcome to tender stumps as a hot stove to a bare hand. While I exercised or sat waiting in my wheelchair, I scanned the assortment of plastic legs, dressed in socks and shoes, scattered about the amputee practice area like spare parts in an auto store. They intrigued me, and I wondered if they felt different to their owners than my numb legs did to me. I gawked at the strapped-on limbs moving between parallel bars hour after hour until the patients seemed glad to escape their stern and persistent therapist.

Tommy was a prototype of too many of the head-injured young

men I have seen in rehabilitation centers and convalescent homes. Loose gravel had skidded his speeding motorcycle into a tree. I imagined my sons in Tommy's handsome face. What would it be like to visit Keith or Paul, unable to recognize me after years of mothering? How many decades lay ahead for this mindless son, strong of body? What cost in money, worry, time and lost possibilities? Tommy's black wavy hair had grown over his head scar, but he was a drooling, uncomprehending infant in a man's body. He grinned a lot or laughed, unless denied a wish which could send him into a raging tantrum. His slurred speech scarcely constituted conversation.

One evening as the snowbanks outside our windows turned orange and supper trays rattled along the hall, we heard a commotion among the nurses. "He's gone. Not in the hall or lounge."

Tommy had eluded the watchful nurses and escaped outside. Through our windows, we saw him tramp in the dusk, ankle-deep in snow, clad in a blue, short-sleeved shirt and gray pants. Within moments nurses caught him under the pines and returned him to his room across the hall.

Patients like Tommy strengthened more than ever my resolve to continue the *no motorcycle, no motorbike* ban we enforced on our children the day they put away their tricycles, straddled bicycles and longingly ogled Harley Davidsons.

My visitors at City were limited by the inconvenient distance from home, but one evening Henry Beiler and his father visited. A quadriplegic, Henry hooked an arm over the back of his wheelchair for stability as we talked.

Henry had been disabled for several years. One night while roughhousing with other teenage boys at a Sunday gathering of young folks, he received a karate chop to the back of his neck. Not understanding the seriousness of the paralysis caused by their horseplay, his friends dragged him home to the kitchen couch. They believed he would recover in time for morning milking.

Bearded Aaron sat beside my bed balancing his black flattop hat on a knee, reviewing news from the Amish community. Theirs was the cream of visits. Henry's younger brothers and sisters had been among my baby deliveries. At one birth Henry's mother and I were both at term. During my years of general practice, I had been the

Beiler's family physician.

Henry had rehabilitated at City Hospital after his accident and knew many nurses and therapists. It was good to see old friends, especially ones who shared a similar problem.

I was glad that my cord injury was not complete like Henry's and my recovery only months away. I was moved by Henry and Aaron's visit, knowing they had paid a driver to bring them to the hospital. How many times the family must have traveled the route when Henry was at City for retraining physiotherapy.

A physiotherapist requires four years of college. Margo, therapist for my roommates and me, had graduated several years before beginning work at City. She was as thin and shapeless as a table knife, mid-twenties and half-a-head shorter than my five-foot-eight. A wintry blast could have blown her scrawny shadow down the street and around the corner. A health faddist, Margo indulged in fasts, purges and unique diets. Blond hair either fell shoulder length around her pale bony face or, fastened with a long metal barrette, cascaded down her back. At home she kept goats and practiced yoga.

"I'm your therapist," Margo said my first day. When she smiled, I wondered if her parents had spent as much money at her orthodontist as I had for my children.

On morning and evening trips to the gym, Margo moved me from one piece of exercise equipment to another strengthening arm and leg muscles. Holding the elastic at the back of my slacks, as Joe had done, she walked me around the gym for gait training. The day she took a movie of my walking, I did not want to believe my loose-jointed hips moving up and down at each step like pistons in slow motion. I had been proud of my accomplishments before I saw the film. Would I ever walk normally, head high instead of eyes focused on the brown tiled floor, concentrating on each step?

Margo was friendly but impersonal. After working on the equipment, I lay on a table while she exercised fingers, legs, arms. Her eyes roamed the room watching other therapists work their patients.

The first weekend she accidentally took my chart home with other papers. Nurses frantically searched our room, the wheelchairs and the gym before beginning a new one.

If Margo fasted too harshly, weakness kept her home and another therapist or an assistant took her place. I resented her absence, her inability to exercise me in my urgency to rehabilitate.

We four quads were Margo's therapy responsibility. While one of us worked at a machine, she supervised another. Often we four were in the gym together. Once she forgot me as I exercised. Exhausted from a full day I dozed, struggled to stay awake, swayed on the seat and nearly fell to the floor. When the supervising physiotherapist noticed my problem, I was returned to my chair and wheeled upstairs to bed. Sleeping was easier than staying awake. Therapy was painless, but the effort left me tired and sore.

When our family dispersed after the Christmas holidays, I did not know that a pet peeve would end my stay at the hospital. If anything ticked me off, it was people who could not keep their minds on the job they were paid to do. When a check-out girl in the supermarket gabbed about Saturday night's date to her friend checking out the next line, I avoided that girl and the store. I had paid for a period of her time and courtesy as she totaled my purchases. Rude ignorance of customers irritated me. Also, the diversion could cause a mistake.

Late one afternoon, the final straw overbalanced my discontent with City. Gym activities had thinned as supper time approached. I lay on a table exercising finger strength against Margo's resisting hand when Cindy's new electric wheelchair arrived.

Margo could not resist a toy. "Excuse me a moment," she said.

I did a slow burn watching her unpack the chair, then ride around the gym laughing, gyrating, backing. When Cory the porter came to push me upstairs for supper, Margo put me in my chair, gym time over but unfinished. I felt as cheated as if a clerk had returned five dollars change instead of ten. Margo's crass insensitivity chafed me.

Another source of dissatisfaction was our ward. A room with two men and two women was tolerable, but I never became comfortable without privacy, particularly during personal care. The thin curtains sieved sounds of bedside commodes, catheterizations, doctor examinations, nightly snores and grunts. It was demeaning. As wardmates we chatted and shared but were of four varied interests and ages. We never became intimate. I had been a good sport long enough.

Cindy and Jimmy complained out loud. They wanted recreational activities, active games, dances and social interaction with other young people. Jimmy agitated to go home. Cindy planned a transfer to a special spinal cord facility.

Group psychiatry sessions, in our room twice a week after lunch, had been a failure for me. "What do you want to talk about?" the doctor had said. "Let's hear what's on your minds."

Cindy and Jimmy requested organized activities for wheelchair patients. I listened several days before revealing my greatest concern. "It's my hands. When will I be able to use them again? They don't feel right."

The doctor ambled from the center of the room to lean over the foot of my bed. "Touch your hands to your face. Do they feel warm? Then they're still a part of you." He moved away to repeat promises that organized games were being considered as an activity for young patients.

An hour's nap at noon was more valuable. After lunch the nurses pulled the curtains around my bed, and I slept until gym time.

During the last month I had become stronger, better able to feed myself without fatiguing or dropping food onto my lap. I could stand longer. My Foley catheter had been replaced by four-hour intermittent catheterization for residual urine, and I was able void on my own. Through digital stimulation, stool softeners and laxatives I had learned what to expect of bowel training. But I was still stand-pivot, could not use fingers, was unable to dress or undress, completely dependent.

I found no fault with City's nursing care, the hospital or physiotherapy. Saturday and Sunday at home were fine, but our house was empty during most of the week. I could not be alone. Also, I needed more therapy. Dissatisfaction and the idea of leaving the rehab center grew like a pinch of yeast in a batch of warm dough. I knew where to go. Community Hospital. The therapists there were as qualified and more caring. Its gym was not as fully equipped and the Hubbard tank could not compare to exercise in a heated pool, the therapy I enjoyed and regarded particularly valuable. In City's ninety degree water I felt less disabled, learned easily to walk between submerged parallel bars, retrained my legs to climb steps, strengthened arm muscles in the buoyancy of water.

Community Hospital was home, where I wanted to be.

Pete agreed. Lancaster was closer to New Holland. I phoned Joe. "I want to leave here."

Joe came to City the next evening, set me in my wheelchair and pushed me into the lounge. We planned the transfer. This time I would be admitted under the service of friend and physiatrist Doctor Richard. Joe and I discussed my requests.

First on the list was a call bell. When I arrived at City Rehabilitation Hospital, Cindy had a call bell that operated by pressing her head against it. Jimmy could call a nurse by using a mouth-operated button. "Ask Cindy or Jimmy to ring for us," the nurses had said when I asked for the same convenience.

Often my roommates were at therapy during the day when I wanted a nurse. At night both slept so soundly that it was impossible to wake them and our door was usually closed. I had to shout to bring a nurse from her desk at the far end of the corridor. Nighttime bedpans often arrived too late, frustrating me as much as the itches I could not reach to scratch. Why could I not have an adapted bell? Was I a second class patient?

"Occupational Therapy can fix one for you," Joe said.

"Is there some way I can take a shower?" This was a luxury I would miss, suds and hot water washing through and over my neck. Below my shoulder I felt nothing, but I smelled as clean as the perfumed soap, felt refreshed and invigorated.

"We can put in a hand shower and have Independent Living from Occupational Therapy give you a shower several days a week.

"Could I have my own wheelchair?" I asked. At my last admission to Community Hospital, repeated searches for a wheelchair irritated the nurses and jeopardized my schedule. At City every patient had an assigned chair beside their bed.

"Yes."

"What about going home weekends?"

"I think we can get home privileges. We'll have to talk to the hospital administrator." Going home on weekends was an important part of rehabilitation. "You will have to sign a release form every time you leave the hospital," Joe explained.

"One more important request," I said. "My back and shoulders are as stiff as a tombstone. Could Doctor Edgel give me osteopathic treatments?" They had been refused under the neurosurgeon's care but Richard understood and would probably agree. I wanted every advantage possible.

"And my hands?" I raised swollen fists.

"I have an idea to reduce the edema in your fingers," Joe said. "We'll give it a try. It will take me several days to get this schedule set up."

"I'll stay here this week, then, if possible, move to Lancaster mid-January."

Joe wheeled me back to my room and laid me on the bed. "This hospital won't be happy when they find out you want to leave."

"You can't leave," my young Korean doctor said. "You're not ready to go." She tapped my chart with her pen. "I won't discharge you."

"Then I will discharge myself," I said. "Sign myself out."

The hospital argued but I would not be dissuaded. A hospital cannot imprison a patient. I had often advised maternity patients to go home after two or three days during the years when the obstetrical department had had a mandatory five-day postpartum stay. For patients without hospital insurance, each day meant another pair of school shoes, a mortgage payment, money to help a needy neighbor. If I signed myself out instead of a doctor writing a discharge order, it released the hospital from any responsibility for the patient and gave City the right to refuse me admission in the future. My decision surprised the hospital.

"What happened? What's wrong?" the staff and nurses asked. "Did we do something?"

Evening nurse Joan took time from her charting to sit beside my bed. She rested a hand on my arm, smiled, sighed. "We're worried about you leaving us so soon." Her unhappy face and furrowed brow bore out her concern. She leaned over my bed. "Is there anything the nurses did wrong?"

"No," I answered. "Nursing care has been excellent."

"Margo?" She rose to leave.

I nodded.

"You are not the only one to feel that way. Won't you stay?"

When I could not be persuaded, the doctor signed my discharge.

"You'll be sorry. You will be back," Margo said. The nurses, the wheelchair porter, the therapist who exercised me in the pool agreed.

Were they right? Was my decision foolish? Would I return?

13

Community Hospital

Work toward recovery began in earnest when I returned to Community Hospital. My first admission to Community had been like elementary school; the weeks at the rehabilitation center, high school. Now I had reached college level.

Three months of disability had passed like a puff of breath. Progress seemed turtle-paced. By now I had expected to be running again, but I could walk only if a balancing hand gripped the back of my slacks. My hips flimflammed like a rag doll in the hands of an imaginative child. It was impossible to get up if seated, transfer myself from bed or chair, dress or undress. Someone had to take me to the bathroom, brush my teeth and cut food on my dinner plate. I longed for the first splintered ray of independence but there was none. Arm numbness persisted. From my chest down through my toes I felt only the vibration of sudden contact. Both hands were swollen and useless. I could move both wrists and the bases of the fingers. Meals were a combination of self-fed, with a fork bandaged in my hand, and nurse-fed. Three to six months remained of the time promised before I could return to office and patients. I was impatient, often depressed, but not discouraged.

All the requests I had made of Joe before returning to Community were fulfilled. Three mornings a week Joan, from Independent

Living of Occupational Therapy, swathed me in towels and pushed me, a wrapped mummy, down the hall where a hand shower had been installed for my benefit. Joan pulled a wash mitt over my hand, soaped it and I dabbed at legs, chest and abdomen. Joan finished the bath and shampooed my hair.

Occupational Therapy jerry-built an ingenious call bell. By squeezing a lever between my shoulder and the mattress, a peg pushed the button that buzzed my room number at the nurses' desk. The problem became one of guarding this prized possession from forgetful nurses who moved the contraption beyond my reach to the far side of the bed or laid it on the bedside table.

For years I had known Doctor Edgel as a fellow staff member, but now he became a friend as he manipulated and stretched my back and limbs. He was not only the most generous, caring, kind man I have ever met, but also unrelenting, brutal and determined as he administered the osteopathic treatments I had requested. He was past retirement age and practiced his profession for the love of it and out of faithful commitment to patients. His fingers were steel bars against my sore spastic areas, but he knew where to apply his art to acquire desired relaxation. Three mornings a week his lanky body bent over me. Sensitive hands, as large as dinner plates, stretched muscles and limbered vertebrae. I lay as stiff as a dead mackerel on the leather-topped treatment table. When Joe and Edgel flipped me from front to back, like a fish in a pan, I screamed with pain. Spasticity came back, but faith in the therapy and determination for improvement kept me returning. Edgel adopted me as his special project, resolved that I should benefit from his years of experience.

As Edgel spoke he had a habit of tilting his head back to see close objects through his bifocals. A clipped mustache arched his upper lip like a brush stroke. White hair framed a square face that reminded me of my handsome grandfather. Carefully enunciated words snagged his speech with remnants of years below the Mason Dixon Line.

A wheelchair of my own. How had Joe managed that when they were a premium possession on every floor? I guarded it. A special water-filled cushion to sit on was a great idea to relieve pressure on my buttocks, but I felt unstable, pitching from one side to the other like a ship about to be swamped in a storm, sure I would land on the floor.

With wheels, the entire hospital was mine. Weak arms could not move a wheelchair forward. I pushed backward with both feet, calling, "Watch out, here I come," as the chair bumped through the swinging doors that separated departments. If they swung only one way, I waited for the next person coming along to open them for me. Until my arms strengthened, elevator buttons were difficult to reach. Everyone was in danger as my wheelchair backed zigzag through doorways, out of elevators and down halls. I visited former patients on every floor, shared their family and friends, enjoyed ice cream and cake parties brought in by visitors. I became a confidant to decisions and problems.

Among my convalescent cards and letters Harvey wrote about his wife's hospital fee of the previous fall. Martha had delivered a baby on the 24-hour plan. Harvey's letter was a taste of practice days. I had pursued so many patient bills that I often imagined the doughy woman in billing hiding behind her filing cabinets as I came through the doorway. When I backed into the office, she smiled, remembering past encounters, ran a fleshy finger down Harvey's itemized bill, checking each item. The $12.50 overcharge correction would be as important as $100 to Harvey. It felt warm and good.

Each day after lunch, an hour in Occupational Therapy strengthened arms and hands. Using cardboard knitting mill cones, piling cone on cone, I broke through restraining barriers of tight weak muscles, until finally, before discharge, I could reach no higher. To strengthen wrist muscles I rested my arm on a 4×4 block of polished wood, attempting to hold my floppy heavy hand out straight. After several weeks I was able to extend it five minutes, then longer.

One day after a stroke patient had cooked a practice meal in Occupational Therapy's kitchen, I asked if I could stand at the sink to wash the dishes. I ached to do actual labor, wanted to try, but the request was denied. Rejection. Only six months before I had fled dishpans for office.

Morning and afternoon I went to physiotherapy, pulling weights attached by leather bracelets to wrists and ankles. I walked for gait training, practiced stepping backwards, sideways or over objects. Several times a week I exercised in the Hubbard tank where the weightlessness of water made motion easier. Joe took me up several floors by elevator so I could practice walking down the steps. I moved slowly, gripped the railing, afraid of stumbling on the steel-edged concrete steps. Every day Joe walked me down halls, but he had to hold me for balance.

Getting down onto mats on all fours was a prerequisite to improved balance. The thought of opening my hands flat enough to bear weight on the palms was as painful as if I had been asked to drive a splinter under a fingernail. Joe brought two book-sized wooden blocks with handles that he placed beneath me on the floor. My spastic fingers clutched the handles. The first day I tried to balance on hands and knees, I shook with apprehension and weakness. A body harness suspended from an overhead frame kept me from falling on my face. Helplessness, the inability to catch myself if I toppled, was omnipresent and feared. Arms and legs shook and wobbled. "Don't. I'll fall. Take me down," I yelled.

"Stay there," Joe commanded.

He would not take me down until he was ready or until I had tried to stay as he put me. I remained on all fours only moments the first day, remembering my father hoisting sick horses with block and tackle attached to leather straps, in an effort to raise them to their feet. They had never recovered. Not me. Within a week I could remain on all fours five minutes without the harness, then ten minutes. The floor still looked hard and cruel. Fear of falling kept me frozen on hands and knees until I shouted that I was about to fall and Joe lifted me onto a chair to rest.

When I strengthened enough, I graduated to mat work. Joe lowered me onto the mats on my abdomen. He lifted first legs, then arms off the floor. I felt like a newborn colt finding its legs for the first time. I learned to crawl on hands and knees, a few feet farther each day until I crept the distance of two mats. Next it was backwards, then over pillows.

Sometimes I upset, rolled like a baby in a play pen, lurched on my face, struggled onto my abdomen. Joe lifted me onto all fours again. The most difficult lesson was learning to get onto hands and knees unassisted. I could draw my knees up with hips in knee-chest position, but I remained stuck in that undignified position with arms pinned under me. Getting onto my arms seemed impossible to coordinate. As soon as I moved to push up, I fell over and had to begin again.

When Joe had a day off, Craig, a younger, sterner therapist, supervised my gym time. "Get up!" he shouted. "Doctor Kaiser, get up! You can lie there all day until you get up." He left me, face down on the dusty mat, while he worked with other patients. My muscles fatigued if I struggled too long. Rest and try again. Finally I conquered the maneuver and struggled into crawl position. "Good," he said. "Now lie down and get up again. Once more before you can go back to your room." If I did fifteen or twenty sit-ups for Craig, he insisted on three more. I always returned to bed exhausted and slept until supper trays arrived.

"Don't you mind Craig shouting at you like that? It's terrible," one of the nurses who attended me on second floor said. "I heard Craig screaming at you from way down the hall." The gym doors were usually open for ventilation.

"No," I answered."It's his way of making me work hard. It's good for me. Besides, I like him. He's really a wonderful person."

With the intensive therapy and time, my wrists, hands and fingers never stopped hurting. I had fewer impulses flying down my arms ending in electric sparks at my finger tips. The most agony was in my back and shoulders until *TENS* was begun. Transcutaneous Nerve Stimulation is a rechargable battery pack connected to two electrodes taped to the skin. A constant mild electrical charge tingles between the electrode pads, relieving pain. Joe easily fastened the electrodes over my painful shoulders, but I had no shirt pocket to carry the cigarette-pack size battery. Finally, I carried it where I used to carry my beeper, nestled in the front of my bra.

When I returned to Community Hospital, Joe believed that he could reduce my finger swelling. My hands were still very limited in motion, also clumsy and swollen twice their usual size due to the nerve damage. At the end of afternoon therapy Joe applied a Jobst alternating pressure machine to both hands. My fingers returned to normal. Tight rubber surgical gloves were pushed on to maintain their reduced size, but after several hours the swelling returned and the nurses had to peel them off because of painful pressure. After a week's trial with no permanent reduction in finger size, we abandoned the experiment. I worried. Would my hands ever be useful again?

The third week of January a wonderful thing happened. It was of such great importance that its discovery remains as vivid as if it had been this morning. Keith, our older son who worked in Lancaster, came frequently over lunch hour to cut food to bite-size for my fork or to feed me soups. It was great to visit with him, and I appreciated the sacrifice of his lunch time. One noon after he had returned to work, I concentrated on hand motion. Suddenly, I could distinguish the slightest motion in my right thumb joint. "That's pretty definitive," physiotherapy agreed that afternoon. I thumbed my flag of victory to everyone I met.

Before long I noticed slight motion in all finger joints of the right hand. Many moments in my bed were spent attempting new mobility and strengthening regained ones. I thought how wonderful it would be if I could only rehabilitate enough to do my own housework from a wheelchair. I had known women who washed dishes or dusted from a wheelchair. I burned with the desire to accomplish menial activities that I had always hated. Daydreaming, I imagined pushing myself refrigerator to stove, preparing a meal. Our kitchen would need remodeling to accommodate work at this new level. I dismissed the fantasy remembering the promise that I would return to office and patients within a year.

Another day as I lay trying to slide my right arm along the sheet above my head, the hand moved high enough to touch my hair. Soon I was able to reach my call button and draw it within grasp if I was lying down, stretch for items on the bedside table, pick up the telephone if it was on the mattress beside me. At least I had one good arm. Each goal became a windmill to battle and conquer.

Drinking from a straw was easy, but I wanted to lift a glass. A nurse filled a styrofoam cup on my tray. Steadying the cup with my left hand, I wrapped the right hand around it. Pressure of the cup against my palm caused the hand to contract. The styrofoam cracked like an eggshell. A disaster of spilled milk on the tray. The next time I held the cup between clenched fists like a baby.

With improved finger function came the desire to hold regular forks and spoons, not ones bandaged into the hand, but I had forgotten how to hold them. It was like trying to manipulate chopsticks the first time. Awkward between my fingers, the tools dropped onto the tray. The nurse held a fork. I analyzed her grasp and imitated it. When my roommate was not looking, I watched her eat and practiced each mealtime until I could manage utensils again.

Success encouraged boldness. I ordered an apple for lunch. It sat on my tray through meat and potatoes, shiny, delicious looking, red. The smooth skin felt good in my hand. I wobbled the weight of it to my open mouth but could not press hard enough to break its skin for a first bite. The apple rolled away like a raindrop down a glass pane and fell onto the sheets. Disappointed at failure, too proud to ask for help, I added apples to my list of goals. The arms would get stronger.

I still wore diapers. "Drink at least eight glasses of fluids a day," nurses at the rehabilitation hospital had warned when I left them. Since most of my day was spent in therapy, I carried a sixteen-ounce glass of liquid with me, usually warm cranberry juice. After the accident, hypersensitivity to salt or cold made iced drinks difficult to swallow. Sipping liquids all day met the quota.

Catheterized every four hours for residual urine, taken regulary to the bathroom, I could not stay dry. Despite urine cultures and antibiotics, intermittent bladder infections plagued me month after month. Embarrassment and depression interfered with therapy. Sometimes I agonized and returned to my room, hiding my tears. I thought how even lowly caged animals had better bladder control.

Urinary tract X-rays were normal. The urologist's explanation of cord bladder was not new, but I had not applied the concept to myself. "A spinal-cord-injured bladder is smaller than before your accident. With contractile muscle innervation impaired, the bladder does not empty completely. The residual invites infection. When the bladder is full, it contracts and spills out urine. Of course the sphincter muscle that closes off the opening between bladder and urethra doesn't function in cord patients. Put yourself on a two hour schedule."

He did not say, "The rest of your life," but I understood. Mary Glick from Gordonville who wanted to marry despite incontinence, the Philadelphia man who carried a catheter in his hatband, medical school's half-awake drowsy afternoon lectures in urology and neurology snapped into unmuddied focus.

Reality must be accepted. My response to living with the problem was reducing the amount of fluids. I quit sipping juices all day and life became more bearable.

After my return to Community Hospital days flew with the speed of hummingbirds. February weekends were razored with cold and clothed in ice that crackled and splintered from the trees in glassy fragments. Snow mantled city streets, and the country roads drifted shut. Trips home were impossible.

During a blizzard nurses unable to go home or be replaced at shift changes bedded down in lounges. Several doctors moved into the hospital to care for emergencies. When the roads were still closed Monday, there was no therapy. The hospital seemed a castle surrounded by a moat of silent white streets. Patients and nurses spoke in hushed voices, as if some unknown disaster was about to tromp down the stark halls.

All patients who could be discharged from the hospital had gone home when the blizzard had been predicted. I had no roommate. Television became tiresome in large doses. I rode down corridors for exercise, watched the wandering drifts, felt the frigid air falling from heavy glass windows or walked my fingers over the bed to exercise my arms. Telephone calls to New Holland confirmed that my family waited out the storm and later that Pete and the boys were shoveling the driveway. The thought that this was one storm which had not called me to a birthing gave me smug satisfaction, but I wondered how many maternity cases had been airlifted to hospitals. How many ditches would have pulled me into their embrace, like the one near Ben and Sara's on a New Year's morning?

14

Ditched

Beginning the new year wheel-anchored in a country ditch, tired and awake too many hours, weary of night calls, wishing I were curled warm and comfortable beside my husband in our four-poster mahogany bed, thinking about the traditional sauerkraut and pork dinner I was expected to serve family and guests that evening was not my idea of starting anything new. It was not the way I would have planned it.

I turned off my engine to await a Good Samaritan with a strong push to unditch me and wondered what life might have been like if Father had allowed the farmer boy, Howard Georges, to court me. What if I had married him and his ninety-acre farm and had hands chafed by garden earth? What if I had a stable full of kids instead of a solo country practice? Would I now sit waiting for a chinook to melt the ice, coating the skin of mud under my Chevy's rear wheels?

The New Year's Eve party had been marked by conformity: the usual doctor associates with wives and friends, the expected complaints about hospital affairs, a little backbiting, midnight glasses raised and toasted, "Auld Lang Syne." One short hour in bed before Amishman, Ben Miller, telephoned to say that his wife's pregnancy was about ready for delivery. Please come to their farm. My head had throbbed. Eggnog and liver paté crawled up my gullet and furred my tongue like the coat on a muskrat.

The downhill of night was jet black with a matrix of drifting mist as I ascended Mountain Top Hill and crossed into Chester County, then north onto a potholed macadam road between Honeybrook and Morgantown. A turn left onto a winding black street, right at the crossroad, a left at a T until I drove east on narrow blacktop. Miller's bullet-pocked mailbox hung drunkenly over the road on a splintered post. Scrawled in a sloping freehand print, only *B   iller* could be seen on i⁺s rusted flank in the beam of my headlights.

The lane was frozen solid, but a warm December 31st had melted a thin coating of mud that stuck to my tires and rattled gravel-like hailstones under my fenders. I parked at the yard fence, pulled my coat tight against the creeping fog and stepped along the walk, edged by last week's shoveled snow, toward a rectangle of kitchen lamp-light tunneling the haze.

I entered the house through the family entrance, a washhouse tacked onto the old colonial home. Chester County has many old colonial houses, built in the early 1900s as summer homes for wealthy city families. Many of the houses were constructed around a wide central hallway. Above a cellar were four large rooms, one in each corner of the house. On the one side of the house were two parlor rooms; kitchen and dining room on the other. On the second floor there was a bedroom on each corner. These great houses of brick or frame were lipped with porches on two or three sides and shaded by benevolent maples. In the post-Victorian era when country estates dwindled, lands were subdivided and farmers moved into the mansions. Many old fireplaces were closed up or removed and the wooden porches torn away in the name of upkeep economy.

In the car I thought of walking for help, but there were no farms or houses nearby. Besides, the road was so slippery that I could not have walked far without falling. I tried again to pull out of the ditch but it was hopeless. I turned off the motor and waited, reviewing my visit to the Miller home.

Millers' house with twelve-foot ceilings and windows to the floor was a typical old Chester County house. I walked across worn kitchen linoleum to a front bedroom and imagined white-gowned ladies moving through the parlors, sipping tea on August porches. What would they say to the sagging floors, scarred cupboards, the boarded up fireplaces with stovepipes running across rooms to the chimneys? I warmed myself gladly at the bedroom space heater, knowing that necessity changes things.

Sara Miller was several hours from birthing. Ben pulled a rocking chair from the cold parlor across the hall into the bedroom. I rocked while Sara, draped in a homesewn pink housecoat, paced between her bed in the front room and the kitchen sink in the rear of the house. Her rounded shape slid grotesque shadows across the walls. She stopped to retie her muslin nightcap. "I hope this is over before the children get up," she said.

"Are their bedrooms heated?" I asked, glad to be inside on a cold night.

Sara laughed. "No. The three little ones sleep over the kitchen where it's warmer. Malinda and Annie are above us where this stovepipe goes through, but the boys sleep on the other side, even have their window open at night. They have plenty of quilts and sheet blankets too. They like it cold."

I shivered, considering a house without central heat. Later I took a flashlight, went out into the black frigid hall and up creaking steps along the chilly banister worn smooth by decades of sliding hands. Years after the house was built, the bathroom had been installed at the head of the stairs where the trunk and storage room had been located. A hissing Coleman lantern burned light into the cold bathroom. The hot and cold water spigots dripped a steady rhythm into tub and sink.

"Why the lantern in the bathroom?" I asked Ben when I returned to the warm bedroom. Flashlights are a necessary accompaniment to Amish bedrooms. The children did not need a lantern. "The faucets drip. You need new washers?"

Ben laughed. "No. A lantern throws a lot of heat. It keeps the pipes that go up through the cold hall from freezing. It sure is a mess if things freeze up. Same reason we let the water drip in the tub and sink." He brushed graying hair from his face and stroked his brown beard with a calloused left hand, his only hand. The right empty blue shirt sleeve was folded back and fastened with a safety pin above the elbow. He noticed me watching him.

From my ditched car I looked east for the first sign of dawn, but only black horizon seamed earth to sky. I switched on the engine to warm the car. The ditch still gripped my rear wheels. It was easy to sit and let my mind wander. Tragedy is a constant shadow of the farmer, children backed over by milk trucks, runaway horses in the fields, lost arms in corn pickers.

"That," Ben had said, lifting the stump in its sleeve, "that happened four years ago. Don't know what makes us farmers do such dumb things. Got it caught in a corn picker, like so many men do. Lost a lot of blood and time in the field at harvest. Good neighbors finished the fall work that year while I lay in the hospital. Guess I was impatient to get going instead of stopping the machine to unclog the fodder when it choked up. We men get mangled arms instead. Eh, Sara?"

But Sara was lying in bed, panting and pushing, her blue eyes squeezed shut and face swollen with effort. Within minutes she delivered a pudgy baby, her eleventh. I wiped mucus from its mouth, clamped and cut the cord before giving the squalling infant a cursory examination as I wrapped it in warm covers.

"Not as easy at thirty-nine as it was at twenty." Sara laughed snuggling her blanketed new son against jowled cheek. "The last boy should be named after his father. We'll call this one Ben." She winked at me, and I knew she hoped that this would be her last birthing. Happiness shone in her eyes and her smile, but fatigue lay in the lines of her face and the way she slumped into her pillow.

After bringing in the new year and sitting with the Millers, I was tired too. Catnaps under my corduroy coat in a pillowed rocking chair beside the Miller's space heater was a poor substitute for sleep in my own bed. I glanced at my watch; still time to get home for several hours between the sheets before my children awakened. I pulled a colorful Dresden plate quilt around Sara's shoulders. The birthing was over and cleaned up, the baby nearly an hour old and Ben would take charge until the teenage girls got up in several hours. Thirty minutes and I would be under my own quilts.

Outside, the air had become much colder. A cutting wind had whisked away the fog and focused stars into a myriad shimmering crystals. I trod the glazed walks as if they were glass bubbles. The car's wheels crunched through the icy skin on the lane, finding the mud beneath.

The black hardtopped road was grease slick. Studded tires did not grip the ice. I crept along steering into skids, glad that no cars shared the narrow byway. Then, after a mile or so, I veered slowly, gracefully, without control into the ditch as if the roadside's stubbled cornfield had swooped me into an embrace.

The ditch that held the rear wheels was not deep. My wheels spun, grinding into the berm, but the car slid sideways, not forward. One little push would have started me toward home again. Surely someone would pass soon. I slumped into my coat in the warm car, narcotized by wailing all-night country music on the radio.

I waited, tried again to climb out of the ditch. My car phone was useless with Mountain Top obstructing transmission. Dawn in an hour. No other cars drove by so early on a holiday.

Day birthed in the east, first like a lantern rising behind a hill, then like a red tongue that slowly rolled into a ball, throwing pink brilliance onto iced briar canes, wild cherry trees and corn stubble. No birds flew. No breeze broke the mystique of dawn or the icicles from the bushes. Only I seemed unsedated.

When the sun had pulled itself into a white fist of light above the horizon, the air warmed. I turned the key in the ignition and tried again to leave the ditch. It relented. The ice crust had softened. Spinning tires gripped the softened berm, and I slowly regained the blacktop, still as smooth as a baby's gums. The cindered main road descended the mountain to an iceless highway. I arrived in New Holland in time to get the family the bacon and egg breakfast I never served when I had to pull myself from bed to cook it.

15

Marriage

As February turned to March and the days warmed toward spring, I imagined from my hospital bed the energetic hustle out in the countryside. Housewives would straddle fallow flower beds with teetering stepladders to wash winter's storms from the windows. The men would be pulling plows from sheds to dip their iron toes into the warming earth. Farm homes, bargained for over winter, would see their occupants moving like checkers on a board as growing families hunted more acreage and fledgling farmers settled their brides onto the land for a first season. Many young men hoped that the new life stirring under a wife's apron might be a boy to help with the milking and hauling manure. I expected that on spring days, Amish wagons mounded with beds and tables and chairs roped onto piled chairs moved along country roads.

Even Jake and Katie Fisher's little Mary must be old enough to be among the newly married. Several years ago the older couple had retired to the small frame end of his house when son John had married. I delivered babies now for John and Amanda in the back bedroom instead of for Jake and Katie, but vegetables still spilled from the roadside stand each summer. My first sighting of an Amish scarecrow had been in that garden.

There it was. I laughed to myself, had never considered the

possibility. Standing between a long row of string beans and a planting of sweet corn, an Amish scarecrow fluttered in Katie Fisher's faded blue dress. Its ample bosom and sun-streaked black bonnet were stuffed with straw that poked through the neck in an awesome yellow beard. Limp tattered skirts swayed lazily in August's heavy air. Two glittering aluminum pie pans dangled on strings from each end of the rough wooden stick that held ragged sleeves in a stiff inhuman pose.

Why not an Amish scarecrow? It was as natural as the considerate way that the Amish cared for their elderly, sick and handicapped. They were kept busy and needed, like Sarah Fisher, the patient I had come to see at Frogtown near the village of Intercourse.

I swung my station wagon around Jake and Katie Fisher's roadside vegetable stand. The wooden shack overflowed with cabbages, glossy purple eggplant, yellow and green peppers, carrots, green-topped beets, fresh bread and shoofly pies in plastic bags, eggs, jars of strawberry jam. Baskets of crimson tomatoes and pale-skinned potatoes sat on the ground beside a wheelbarrow of sweet corn, spilling unhusked onto a pile along the lawn.

The bushel of lima beans I had ordered would not be popular at my house. All hands had been warned to be ready for work when I returned home. The children hated lima bean sessions more than corn husking or pea shelling.

Fisher's gravel lane lay between the empty tobacco barn and a long vegetable garden. Leah, the oldest Fisher daughter at home, hoed a row of potatoes with a vigor no weed could survive. Mary bent over lima beans, filling a basket with the thick green pods. Her twin Sylvia, on hands and knees, weeded a long row of fragile young celery plants. The sisters wore pink short-sleeved dresses. They were barefooted. Their heads were covered by bandana handkerchiefs knotted at the nape of each neck below the hair bun. The girls waved. Leah nodded, walked past the weak-necked scarecrow and propped her hoe against the wire yard fence on her way to the house.

At other visits I had seen the girls push the reel mower that kept the Fisher yard looking as if it were manicured with a scissors. A brown ribbon of bare earth edged the walks to kitchen and wash-house, eliminating the need to clip grass along the concrete. Flower beds against the house were a profusion of geraniums, petunias and zinnias. Astors, delphiniums and dahlias bloomed along the fence and continued to a bed of impatiens and varigated coleus on the sunless north side of Sarah's wing of the house.

"Hello Sarah," I called, entering her cool shaded room through the screened door. The east and west shutters were closed against the sun. "What are you working at today?"

She smiled. "This is green day. Mary poured a new batch of animals for me yesterday." Twisted knobby fingers gripped a small brush wet with green paint. On the newspaper-covered table, plaster chickens, cows, horses, pigs and ducks stood on freshly painted grass. "This work keeps me busy. Seems I can never keep up with the orders." Sarah fumbled the lid onto the jar.

Sarah Fisher had been disabled several years before I began routine house calls. Once a teacher in an Amish school, she had to retire because of severe arthritis which had finally limited her to bed and wheelchair.

Sarah's youngest brother Jake had added an ell to his house. A bachelor brother Jonas, who talked with a lisp when he spoke, which was seldom, slept upstairs. Jonas paid board at Jake's table helping him at harvest time. He worked nights catching chickens for Victor F. Weaver, Inc. in New Holland. I rarely saw the rotund and rusty-bearded middle-aged man.

Sarah was always home, except during times she visited her eleven younger siblings. Home was at Jake's. Katie and the older girls were accustomed to Sarah's care and took turns sleeping on a cot in her room. Even attending church was impractical and painful for Sarah. She only attended when the Fishers took their annual turn to host the district's church service.

"This is my week to care for Aunt Sarah," Leah said, wiping garden dirt from her toes onto the doormat. "I like to help over here." The girl washed her hands at a corner sink. "Have her in bed in a minute."

Leah's slim body moved with grace and the skill of her work. She pushed Sarah's wheelchair to the bed, hooked the canvas backsling and seat to the hydraulic lift, deftly pumped the handle and swung her patient over the bed. Pressure released, Sarah's thin rigid body rested on the log cabin quilt. Sarah grimaced when her niece straightened her black dress and apron, pulling out folds under hips and shoulders.

A wrinkled, child-size little woman lay on the bed. Her white cap, fastened to a narrow black band by a straight pin at the midline part, emphasized the thin white hair. Black-stockinged legs maintained sitting position. Sarah clutched a white handkerchief in knotted fingers.

Finished with my patient, I turned to Leah. "Leah, that's a big celery patch in your garden." I imagined fall with the rows of celery bleached and protected from frost by mounded earth and covered with long rolls of plastic. "Your family going to eat it all, or is there a November wedding?"

My victim turned away, pretending to examine the plaster animals. "Takes a lot of celery for this family. You're just guessin'. I'm twenty-two. That's old enough to marry." She brushed dust from her skirt and leaned against the white wall. Her brown eyes and lean face were innocent. "Besides, wouldn't need to be me. Could be the twins."

No confession from Leah. Most Amish marriages do not become public knowledge until the banns are announced in church about a month before the wedding and long rows of marriage licenses with traditional Amish names begin appearing in autumn newspapers.

During our early years in New Holland Pete and I often passed through the village of Intercourse Sunday evenings to see the Amish young folks gather. Many came to the triangle in front of the bank and went from there to the evening sing held in the home of a friend. We watched horses pulling open courting buggies, clogging the streets. Sometimes the skittish animals tempted their drivers to race. We watched brothers drive sisters to the gatherings, two sitting on the seat, the third passenger astride the middle knees of those on the bottom. We watched the young men with their girlfriends, knowing they would escort them to the singing, then take them home, often not arriving at their own homes until morning milking time.

***

"Leah wants to marry this fall," Katie said at the October prenatal visit. "Last year it was Sallie. She's expecting early December; me in the middle of November. Problem is setting a date for Leah's wedding." She grinned a dentured smile that deepened wrinkles under blue eyes and along her cheeks. "Guess you can't say yet if I'll be early or late?"

I shook my head. "At least you have plenty of help with eleven at home yet."

Katie exposed her sagging abdomen for examination. "I'll be able to boss them." She shifted to sitting position with a long grunt. "Little Jake is two. Time we had another baby to spoil. Guess this'll be our last. Thought so last time." Slender fingers searched the depths of a voluminous blue tapestry bag and found a man's pocket watch. "Time to get home for dinner. Jake went to Kauffman's Hardware for nails and caulking. Guess he's waiting out back at your hitching rail." Katie turned at the door. "Would you and your husband like to come to Leah's wedding?"

I felt honored to be invited to an Amish wedding. By tradition they are held on Tuesdays and Thursdays. Tuesday allows Monday for washing, cleaning up and catching up with chores after Sunday. Wednesday is a day to work after Tuesday's activity and prepare for Thursday. Thursday ceremonies allow Friday and Saturday to work and prepare for a day of rest on Sunday. During wedding season folks often brag about their number of wedding invitations, and only essential work is done around farm and home.

Amish church rules require that a bishop officiate the wedding ceremony. This limits the number of weddings per day and if there are many weddings that year, requires some marriages to fall into late October or early December. November customarily lies between the work of corn picking and tobacco stripping. Fall weddings allow families to prepare young couples for housekeeping in March when farms become available. Widows and widowers, in their need to restore family life, marry any time of the year.

In addition to the Tuesday and Thursday limitations, families maneuver dates to avoid conflicts with weddings of cousins and friends as well as family birthings. Jake and Katie set Leah's wedding for late November hoping to beat Sallie's baby and have Katie's birthing past by several weeks.

The first week in November Jake called me to Frogtown. "Can you stop near the cheese plant on the way over and pick up Mommy

Glick? We'll need a granny."

It was after midnight but Katie's mother, slipper-footed and dress unpinned, climbed onto my front seat only minutes after I knocked on her kitchen door. There had been no time to pack her bulging green tapestry bag. I never stopped for a granny who did not come with a bag of cookies, a jar of fresh jam and the craving to be included in the action of new birth. "I didn't want to keep you waiting. Katie might need us. Remember how fast she went with little Jake? I've had this bag packed for the last week or so."

Rachel Glick managed to tug on black stockings and shoes as I rounded curves and bounced potholes, added straight pins to finish closing her dress and cape over a matronly bosom. She pinned a narrow black cotton ribbon around her head and with a straight pin fastened her organdy cap to it at her central part. After the black hardboard bonnet covered her white hair, she settled against the seat and seemed ready to be granny. That meant receiving the new baby into warm blankets, dressing it and staying with the family to care for Katie until a maiden Amish woman came as nurse. Rachel would fetch a basin, old rags and baby clothes, then sit and tell me of her eight birthings, her multitude of grandchildren and how Amish folk from Quarryville to Lititz were doing, while we awaited Katie's birthing.

By 4:30 a.m. when Jake called the boys downstairs for morning feeding and milking, Katie hugged a new daughter in her arms. "Little Katie," Jake said. "Katie G. Fisher."

Leah and Mary came down to admire the baby, then fried mush and eggs for breakfast. Amos, John and Ezra put on old coats from hooks behind the space heater, pushed work-stained wool hats on their heads and went to the barn. Sylvia came from Sarah's room to hold the baby, then carried it back to her aunt for approval before helping little Martha and toddler Jake button clothes and tie shoe-strings.

"Now all we have to think about is Sallie holding off until after Leah's wedding," Katie said, looking at a calendar on the bedroom wall.

***

Leah G. Fisher and Levi B. Ebersole were married the Tuesday after Thanksgiving. I could not spare time from morning office hours to sit through services that began at eight and lasted until noon and I would not have understood the High German. My afternoon was needed for patient rounds. Pete and I agreed to attend supper and the evening sing. We arrived at four o'clock, waiting at the end of the lane to drive to the house. Families leaving the wedding to go home for evening feeding and milking clogged the lane. Carriages stretched toward South Queen Street in a gray undulating ribbon. At the barn teenage hostlers helped hitch and unhitch horses to the wagons that dotted the pasture beside the stable like raisins in a pudding. Horses were tied in the stable and along the second floor of the barn between the haymows and beneath unstripped tobacco, hanging on laths along scaffolding that rose to the barn peak.

Pete and I parked between a large black van and the gray bench wagon that stored and transported the folded benches of a church district. A dozen shawled and bonneted girls and jacketed boys ran in the yard. Clusters of men in black overcoats and wide-brimmed black hats stood about talking. They said "Hello" or nodded as we passed to the kitchen door.

The Fisher yard had been combed of stray leaves, summer's flower beds cleaned of every brown frozen stalk. The boarded-up vegetable stand looked cold and bare against the empty garden. I wondered where the scarecrow had gone. The earth lay dark and fallow until spring. A straw bale covered each cellar window keeping winter winds from the house. The large front porch had been enclosed with plastic sheeting. Through it I could see benches for extra seating and two cupboards moved from the house.

A wall of hot air bearing odors of cooked onions and celery, roast chicken and the stuffiness of a crowd met us at the open door. The Fisher house had changed. The stone farmhouse had always seemed large, but on this wedding day it rivaled the barn floor. The varnished wooden partitions between Jake and Katie's bedroom, the parlor, the large kitchen, even into Sarah's frame end of the house, had been removed to make one large room. Beds had been taken down, bureaus and cupboards taken out or pushed against the wall. Parlor rugs were gone exposing wide pine boards. Only the usual three space heaters remained. I wondered if they were needed or if the knurls of black-garbed women sitting about chatting in Pennsylvania Dutch would have warmed the room. A great U of tables, covered with a variety of cloths, encircled the room.

Katie came to greet us, changing from Pennsylvania Dutch to English. "Glad you got here. We'll have supper soon."

I had seen many of Katie's and Jake's sisters and the neighbor women in my office. As married women they wore a Sunday dress, cape, black apron and a white cap. They smiled and offered a chair. One woman held a baby girl. Amish mothers wore dresses similar to their own on babies when they brought them to my office, but I had only heard of nearly bald infant girls wearing white caps to church and was amazed the tiny child did not pull it off. She did manage to get its wide strings into her mouth. Because of the large number of adults invited to weddings, only children of the bride's and groom's immediate family or nursing infants could attend.

I greeted Katie, Sarah, then the other women with a handshake. Sarah looked happy surrounded by friends and family. I wondered how many pain pills she had taken that day, how many plaster animals she had sold, how many orders she had taken for Christmas.

"Jake and I don't work today," Katie said. "But you can see everybody has been busy this week. Yesterday we scrubbed three washtubs of celery. The best goes to the bride's table. We cooked fifty chickens and ducks, cut them up with the bread for the roast. Mary and Sylvia made two lard cans of applesauce Friday. Neighbor Henry Beilers made all the doughnuts." Katie accepted my wedding gift, a nest of bowls, and handed them to a young girl.

"Get Sylvia to take you to the cellar to see all the cakes. Leah's girlfriends decorated cakes with fancy icing and nuts. Some have figures of barns, fences, animals and people. We'll freeze the ones we don't eat today. Mary and Sylvia put colored candies and nuts in the secret wedding cake they baked." Katie stopped to shake hands with newcomers in black shawls.

"Too bad you couldn't get here this morning. We sang, the ministers spoke. Last came the marriage ceremony by Bishop Daniel Stoltzfus, then Levi and Leah went upstairs until some benches were made into tables and the rest used to sit on. When they came down, they were happy to see the different cakes, nuts and fruit at the *Eck*, the special corner of the table where bride and groom are served."

I nodded to Katie, trying to absorb everything she said, comparing it to weddings in our culture. When Pete and I were married, Mother, Grandmother and I had made platters of crustless fancy sandwiches, made punch and bought ice cream to go with the baker's wedding cake. "Glad I don't have to manage and prepare food for three or four hundred people. And two meals. Guess you're glad for any help you can get."

Katie continued, "The week before the wedding an Amish groom comes to the bride's house to help work, so we had Levi here to help out. Tomorrow Levi and Leah will clean up and do the wash if the children here will let them. Leah's brothers and sisters will tease them, tie the tablecloths in knots, dump out the wash water. It will be a lively place. I think Levi hid the washing machine so nobody could steal the gasoline engine or wringer.

"This afternoon a bunch of girls tricked Leah into jumping over the broom so she's a *Hausfrau* now. They were going to sew her fork and knife fast to the tablecloth but they got caught. Jake heard Levi's friends say they were going to throw him over the fence to the married men. Don't know if they got it done.

"Tonight you and your husband will sit at a special table with others who just came for the evening meal. You'll be served leftovers from the noon meal along with supper."

Pete sat across the table from me with the men. Ivan Smucker, a Mennonite from Nine Points, sat beside him. Ivan, a retired farmer, had driven his black van full of Amish neighbors to the wedding. Frequently, for extra income, retirees rented time and transportation to buggy-driving folks, charging a set price per mile per person. "This is the third wedding my passengers have been to today," Ivan said. "I drove to Christ Zooks at Georgetown for the service and noon meal, stopped at John Riehls near Skelp Level this afternoon and now here for supper."

The tables were set with a mismatch of metal plates and stainless steel flatwear in a variety of patterns. Later Mary told me that they belonged to the church district and were kept in a chest to be used for church, weddings and funerals. Water glasses were plain, printed, octagonal, tall, short and even some jelly glasses. I wondered if the neighbors had contributed theirs for the day.

Everyone bowed their heads for silent grace. We lifted them to a slice of bread on each plate. As if a starting gun had sounded, a network of flailing arms reached for jam and butter to spread on the staff of life. Dishes of roast, gravy, creamed celery, beans, coleslaw, chowchow, noodles, chips, mashed potatoes, pickles and fruit salad rushed past. Supper's menu also moved hand to hand along the table. Raw celery, doughnuts, cornstarch pudding, cookies, cake, pie, ham, macaroni and cheese, all dished onto the same plate. We were overwhelmed. This was no time for gawking or talking. If anything impressed me, it was the speed with which food was shoveled into mouths. I had never seen anything like it. Within minutes it was over. My plate was not empty when hands around me rubbed crumbs from beards and chins.

Those who served tables were friends of the newlyweds who had married the year before. Several women carried unmistakable bulges beneath their aprons; others I knew had small babies in a bedroom upstairs.

We bowed our heads in another silent grace and rose from the benches to make room for the next seating. We found chairs along the wall. Two galvanized laundry tubs on casters, one with suds, one with hot rinse water, were rolled to the center of the room. The helpers, men and women alike, washed, rinsed and dried dishes at a furious rate, resetting the tables as they worked. Others refilled empty serving dishes. Katie said there had been more than three settings at the noon meal; two fed everyone at supper.

The young folks had come in from the tobacco stripping room and barn, where they had been socializing, and gone upstairs to wait until they were invited to come down for supper. We watched as the bride and groom emerged from the upstairs door and walked to the bride's corner. I expected Leah to have a special bride's dress, but she wore a new navy blue one made in the style of all her other dresses. Levi wore a new black Sunday suit. As a married woman Leah would now wear a black apron to church instead of the white one worn by single girls.

Next the two young men and two young women, who were the attendants, descended the stairs hand-in-hand. The bride and groom and these attendants had spent the late afternoon hours pairing the remaining young folks, usually asking for both the boy's and girl's consent. These couples now also came down the stairsteps holding hands and filed to seats along the heavily laden supper table. We visited while the young folks ate.

I wondered how Katie managed everything: dowry furniture, rugs, quilts over the years, the wedding, even a baby scarcely a month old. Last year daughter Sallie was married; now Leah; more daughters to marry in years to come. Jake and Katie should be glad that half their children were sons. Would Pete and I have fewer responsibilities, or only different ones? I chewed a pretzel and took an apple from snacks passed around after everyone was fed and thought of our children's college years ahead, our daughters' weddings.

The pleasure of the evening sing with the young couples joining in rounded out the happy occasion. Sallie handed Pete and me an Amish hymnal. I do not know what we sang, each verse begun by a leader, the wedding guests joining him in a singsong chanting wail without musical accompaniment. I knew enough German to follow the singers and mutter a few words. All tunes sounded alike as I blundered along. I looked at Sallie. She laughed at me. Others grinned and I laughed too.

When women began climbing the stairs to sort out black bonnets and shawls with their initials embroidered on the corner, and the men slipped on heavy black overcoats and wool hats, Pete and I thanked our hosts. We shook hands and left amid the carriage traffic. We were home by eleven o'clock.

If there was any lesson learned that Tuesday after Thanksgiving, it was that if I should ever again be invited to an Amish wedding, I would eat faster and not miss the cherry pie that passed me by, making room for it on my plate amid the roast and gravy.

***

Snow patched the hollows of fields and lay in dirty black ribbons along the roadsides where it had been thrown up by last week's plows when I visited Sarah Fisher on January's foggy morning. It was a long-awaited wet day that allowed laths of fragile brown tobacco to be taken down from their scaffolding and placed in the damp room beside the stripping room.

The stripping room in the basement of the tobacco barn was a busy place as I drove past its windowed front. Jake, with sons and daughters too old to be in school, pulled the finger-staining tobacco leaves from stalks and laid them in piles to be pressed into paper-wrapped bales. Mary saw me and waved as I walked toward Sarah's room.

The windows in Sarah's space heater glowed red from the burning coals that radiated comforting heat into the room. Odors of freshly baked bread or cake filtered into the room from Katie's kitchen beyond the varnished partition. I recognized Leah's and Katie's voices in muffled bits of laughter and conversation in the next room.

"It's my week to help Aunt Sarah," Mary said, removing her jacket and scarf. "Sylvia works three days a week making jam at Kitchen Kettle and Leah is pretty busy these days." She lowered Sarah onto her bed.

Katie opened a door in the partition, held flour-covered hands in mid-air. A blast of spices, apples and cooking meat came in with her. "When you're finished with Sarah, come over to our side if you can spare a minute. Something I want to show you." She hesitated, directed her attention to her daughter. "Mary, can you help here in the kitchen until dinner?"

Finished with Sarah, I entered Katie's kitchen. Cloves and cinnamon surged from the black gas stove oven as Leah removed a tray of brown-rimmed buttermilk cookies, knobby with nuts and raisins. "Our boys like their sweets," Katie said, offering me a cookie the size of a doughnut. "Mary, can you change the baby then mash the potatoes?"

I resolved to add Katie's recipe to those from other Amish kitchens as my teeth sank into the soft warm cookie. "What is the dough hanging on the wooden clothes rack?" I watched Katie roll out the last large paper-thin oval on the kitchen table and hang it to dry before rinsing her hands at the sink.

"I'm making noodles. Later when they're dry I'll take the noodle cutter, finish them off and store them in cans. Leah will need some too when she goes to housekeeping." Katie shook her head. "Trouble is Jake wants the girls to help finish the tobacco stripping, and I need them in the house. Sold his tobacco for a good price this year, took the last of it down this morning. Soon as stripping is over, we have a pile of sewing ahead."

"What do you have on the wire racks?" I asked, examining dried up, brown nubbins in a three-layered homemade dehydrator on the back of the space heater.

Mary laughed. "Taste one. Dried apple snitz for snitz pies. About dry enough to put away now. We cook them to a sauce with sugar, cinnamon and cloves for a two-crusted pie that we serve when it's our turn for church. Ever have a snitz pie?"

I nodded, savoring the chewy apple lump. A mouthful could occupy a person most of an evening. A snitz pie was a real treat.

Katie dried her hands and turned down the gas under a chattering kettle. "I called you over to show you the parlor. Come see."

The air in the unheated parlor was damp and heavy with the odor of varnish, harness oil and new things. Katie's green couch and rocking chairs, with their bright needlepoint cushions, had been pushed against the wall beside the Dutch cupboard and drop-leaf table. Trestle and board tables occupied the space between a dismantled bed and six new kitchen chairs painted with clusters of fruit on their glassy varnish.

"Leah's *Hausschteier*," Katie said, sweeping an arm over the tables of pots, pans, nests of bowls, stainless flatwear, hand-painted dishes, mirrors and a plywood letter rack. A stack of embroidered tea towels and pillow cases lay between dishcloths and sheets still in plastic wrappings. "That other table is Levi's things." She pointed to hammers, several saws, a bridle, a pair of reins, two oil cans, buckets and more than my eyes and brain could catalogue.

"Wedding gifts? I didn't see these at the wedding."

"No. We Amish don't bring gifts to a wedding. Until March when their rented farm will be free, Leah lives at home like usual during the week. Levi stays as hired man for his brother Daniel K. Zook at Buena Vista. Ever since the wedding Levi picks Leah up Friday evenings, and they visit around at wedding guests' houses and get the wedding gifts. Uncle Amos R. Glicks gave them that nice mantle clock. Levi brings her back home Sunday nights."

I knew that Amish women liked nice china. "Do they have a set of good dishes?"

"Levi gave them to her the Christmas before they were married. It's almost like an engagement gift."

We both knew of Leah's early pregnancy with its morning nausea but did not discuss it. "Do people know they're coming for dinner, spending the night and collecting a wedding gift?"

"Oh yes. We know when to expect young folks. We've been working all winter scraping, varnishing and polishing old bureaus, tables and chairs, getting them ready for Leah and Levi. Bought most of them at sales. Got Leah her own sewing machine coupla years ago. Handy to have several in the house. Mary and Sylvia have them too."

"What does Levi's family do?"

"They help them get started farming. Levi's brother Isaac is moving off the sixty-acre farm their dad bought near Nickel Mines so Levis can move in. Levi's mother made him several quilts too."

"It sure takes a lot to get started."

"Yes. Cows, horses, plows and machinery to buy yet too. It was the same for Jake and me. We took Leah's last quilt out of the frame a week ago. Had a quilting bee for my sisters, then Jake's sisters after Christmas to get it finished.

"Everything finished now?"

"All but the carpets. We keep all the men's old shirts and the girls dresses, tear them in strips, sew them end to end, stitch the edges in and roll them in balls. We took them to Big Ben Beiler at Leaman Place, but he is so busy looming rugs this time of year. Guess Leah will be without rugs awhile. She can use the hooked ones she made. We'll have the infare in two weeks. That's when the groom's family invites Leah's whole family to dinner."

Last year Katie and Jake had gone through this process with Sallie. This year it was Leah. Next year it could be Mary, Sylvia or even a double wedding, and way down the years little Katie.

Aunt Sarah had watched November pass November. Was it by her choice that she never had a wedding, never had collected a *Hausschteier*?

16
Ripples and Reflections

After four weeks of hospital confinement by weather, March came to me as a welcome change. Its warmer days unfolded toward April, like the blue and white crocuses blooming on our New Holland lawn. Finally, I saw weekends at home again.

Not that I was bored or lonely in the hospital. Therapy occupied most of the day, family and friends came to visit, frequent telephone calls kept me in touch with the outside world. But phone calls were stormless waves in comparison to the, "hurry over my wife's having her baby now," or the humorous and jaunty calls I had received during the years of practice. I laughed remembering the 5:00 a.m. raspy voice that panted, "Can you come over right away? I got a cow down with mastitis. Wanted to get ya before I started milkin'." The caller did not give his name but the throaty voice was unmistakably Jake Riehl's. He had called every time his wife Malinda had birthed one of their seven children. We had spent hours in the Riehl's warm kitchen, chewing over intolerable milk inspectors, the quality of that season's hay and tobacco prices. I knew Jake's voice.

"You want the vet," I told the excited Amishman, fumbled the phone back into its cradle and hunted the warm hollow under the covers. I envisioned Jake in his ragged barn clothes and stained straw hat, squinting deep-set blue eyes, scanning the graffiti of scrawled names and numbers in a telephone shanty hanging over a road bank someplace east of Churchtown. The waning yellow flashlight beam had not distinguished the vet's name amid the overwritten jumble of names.

Another day Josiah Glick called, concerned about his newborn son's unhealed umbilicus. Josiah's name had not sounded familiar, even in a community in which the names on mailboxes were duplicated many times.

"Did I deliver your baby?" I searched my memory for the recent delivery.

"No," Josiah answered. He hesitated, laughed nervously. "We didn't have you for the baby. The vitamin salesman that comes around regular delivered it. Didn't cost as much. He did it for just a donation."

Too often people carried health and illness in their pocketbooks. I sighed, shuddered and gave Josiah's baby an appointment. I rarely scolded a patient for delaying visits, for using home poultices or for seeking help from a donation-fee, self-educated country healer. Instead I listened.

Lecturing patients about overdosing on expensive vitamins and health concoctions, self-treating wounds or delaying prenatal visits would only have blurred case histories, and I would not have learned that *salva* (sage) tea, available in most home gardens, helps diarrhea. I would not have heard that before calling a physician for a child's earache, a father might blow tobacco smoke in its ear to relieve pain.

When Elsa our oldest child was small, I took her with me so frequently on house calls that it became part of the visit. "Guess what Mary and Sadie were playing yesterday?" Susie Stoltzfus said in my office. She smiled, remembering her daughter's antics. "Doctor Kaiser and Elsa on a house call. Mary was you. Sadie was Elsa and she pulled her along by the hand. They pretended to examine a doll."

Sliding a stethoscope along a wheezing chest could coat scope and fingers with tarry Ichthymol or pink Antiphlogistine's gummy paste. A spoonful of Great Find was used to cure innumerable ailments. Pregnant mothers rubbed Mother's Friend over their abdomens to prevent stretch marks, or they drank raspberry leaf tea for easier delivery of the placentas. If home remedies did not conflict with acceptable medical treatment, I shared the case with tradition.

In the hospital I enjoyed the visits of friends, like the evening three Amish ladies, Annie Stoltzfus, Ruth Fisher and Hannah Beiler, hired a driver and came to visit.

Annie and Ruth unloaded their black bonnets and shawls onto the vacant bed beside mine. Annie pulled an unfinished pillow case from her voluminous bag, plucked a needle from the fabric and began to embroider. Ruth's hand emerged from her tapestry tote with a new shirt for her husband. She began to stitch buttonholes.

Hannah sat as if afraid to remove her wraps. "Guess what I have?" she said, her brown eyes bright in a round face. She dimpled with a secret she could not wait to reveal. Beneath her shawl, her right arm bulged with an obvious package. Slowly, she lifted the black wool. A small dark shape lay on the crook of her arm. "Thought the nurses might not let me bring this in to show you." The infant wore a tiny blue bonnet and a black shawl over her pink dress, white stockings and booties. "Her name's Malinda."

Another day a group of Amish ladies, who completed a beautiful Texas star quilt in shades of blue, spread it across the vacant bed beside mine. I had delivered at least one baby for each woman, some with special experiences. The quilt was admired by hospital personnel and visitors before I sent the love gift home. I resolved to invite the quilters to New Holland for ice cream and cake when I was discharged.

There were other ways in which I felt special. On my birthday the hospital administrator and the dietitian, an old acquaintance who shared my birth year and month, marched into my room with a candled cake. I never learned who wore the white pile skin at Easter when a giant rabbit hopped into therapy and handed me a basket of candy eggs. One day Joe and I had our pictures taken for the hospital newspaper.

Joe still spent evenings with me when he was in town. He stressed the importance of a good diet to gain strength, told me how to move up in bed when I slid down. I learned to cover myself by gripping the sheet with my teeth. If ever I write about my hospital days, I will title the book *Hang on to Your Teeth 'Cause You Can't Gum the Bed Sheets*.

If another patient occupied the other bed in my room, time moved faster. We talked and watched television together. During February when I could not get home, I became hooked on football. Over and over my roommate and I saw tangles of heaped and twisted bodies unravel, marveling that the gladiators got onto their feet to regroup and clash again. The thuds and grunts as hurling bodies met bodies, the clunk of helmet on helmet, made me wince as I remembered the force and orange shock of my fall. I wondered how even seasoned men could survive impact after impact and was thankful my sons were not football players.

We roommates cheered the teams and held our breaths as yardage was measured for a first down or players struggled on the one-yard line as the clock ran out. Some weeks saw more warriors than others limp from the field or hauled off on stretchers. At one game, when a favored player was carried off, it was announced that he had a possible spinal cord injury. During the next Sunday's game the diagnosis of quadriplegia was confirmed. The hero's name was never mentioned again. He was just one more number among the 10,000 spinal cord injuries a year in the United States. It was as though he had never existed. I knew that his future had been snapped like a whip from under him. After possible surgery for fracture of his neck and months of physical rehabilitation, life in a wheelchair lay before him. The most important and difficult change would be adjusting from a life of activity and fame to one of oblivion and anonymity.

The game's announcer did not elaborate whether the injured player was married. If he was single, I imagined anguished parents rushing across the country, travel and hotel at their expense. There would be anxious hours and days as he rehabilitated, unexpected responsibility for a son they believed gone from the nest. If he had a wife and children, their futures would be altered forever. Many marriages do not survive the change. Some wives cannot endure a husband unable to embrace them or make love to them as before the accident. The possibility of fathering children is dim.

I thought about my former roommates at City, how Jimmy's parents had changed their hopes for his future, built a wheelchair-accessible wing to their home. Cindy's nursing career had ended at midpoint. Every evening during visiting hours her bed had been surrounded by concerned parents and friends.

While attention is focused on the injured, families spend a multitude of hours and many dollars traveling to and from the hospital, depriving themselves of valuable time. They wonder what the future holds, worry that they act and plan properly under the cloud that has suddenly cast its dark shadow over everything they do.

My family passed under that long shadow the night of my injury. After I was loaded into the ambulance, Pete drove to New Holland to tell our sons, Keith and Paul, what had happened to me before driving to the hospital. "The longest drive in my life," he said later. He did not return to the campground to help with the festival weekend we had planned. The next day Pete and Paul folded the trailer and took it home.

Our camping friends were upset and concerned by the accident. Pete telephoned Elsa in Denver and she called her sister Lorelei, a freshman in college several blocks away. Disbelief, a desire to fly home, then a more practical wait-and-see attitude followed. How fortunate that our children were grown and no longer mother-dependent. The days of ball games, school concerts, PTA were past. I had been den mother for the boys. Camped Girl Scouts to Washington, Colorado and Wyoming.

Keith had returned home to live after college. Paul was a high school junior. Always independent, now he became more so. During my first weeks in the hospital he visited to complain about the battered Toyota with unstylish torn upholstery that I had bought for Lorelei and him to drive to work at Red Run Campground. His eyes glowed with desire as he told me about the wonderful Bradley GT car in the garage of his scoutmaster. "Sorry, Paul," I said. "I'm in no position to help you. But, if you can sell the old car and swing the deal without additional funds, the Bradley is yours." Paul matured as he advertised, then sold the Toyota, as he worked hours getting the Bradley road-ready.

We learned months after the October 13th accident that there were speculations our marriage would not endure the crisis, that Pete would tire of my change from independence to complete helplessness. I never gave the idea a moment, assumed he would be at my side as I had supported him during his three hospital months and recuperation when he had had a leg masticated to kibble by a backhoe at our Spring Gulch Campground.

It is not always easy to be a doctor's husband. At times he is expected to pass out free medical advice or give inside information regarding the life of his wife. The myth that doctors, by reason of their profession, are affluent, prospering at the expense of victimized patients, overshadows the need for a husband to earn a living. He is sometimes seen as living in the luxurious lap of his wife.

Pete was crushed, literally and emotionally, soon after my hospitalization. An Amazon, a nursing supervisor, cornered him, her large arms and huge body stapling him into a corner. "I'm so sorry about your wife's accident. What ever will your family do now? How will you get along?" She did not release her grip on the wall until he assured her that the Kaisers were not headed for the county poor house. He hurried down the corridor without telling her that since college he had never been without a job. Why bother? She had injured his ego and no hospital insurance compensated for that.

At home in New Holland reorganization kept the wheels oiled and turning. After the weekly cleaning lady washed the dirty laundry, dusted the chairs and swept the floors, there was only grocery shopping and the evening dinner to appease three male appetites. Pete was no cook. He had often laughed and bragged that a clause in our wedding certificate stated that providing meals was my wifely duty.

Pete's mother to the rescue. Oma, at seventy-eight, took on the responsibility of planning, shopping and supper. Every day at three o'clock she crossed our backyards to begin the evening meal. After cooking only for herself the past twenty years, she was flabbergasted at how much food three hungry men could eat and worried about the total at the checkout counter.

When tragedy strikes, it stirs up not only one ripple but is like a stone skipped across a pond, producing multiple ruffles. I lay in the hospital remembering obligations. The first week of hospitalization a nurse dialed numbers and held the telephone against my head while I unburdened duties.

When the obstetrical group of doctors assumed my office hours and hospital cases until a permanent physician could be found, it relieved a great responsibility. Patients expecting home births had to hunt other physicians. Patients at term or with special problems requiring house calls occupied my thoughts. I had let them down, abandoned them. I wondered how they felt.

At Community Hospital a substitute had to be found for the staff office I was to assume. I deserted hospital committees that had occupied time and thought. A stack of charts became weeks overdue until brought to my bedside at City Rehabilitation Hospital for completion.

The capable vice president of the County Parks Board assumed my responsibilities and became its next president. I remained an active member until I left Lancaster County.

In the village of Terre Hill a men's prayer group met weekly for breakfast in the back room of a restaurant. They placed me on their prayer list, one of many prayer chains and lists composed by local friends and cousins from New Jersey to Florida.

Patients and friends stopped during a day's activities to visit me in the hospital or send a card. Pete visited regularly, seldom missing a day. He, Keith, Paul or a friend opened and read each card. Many contained notes. I enjoyed cards from Amish and Mennonite friends who took the time to write detailed letters describing the weather, what the housewife prepared for the next meal, how garden and field crops fared. Often they contained lists of their children with birth years, indicating the ones I had delivered.

***

By mid-March, five months after the accident, I was stronger and able to wash and feed myself, use the telephone, move in bed and sit on its edge unassisted. I could not walk without help.

"Let's use a walker," Joe said. "But only if someone is with you."

Another step toward independence. Someone still had to stand me up before I could take a step. My hands on the walker gave me stability but my left arm was not strong. Evening nurses took me for walks in the hall. The walker period was brief.

"Now we'll go to Canadian crutches." Joe pulled me to my feet and slipped my forearms through the U-shaped supports. I grasped both handles. The right hand held firm and lifted the crutch as I stepped forward with the left foot, but the weak left hand slipped its hold. The crutch fell away. Joe taped the hand to the crutch and I moved across the gym, right crutch and left foot forward, left crutch with the right foot. The rhythm came easily, but I worried about falling and was glad that Joe stayed close in case I lost balance. By the next therapy period a wide strap had been glued to the left crutch. Velcro held the insecure left fist tight to the handle. The wheelchair remained my daytime residence, the Canadian crutches became my means of walking. After I fell crossing an alfalfa field one weekend, my concern grew about not being able to shuck my arms free when I tumbled. A forearm fast in a crutch might mean a sprained or broken arm. Several months later I graduated to a cane.

It was time to think of going home more than weekends, a necessity when my hospital insurance came to an end. Pete became my business manager when I was hospitalized, learned the mystery coding system on the monthly bills. He scrutinized each one, asked me about medications and treatment, questioned dubious items. Frequently he found overcharges that took him to the billing department for correction. The computer number for the disposable catheter the nurses used four times a day was one digit different from an indwelling Foley catheter, but the price difference was five dollars compared to twenty-five for the Foley. Mistakes were unintentional, but the corrections made possible more days of hospital care.

The third week of March I backed my wheelchair into Doctor Richard's office. "I'll have to go home. My insurance is used up the end of this month."

"You're not finished with therapy yet. We'll have you come in as an outpatient three days a week."

"Yes," I agreed. "And I'll find a bed someplace in this hospital to rest over noontime." How could I work in therapy all morning without a short noon nap to recharge my battery for the afternoon workout?

More adjustment for the family in my full-time care. How would it be to live at home? Weekends when Pete was there to care for me were easy — but every day? For five and a half months I had lived within the protective womb of the hospital. Nurses came when I rang, washed and dressed me, moved me from wheelchair to bed and back again. Could I live with a family where people had their own interests? Could they care for me? The more I thought about it, the more apprehensive I became.

Time tromped toward April.

17

Home

Home to stay. I felt as wobbly-legged and insecure as the day Joe pulled me to my feet after my accident and told me to take the first step. The prospect of life permanently out of the hospital womb, away from nursing care, appeared as cold, hard and unpredictable as the floor had looked those first shaking moments.

Life at 561 West Main Street adapted for my needs. Pete had installed a second stair-railing so I could grasp one in each hand as I went upstairs to bed. Each evening I ascended with Pete behind me, should I lose my balance. In the morning I descended one riser to sit on the top step before bumping down the rest of the stairs, one carpeted plank at a time, on my bottom. Months passed before the long incline ceased to look like a parachute-less free fall, and I could walk down the thirteen treads.

Changes began in January during my first weekend home from City Rehabilitation Hospital. An ancient oak bedside commode that had belonged to my great-grandmother (I descended from generations of attic hoarders) made the three or four nighttime excursions easier.

Each morning Pete catheterized me from a supply of sterile packs. He tugged slacks over my hips, slid on a blouse, shoes and socks before I descended the stairs to a wheelchair borrowed from New

Holland's American Legion. They generously supplied the town with crutches, walkers and wheelchairs on a donation basis.

On the four days a week I now spent at home, Pete stayed around the house or ran short errands between my trips to the bathroom. He made us toast or cereal for breakfast and fat ham and cheese or tomato and lettuce sandwiches for lunch. At three o'clock Pete's mother came to prepare supper and discuss the next day's menu. Oma insisted that it was my house and I was the boss.

During the day I backed my wheelchair through the house to answer the telephone, load plates and flatwear on my lap to set the table, watch television or entertain visitors.

Pete set posts in the ground under the walnut tree behind the garage, fastened stair-railings to them and constructed twenty-eight feet of parallel bars. April softened the days. Every clear day Pete hoisted me to my feet, and I practiced walking. The laps increased and the grass between the rails wore to a rut as the walnut, persimmon and elms budded, then leafed and colored to fall's amber and mahogany. While I walked, Lady Dog sniffed the hazelnut bushes or chased squirrels into the chestnut trees. The neighbors came out to talk. It was good to see old friends but I was uncomfortable, felt like society's fallen crumb, sensitively aware that while I was once a doctor in the community, now I could not stand tall.

Was it purely pride, foolish pride? Perhaps, after months of bed and wheelchair, weeks of submitting to care by others, I still had a mind set against being handicapped. I had not overcome abhorrence to disability. Stroke patients recovered their ability to walk by leaning on four-footed quad canes as they limped around the gym, often one arm hanging in a sling. My sympathy for them burned so deep that I did not want to touch the embers of pain, did not want to be counted with them as they too bent over to watchdog the movements of each step across the floor.

A regular cane was too unstable for my tottering balance. In June Joe took away my Canadian crutches and placed a quad cane in my right hand. I crossed the gym after several uncertain tries. It was a great triumph, but the quad cane gave me a crippled pathetic feeling. A friend wrote about a cane with a large plunger-like foot. I searched out and bought one. It was clumsy and unusual, but it stood by itself and was not a quad cane. I practiced with the cane only in therapy.

Without crutches or someone holding the top of my slacks, I felt like a tower seesawing without guy wires, about to crash, until Craig tricked me. He followed at my heels as we started across the gym. A minute later he stood ten feet before me, his boyish face grinning gleefully. The walk had been solo. Concentrating as always on my feet, I had not heard him run behind a partition to face me. "Here I am." He laughed.

The cane became my companion. Finally I had a free hand for carrying a pocketbook, but that divided my concentration between walking and maintaining a grasp with the left hand. "I carried an envelope home today," I bragged to Doctor Richard. "Didn't drop it." It was a marvelous feat. I worried about the inevitable day when I would let my cane fall. I had never picked anything from the floor, worried that leaning so far would unbalance me.

"I dropped my cane yesterday," I boasted to Craig. Picking it up had been as wonderful as the first time, months before, when I had conquered paging the great leaves of the Sunday paper.

"Then what?" Therapists Joe and Craig shared my victories.

"Picked it up by myself," I said, remembering how gingerly I had bent from the waist, slow and stiff as a rusted hinge, fingers extended to fumble the cane into grasp. With as much care I had stood erect again.

***

With warming Pennsylvania weather came spring fever. In all our New Holland years, not one season had passed where I was not behind the rototiller as soon as the drying soil could be aroused without producing curdled clods. I lost the annual battle with weeds, but when my freezers filled by September, the victory was mine.

Disability does not hammer down desire. May's warm sunny days churned the earth-blood in this farmer's veins. I could not get out of the wheelchair by myself, let alone think of stirring up last year's stalks and weeds.

Now Pete, who had tilled the rose bed but set his size thirteens firmly against collaborating with peas, carrots or onions, except on his plate, made his ultimate personal sacrifice. He offered to plant a vegetable garden in the plot of last year's skeletal vines if I would supervise. I sopped up sunshine while my husband turned the ground, then dropped peas, carrot and spinach seeds, plus cabbage, broccoli and lettuce plants. That summer I hand weeded from the wheelchair while Pete hacked with a hoe. Nothing inside the house could replace the damp odor, the satisfying grainy feel of fresh earth between my fingers, as I pulled lamb's-quarters and crab grass along rows of beans on the days I did not go to therapy at the hospital.

On the three hospital days each week, we arose early so Pete could catheterize, dress, breakfast and deposit me by wheelchair at physiotherapy. After time in the gym with therapist Joe or Craig, I lunched in the cafeteria. Nurses, medical staff or employee friends took my tray through the line and found a space for my wheelchair at their table.

Old friend, generous Barbara, nursing supervisor of the obstetrical department, took me to the lavatory after lunch and found an empty bed. She covered it with a sheet blanket for my short nap before time to go to Occupational Therapy. Barb returned me to the wheelchair, and I wheeled away to stack cones, increase the strength of my wrist and improve finger function by pulling them against the force of rubber bands. Another hour in physiotherapy before Pete came to return me to New Holland. Enroute we discussed plans for our trip to Arizona.

After Pete sold Spring Gulch Campground, he began planning a move to Arizona, claiming that the warmer climate would ease the aches in his injured leg. I licked my finger and held it to the wind. It blew toward the Southwest. The velocity was increasing. Previously absorbed and busy in my medical practice, the move had not interested me. I preferred to think of living in Arizona in the far distant future. Not my husband. After searching through the state, he had invested in a taxi business in Scottsdale. At intervals he flew to consult with his manager. Mid-April was his next trip.

I would go with him, take Barbara with us. Barbara had helped Pete decipher my monthly bills, been my nurse in the ambulance when I was transported to City Rehabilitation, improved my comfort daily in a multitude of ways. She was unmarried and could arrange time off. Barbara and Pete looked forward to the trip.

Only two weeks out of the hospital and traveling in a wheelchair, my dependency on others gave me a bottomless apprehension. How could we manage in the small toilet of an airplane? Even with help I was not steady enough to walk down an aisle in-flight. Could we make the long trip through the Chicago terminal in time to catch our connecting flight? All unfounded fears. We checked my wheelchair as baggage. The airlines provided a wheelchair and someone to push it from curb to plane door. On the tarmac at Harrisburg Airport two attendants strapped me to a narrow chair, carried me up the steps into the plane and to my seat. In Chicago and Phoenix a wheelchair and attendant met the 737 in the jetway, pushed me to the baggage claim area, then the curb.

Mornings at Scottsdale I waited in bed until Pete or Barb dressed me and pattern-exercised my arms and legs as Joe had instructed. I cannot say if patterning had any long-term effect, but it did improve my walking for an immediate period. The remainder of the day Barb pushed my wheelchair as we browsed Scottsdale's fascinating shops or took drives into the desert.

When Pete toured with us, I rode on the back seat where I could stretch out my stiff legs. As the car sped past cacti and paloverde, I flexed my hands against the resistance of a rubber-banded exerciser; squeeze-release, squeeze-release, until both hands demanded rest. My goal was to clench them, to touch finger tips against the palms by the time I left Arizona for our next stop in Colorado to visit our daughters.

In Denver we also stopped to see my former roommate, Cindy, at Craig Hospital for the spinal-cord-injured. Cindy had transferred there from City Rehabilitation. Barb and I were amazed and fascinated to see the adaptive aids and computer appliances making life easier and more independent for quadriplegics. They even danced and played ball in wheelchairs. I left Craig Hospital relieved that when fully recovered, a wheelchair, Canadian crutches or adaptive aids would not be a part of my life. My hands were becoming more useful and I could contract them into a fist. Rising out of a chair was my next goal.

I yearned more than ever for the day I could rise unassisted from the wheelchair, to transfer from bed to chair alone, to stand up whenever I wished. Doubts, like the first wisps of clouds on the horizon before a rainstorm, were beginning to form. I brushed them away, still believed that within the next five months all my disabilities would be overcome, and I would return to full practice again. It had been promised six months ago.

Back in therapy Joe and Craig concentrated their skills on teaching me to rise from the seated position. Not every milepost was easily passed. Craig exercised and strengthened my legs by attaching rubber tubing to the rowing machine. My legs seemed more than strong enough to push my body up, but I could not coordinate the procedure. "Throw yourself forward from the chair," Joe insisted. The tile floor looked hard. I feared falling face down. "I'll catch you. I won't let you bounce more than twice." All the grunting, thrusting and pushing failed. My bottom seemed too heavy.

The last week in July I finally accomplished it in Occupational Therapy. With a table before me I stretched to reach a cone. By bending forward, then pressing hard against the locked wheelchair with both legs while pushing up with my hands against the chair arms, I gradually stood. "I did it. I stood up without help," I shouted. The occupational therapists called Joe from the gym next door. With concentration and effort I repeated the rise in slow motion. Now everything would be different, the world bigger, the world mine. Coming and going would be mine to control. There would be no limits to progress. A great victory, the second one that month.

The first had been during July's third week. I wheeled triumphantly into therapy to announce, "Guess what? I dressed myself this morning. All Pete did was tie my shoes." Sitting on the edge of the bed, I had pulled on elastic-banded underwear and slacks. Lying on the bed, I wiggled them over my hips, losing hand grips several times. Getting into a brassiere unassisted was a concern. First I ordered one that hooked in the front, but generosity in that part of my anatomy made stuffing and closing more than I could manage. Then I recalled fun bets among nurses about whether more women closed their bras by reaching behind their back to hook them or snagged them in front and slid them around. Problem solved, seizing both ends in front, elastic snapping from my awkward hands several times, I maneuvered the hook-and-rotate step before wrestling and wiggling the straps over both shoulders. Blouses or sweaters were all "over the head, no buttons or back-closing zipper" style. Capturing a foot to battle a stubborn sock over it was the next feat to be conquered. My stiff legs did not want to bend enough to bring the toes within reach. After several tries I bagged them and finished the job.

Successful dressing is ruled by choice of clothing. Back zippers are allowed now, but no buttons where I cannot see to direct fingers that slide away with a will, direction and life of their own. No side closings where I cannot watch a left hand with no sense of where it is in space (loss of proprioception). A solo game I play is moving the left hand under the bed covers then guessing where it lies. If I think abdomen, I find it stretched by my side, or if I believe it beside me, I find it resting on my left leg. When slicing anything in the kitchen, the position of my hand becomes crucial. Pete often clips a left earring into place. Small blouse buttons are an aggravation. Fingers slow in tying shoes prefer granny bows to square knots. But I dress and undress every day. I do it myself!

It had to be difficult, a strain for the family to watch me struggle with the effort of daily routine. Sometimes I slapped at Pete's hands if he wanted to pick something from the floor that I had dropped. He became angry at my "me do" attitude. My husband wanted to help me but I became irritated, wanted to do things without assistance and wanted no impatience on his part or lack of belief that I could do it. Other times he said, "Do it yourself," and walked away. When we had an angry confrontation, I became more determined to be independent and my abilities improved through rude stubbornness. I suffered unnecessary assistance from strangers, but wondered how I could recover if people insisted on doing even little things for me.

Recovery was the word inscribed on my mind like a billboard. Able to get out of any chair firm enough to push against as I rose, I determined to drive the car. The prospect of maneuvering so much power was awesome. What if it was too much for me? What if I lost control, hit someone, had a flat tire along the road? I had to try, had to find out if I could do it.

Mid-August, a Sunday afternoon when the big parking lot at the shopping center east of town was empty, Pete parked in its middle. "Let's see what you can do," he said, turning off the engine.

I slid behind the wheel of my Pacer station wagon, a familiar and comfortable feeling. My fingers were too weak to turn the key in the ignition. A great start. By bracing the stiff wire key ring against the key, I pulled toward the floor, levering it like a handle, until the engine turned over. The only other obstacles were the lamp standards. No problem. Of all my goals, of all the markers I had passed, driving the car was the only skill that did not need to be relearned. My right leg responded to brake and gas by reflex action. The Pacer moved victoriously around and around the big lot, then out onto the street toward home, slowly, carefully and as tensely as an overstretched slingshot. I tilted the steering wheel far forward to stretch my stiff arms. Only the right one controlled the wheel. The weak left one moved the turn signal.

I could now drive myself to physiotherapy sessions! Parking near the entrance, I slid my feet to the ground, pushed both calves against the car and became upright. Walking with slow deliberate steps, avoiding a curb, I skirted wide around an open stairwell and hugged the building. Pete was not there to catch or balance me. If I lost my balance, the wall was close. Often my elbows were skinned raw and scabbed from rubbing against the rough bricks as I passed. If I fell, getting up without help was impossible. Vulnerability begets fear. Each hospital trip I walked slowly, with deliberate care. I never fell.

Some moments in life are sculpted on our minds like letters engraved on a monument. How long the aisle in our country church had seemed as I clung to Father's arm before the wedding march began. How I wished Mother had stitched the hem of my gown two inches shorter as I tripped toward the altar. A bomb might as well have landed in the church yard the Sunday we emerged from services to learn about the disastrous attack on Pearl Harbor. Later as an inner race groove grinder during the war, I remember standing in the lunch line at SKF Ballbearing Plant as the cafeteria loudspeaker blared the A-bomb drop on Japan. Never forgotten during a frigid January inauguration, the memorable words, "ask not what your country can do for you," as they beat like a drum from our black and white TV. At that inauguration I watched poet laureate, Robert Frost, stand white-haired in the cold breezes as the pages of his poem drifted away in the wind. As if only yesterday, I pushed a dime into a parking meter on Ephrata's Main Street and overheard a man on the sidewalk say, "Shot during a parade in Dallas. Don't know if he's alive."

It was like that with the inevitable truth that I would never return to my office. During gait training. Walking exercise time. The month of August. I walked two tiles into the hall beyond the gym door, my left foot stepping forward. Joe, close behind me, verbalized the truth which had lain beneath the sea of recovery, a muddy wreck of suspicion, a reality I had not wanted to eyeball. "Your progress has been good," he said. "You will continue to improve. No one can say how much. You won't be the same as before the accident."

I held my breath, stunned, waiting for Joe's next prediction. "You will be able to get around by yourself," he continued, his voice quiet, as calm and factual as if he had told me that rain was forecast. "Your hands will be able to do most things, maybe not sew fine stitches."

"Oh." I answered with the same matter-of-fact professional voice. Who cared about mending or dressmaking? I hated any kind of sewing except the thrust of a needle and the knotting of thread at a perineal repair after the delivery of a baby

We continued down the hall. The mud had washed away. The wreck was my medical practice—standing at the delivery table encouraging a woman, the pulse beat of a fetal monitor, the flush of excitement on hearing a newborn cry, the baby's slippery warm body on my arm. There would be no more night calls in winter storms and summer heat, familiar trusting faces across my desk.

For most of a year I had put my future on hold, letting the world glide by, imagining that I sat on a limb above everything, watching but not participating. In psychology class we had learned that it was mentally unhealthful for a person to observe the world as an out-sider. It was time, necessary now, for me to slide out of the tree and back into life. But when my feet attempted to touch solid ground, the world had kept moving; it was not the same place I had left. I had expected to resume life at home and office without losing a step. Never in my wildest dreams was there a vision of the future with limitations, a cane to walk, the years ahead without stethoscope and black bag. Retirement was not supposed to begin now but when I decided, at my control, after gradual reduction of patients and responsibilities, years ahead. This was too soon. Rocking on the porch, cuddling grandchildren, driving to visit old friends better fit my plans for retirement. I felt like a new mother who expected to birth a perfect infant and was told that her baby had a deformity. What I had perceived as a mere detour in life, a bypass that would return to the main route, had become the permanent road, the only one. Surely incomplete recovery should have been the prognosis as early as the night I fell in the camping trailer.

"Why didn't you tell me the truth, that my medical practice was over the night of my accident?" I asked the neurosurgeon who had attended me in the emergency room. We met in the hall one day. During his numerous hospital visits I came to know him as friendly and concerned.

"I had never met you. I didn't know how you would react," he said. "Maybe you would have given up without trying."

His explanation was medically justified, but I have always felt cheated, lied to, concerning *my* life. Would things have been different? I also pondered if anything would have changed if the psychologist at City Rehabilitation had delved into my reason for believing that I did not need help in adapting to life as a person disabled.

The word DISABLED burned like a fresh brand; this scar would belong to me forever for everyone to see. There had been tears, frustrations, disappointments, low periods in my recovery, but through everything I had held to the vision of total healing. Running in my dreams first slowed to walking, then locomotion disappeared, and I no longer moved on my feet when asleep. I wanted to know that the nightmare was over, but now both feet touched the ground and this was forever.

I slipped into a depression hidden from family and friends. Joe had told me that a percentage of spinal cord patients resort to suicide. I resolved never to allow this although the thought came frequently. There must be good days ahead, some cause for which to live. A strong feeling of purpose had confined me within the walls of college for eight years. The pull of destiny helped me through internship and the struggle of early practice years. What now? The children were grown and did not need me. I could not return to my office as it had been, and too many years had elapsed since general practice days. My ego kept whispering that life was not over, that there was something for me to accomplish.

In September a friend died in an accident. Why did the able-bodied die while I was left with wheelchair and cane? Alone in the kitchen, I laid my head against the counter top. My wedding and engagement rings, now returned to my finger, stabbed my forehead. Tears dropped onto my lap as I wished that fate had taken me. A row of evil knives dangled in a rack near my head. My resolve held firm.

If destiny had served a good purpose before, I should trust it now, but this blanket of self-pity seemed too heavy to shake off. I wondered why sadness insisted on shadowing me.

Then, as if an unseen hand pointed the way on a map, my eyes opened and I remembered a maternal infant-bonding seminar years earlier at the Bond Hotel in Cleveland. It had been a wonderful and diverse congregation of doctors, nurses, midwives, long-haired commune members and mothers sitting lotus-limbed in hallways nursing babies. One session dealt with the loss of body parts such as an arm, leg or breast and the resulting grief.

Remembering the seminar, I raised my head from the counter in disbelief and recognition. Grief! Me? Yes! Grief for a lost yesterday, a second Thanksgiving without independent walking and soon Christmas without running. The running I had predicted by my first hospital Christmas was impossible. I was in mourning.

In retrospect I recognized Elizabeth Kübler-Ross's stages of grief. First, shock and numbness, followed by denial. Being a physician, I should have had insight into my prognosis. Was my consistent belief that I would return to my office in a year actually denial?

Anger is the second stage; anger because plans and activities are interrupted. What could have been more interruptive than being unable to give medical attention to the many women depending on me to deliver their babies? The guilt of letting them down led to greater anger.

I envied those who could still enjoy life. Drunks and criminals walked across the TV screen during the six o'clock news, and, playing Pharisee, I resented their freedom and mobility. Was the disappointment felt at my pastor's first visit unjustified anger? The accident had been a solo performance. Only I had tangled a foot in the electric cord, and there was no one to blame, to vent anger on.

The third stage, bargaining, I resolved to omit. There are stories of soldiers in trenches, people who face death due to accident or disease, who bargain with God. Disability, not death, was at issue. I had nothing to promise God but my body and my future. He already controlled them. Feeling beaten down by my disability, I feared entering a pact.

The fourth stage is depression. In its twistings and turnings depression began within days after my accident. Its tentacles are still visible, braided with frustration and anger. Plans still crash or must be altered because of physical limitations. Food preparation and cooking are accomplishable, but I cannot carry dishes to the table. On a vacation in Bavaria I climbed a steep hill to tour Neuschwanstein Castle. Then I fell in the restroom and was carted away in an ambulance to an emergency room before I saw the wonders of King Leopold.

On television I watched a young quadriplegic request the right to end his life. Unable to move from his neck to his toes, he asked for assistance in suicide. After therapy with three psychologists, he felt there seemed no reason for him to continue living. Psychologists have been invaluable in helping the handicapped adjust to new lives. Hearsay states that if suddenly a cure were found for spinal-cord-injured patients, the estimated number of psychologists required to counsel them during their readjustment would be astronomical — more than available.

The fifth stage of grief is acceptance, during which neither depression nor anger exists. I must accept my limitations, but like the quarry slave, I do it kicking and fighting. Often the risks I take are foolish, like driving solo from Phoenix to Alabama for an Elderhostel week. Alone, I pumped gas, hunted motels and restaurants. Struggling to open a heavy door at the Montgomery college, I fell and fractured a bone in my foot, making traveling more difficult. Driving home, at a rest stop along Interstate 70, I lost my balance and seriously injured my back.

Learning to suffer the indulgence of others when for years I had been the care giver has been a bitter dose. People rush to assist the handicapped. Family members know better after my cross words or the rude swipes of my hand. From strangers I politely accept assistance, needed or not. Pity is unendurable. There is no room for it.

Steps without a railing and heavy doors are my worst problems. I frequently ask strangers to hold doors open. A lady in the Tulsa Airport held my arm to help me onto the escalator, released my arm too soon and I sprawled out as the stairway moved up to the gates. A man heard our screams and stood me up like a jointless manikin in time to walk off at the top, unhurt. The thought of what I must have looked like riding feet first up the escalator still makes me chuckle. Our son Paul who was busy checking luggage laughed too and regretted missing the event.

I was deeply self-conscious about my appearance. Acceptance came hard. It did not keep me at home. Slow paced I move along, conscious of watching my feet; it is impossible to make eye contact with people unless I stop walking. I find many pennies along a path. Acquaintances pass unnoticed.

Most difficult to reconcile are attitudes about the handicapped. People act as if we are not as mentally bright as other people or as if we are indigent. Detailed explanations about obvious matters amuse and disturb me. Strangers tend to talk over my head to my companion.

People often stuff the proverbial shoe into their mouths! One day after therapy Joe placed me in a regular seat instead of a wheelchair. The porter who transported patients from room to therapy entered the room and said, "You look normal sitting like that." During sound sleep, when I first went home, my respirations became very shallow and quiet. Pete said one morning, "You breathe so slowly at night that I have to look to be sure you're alive. Last night I couldn't see the motion and thought at last . . ." It was the only time he acknowledged my innermost desire and had blurted it out before he thought. When I went to a photographer for a passport photo, he asked, "How long are you going to be laid up like this?" A glimpse of how I appeared to others startled me because I was so proud to be able to come and go places as I wished.

Throughout recovery nothing could be done about my handicap, but the future could still be molded by choices. Control was still mine. Joe once told me that most of my progress would probably occur within the first year. Improvement would be slower after that period. "You must relearn in a year what a baby develops in several years," he said. Often I identified with my children, remembering how they had rolled about in their playpens. I also struggled on the mats or lost balance as I walked. Every day I chose to keep trying, keep walking, keep exercising. Active longevity has been a family trait, and I did not like the alternative image of a woman shawl-wrapped, seated in a wheelchair, needing help for every activity. The choice is mine. Everyday!

Through it all I felt blessed. I was not confined permanently to a wheelchair. My legs were numb. The left arm and leg were still lost in space, but my brain was unaffected. The use of my hands had returned. Running was impossible but I could walk, slowly at least. I was fortunate.

***

When I lifted my head from the kitchen counter's chopping block and grasped the idea that I was in a state of mourning, I had at last something to hold in my fist. It was time to end this grief. The cure was obvious but not easy. The remedy for me was to become busy, so deeply involved outside myself that there was no time for grief. I needed a project, something to do, a goal.

The difficulty lay in breaking out of my cage. For most of a year all effort had been concentrated on recovery. Each week I yearned more to take charge of my kitchen, but Oma enjoyed her responsibilities and the daily family companionship. "You can't do it," she insisted when I pressed to get a meal. Our differences of opinion chafed until it became an open sore.

Finally, Oma needed a day off to go on a senior citizen bus tour. After many explicit instructions, I was allowed full kitchen duty for an evening. I locked the wheelchair behind me as I worked at the counter, stove or sink in case my knees buckled and I flopped backward. Supper proved not only possible but successful. Daily kitchen involvement increased. Oma went away more often.

Bread-baking became a regular duty as I exercised my arms kneading and rekneading each batch. I baked a box of loaves for the Boy Scout blue and gold banquet. When my legs collapsed, the wheelchair caught me. Each week my legs endured longer standing periods and my arms became stronger. Pete and our sons reveled in fat slices of crusty whole wheat bread slathered with butter and jam.

Not only was I not confident enough on my cane to become involved in any community work, which ceased the night I fell, but attending park board meetings or hospital functions was also not the same from a wheelchair. The winds blowing toward the Southwest were picking up. Pete was determined to trade his lawn mower and winter coat for life in warmer Phoenix, Arizona. Without a medical practice to hold me in Pennsylvania, I reluctantly agreed. We would fly west in October and hunt a new home in the desert.

18

New Beginnings

Racing blithely down the road, my eyes focused only on steering the course. I did not see the detour signs. I had had two objectives before my shingle became weatherbeaten and fell onto the grass.

First, although I had not kept a count of the numerous sets of twins I delivered, my frequently expressed desire was a set of triplets, all babies surviving.

Mary Stoltzfus's last child was several years old, and she hankered fruitlessly for a baby. Finally a bulge under her apron became obvious and larger than estimated for her stage of pregnancy. But Mary was a short woman, slender as a pump handle, with shafts of legs that ran from kitchen to garden to barn and back again. She had always looked like a distorted string bean when pregnant. At seven months I hospitalized her with leaking membranes and a suspicion of twins. Triplets confirmed. Several days later she delivered two boys; one whose middle name was Harold for the pediatrician, one the middle name of Joel for the obstetrical resident and a girl bearing Grace for a middle name. The boys spent stormy weeks on life-support systems, then incubators, but all babies were welcomed home by a happy family.

My other wish was an avoided situation, a brag. Despite many near accidents no woman had delivered a baby in my car. Amniotic fluid had been mopped off my plastic car seats leaving deposits of salt impossible to scrub away. But I boasted that despite cop chases and escorts, running country roads at full speed with high beam headlights and horn blaring through crossroads, no panting mother had ever birthed enroute to the hospital.

Not until Anna Beiler, in January of my last year of practice. She was to have her baby at home, on the edge of Lancaster City. When I saw her with irregular mild contractions, leaking amniotic fluid for two days and running a mild fever, I insisted on a hospital delivery. I would take her there immediately. My car was a small two-door Pacer station wagon. Her husband and I pillowed Anna on the back seat. Aaron sat beside me. We bumped no further than the Beiler mailbox at the end of the lane before Anna had her first hard contraction. Six miles were sixty. We flew over the macadam, shortening curves, lights on. Speed increased with the frequency of contractions and intensity of panting in the back seat. Two blocks from our destination Anna shouted, "It's comin'."

"Not yet. Pant harder," I yelled back, concentrating on turning a corner, worrying what might happen to a baby delivered in the confines of the back seat.

It came. It cried. I swung onto the hospital driveway.

Forewarned from my car telephone, attendants pushed a stretcher out as I stopped against the emergency room doors. We untangled the baby from Anna's clothing and cut its cord before whisking the wrapped squalling newborn off to the pediatrician. I delivered the placenta, homestyle in a basin, before Anna was pulled and slithered off the back seat and onto a gurney. Mother and baby went home in several days. Cleaned up, the Pacer was ready for its next wild trip.

Only in retrospect are adventures amusing. At the time, spiraling down icy hills, dusting stork feathers from a shoulder as I dashed between deliveries, flat tires along country roads were frustrating inconveniences. But it was the excitement, the tension, waking to the promises of each unborn day that I missed at unmapped retirement.

As Pete and I planned a house-hunting expedition in Arizona, his next business trip in October, I felt like a tree slowly and painfully being extracted from the ground. The soil I had sunk my roots into was Lancaster County, subtitled "Garden Spot."

In Phoenix Pete left me at a senior center to watch television, read and write letters while he made business calls. We toured five houses one day with a realtor. Accustomed to the unfenced expanse of backyard against backyard, the high-walled properties of Phoenix seemed like Alcatraz. "Walls are for privacy," Mister Salesman said. No neighbor had ever squatted on our acre or violated privacy in New Holland. Not one house shown us gave the comfortable feeling that I could call home.

"There is a place for sale by the owner, near my house," the salesman said. He looked as weary as I felt.

There it was. The only place I wanted. Through a wire fence we saw the pool, palms, orange and grapefruit trees and six varieties of cacti. The ranch-style house was surrounded by an acre of wild desert. Contrary to easterners' mistaken belief that the desert is mile after mile of sand without fauna or flora, mountains lip the horizon everywhere in Arizona. Twelve miles away from the prospective real estate the McDowell Mountains, as if they belonged to the property, played changing colors with the sun.

"We'll take this one," Pete and I agreed. "Don't let it get away from us."

"Don't you want to see the house?" the agent asked.

"Not necessary. It can't be so bad that we can't live in it or change anything we don't like."

The next morning we toured the house and set settlement for January. That afternoon we flew home to sell our New Holland house and begin the gargantuan task of honing down thirty years' accumulation of beds, sofas and kitchen knickknacks so we could begin again. What had we done?

As misgivings about moving came and went, I picked up my cane and attended meetings. The hospital medical staff met at night. Driving to the restaurant gave me no problem, but unexplainable panic grabbed me as I crossed the dimly lit parking lot, hugging a line of parked cars until I reached a railing and safety inside the lit building. After moving to Phoenix, I grabbed the kitchen counter and nearly fell over when an electrical storm blackened the house. Only after I fell in a grocery store parking lot one night and cracked a kneecap did I realize that, because of my spinal cord damage, my balance depended solely upon vision. Night walking is a problem.

A problem, also, was the whole-day auction we held in May to shrink a fourteen-room house to a six-room house in Phoenix. So many memories, struggles and happy moments. The auctioneer fingered each one as dishes, sofas, beds went to the highest bidder. Sentimentality made us keep too much. Moving day rushed toward us.

Two pieces of unfinished business remained. Since I had delivered the last baby, the final time I changed my scrub suit for street clothes, my locker in the nurses' lounge had remained unopened. Cleaning it out was a thud of earth in an open grave, the farewell. I fingered the limp lab coat with DR. KAISER embroidered on the pocket before tossing it into the soiled linen hamper. Like a handful of flowers, my splattered white clogs went home to gather dust in the back of a closet. The funeral was over.

I walked everywhere with a cane, but at home it was quicker and easier to back the wheelchair forty-five feet through the living room into the kitchen. The chair was like a baby's pacifier clung to beyond necessity. The week before we left New Holland, I surrendered it to its lender.

The entire nation burned under the fiery thumb of an endless and record-breaking heat spell the July seventh morning we left Country Squire Motel in New Holland to walk through our house on Main Street one last time. Our echoing footsteps in the vacant rooms drummed discordant accusing beats. We spoke little. Pete, Oma, Lady Dog and I climbed into my Pacer and took the road west.

The little station wagon dragged behind it a ton of U-Haul trailer containing odd-shaped and extra items that would not fit into the full moving truck. We traveled no further than the mountains of Pennsylvania before realizing that using the air conditioner overheated the engine. The humidity is aquatic in the eastern states during July. People gasp for breath like fish. In Ohio Lady, riding behind the back seat in the sun, was the first to rebel. Enough was enough. The dog bounded over Oma onto my lap. I did not need a yellow Labrador fur piece. No coaxing, shouting or shoving could move her. In Indiana we bought white contact paper to cover the expanse of glass behind us and Lady returned to her place.

Pete mopped his face and leaned forward to cool his back. The heat turned Oma's face red. Lunching in a park the second day, I flung myself onto the grass and poured ice water over my neck and down my back in a panicked effort to cool off. Riding the long steep rolls of western roads, nothing but blasts of furnaced air swept through the open car windows. We stopped in McLean, Texas for an afternoon drink and to enjoy a few minutes of air conditioning. Everywhere people talked about deaths due to the extreme heat. I felt as if I would explode. Pete put cold towels to my neck. "Get me an ambulance," I said, half-conscious. An hour or so in a cold emergency room, cold compresses and an intravenous infusion cooled me down. Later I learned that spinal-cord-injured patients are more susceptible to heat prostration.

The third day we traveled through cooler New Mexico mountains and arrived in Phoenix at night. The moving truck, backed into the dry wash before our new home, had beaten us. The next day we unloaded in 115 degree heat. Again I wondered, what had we done? Would it ever get cold in Arizona?

Cold is as intolerable as heat for me. I am a snake in a snowbank and do not realize that I am cold until I cannot move and my fingers need to be pried open. One October we spent a day traveling beautiful Canyon de Chelly with ancient dwellings under the brows of patina-streaked cliffs. Although the northern Arizona sun reflected off colorful wind-sculpted formations, layers of blankets bundled and tucked did nothing to warm us. By mid-afternoon I was as stiff as a corpse. The guide allowed me to ride with him in the heated cab of the open truck. All afternoon I thought of returning to the motel and soaking in a hot tub. I imagined the wonderful flush of heat as I sank into the water. Disappointment! I forgot my loss of sensation. Until immersed to my shoulders, there was no comforting satisfaction, but the warming made me relaxed and happy.

Happiness did not rule every day in Arizona. We knew no neighbors and had no close friends. I brought out the new sewing machine I purchased before leaving New Holland. The first item I mended was the brassiere cut from me the night of my accident by a nurse in the emergency room. Zigzagging over and over left a thick scar but it was stronger than before. I sewed several summer blouses and slacks but soon learned that I did not like the seamstress trade any better than when Grandmother bossed my pinning and ripping as a teenager.

It takes time and work to fit into a new community. Pete had business associates. I found a church and attended a women's circle. The Heard Museum, concerned with Indian art and artifacts, offered the opportunity to take a guide course which taught much about the Southwest and admitted me to a valued circle of friends. I needed more.

In the fall Pete fenced in a plot of ground and ran irrigation lines for a vegetable garden. I contacted the state agricultural division, read the gardening section of the paper and learned when and what flowers and vegetables to plant in our new Arizona climate.

Life was busy but there was still something missing. Hoeing grass from broccoli and cauliflower, dusting the house were not enough. A writing career still pooled in the back of my mind. There were stories to be told if I had the skill to write them.

February 1980, before we moved, I had attended a one-day writers' seminar at The People's Place in Intercourse, Pennsylvania. Author Katie Funk Wiebe stood before us and told of her beginnings, how only a few years earlier she could not have imagined speaking before a group of writers. "Not me," I whispered under my breath. "I'll never stand up there." March 1987, after *Dr. Frau* my first book was published, I stood there.

After two weeks of Dorothy Lykes's writing class at Scottsdale Senior Center, I bought an inexpensive electric typewriter at K Mart. My writing career was born. Like any newborn, it cried a lot and needed frequent feedings. Dorothy was a doting mother. The next semester she helped me enroll in the first of many creative writing classes at Arizona State University. My first homework contained all the "do nots" of writing. The carnivorous professor had a feast.

I read articles and books about my new career, saw the same intense hopeful faces at every seminar, heard the same advice sliced and mauled over and over until truths emerged like old tree roots breaching the earth. This adolescent writer rebelled. Seminars, reading, college were of no benefit unless I put pen to the paper, corrected my sins without shame, wrote and rewrote seventy times seven.

I have watched writing aspirants flounder in ink like sparrows splashing in a puddle. It feels good, but some feathers never become wet. For me getting a little wet seemed better than never jumping in.

My involvement in writing became deeper, but I still mourned my physical losses.

Five years into my detour, I explained to a friend how I felt about needing to watch each footstep, my faltering pace, the frustrations of limited activities particularly at night. "I am like a great stump in a forest after the ravaging fire has passed," I said. "Burning embers still smolder deep at the roots, ready to break out again, but now I am too busy to look over the charred edges." Returning to college was my best move.

The university campus is designed for access to the handicapped; each building is ramped and has electrically operated doors. Wheelchairs of quadriplegics, paraplegics and other disabilities are everywhere. Seated on a bench, I watched them wheel past and wondered how they felt beneath their facades. What were the private thoughts and desires behind the young faces? How did they get through a day?

"Working students come to my room each morning to dress me and get me ready for the day," a young classmate, chair-bound since birth, told me. "Another helper puts me to bed at night. I pay five dollars in the middle of the day for someone to take me to the toilet. I could write a book about toilets."

This subject among handicapped people brings head-shaking and sarcastic grins. Each one offers a book of experiences. Pete and I could not go out to a public place when he had to stand-pivot me in a restroom. One afternoon at an Arizona park above the Mogollon Rim I could not rise from a low pit toilet seat. In my struggles I caught my arm behind the assist bar. Worried about a fracture, I yelled for Pete. The woman in the next open stall hugged her jeans around her hips as my husband came dashing around the barrier. Most restroom doors displaying the handicapped insignia are too heavy for me to open. Risking black suspicious stares, Pete frequently pushes them for me. Restaurant restrooms are often up or down steep steps and along twilit hallways. My secret fear is to descend onto a hopper too low to rise from. How long before I would be missed, before someone came along? What a fate. Restrooms along interstates are usually well planned except the flush mechanism which is either inaccessibly embedded in the wall or too stiff for my fingers to operate.

On my April Arizona trip with Barbara, who alone fills an airplane toilet space, she took advantage of ground time to help me to the lavatory. The absurd stewardess insisted on latching the door. Unable to get up or down by myself, I pressed my tummy against Barbara, who could scarcely fumble my slacks from her skirt while we took turns breathing.

In one restaurant Barbara heaved her weight against an unused jukebox to push my wheelchair past the obstruction to the handicap restroom. At a national park listing handicapped facilities, the barrier was so close to the entrance that Barbara had to stand me against the wall while she folded the wheelchair enough to enter the washroom, then reseat me.

I was on a walker after a hip replacement when I flew home to Lancaster County to promote *Dr. Frau.* I wrote *Dr. Frau* because I wanted to preserve in ink how I saw things. I wanted to tell the world that although the Plain People dress differently, they have the same basic pleasures and interests as folks everywhere. I wanted my Amish and Mennonite friends to read the stories and laugh with me. They did. Letters came, guessing the identity of characters in the stories.

People came to a reception held in New Holland's fire hall on a rainy night. On another evening the firehouse in Intercourse was shadowed with black hats and shawls waiting thirty minutes for the doors to open. Friends of the New Holland library sponsored an evening at the Lutheran Church of greeting and book-signing. I wanted to talk over old times with each family, but the crush of time and people barely offered an opportunity for a greeting. It was not only the women seen through pregnancy and delivery whom I remembered with rosy thoughts, but also their husbands who had toasted me with homemade rootbeer, shared cookies at midnight or opened cans of pretzels and chips while their wives paced and panted. My love of fresh bread spread with peanut butter, amber molasses dripping off crisp crusts, came from waiting a night with Joe Stoltzfus.

John and Sara Weaver lined up to shake my hand. John called me too late to take his wife to the hospital for a breech delivery, their ninth baby. "Wait a minute," John said when Sara and her newborn rested comfortably in bed. "You deserve something extra tonight." I waited with curiosity as John took a flashlight to the cellar. Minutes later he reappeared with two glasses of amber liquid. That applejack wore fingers of golden satin as it slid across my tongue. John told me how he made his nectar with apple juice, raisins and brown sugar.

At the Intercourse reception, Eli King stood with the men against a back wall of the firehouse. I will never forget Eli, how he started my car at one o'clock in the morning. It took no special intelligence to understand that tired whirr as I turned the key in the ignition.

I looked up the slate walk to the old brick farmhouse where I had slumped four hours on a hard chair in the Amish kitchen waiting for Lizzie to birth number four. Eli would have to help me.

My flashlight beam guided me back through the cold washhouse, past the great iron kettle that heated Monday's wash water, past a table of half-consumed pies, bowls of leftover food and empty canning jars. I gave a warning knock and stepped into Kings' kitchen.

Eli, stocking-footed as he had been all evening, stretched a hand toward the stair door. "I was just going to bed," he said. "Time to get up for milkin' in four hours. What brought you back so soon?" He squinted at me. The dull light of a lamp on the kitchen counter sank his brown eyes deep under a broad brow and spread his straggly beard into the shadows.

"I'll need help to get my car moving. Battery's dead."

Eli's mother stopped mid-kitchen. "When I came home from daughter Anna's last night at ten, your inside car lights were on." She walked toward the bedroom beside the kitchen with hot tea for Lizzie. "I thought you knew about it."

"No," I said. "That would do it. I was in a rush when Eli told me to hurry over here. Guess I didn't close the door right."

Eli laced up work shoes. He took an old coat from a hook behind the black space heater and clapped a tattered broad-brimmed hat on his head before going to the barn. I heard his soft voice speak gently to the horses as he drove them from the stable to my car.

Eli slid under the bumper. His coat grated gravel and ruts at the edge of the barnyard. "I'll find a place to hook on," he called from deep under the front end of my station wagon. Looping a chain over the frame, he crawled out and snapped the other end to the double-tree behind the horses. Eli leaned into the open car window, his breath a wispy cloud in the March air. "Couple hundred feet you'll be through that pasture gate. Soft there. Even this team can't pull you outa that muck." He slapped leather reins against the shaggy brown backs. "Get up Joe. Go Bud."

The Chevy moved, picked up speed. I let the clutch out. The engine sputtered stinking explosions, coughed, smoked, died halfway to the pasture. Again the horses leaned into the traces. I rolled forward, let the team get to the gate. Clutch out. The engine roared and held.

"Okay," I yelled to Eli, slithering after his chain. "Thank you," I repeated as he drove Joe and Bud into the stable.

I drove home, humbled that all the gas-driven horses under my hood had been helpless without two oats-eating ones.

At the receptions I greeted friends with humility and pleasure. They lined up to shake hands, exchange a few words. Mary Weaver handed me a sack of fresh raisin cookies, Eva Horst a dozen tollhouse. Grace Stauffer brought apple snitz. "Just took them off the drying racks today," she said.

Taking the plastic bag of preserved sweet apples still warm from her hands, I fingered savored memories.

Epilogue

Trouble sneaked in like a cat burglar during the summer of 1989. It began with pain down the right leg into the big toe. A little sciatica, I thought, and waited for it to disappear. In October I flew east and blamed my poor balance on an injured foot and on neglecting to visit the gym regularly for exercise. But when I returned to Phoenix, gym exercise aggravated the growing weakness in my arms and legs. Nighttime spasms returned. I had painful cramps in the right forearm which I believed were due to sleeping with the arm flexed against my chest.

Could I possibly lose everything I had gained the last eleven years? Rapidly, my arms and legs grew weaker. As I wrote *Detour*, rejoicing in my recovery, I wondered if I would have the motivation and energy to repeat physiotherapy with its slow gains and muscular agonies.

By Thanksgiving I fell easily. Next, I could not reach the top cupboard shelves, then the lowest ones. Pete had to set items I needed on the counter where I could reach them. Surely the next day would be better. It was not. I had stepped back in time to rehabilitation and the days of therapy. Physiotherapy; that would mend my problems. I would visit the physiatrist, whom I had not seen for several years. Mid-December I entered his office using a walker, my hands contracted and stiff.

Two days later MRI (magnetic resonance imaging) in an X ray facility revealed pressure on the spinal cord in the neck area due to arthritis and four intervertebral disk herniations.

Before Christmas the final rewrite of *Detour* was tedious, my arms struggled to reach the keyboard level of my word processor, my fingers barely able to peck out letters. Pete and I flew to Tulsa to spend the holiday week with Lorelei and her family. Unable to rise from a low seat, hands uncoordinated, I could not help. I was a guest. As I huddled by the yuletide fire or wandered clumsily through the house, I remembered the same kind of Christmas eleven years before.

Returning to Phoenix, I kept my appointment with a neurosurgeon, understanding too well the surgical procedure and his grim warnings about the reaming removal of the offending disks. "With all spinal cord fibers descending the spinal canal through the neck, any area below it could be permanently affected," he said. "And you could come out of surgery a quadriplegic."

Put into words, surgery sounded even more ominous than when I had visualized it. Any slip of the drill as it ground toward the spinal canal could cause instant irreparable damage.

The surgeon continued, "I can use the posterior approach to the cervical disks, but I prefer to enter through the front of the neck. I get far better results with an anterior incision. There is the possibility of permanent voice loss since we work so close to the larynx. You could end up with a large scar on the neck."

I had anticipated danger to the spinal cord. But being unable to speak! Pete and I looked at each other. "Without surgery I will soon be a quad," I said. The doctor nodded. The decision was not easy, but I had made it even before seeing the neurosurgeon. If surgery went well, a neck scar would be insignificant.

The future was like stepping into a great void. Often as I watched paratroopers on television step into space from high above the ground, I had wondered how they felt at their first jumps. As the earth hurdled toward them, were they breathless with fear? Did they worry about their chutes jamming? Did the thought of landing terrorize them? All I saw was a graceful string of parachutes drifting earthward in a lacy tail, like a line of dandelion seeds fleeing before a puff of breath. Could I step into vacant air? What would the landing be like? The plane I rode was in a tailspin. Crashing was certain.

"There isn't much choice. The sooner we can schedule surgery, the better," I told the doctor. The earth reeled toward me. Time to jump. "I hope I can regain lost ground, use my word processor again."

"You may have to make other arrangements." He gave no promises.

Surgery was scheduled for the following Wednesday. I went home to package my life. Tie it up in case I did not survive. Laboriously I inventoried the family antiques so my daughters would know from where they came and to whom they should go. I sent both girls a copy of our family history and wished I had put other genealogies on the computer. I telephoned friends, emptied the refrigerator and packed my bag for a long absence.

I entered Phoenix's Barrow Neurological Institute. The X ray department was generous in showing me my myelogram film. I saw nearly complete occlusion of the spinal canal and knew that surgery was the right decision.

Some people do peculiar things as they come out of anesthesia. After nearly nine hours I awoke in the recovery room. I tested my voice, not by speaking, but by giving a feeble rooster crow, a game I often played with my grandchildren. The sound bleeped out; audible, weak and husky, if not identifiable. No neighboring cock answered. Within days I could speak without sounding like a bullfrog. My voice seemed normal until I attended church. The first stanza, first hymn quacked out like a mallard at mating season. I looked around to see if anyone noticed, wondered if I should continue and hope for improvement or stop singing and mouth the words.

Fresh from surgery, my hands were swollen. The painful forearm contractions were gone, my fingers relaxed and unclawed. No pains shot into my foot. I had a Foley catheter. Wonderful. I was alive and could move everything.

Several days later the resident in neurosurgery explained the marvels of the high speed drills used in the microdiskectomy. "In learning we practice on an egg," he said. "Grind off the shell, leaving the membrane." I remembered the occasional soft-shelled egg found in Father's henhouse, its pliable white membrane which punctured easily. Carrying it into the house unbroken had been a feat of gentleness.

"Can the problem of ruptured cervical disks recur?" I asked the surgeon. "How long will I be in the hospital?"

"No," he answered. "They cannot recur. You may be discharged to rehabilitation on your fourth day."

I spent the next month at Good Samaritan Rehabilitation Hospital. Every muscle was weak. I found it impossible to rise from a seated position. At first nurses dressed me. My arms were feeble and limited in function. The agonies of twice-a-day therapy returned. I remembered Community Hospital. The slogans "no pain, no gain" and "anything physical is therapy" still applied. I requested no visitors so that I could rest after therapy sessions. The hospital wheelchair van took patients to shopping malls, out to dinner, to therapy swimming. These outings integrated us into the community, made us aware of the hazards of steps, doors or barriers and educated us to plan trips. I took advantage of this training as well as the games and entertainment in the lounge. The more time I spent out of bed the stronger I became. Evening television is a sinister tempter.

If temptation for self-pity raised its scrawny head, it was only necessary for me to look around the gym and watch other patients at therapy. Amputees practiced walking on combative stumps. Patients requiring oxygen carried tanks and tubing with them as they practiced walking or strengthened their arms. Quadriplegics, married to their wheelchairs, learned to adapt to the non-handicapped world. In several weeks I could dress myself and had shed the wheelchair for a walker.

After four weeks I left the hospital to continue therapy as an outpatient. I still have much to accomplish by retraining weak muscles. Using my word processor is not as easy as it was six months ago, but it is possible and I need not make other arrangements.

My parachute did open. The landing was not soft. I became entangled in shrouds but I survived. I gather up the details and equipment of the jump hoping there are no more.

RADIO
SHANGRI-LA

What I Learned in the Happiest Kingdom on Earth

RADIO

SHANGRI-LA

LISA NAPOLI

Crown Publishers • *New York*

Library of Congress Cataloging-in-Publication Data
Napoli, Lisa
Radio Shangri-la: what I learned in the happiest kingdom on earth /
Lisa Napoli.
p.   cm.
Includes bibliographical references.
1. Bhutan—Description and travel.   2. Napoli, Lisa, 1963—Travel—Bhutan.
I. Title.
DS491.5.N37 2010
954.98—dc22
[B]   2009049176

ISBN 978-0-307-45302-0
eISBN 978-0-307-45304-4

Printed in the United States of America

Book design and title page photo by Lauren Dong
Jacket design by Laura Duffy

10 9 8 7 6 5 4 3 2 1

First Edition

For Kinga Norbu and all the children,
may they find a happy path in a peaceful world

∽∞∾

For my friends,
may they feel as much love and support as they've given

∽∞∾

For my parents,
who taught me that family doesn't have to be biological

∽∞∾

CONTENTS

Grant your blessings so that confusion on the path
may be eliminated.
Grant your blessings so that confusion may dawn as wisdom.
Please bless me so that I may liberate myself by attaining
realisation.
Bless me so that I may liberate others by the strength of
compassion.
May all connections I develop be meaningful.

—His Holiness the Twelfth Gyalwang Drukpa,
The Preliminary Practice of Guru Yoga

We are the station that makes you smile.
We can help you walk a mile
And even when you stop and think
We can make you dance and sing.
Always do your thing, on Kuzoo FM.
Always do your thing, on Kuzoo FM.

—Kuzoo FM promotional jingle

PREFACE: THREE GOOD THINGS

THE APPROACH TO the most sacred monastery in the Kingdom of Bhutan is steep and winding and, especially as you near the top, treacherous. You are sure with one false step you'll plummet off the edge. Had I been here during certain times over the last few years, I might have hoped I would. It is a cold winter's Saturday, dark and overcast. Misty gray clouds, pregnant with snow, hug the mountains.

My companions are several of the twenty-somethings who staff the new radio station in Bhutan's capital city, where I've come to volunteer. Kuzoo FM 90: The voice of the youth. Pema is wearing jeans and a sweatshirt and flat white dress shoes, the kind you might put on with a demure frock for a tea party. Ngawang's wearing the same stuff on top, but she's got sneakers on her feet. Each woman carries a satchel stuffed with her *kira,* the official national dress, requisite attire for Bhutanese who reach the summit. Kesang is already wearing his *gho,* the male equivalent. Over it, he's carrying a backpack filled with ten pounds of oil to fuel dozens of butter lamps, offerings to be left for the gods. Me, I'm twenty years older, and practicality reigns: I've got on my thick-soled boots, an ugly long black down coat with a hood, and six layers of clothing underneath.

So much for the strength I've gained from my daily swimming regime; I am huffing and puffing against the altitude and the intensity of the climb. My new friends modulate their sprints to let me keep up.

Bhutanese are hearty in many matters—they are used to living off the land, the hard lives of farmers—but they are particularly strong when it involves making the trek to this place called Takshang, built on a sheer cliff that soars ten thousand feet into the sky. The depth of their devotion becomes abundantly clear when, out of nowhere, a radiant twelve-year-old boy scurries down past us, stark naked, completely unaffected by the temperature and the incline. He's trailed by a solemn entourage of grown men. Not one of them misses a step. Later, we learn this beatific adolescent is a reincarnated lama on pilgrimage from the remote eastern reaches of this tiny country.

A pilgrimage to Takshang is the highlight of a trip to Bhutan, but it is commonplace for the Bhutanese. They are carried here from babyhood. Slight, frail seniors navigate the twists and turns and inclines deftly from memory, in a fraction of the time it takes foreigners half their age. Tales are told of people with physical disabilities who labor for twelve hours so they might reach the top, where a cluster of temples awaits. The most sacred of the altar rooms there is open to the general public only once a year.

It is believed that meditating for just one minute at Takshang will bring you exponentially greater blessings than meditating for months at any other sacred site. If you travel here on a day the calendars deem to be auspicious, the merit you accumulate will be even more abundant. Ngawang tells us that the first time she remembers visiting was two decades ago, when she was four years old; her mother had died and the monks sent her here to pray.

What Takshang promises all who visit is cleansing and renewal. Into this valley in the eighth century a sage named Guru Rinpoche rode in on the back of a tigress. Then he retreated to a cave for three months and, with the most powerful weapon there is—his mind—swashbuckled away evil spirits. In so doing, he persuaded the Bhutanese to adopt Buddhism as their guiding light. Hundreds of years later, to mark the feat, a colony of structures was built in this precarious location—testament to how the people of Bhutan have long revered him, this being they consider the Second Buddha.

As we climb higher and higher, and as the gold-topped Takshang comes into view, I can feel Guru Rinpoche's strength bolstering my own, diminishing demons, softening my heart.

THIS IS THE STORY of my midlife crisis—and how I wrestled with and then transcended it, thanks to a chance encounter that led me to a mysterious kingdom in Asia few have visited. In the march of years leading up to my fortieth birthday, and on the rapid ascent into that menacing decade, I'd found myself Monday-morning quarterbacking every step of my life, haunted by the revisionist history of regret. A near-continuous looping chorus of "what ifs" and "if onlys" became my soundtrack:

> *Why had I failed to have a family with a man I loved?*
> *Why had I squandered my youth so haphazardly?*

Why had I stuck with a profession that infuriated me so
    intensely?
What could I do with the second half of my life to make it
    more meaningful than the first?
How was I going to grow old gracefully?

Inhaling the cold, clear air on that trek up to Takshang, on the other side of the world from home, the pain and noise of those questions began, finally, to melt away. To morph into a sense of acceptance and peace. No longer did I feel stuck on a treadmill of emptiness; now my life story read as full, exciting, wondrous—with limitless possibilities for the future.

And we hadn't even reached the most sacred spot on the mountain.

THE GROUNDWORK FOR this awakening had been laid months earlier, when I had only the vaguest of ideas where this place called Bhutan was on the planet.

Every Wednesday evening, I headed west on the clogged I-10 freeway in Los Angeles for an experimental workshop in positive psychology. In classic therapy—where you endlessly review all your personal history—you work to gain a better understanding of why you are the way you are, have done what you've done. But it isn't necessarily designed to help you move forward, much less reframe the way you look at the world. By now, with the help of various counselors, I'd navel-gazed a giant gaping hole in my belly button, dissecting my own personal history the way a Proust scholar did *Remembrance of Things Past*. And yet I still found myself swirling in a vortex of despair.

I summoned a sense of optimism about this "happiness" class and hoped that it might at least be a salve, if not a cure, for how poorly I'd been handling the approach into middle age. It seemed unlikely, though, that a six-week class could possibly jolt me into contentment, or anything approximating "happiness."

Since the workshop wasn't yet fully developed, the teacher, Johnny, asked for our patience. We'd be acting as guinea pigs for this program, he said, and there wouldn't be any charge. A romp into positive thinking—gratis? I couldn't resist.

One of the first things Johnny taught us was a Zulu warrior greeting. Everyone paired off, standing an arm's length across from his partner. Then we looked deep into each other's eyes. When you felt a connection, you were supposed to say, "I have come to see you." The other would respond, "I have come to be seen." The gazing would continue until that person felt the click and proclaimed, "I have come to see you." Then, you moved on to the next classmate. Each session began this way, to affirm that we were here for real, pure, honest interaction, heart to heart. You weren't supposed to say you had come to see and be seen until and unless you really meant it.

Doing this exercise made me want to stare right into the eyeballs of every single person I encountered, to make up for all the times I'd distractedly engaged in "conversation." Gazing intensely at people I hardly knew reinforced how rarely I looked directly at the people I did know. We were all perennially distracted, attempting to triage the various competing demands on our time, multitasking our days away. Almost worse was communicating with the family and longtime friends who lived in other zip codes and time zones altogether. Static-filled cell phone conversations and emails were the hollow tools that connected us, eye contact sorely lacking. I craved meaningful human contact.

Other simple assignments from Johnny were crafted to help us discover what we appreciated in ourselves, and what inspired us about others.

"Describe in detail a person you love—and why"; "Write a toast to four difficult periods in your life, and how you handled them"; "Summarize your life story as if you were ninety and telling a child."

The themes were the same for me each time. I could see that it was a triumph to have made my way in the world, despite various misguided choices with men, the random steps that comprised my career, even an act of violence I'd experienced as a young woman. I saw how fortunate I was to have been cloaked in love and support all along. How, in the absence of creating a traditional family for myself, I'd cobbled together an army of dear friends around the world with whom I enjoyed rich, textured relationships. It moved me how many of the people I knew ended our conversations with the words "I love you." That counted for something. It counted for a lot.

No, it wasn't perfect. What was that, anyway? No one I knew would say their choices had yielded an ideal existence. Maybe my life wasn't conventional, by some old-fashioned definition of convention. The years had been flawed, but they had been leavened with much good. Such were the ingredients of a life.

At the end of the third session, almost as a throwaway, Johnny assigned an exercise that really started to bring the jumble in my brain to order. It was a simple nightly ritual, and it taught me how to appreciate life in the most basic terms.

"I want you to keep a notebook by your bed," he said. "And every night, before you go to sleep, I want you to review your day. Make a short list of three things that happened that were good."

"What if three good things didn't happen?" several of us asked in unison. Clearly, we weren't naturally wired with a positive way of looking at the world.

"Well, that's the point," he said. "This exercise challenges you to find three good things in each day. They don't have to be big things. In fact, most of the time they're *not* going to be big things. Big, important things don't happen to us every day. Winning an award, getting married, starting a new job, going on vacation. It's the big spaces of time in between those monumental events that make up life. Right? The idea here is that little things have power. An interaction with someone in an elevator, or a clerk in a store. Small victories, like fixing something that's been annoying you in the house. Going for a really long run. I want you to see that every single day, three good things do happen. It will help you discover that goodness exists all around us, already."

You could feel the more skeptical of the class participants sigh. They wanted a different formula for happiness than that, the equivalent of a diet pill for the spirit. A "do this, do that, don't do this" list of action points, where they could just fill in the blanks and come out on the other end in a matter of weeks, angst-free—blissful. But what Johnny said resonated with me, immediately. An image of my UPS man popped into my mind's eye, one of the few consistent characters in my life; each day, he delivered packages to both my apartment building and the office complex just across the street that housed my em-

ployer, a public radio show. Even though our exchanges rarely amounted to anything more than pleasantries and chatter about the weather, his kindly presence was often one of the day's highlights. Especially when I was working the graveyard shift and trying to adjust to sleeping during the day, he was often the most pleasant human interaction I'd experience.

People wouldn't be all I'd consider for my three good things. Since I'd moved to Los Angeles, no matter how uneventful or difficult the day had been, I'd marveled at the dance of light at sunset from my apartment on the eighteenth floor. That would undoubtedly make it onto my lists.

One of the more optimistic in our group asked, "What if you have more than three good things?"

"Lucky you!" said Johnny, laughing. "Well, write them all down. But try to pick the top three. Over time, you'll start to see which things make you happiest. It probably isn't what you think."

That night, I couldn't wait to go home and go to bed with my notebook.

THREE GOOD THINGS
1. Chris the sound engineer saying he was looking forward to working with me again
2. My friend Michael, who I never get to see because of work schedules and L.A. geography, taking me to a pre-birthday lunch
3. Happiness class

Throughout the next few days, I found myself taking mental notes of the interactions and experiences that might make

my written list each night. There were many bedtimes when I had to search for the good things, when the three items of note might simply be my daily swim, the Goodyear blimp gliding by my building on its way to nearby Dodger Stadium, and the taste of a pork chop I'd fried up.

Food items, the glow of the magnificent Southern California "golden hour," and quick, often silent exchanges with strangers frequently made my lists. So did shared meals, especially shared lunches, which I got to have only when I worked those overnight hours. Writing down that the food and the friend I'd enjoyed it with were great countered all that wasn't about having to get up and go to work at one in the morning as often as I did.

And, of course, this was the point. Something good actually happened, even on the crummiest, hardest days. And those good things, the simplest things, were the most nourishing.

The ritual of this nightly exercise worked like a gym for the brain; over time, the lists started to strengthen me, to reverse my march of distress. I began to reframe the way I'd been thinking about life the past few long, heavy years, excavating the positive developments that had come out of it: How, after a painful end to an engagement when I was thirty-seven, I'd learned to swim, and now made the activity an essential part of every day. How, during a long period of unemployment, I'd taught myself to make soufflés, so I could continue hosting friends for dinner while not breaking my very tight budget.

Most important, I was learning to slow down, to sit with myself and the uncertainties of the future. To enjoy not knowing what was next, instead of fearing and panicking over what might be. To appreciate the successes I'd had, instead of dwelling on my failure to have accomplished more.

As I sat in bed each night with my notebook, I didn't completely understand what was happening. I didn't see that I was making peace with myself, relaxing after a long war. Then came that day on the mountain in Bhutan, when my fog began to lift, and my life began to focus.

Radio
Shangri-La

1

THE THUNDERBOLT,
PART ONE

ARRIS SAID HE'D BE AT THE COOKBOOK PARTY BY 7:00 p.m., which gave me an hour to hang out with him there before I headed uptown to have dinner with another old friend and his family. The party was a bit out of the way, and I almost skipped it, but since I was only in my hometown, New York City, on rare occasions, I figured I might as well get out and see as many of the people I loved as I could. What had brought me here from Los Angeles was the chance to fill in for a month at the New York bureau of the radio show where I was on staff as a reporter. I bolstered my energy for a busy evening of flitting around the city in hyper–social butterfly mode—a way of life I rarely indulged in anymore.

The walk from the office on East 47th Street to the party on 66th Street filled me with wonder and made me wistful for this place I loved so dearly. In early autumn, twilight in New York is magical; the sky glimmers and there's energy in the streets. You feel powerful, invincible, as if every gritty bit of the city is yours. I found myself doing a mental trick I hadn't

done since I'd moved away: reciting the address of my destination while I walked as if it were the lyrics to a song. *Two-three-
four / East Sixty-sixth Street,* I sang to myself over and over
again this September evening, the clunky tune mingling with
the click-clack of my bright pink "comfort" high heels. Inevitably, after all that repetition, I would muck up the street number, and I did this time, too. But there was such a crowd in front
of one particularly gorgeous old brownstone, I didn't need to
check the little slip of paper in my purse to know I'd arrived.

Crazy busy. Some swanky food magazine editor was debuting a new cookbook. Harris had long been a foodie, and in
the last few years had broken into writing about all things
gourmet. Good for him to be mingling in such well-fed company. Now it seemed I'd have to fight a dreaded crowd to find
him. How could I be a city person and hate mob scenes?

As I made my way to the front door, I took a look up the
staircase. It was packed with a crush of people. In the thick of
it, facing in my direction, was *the* most handsome man. He
had a shock of brown hair and big brown eyes to match. I
know it sounds ridiculous, but in that instant, the mob seemed
to disappear. Much to my surprise and delight, I saw him looking right back. Not just in my direction, but at *me*. Our eyes
locked, and, even from a distance, I could swear a sort of
chemical reaction erupted between us.

I'd read about these celebrated *coups de foudre,* thunder-
bolts, where people met and fell in love at first sight. I knew
from experience that an instant attraction could be intoxicat-
ing—and dangerous. As was the impulse to imagine that a
momentary connection was something larger. But this thunderbolt felt different. This was a beautiful, instant intensity I'd
never, ever experienced.

Practical me prevailed: I had to find Harris. Time was tight. I peeled my eyes away from the handsome stranger and pushed through the thicket of people. After a series of wrong turns, I spotted him holding court in a corner of the room, smiling and gesturing as if he owned the place. Harris was so good at making people feel welcome, connected. Everyone clutched goblets of wine—no disposable plastic cups for this crowd. My friend did a round of introductions, and as he got to the end of the group, I was happily surprised to see the man from the staircase.

"Lisa, this is my friend Sebastian I've been telling you about, who I'm going to Asia with next week. You know, for that story I'm writing for *Gourmet* magazine. And Sebastian, this is Lisa, my friend who works in public radio out in L.A."

He was better looking now that I could see him up close, and there was a warmth about him, an easy friendliness. I felt a bit self-conscious and suddenly a little off-kilter in my pink shoes.

Long ago, I'd been one of those kids who hid under her mother's armpit to avoid looking at strangers. Then I went into the news business. Earning my living posing questions to people I didn't know had cured me of my innate shyness. Confidence was a good quality, one I was happy to have cultivated—especially now faced with this handsome man. Right at this instant, though, I found myself feeling unsure about how to proceed. I wanted to say something clever and prophetic, but I couldn't find the words. So I stuck out my hand, and he stuck out his, and we shook. Sebastian asked if I wanted a drink, and I said yes, and he said he'd get me one from upstairs, and I said I'd go with him, and there we were, presto, in our own conversational bubble. We talked a bit

about public radio—always reliable upscale cocktail-party
chitchat. With everyone captive in their cars, and smart programming in short supply thanks to budget cutbacks and media consolidation, the public-radio audience tuned in with
almost cultlike devotion. Personally, I was sick of the news,
and tried to avoid it as much as possible. At the same time, I
appreciated the attention those commuters paid our show, and
was grateful to have a job at a news outlet that had such an
enormous, attentive audience. Better than having no audience
at all. I'd been out of work a number of times, and underem-
ployed, so I knew well what that was like. I also was very
aware that in situations like this one, my profession converted
into useful social currency.

Once we had my wine and a refill for him, I started plying
Sebastian with questions about his upcoming trip to Asia. He
ticked off the itinerary: a swing through Hong Kong, a few
provinces in China I had never heard of, two places in India
whose names I knew simply because of their tea—Assam and
Darjeeling—and, for a few days, the tiny neighboring Kingdom of Bhutan.

"Ahh. The happiest place on earth," I said. I hoped my being dimly familiar with one relatively unknown country in all
of Asia—and knowing the factoid that it was purportedly
filled with blissfully happy people—might impress him. Although I'd never come anywhere close to the continent. I
wasn't even certain just where on the continent Bhutan *was*.

"Yes," he said, smiling. "Exactly."

"I've always been curious about this happiness thing and
Bhutan. It has to have something to do with the fact that television is banned there, right?" I'd now exhausted the extent of
my knowledge about the obscure little nation.

"Right, although His Majesty did let TV in a few years back," Sebastian said, his smile broadening and his eyes intense. "But it's still a very happy place. Hey, get a visa and come with us. Harris and I will be your guides."

What I wanted to say was that I would have driven to the airport and boarded a rocket to another galaxy with this man, whether or not my dear old friend Harris came along as chaperone. We kept talking, but I really don't remember what we said. I was lost in Sebastian.

Then, a sort of internal alarm rang and jolted him into remembering he was looking for quarters for the parking meter. After I dug a bunch out of my purse and handed them over, I asked the time and discovered that the clock was ticking for me, too. I needed to head to the other side of town for dinner.

A quick good-bye, and off I ran. The friend I was meeting turned out to be running very late; I sat at the restaurant with his family as he called every five minutes with updates from the traffic jam. Ordinarily this would have annoyed me, but not tonight. Just knowing Sebastian was out there in the world improved my disposition immeasurably.

THE NEXT DAY, I sat in our midtown offices trying to motivate myself to research a story about rich young couples who were trading the plush suburbs surrounding New York City for a new crop of multimillion-dollar kid-friendly condo complexes being built right in the heart of Manhattan. With enough money, you could now have a family without disrupting your metropolitan lifestyle. Among other luxuries, like on-staff dog walkers and a wine cellar, these buildings offered concierges to assist the nannies. An email popped into my inbox and saved me from my internal rant about conspicuous consumption and the decline of civilization. The very sight of the man's name made my heart beat faster.

Dear Lisa:

It was great to meet you last night. I owe you a drink for all that change you dug up for me. When can you get together?

—Sebastian

Sebastian and Harris were leaving on their journey in just a few days, and by the time they returned, I'd be back home in Los Angeles. I could find a way to see him tonight. My calendar was totally open after work. I liked it that way, and this invitation reinforced why: The most interesting experiences seemed to happen spontaneously—just the opposite of how most everything worked in New York City, where every moment had to be planned by the quarter hour, lest you felt as if you might be "wasting" a bit of your precious time.

And yet I found myself hesitating to accept this invitation. I'd witnessed many a friend as they sabotaged or just plain avoided opportunities out of some sort of unexpressed fear that success or happiness might result. They became riddled with anxiety and self-loathing before they'd even sent in that cover letter or gone on that date. Now here I was, similarly paralyzed.

The voice of this other me politely declined. It was easy to justify not seeing him. We lived on opposite sides of the country; launching into a relationship that was destined to be long-distance was preposterous, a mistake I'd made in the past that

I'd vowed not to repeat. My, I was getting way, way ahead of myself.

Of course, none of this meant I just forgot him. Clicking out of the Web sites about yuppie family-friendly condos, I did what any smart, savvy person in the age of the Internet would do. I Googled him.

He appeared, from what I could deduce, to be about my age. He had been in the tea business for a decade: He had been going to Bhutan, it seemed, for twenty years. It looked like he'd started as a guide, leading people there on exotic treks.

Exhausting what I could dig up about him, I then searched for "Bhutan," and realized his offhand comment about my tagging along was a joke. There was no just "getting a visa" to this remote Himalayan nation. Tourism to Bhutan had been permitted only since the 1970s, a time when the nation began to step out of its long-imposed isolation. An airport hadn't been built until 1984, and even now there were many restrictions; the government-run airline owned only two planes. You couldn't just tool around the country unescorted; you had to hire a guide to travel with you, and some areas still remained off-limits. To keep out all but the wealthiest visitors, a $200 per person, per day tourist tax was imposed.

Other colorful, curious facts unfolded: Bhutan was considered the last Buddhist kingdom, as others around it like Tibet and Sikkim had been swallowed up in political battles waged by giant neighbors China and India. Little, independent Bhutan had been known as the Land of the Thunder Dragon since the twelfth century, when an important religious man heard a clap of thunder—believed to be the voice of a dragon—as he consecrated a new monastery. The nation had long deflected colonization and outside influence. Christian missionaries had come calling in 1627, but the only lasting legacy of these Jesuit priests from Portugal is a detailed written description of their travels there and the hospitality they enjoyed from the locals, who politely resisted conversion.

Today, the majority of the people subsist by farming. There isn't a single traffic light anywhere in the country, not even in the capital city, the only capital in the world without them; instead, a uniformed police officer directs cars at a handful of particularly tricky intersections. As part of a campaign to preserve the culture, citizens are obliged to wear the traditional dress—intricate, colorful hand-woven pieces of cloth called *kira* and *gho*.

The reigning king had married four sisters simultaneously—the queens, they were called. Among them they had had ten children—eight of them born before an official marriage ceremony had taken place in 1988. There was a surreal portrait of the women standing shoulder to shoulder, wrapped meticulously in brightly colored *kira,* perfect as dolls, each one gorgeous and just slightly different from the next. What was *that* family dynamic like? Multiple simultaneous marriages weren't reserved for royalty, it seemed; this practice was allowed for all the citizens of Bhutan. Men and women, both. An Internet search didn't reveal how common this was.

King Jigme Singye Wangchuck and his father before him had been progressive in a variety of ways: They'd been responsible for nudging, then catapulting Bhutan into the modern world after years of seclusion. Hard currency, roads, schools other than that of the monastic variety—all had been introduced in only the past forty years. Since Bhutanese would now need to study abroad to become doctors and lawyers and scientists necessary for the health and measured growth of the nation, the native tongue, Dzongkha, was replaced by English as the language of instruction. The ability to speak English was perceived as a passport to almost anywhere, a vital connection to the outside world as Bhutan moved into an era of progress and relative openness it had previously worked to avoid.

Despite its isolationism, Bhutan had been at the vanguard in other ways. Long before the rest of the world started flaunting environmental concerns as a trendy marketing strategy, Bhutan's king had been winning awards for his genuine commitment to conservation. Clear-cutting was not allowed, and if a single tree was chopped, three had to be planted in exchange. By royal covenant, he had committed that 60 percent of Bhutan's forests would always be preserved. Unlike many Asian countries, Bhutan had not been transformed into a giant pollution-generating smokestack, nor was it overpopulated, with only 650,000 citizens. It was poor, but it prided itself on the fact that no beggars were on its streets. Babies weren't left on the doorsteps of orphanages; such institutions didn't exist. Everyone had roofs over their heads and something to eat. The people took care of one other. A royal form of welfare called *kidu* allowed citizens in the most dire circumstances to petition the king for help.

Perhaps the most unusual and intriguing aspect of this Land of the Thunder Dragon was its attitude toward development and consumerism—the policy that catapulted Bhutan to the formidable (if unqualifiable) distinction as a place populated with supremely happy people. Instead of measuring its economic progress by calculating the gross national product— a complex matrix detailing the monetary value of what a country churns out—His Majesty created a different scale. He proclaimed this philosophy, ironically, poetically, "Gross National

Happiness." Economic progress at any cost, went the thinking, was not progress at all. Any force that threatened Bhutan's traditions or environment was cause for concern—and not worth inviting into the country. The well-being of the people was to be considered before the sheer generation of goods and cash, before rampant growth just for the sake of an upward slope on a graph. Quality of life was to take precedence over financial and material success. Compassion toward and cooperation with your fellow citizens was fundamental, essential, rather than mowing down the other guy with abandon so you could succeed.

Social scientists and economists around the globe curiously studied GNH and this place that because of it had been dubbed "the happiest place on earth." What would the New York City couples buying $2.7 million apartments with nannies to assist their nannies think about these ideals? How about the audience and staff of the radio show where I worked, where the theme was money and business? Being, not having. Happiness above wealth. It sounded great to me; Bhutan certainly appeared to have its priorities straight. At least, it seemed to have the same priorities I was craving more of in my world.

Could it be real? Or was it brilliant sloganeering, a marketing mirage? Maybe I'd figure out a way to get to Bhutan one day, to find out for myself.

THREE WEEKS LATER, I'd returned to Los Angeles. One particularly frustrating day at work, I was sitting around, trying to invent some idea for a fifty-second story that would please the editors and fill the news hole in the next morning's show. Once the idea was approved, I'd begin chasing down sources by phone and begging for just five minutes for an interview.

At least this wasn't one of the weeks where I had to go to work at 1:00 a.m. That shift required a different sort of madness than wrangling sound bites into radio news blurbs.

Sebastian's name in my inbox provided relief once again. It was ridiculous how excited I got just seeing an email from him. I didn't think I was capable of being so smitten.

> Hi Lisa. How are you? Hope all's well in L.A. Harris is being an excellent sherpa on this trip.
>
> How would you like to go work for a start-up radio station in Bhutan? If so, let me know and I'll make an introduction to a friend of mine here who knows someone who needs help. Seems like a good way to get to Bhutan and up your alley, too?
>
> —Sebastian

Was this for real? He couldn't be making up this kind of offer just to impress me. Could he? Suddenly, an exotic foreign experience seemed the antidote to my malaise; without thinking it through I wrote back and said yes.

As soon as I hit Send, the questions surfaced: How would I take more than a week off? I was constantly reminded at work that younger and therefore less expensive talent lurked in the wings; I'd been unemployed for so long before taking this job, I couldn't just frivolously run away. Besides, impetuous work-related decisions weren't my style. And yet, even though I had no idea how it would sort out, I didn't worry for long. The possibility that my few skills might be useful to people in this faraway "happiest place on earth" warmed me.

Sebastian virtually introduced me to a Mr. Phub Dorji and we began an email correspondence. He asked for my résumé, inquired how soon I could get to Bhutan, and told me that if I paid my own way, the station would cover the cost of my room and board. A plane ticket seemed a small price for this kind of experience; who knew what it might lead to? Mr. Dorji sent along a list of goals he hoped I could achieve: taking the station national, improving the professionalism of the on-air talent, figuring out how to better report on and deliver news, creating and selling radio advertisements.

The station was called Kuzoo FM. *Kuzu zampo* was Dzong-kha for hello, which is how in truncated form it became the name of the radio station. The accompanying Web site, Kuzoo.net, looked to be a kind of social-networking hub for Bhutanese kids—as if that would cordon them off from everyplace else on the Net, keep them from interacting beyond Bhutan's borders, I thought cynically.

"Kuzoo was started by the crown prince for the young people of Bhutan," Mr. Dorji wrote.

Naturally, I thought, in this happy kingdom, the royalty would be in touch with the youth. When I asked him his exact role at Kuzoo, he was elusive: "I will keep that a mystery until you get here."

As I worked out the details with this mysterious man on the other side of the world, a steady stream of communication with Sebastian erupted. He became my live human resource for all things Bhutanese. Was there really a radio station? Had he heard it? Were women respected? Was it safe for me to travel to Bhutan alone? While he patiently reviewed my many questions and offered as many answers as he could, I got the sense that he didn't understand what I was worried about.

When you've been visiting a place for so long, very little about it seems daunting.

One query Sebastian didn't (or wouldn't) answer was how he first got involved with Bhutan. Becoming a tour guide in Bhutan twenty years ago wasn't like picking up and heading to Tahoe to be a ski instructor. You had to have an in. "Ask one of these guys to tell you the story when you get there," he said coyly, and he attached to his email a list of people to look up when I arrived.

Soon, our trip consultations graduated to the telephone. We were talking practically every day. He'd call with a quick thought or reminder. Like the importance of bringing long black socks as gifts for the men I'd meet; Sebastian said this leg covering was essential not just for warmth in winter but for style.

"Buy half a dozen pairs, or more. They prefer the Gold Toe brand, because they stay up better and last longer. Get them in solid black. Bring lip gloss or boxes of tea for women." Not fancy Asian loose tea, he added. Plain old tea bags from America would impress. I trekked to Target and loaded up on a dozen pairs of Gold Toes, boxes of Celestial Seasonings, and various lipsticks.

Finally, the most important detail of the trip had been arranged: I had in my hands a faxed copy of my visa from the Royal Government of Bhutan permitting me to enter the country. Now it was official. That's when I marched into my boss's office to propose an unpaid leave of absence of no more than six weeks. I was surprised at how easily he said yes. "Isn't that the place where there's a two-hundred-dollar-a-day tourist tax? And you don't have to pay? Go for it. What an amazing opportunity." Then he muttered something about an old acquaintance who'd visited the place a decade before, and how while I was there I should try to file some stories for our shows, before he swung back around to his mound of paperwork.

The only not-so-smooth part of the plan came from my father, who couldn't quite grok the adventure I was about to have:

YOUR GOING TO A THIRD WORLD COUNTRY TO DO WHAT FOR FREE? he wrote in an email, which, given the block letters and misspelling, conveyed the concern he felt about his dear and only daughter going off to a foreign land he'd initially thought was in Africa. (As did many people, although most were too timid to even venture a geographic guess.) What had happened to me as a young woman years ago weighed heavy on his heart. The fact that he'd read online that the United States didn't have a diplomatic presence in Bhutan made this already faraway place seem even riskier. I assured him I wouldn't be going if I didn't feel safe.

But my safety wasn't what I was thinking about. I had absolutely no idea what I would find on the other end—and that was the point.

A FEW WEEKS before my departure, I did a routine online check of the government-owned Bhutanese newspaper *Kuensel.* It published in hard copy twice a week, but new stories were added online every day. In anticipation of my trip, I'd taken to looking at the Web site every morning while my editors decided the fate of us reporters for the day. I hadn't read the news in my own country so closely or with such interest in years.

Even for a newbie to "Bhutanalia," the enormity of the newly published lead item was evident.

"His Majesty Jigme Khesar Namgyel Wangchuck becomes the fifth Druk Gyalpo," read the headline. *Druk Gyalpo* meant "Dragon King." The tone was so subtle, it read like a whisper. No *New York Post*–style fanfare trumpeting this news. The matter-of-fact report detailed how the fourth king had announced his abdication during a speech to a group of yak herders in a remote village. By handing over the throne now, he would allow his eldest son to reign for a few years before democratic elections would be held.

A constitutional monarchy, the king rationalized, was a more modern form of government, one he wanted to gift to his people during a peaceful time. He'd been slowly giving up power over the last two decades, establishing councils of advisors for various matters. Now, he said, was the time for his son to lead, and he was confident that under his guidance, "the Bhutanese people would enjoy a greater level of contentment and happiness."

The newspaper described the reaction of his subjects as "stunned." They wanted nothing of this, no dilution of power for their monarchy. They weren't ready for this ruler to step down yet, either. The king was only fifty.

The only person I could talk to about this—the only person I knew who would care—was Sebastian. He wasn't a slave to a computer all day and probably hadn't seen the news, so I called him. My hunch that this was big and unexpected was right.

"*What?*" he exclaimed. "Can you read that to me, please? Every word!" And I did.

"I just can't believe it," he said.

"But it's not that big a surprise, is it?"

"Well, yes, in a way. Everyone loves the king."

I imagined Sebastian shaking his head, stunned—the same reaction as the people of Bhutan. "But, no, of course we knew this would happen eventually," he said with a sigh. "Now it'll be impossible to see him anymore."

"Him, like the new king?"

"Yeah."

"You know the crown prince?"

"Yeah, he's a nice guy. I've known him since he was a kid. But he'll be off-limits now. Wow."

My curiosity intensified. Sebastian knew the crown prince. The crown prince had founded the station where I was going to work. Now he would rule as king. Was this who had asked Sebastian for an American radio volunteer? Was Phub Dorji connected to the king? Maybe Phub Dorji was a pseudonym for the king! Of course, that was ridiculous. But who knew? There were so many vagaries, so many dangling threads. These speculations made me even more eager to go.

And so, in January 2007, I embarked on my journey to Bhutan. Where I would be working with the eager young staff of newly launched radio station Kuzoo FM. Which I took on faith actually existed. To do what exactly wasn't clear. All because of an email introduction from a devastatingly attractive man I'd met once, for twenty minutes, at a party I almost didn't bother attending.

It all seemed completely strange, and yet, completely normal, the way huge, life-altering experiences can feel almost like an invention, or a dream. Except that never in your wildest imagination could you have made them up.

2

"WELCOME, JANE!"

GAWANG PEM TOOK HER ASSIGNMENT TO FETCH me from the airport in Paro very seriously. If the threat of security guards tackling her hadn't loomed, she probably would have made her way out onto the runway so she could hold my hand and escort me the second I stepped off the plane. Despite the regulations, she got pretty close. As I walked across the tarmac to the terminal entrance, there she stood, *kira* crisp, her long, thick black hair piled on top of her head, cell phone in hand, neck craned expectantly.

"Madam Jane!" she said as I walked past her into the customs area. When she got no response, she tried again. "Lady Napoli?"

"You must be from Kuzoo?" I said, reaching out to hug her. I was so happy someone knew who I was, even though we'd never met. I didn't know how to pronounce her name, which had been sent to me in an email a few days before I left on the three-day journey. And I was too exhausted to correct her about mine; I figured she'd assumed my middle name was my first. I liked the mistake.

"Yes, and I recognize you from your passport photo," she said, and giggled. She sounded like a teenager, and didn't look much older than one. "I was in charge of getting your visa. Welcome to Bhutan."

She said I could call her Ngawang—*Na-wang,* we practiced saying together. It was much easier to pronounce than I'd feared. Or I could use her second name, Pem—whichever I preferred.

With the pluck of a New Yorker navigating the subway, Ngawang whisked me into the line marked "diplomat," reserved for those with official visas; tourists used another line. The airport held a handful of Westerners, who emitted that eager and bewildered look vacationers have when they've just arrived at their destinations, and several people who were clearly Bhutanese. Like Ngawang, they wore the official national dress—the kilt/bathrobe-like *gho* for the men, a belted neck-to-floor swath of beautiful fabric called a *kira* for the women, accentuated with a bright blouse and color-coordinated silky jacket. *Kira* are colorful and elegant, simpler than a sari and more practical than a kimono. This formal wear left me feeling underdressed.

"They can be difficult here, especially with foreigners, and I didn't want you to get stuck," Ngawang said, smiling with the knowledge of her conspiracy. "So I used my connections." She gestured toward someone behind the stalls where passports were being checked as a way of explaining how she'd talked her way back here. "See him? He's my brother."

I wasn't sure if she meant one of several men wearing military gear, or a man who was wearing what looked to be a police uniform, or, for that matter, whether she was pointing toward an older gentleman clad in a dark-colored *gho*. I had arrived safely in Bhutan to a warm welcome, and that was what mattered. Soon I'd learn that Ngawang knew someone everywhere we went, or anywhere that I needed anything. This made her not only an excellent candidate for her job in radio but an indispensible guide for me.

The hours of endless travel had addled my brain. Instead of being elated about this adventure, I had succumbed to the perilous trap of feeling sorry for myself as I trekked around the globe alone. What was I doing? Where was I going? Why was I headed to this strange little country most people hadn't heard of and couldn't find on a map? Shouldn't a woman in her early forties be doing something normal, like taking her kids to Disneyland? Or enlisting the grandparents to babysit, so she could steal away on romantic trips with her husband? Or, if the husband and kids had been around for a while, plotting spa getaways with her similarly beleaguered girlfriends?

This grand adventure seemed, all of a sudden, pathetic and sad and a bit rootless. To be running to the other side of the planet at age forty-three to volunteer with a bunch of people I didn't know, in a country that had fewer people than there were students in public school in Los Angeles—all in the hope that the experience might justify my existence, fill the emptiness in my heart. A normal single woman would have met a handsome man at a party and been whisked off on an exotic whirlwind affair. Wouldn't she?

Every step of the long journey here, I was regaled with a chorus of "if onlys" and "what ifs" I thought I'd silenced. My trusty exercise of making a list of three good things only briefly helped halt the noise: *(1) Lunch at the airport with my friends*

Hal and Phil; (2) Seeing The Darjeeling Limited *and* Into the
Wild *on the plane; (3) The surprisingly lovely airport hotel in
Bangkok.*

Ngawang snapped me back to the present with an offer of a
stick of chewing gum. The sweet, fruity taste felt good after
days in transit, hours cooped up on a plane. Wasting time wallowing, here, was just dumb.

In addition to her work as a radio jockey at Kuzoo FM,
Ngawang had also been assigned the important job of watching over me during my stay, helping with whatever I needed.
After I presented my visa papers to the customs official, po-
nied up the $20 fee I'd been told to expect, and officially en-
tered the country, we made our way toward the baggage claim.
The airport was so tiny it needed just one carousel. Even
though she was clacking along in her heels, Ngawang insisted
on grabbing my bag, as well as the heavy backpack I was carrying, and wheeling the load outside.

Ringed by mountains, Bhutan's only airport has been called
the scariest in the world. Only eight pilots are certified to navigate it. The runway is narrow and visibility is often a problem,
apt metaphors for the official and cultural barriers that make
it difficult for a person to enter Bhutan's borders. Once you're
on the ground, peaceful simplicity reigns. With just two planes
in the Druk Air fleet, there's little danger of collision when an
aircraft, after it lands, does a one-eighty to move closer to the
terminal.

My travel began with an eighteen-hour flight to Bangkok, a
brief overnight layover, a five-hour delay due to fog hovering
over the airport in Paro Valley, and a four-hour flight that
hopped through India. That allowed for the plane to be stuffed

with Indian businessmen, their eyes dark and expressions stoic. Besides being an economic necessity for the airline, this brief layover served another, unintended purpose, at least for me. A glimpse from the tarmac of smoggy, congested Calcutta raised the prospect of the stark, empty landscape of Bhutan to an even higher level of mystique and otherworldliness.

By the time we landed, I was so blind from the overstimulation and exhaustion, I couldn't keep track of what hour it was or how long Ngawang must have been hanging around. I apologized for keeping her waiting.

"No problem," she said. "We went into town to my sister's place when we heard you would be delayed and ate breakfast."

A sister, a brother. I wondered how large Ngawang's family was. As we approached a tinny white passenger van with the orange Kuzoo FM logo painted on the side, it became apparent who she meant by "we." A handsome *gho*-clad young man with a Kennedyesque square jaw hopped out and bowed slightly. I felt like the newest member of the royal family.

"Madam Jane," he said shyly, averting his gaze. My eyes were drawn to the black socks that covered his calves. I looked forward to fishing out a few pairs from my Gold Toe stash and presenting him with them.

"This is Kesang, the Kuzoo driver," said Ngawang. "But he doesn't understand English. I made him practice your name."

"Kuzu zampo," I said. My first attempt at speaking the only words I knew in Dzongkha was easy. I'd been thinking this word *Kuzu* for months; now here I was saying it out loud, to someone for whom it actually had meaning.

He smiled, whisked my bags into the back of the vehicle, and hopped behind the wheel, as Ngawang installed me in the front seat next to him. It was a British-style vehicle, driver on the right. It had been ages since I had ridden as a passenger on the left side, but I was so disoriented that it didn't feel as off balance as it otherwise might have.

"We have to go now or else we'll get stuck on the road," Ngawang said, sliding the van door shut. "If we can get behind Her Royal Highness, we can proceed on to Thimphu. If we do not, we'll have to wait for the go-ahead. Maybe a few hours, even."

She explained that construction was under way to widen and smooth the forty-mile stretch between Paro and Thimphu, the capital city. Paved roads were chief among the modernization plans launched forty years ago, yet still only six main arteries traversed the entire country. Though they were called highways, this one resembled a rocky country thoroughfare you hoped lasted only a few miles. Improvements to this essential stretch of road were among the projects in anticipation of the coronation of the new king; the date had still to be determined, as the royal astrologers hadn't yet weighed in on the most auspicious moment for the occasion. But in anticipation, and to meet the country's growing dependence on motor vehicles, traffic was stopped for several hours every afternoon in order for the work to proceed. Of course, royalty would not have to be subjected to this inconvenience.

"How do you know a queen is on the road?" I asked, bewildered by the thought of being so close to royalty—I, who didn't even notice or care about the inevitable celebrity sightings that occurred at various spots around Los Angeles.

"Not one of the queens. A princess. Elder sister to the new king. She was on your plane."

Which of the Bhutanese women on that plane could have been a princess? I mentally ticked through the few passengers stuck in the waiting area in Bangkok. Ngawang read my mind.

"A lady with a baby, wearing *kira,*" she said. "And several ladies helping her."

I had seen a baby being passed among several bored Bhutanese ladies. We waited at the gate for so long I was surprised I didn't play with the kid myself, much less memorize the face of every single passenger. Much of the delay I'd spent talking to a physical therapist named Beda, who was returning home to her husband and two kids after six months of study in the United States.

We'd met before dawn at the Druk Air check-in line at the edge of the vast departure area in Bangkok's brand-new billion-dollar Suvarnabhumi Airport. Both of us were crossing our fingers that our baggage didn't exceed the allotted thirty pounds each. When Beda's did tip the scales, we pretended to be traveling together and I took up her slack. Between that and the cappuccinos I bought us with the little bit of Thai currency I had in my purse, my first attempt at Bhutanese-American relations proved a resounding success. Together we kept each other company in the gleaming glass-enclosed terminal D. The airport was so new that the water fountains and televisions in the waiting area still bore labels. We picked at the free lukewarm Burger King sandwiches the airline had provided as an apology for the inconvenience. And we used my laptop to check for more information about the weather. Since I had no idea how long it would be before I got online again, I fired off an email to my nervous family, too. *Almost there,* I wrote.

Though the longest leg of the journey was over, I didn't realize the most dangerous part of it was ahead.

THE RICKETY WHITE Kuzoo van was making its way onto the "highway." This thoroughfare was the automotive equivalent of the approach to the airport: simply treacherous. The difference was that the pilot took great care to steady the plane as it wobbled in the wind; the drivers here seemed to fancy themselves participants in a demolition derby. Immediately, the need for widening the road became obvious. Instead of two lanes there was a slightly wider-than-average one-lane sliver of bumpy pavement. Making it all the more precarious was the fact that every other vehicle was a giant brightly colored truck that looked like it had driven out of a Bollywood-style cartoon. Hand-lettered words on the fronts ironically proclaimed, LONG LIFE; the bumpers admonished BLOW HORN. Blowing a horn wasn't going to do a thing to facilitate passing, since the oncoming vehicles were obscured from sight. Still, Kesang impatiently—but expertly—barreled past every vehicle in our path. Cars precipitously hugged the road's edge. And that edge was unprotected by guardrails to keep you from careening off and dropping hundreds of feet, straight into the valley. Just when it seemed the road might go straight for a bit of a reprieve, on came the snakiest S curve. Without exception, all the vehicles were traveling at high speeds. No ride on the autobahn could match this. I was happy the passenger-side safety belt worked. But as we kept moving, it hit me that even being straitjacketed to the seat wouldn't help a bit were the van to slip.

I fought the urge to bite my nails; I wanted nothing to

dwarf my absorption of the scenery and the feeling that I'd landed on another planet. Bhutan's tourism industry sold the place as the last Shangri-la, and it became clear from what I saw out the van windows that this was indeed a land that time and rampant development had forgotten. Rolling hills punctuated by spectacular mountains, vast expanses of meticulously terraced land and the clearest river rushing through, interrupted only occasionally by a cluster of unusual-looking houses. Within the array, a tiny store, marked by a simple blue sign bearing white hand-drawn letters, provided a hint of commerce: KUENGA WANGMO GENERAL SHOP CUM BAR.

All the signs were in English, topped with the squiggles of Dzongkha letters, painted in royal blue with white, and they all looked the same. The buildings themselves, too; every structure had sloping roofs and ornately carved orange wooden frames around the windows. They weren't ugly in their uniformity, nothing like a Levittown suburb or subprime development might be, but rustic and charming—like Asian-infused Swiss chalets. The view repeated itself over and over again so that it began to feel like a driving scene from a *Flintstones* episode, in which an occasional variation pops up every tenth frame to remind you there is indeed forward motion.

Every mountain and valley was so picturesque I half expected Julie Andrews to emerge, singing sweetly about the sound of music. Except that there wasn't a blonde as far as the eye could see. To my American eyes, the ethnic homogeneity of the people was as unfamiliar as the houses, an endless chorus line of humans whose heads were topped with thick, shiny jet-black hair, close-cropped even for the women, longer for the children. From babes in arms to barely school-age kids all the way up the generational line to weathered old men and toothless old women. Regardless of their age, each was wrapped in colorful variations of the national dress, in bright blues and oranges, yellows and pinks.

The erratic madness of the road didn't seem to cause concern; kids sat at the edge of it, older people meandered across it, cows clustered serenely in the middle of it. Even as we whizzed by and stirred up dust and pebbles, both the human beings and the animals went about their business, undisturbed.

And then there was a visual punch line, adding a bawdy comic-strip-like touch to the landscape: Houses were adorned with giant, brightly colored paintings, sometimes of a rooster or a lotus flower or, occasionally, a ten-foot giant winged phallus, wrapped sweetly in a bow. When I'd found pictures of these online, they'd appeared humorous; here, they seemed ordinary, just part of the scenery.

As we drove, Ngawang was like a windup doll, chattering from the middle row of the van. She narrated the sights: Animals lived on the ground level of a house, she said, and the people one flight above. You could tell we were in Paro, and not Thimphu, because the houses had three rows of windows, not two. From the license plates, you could distinguish whether a vehicle belonged to the government, was a taxi, or was a private car. She had earned a tour guide license, she explained, so if I had any questions, she was equipped to answer them.

I had one. "What exactly is the meaning of the giant penises?" There had been various discussions on the Web about their meaning. They weren't fertility symbols, nor were they indicators that prostitutes were available inside, as was the case in other countries. It had something to do with a bawdy mystic named Drukpa Kunley, also known as the Divine Madman, who tamed demons (and just about everyone else he came into contact with) using his abundant sexual powers. But the reason for their prominence on the sides of houses hadn't been properly explained on the Internet.

Ngawang deciphered the mystery. "We believe it is wrong to envy what someone else has. When you have a phallus painted on the house, people will be too ashamed to look and to covet what they don't have," she said. "In this way, the phallus wards off evil spirits."

This had to be the most beautiful circuitous logic I'd ever heard.

"I imagine a lot of visitors ask that question, huh?"

"Yes," Ngawang said, giggling, lingering on the *s* for emphasis. "They think it's strange. For us, it's just a part of Bhutan." Then she explained that having to answer the same question over and over showed her that a career as a tour guide was not for her, which is why she was so excited that she'd been hired at Kuzoo. And when she read my résumé, she decided she wanted to learn everything I knew.

"I want to be the best radio jockey ever," she said. "Please teach me how, Madam Jane."

Kesang interrupted the flattery, the pitch of his voice indicating it was urgent. Ngawang translated that we had indeed gotten stuck in the roadblock.

For the next ninety minutes, parked on the side of the very scary, very narrow road, surrounded front and back by several dozen other vehicles, and in between the almost constant trill of her cell phone, I learned a lot more about Ngawang.

Her mother had died when she was four. Her father proudly served in the Bhutanese army. It seemed a curiosity that a peaceful Buddhist nation would require a military, but perhaps that was how the country had avoided being annexed by neighboring China or India. Since her father was stationed in the west at a military base on the border, Ngawang had been living with her uncle and aunt in Thimphu. She had attended college in India. In her large extended family, she had many, many "cousin brothers and cousin sisters." She was twenty-three. She dreamed of visiting America. And of having a baby.

"Oh!" she exclaimed, interrupting her autobiographical monologue as if she'd remembered something more important. "How did you come to know about Bhutan?"

I told the story of that fateful night in New York. "Do you know Sebastian? He's in the tea business."

"American?"

"Yes, yes. Tall, thin man. American," I said hopefully. I imagined Sebastian must be a revered figure here.

"Nope," she said, as if she were flipping through mental images of people he might be. "Don't know him." She paused for a moment. "So it was your karma that brought you to Bhutan. That's cool."

"No, it . . ." As I disagreed, I understood. "Yes, it must be because of my karma that I came to Bhutan."

"What do people know about Bhutan where you are from?"

"Well, I knew about Bhutan because I heard you didn't have television," I said, refraining from launching into a rant against the evils of the boob tube. It didn't seem good form to introduce myself in this way, particularly given the reason for my visit. "But honestly, most people don't know very much about Bhutan."

I also didn't mention that several family members were concerned I might be held hostage here simply because they worried about everything. Or that my father had warned me in his bon voyage phone call that I'd likely have to carry my own toilet paper, as if that were the most barbaric proposition. There wasn't any need to tell Ngawang, either, about how one of my more sour coworkers deemed Gross National Happiness "old news," and "a gimmick."

Ngawang laughed. "We have television now!" she said. "The fourth king allowed it. I love watching TV!"

That's what I was afraid of, I thought. "The fourth king?" I asked.

"The father of the new king, who is Bhutan's fifth king," Ngawang explained. "Our monarchy is one hundred years old, and His Majesty is the fifth in his family to serve."

"Do you like the new king?"

"Oh, yes, very much. Everyone loves our king. He is a man of the people and devoted in his service to Bhutan." The words sounded as if they'd been lifted from a brochure, and yet the tone was heartfelt.

Her scattershot line of questioning continued. She brimmed with the energy of a teenager. How big was my family? And oh, did I believe in God?

My parents were both alive, I told her, and I had a younger brother with whom I was close. We had lots of aunts and uncles and cousins, but none of us saw one another much. As far as what I believed, I wasn't sure, but I liked the idea of believing in something. What little I knew about the Bhutanese faith, Buddhism, seemed to make a lot of sense to me.

"What about you?" I asked. "Do you believe there is a God?"

"I don't know what I believe, either," Ngawang said. "But being raised Buddhist, I follow what my family tells me. If it's an auspicious day and we have to make offerings, I obey. So have you ever been in love?"

That's complicated, I thought, glad she hadn't asked if I'd been married, because I hated answering that question. "In love a thousand times with silly infatuations, but for real, yes, twice. And you?"

Ngawang said she'd had a boyfriend who'd taken up with her best friend. She didn't believe in love anymore. What mattered to her was having a baby.

"Well," I said, "you've got plenty of time . . ."

At last we were moving again. It seemed that each time Ngawang's cell phone trilled, it played a different tune; now it was playing "Hotel California," and I wondered whose ringtone it was. The interruption saved me from being asked about my interest in children, which was even more complicated to answer than the love question.

On the phone Ngawang was speaking in her native language, but every so often I'd make out a reference to me, "Madam Jane." Listening to the cadence of her voice and trying to discern the tone provided further welcome distraction from the terrifying roller coaster that passed for a road. As did more unusual visions punctuating the landscape: groups of monkeys skipping alongside the river that ran below, a gold-topped temple emerging from the side of a mountain, clusters of skinny cows sunning themselves.

"We're coming to the checkpoint," Ngawang said.

The government kept track of who traversed these roads, inspecting whether visitors were in possession of the proper permits. Bhutan had opened up, but that didn't mean total freedom of movement. Thanks to the government's increasing engagement with the outside over the past few decades, including the introduction of modern air travel, and, apparently, my karma, here I was in this faraway kingdom. With each passing kilometer, it became more evident just how distinct this universe was from my own.

Gazing out at the foreign landscape dissolved my worries, my failures, my triumphs. I was humbled by all that surrounded me. What difference did it make what I had and hadn't accomplished, under what circumstances I had come here, or that I had come here alone? I was here. I was fortunate to be here, to see how other humans lived in a place unlike anywhere else in the world. I had the chance to interact with people from an entirely different culture, on this planet we all shared. My world had simultaneously become infinitely larger and smaller, and the very anticipation of what lay ahead drowned out my usual litany of concerns and self-criticisms. Worries petty and large began to shrink away. No longer was I some burnt-out career journalist with no idea how to escape the grind. No longer would I see myself as a failure as a woman, either, for not having had a successful long-term romantic partnership that yielded a happy home filled with children. This long-crafted definition of myself, of a nice gal who had made a mess of her life, started to melt away. Replacing it now was a new vision of me: one part proud ambassador from the United States, one part curious anthropologist, 100 percent human. I resolved to be the best person I could be—and to stay alert to the possibilities before me.

TWINKLING LIGHTS ACROSS the landscape signaled that we had entered the capital city of Thimphu. It was dusk now. A cold gust of wind blew through the valley, as if to welcome us and remind us it was winter. Eight hours later than our anticipated arrival, the Kuzoo van drove through town and up a short hill to the Rabten Apartments, a small two-story building that was to be my home.

Ngawang let us in with an enormous brass key, and Kesang hauled my suitcase up the steps and into my apartment, then downstairs to the bedroom. Ngawang plugged in the space heater in the living room, the only source of heat. As the sun set, the air cooled fiercely. She asked how I liked the place, was it okay? As long as there was a bed for me to collapse into, I was sure it was.

I did a quick survey of the accommodations. The focal point of the living room was the television set. Pushed up against the wall to provide the perfect line of sight was a worn old wood-framed couch, two matching chairs whose cushions had seen better days, and a wall of mostly empty bookcases, fringed with colorful, ornate Bhutanese woodwork. All that sat on the shelves was a pamphlet from the Center for Bhutan Studies explaining Gross National Happiness and two old Bhutan Telecom phone directories, neither volume thicker than an inch. So accessible was the royal family that the king's private phone number was said to be listed; I'd have to take a look for that later.

"I picked out this apartment for you," said Ngawang with pride in her voice. She clunked around in her heels, flipping switches, and determined the TV remote control was dead. "That's bad. We'll get that fixed." Then she hurried out the front door while dialing her mobile phone, explaining that she was off to fetch the landlady to bring me tea. "Sir Phub Dorji asked me to call as soon as we got here," she added. The twin impact of jet lag and bewilderment weighed on me now that we were "home." As eager as I was to meet my official host, with whom I'd been corresponding almost daily for months, I couldn't imagine having to talk in a professional or formal way at that moment.

A young lady carrying a tray filled with steaming cups entered the front door. Ngawang talked to her urgently in Dzongkha as she served us. I could tell the faulty remote was at issue; I didn't confess that I wouldn't need it, certain that when I bothered to turn on the set, I'd keep it glued to the Bhutan Broadcasting Service. The warm cup felt good in my hands and I wandered into the tiny kitchen. No oven, just a two-burner hot plate fueled by a propane canister, the kind you might find attached to a barbecue grill. A worn-looking half-size fridge by a window, and a rice cooker sat on the counter. In a plastic dish drainer were a couple of plates, a few forks and bowls, and some unmatched glasses. Ngawang watched me drinking it all in.

"You have a geyser in your kitchen—that's very fancy!" She meant the sink, which hardly seemed fancy until she said her place didn't have one. For many Bhutanese families, even in the city, she said, their water source was outside. What seemed very modest to me was very lavish to her, which made the gift of this apartment all the more grand.

Down a short flight of stairs was the bedroom and bath, and they were simple, too: A blanket covered twin beds pushed together to make a king. A tired old cabinet resting against the wall served as a closet. A stall shower covered by a moldy plastic curtain, two thin white towels, and a sad wooden shelf made up the bathroom. This is fine, I thought. I can live anywhere—as long as there aren't any mice, or worse, rats. Everything seemed too tidy for that.

A tall, slender man in his late thirties appeared in the

doorway, a commanding, if solemn, presence. If his dark gray *gho* had been a suit, he could have stepped out of a bank in midtown Manhattan. It was Sir Phub Dorji, my benefactor. He had an air about him of a grown-up choirboy. Innocent, sincere, earnest, strictly business. After a flurry of greetings, he asked Ngawang to please make sure the landlady got me something to eat now—and to be certain she brought breakfast in the morning, too. With the plane arriving so late, we hadn't had time to go shopping for kitchen provisions.

"We are so grateful that you are here," he said. His tone wasn't warm as much as it was serious and matter-of-fact, the same as in his emails.

"I can't quite believe I am."

"It's a very exciting time for us right now. Kuzoo FM is causing quite a sensation. But we really could use your professional guidance."

"I'm ready to help, however I can." I sat straight up in my chair, thrilled to be of service to these kind people in this unusual place.

"I am sure this is quite modest, quite simple, these accommodations, compared to what you have back home," he said. "My wife watches *Desperate Housewives,* and I've seen the kitchens. I hope this will be suitable."

"This place looks to be about the same size as mine in Los Angeles," I said. "Including the kitchen. Trust me—most of us don't live like you see on television."

The look on his face suggested he didn't believe me. Or that I didn't quite understand the extent to which daily life here was different from that in my world.

A plate of pinkish rice arrived; alongside it was a little bowl of what looked like stewed vegetables. They were fiery hot, and a bit too gloppy for my taste—covered in a runny, oily cheese sauce. So I concentrated on the grains.

"Let me tell you the story of Kuzoo," said Phub Dorji. "It was a pet project of His Majesty the fifth king, created when he was crown prince. What happened was this: The youth wanted a radio station, and they approached him. He had been given the gift of a BMW car. He sold it at auction to raise funds, which he donated to start Kuzoo. And that is how the station began, as a gift from His Majesty to the youth of Bhutan."

He paused. This was all so radically different from the big media universe in which I'd been dwelling for over twenty years. The media here seemed pure, neat, a public service—not another quiver of power for a mogul like Rupert Murdoch. Providing a voice for the people, plumbing the depths of the community, that was what newspapers and radio and television were supposed to do, what had attracted me to the news business in the first place. "Remember you asked my specific role at Kuzoo, and I said it was a surprise I would reveal to you when you got here?"

"Oh, yes, I do." I put down my teacup and moved forward a bit in my chair.

"Well, the secret is that I have nothing to do with Kuzoo." Phub Dorji smiled a bit, the most I'd seen of his teeth so far.

I was intrigued. "I don't understand. You sent me all those documents about what you needed . . . and you said you oversaw the station."

"Yes, I do. But from a distance. It's okay. You are in very excellent hands. Mr. Tenzin Dorji will be here in a few minutes to say hello. He is a former high school principal now in charge of Kuzoo. No relation to me. You won't see me every day, but if you need anything, I insist that you call. Or have Ngawang call me."

Phub Dorji motioned to a piece of paper taped on the wall near the phone. "Ngawang, can you write down my mobile number for Lisa? Can you lend her a mobile phone so we can reach her?"

"Yes, sir," said Ngawang, with her head bowed respectfully, before I could refuse the offer. I'd been looking forward to not having a digital leash during my time here, but I supposed a cell phone wouldn't be a bad tool to have.

Just then, the front door opened, and a cyclone of energy in the form of Mr. Tenzin Dorji entered the room with his eight-year-old son and a little white Maltese in tow.

"Welcome, Jane!" he bellowed.

3

RADIO SHANGRI-LA

A RADIO STATION MAY SEEM QUAINT AND RETRO, AN old-fashioned medium in this age of all things digital and pod. But in the last Shangri-la, it proved to be an invention as modern as a spaceship.

As soon as Kuzoo FM started broadcasting on September 28, 2006, the entire population of Thimphu tuned in. That's not an exaggeration. The few stores that carried radios promptly sold out their stock. Farmers in the nearby valley twisted the angles of their antennae in order to tune in a signal so Kuzoo could keep them company as they worked the land. Drivers of the kingdom's growing number of motor vehicles (up from just under four thousand in 1999 to well over thirty thousand less than a decade later) were happy to have Kuzoo's radio jockeys entertain them as they cruised the capital city. Many of the cars proudly displayed Kuzoo bumper stickers in enthusiastic support of the new station.

Before Kuzoo came along, there wasn't much else to listen to. Recorded music—if you could even get your hands on it— was far more expensive than modest Bhutanese incomes would allow. Up until Kuzoo, the only sounds transmitted over the airwaves had been the dull news and announcements, punctuated by the occasional music program, churned out by the government-launched Bhutan Broadcasting Service. It didn't even broadcast all day. The rest of the dial was filled with static.

Suddenly, a radio was a hot item, and Kuzoo FM was a real station, playing all kinds of music that most Bhutanese hadn't heard before: the saccharine epiphanies of pop divas, the aching twang of country music, the interlocking rhythms of rap, rock, hip-hop. All presented by friendly, if inexperienced, Bhutanese radio jockeys, who shyly stumbled through their pronunciation of English words, making it clear this was not some slick feed imported from afar.

Even so, the capital city was a world away from the rest of the country. Villagers might visit Thimphu once in their lives—and only then for formal business or to be tended to at the hospital. Travel in Bhutan had long been utilitarian, not for pleasure. Leaving home to scratch through forest paths in order to venture to the next town meant time lost working the land, which yielded the food and other necessities that sustained the community. Only in the last few years had the beginnings of a leisure class blossomed.

That the citizens of Bhutan could now be connected to one another through radio, without actually *going* anywhere, was nothing short of magic. This eager audience immediately began to phone in to give thanks for the music, and to chatter on the air—simply because they could. To dedicate songs not just to their friends and family but to fellow callers whose voices they'd found pleasing. When nature intervened and the signal was temporarily disrupted, Kuzoo fans called and begged so plaintively in despair at the interruption that you'd wonder what they'd done before the station existed. "Please, my wife has stopped eating because she's so sad without Kuzoo," implored one man after a storm knocked the station off the air. "You must repair it."

Perhaps the most fascinating aspect of the Kuzoo experience—the quality that endeared it to its audience above all others—was that listeners were allowed, even encouraged, to participate on-air. Besides making dedications, they could sing songs and talk to friendly radio jockeys. Or ask questions about Buddhism on a weekly show called *Dharma Bites,* hosted by two young self-styled "spiritual jihadis." Disappointed that their fellow youth were becoming less engaged with the national religion and showing more of an interest in the trappings of the material world, they'd cooked up the idea for this program and showed up at the Kuzoo studio one day to ask for airtime. Like legions of evangelists around the world, they saw the power of the medium to educate and persuade.

The excitement wasn't just because media in Bhutan hadn't been interactive before. For generations, the tiny, landlocked Himalayan kingdom had practically no media at all, and very little in the way of modern communications. It had been literally sealed off from the rest of the world, and virtually sequestered, too. TV had long been outlawed, lest the insidious forces of the outside infiltrate and pollute the minds of the people—dilute their unique culture, intoxicate them with images of an outside world to which they'd yearn to belong.

Some of the bolder and more affluent citizens hooked contraband televisions up to video recorders, traded taped films they managed to smuggle into the country, or slipped cash to enterprising Indian businessmen who smuggled dismantled satellite dishes across the border and reassembled them, discreetly, around their customers' homes. The number of people who could afford such a luxury was few. Even as the burgeoning World Wide Web had been taking root most everyplace else, it had not been allowed to make inroads into Bhutan. Not that every person in every corner of the nation could have availed themselves of the service even if cost weren't an issue. A quarter of Bhutan's villages still lacked electricity—and half the population had to walk at least four hours just to get to the nearest all-season road. When mobile phones were introduced in 2003, the number of houses with landlines totalled in the hundreds.

On the morning of June 2, 1999, King Jigme Singye Wangchuck issued the decree that would change Bhutan indelibly. At the silver jubilee celebration commemorating his twenty-five-year reign, he delivered a speech in which he bestowed several gifts on his constituency. Roads and bridges, he declared, would be built in the remotest corners of Bhutan, to give the people greater mobility. To accommodate a larger plane for the nation's airline, a new airport terminal would be constructed—another enticement to would-be visitors. As part of Bhutan's continuing environmental stewardship, the king announced that plastic bags would be banned—for the good of the planet and, ultimately, all people.

The bombshell of His Majesty's address that day, the revelation that elicited cheers from the otherwise solemnly reverent assembled guests, was this: After years of self-imposed isolation, of gently dipping its toes into the outside world, of carefully restricting which foreigners entered the country and which Bhutanese left, the almighty superpowers known as television and Internet were to be permitted into the happy kingdom. With that, the switch was thrown on the brand-new televised Bhutan Broadcasting Service, which would run alongside a selection of international channels. From that day forward, the BBS television signal—transmitted, like its radio counterpart, for just a few hours each morning and evening— would mix with the pristine air and low-lying clouds of the Himalayas. Cable television would render those illicit satellite dishes obsolete; now they would perform another function as a handy surface on which to dry the nation's staple food, chili peppers.

In his speech, the king acknowledged the Pandora's box he was unlatching, the effect media might have on his carefully crafted policy of Gross National Happiness. Television and the Internet, he reminded his audience, possessed both positive and negative qualities. Their use required good sense and judgment. When it came to their consumption, the king trusted his people to deploy what the Buddhists call the Middle Path: moderation. He believed firm religious footing would ultimately hold more sway than the mesmerizing power of the screen.

Whether that made the king an idealist or simply naive would be revealed soon enough.

THE NOTION OF Bhutan as Shangri-la has to do with its unspoiled landscapes and striking views of stunning Himalayan mountains, believed by some to be the dwelling place of the gods. Adding to the mystique is its fierce commitment to the preservation of age-old traditions that are the mainstay of the country's cultural heritage. Western Buddhists plan once-in-a-lifetime visits to worship at the hallowed historic monasteries scattered throughout the land and soak in the energy of the country's storied religious festivals, called *tsechus*.

None of this was what drew me to Bhutan.

For me, the prospect of a relatively media-free universe was as close to utopia as I could imagine. No wonder the country was considered the happiest on earth! The promise of a place where life was simpler—unsaturated by the menacing forces of mainstream media, which had kept a roof over my head for years but which I found increasingly noisy and bothersome to consume—appealed to me. That Bhutan was guided by intense spirituality, by connection to home and community, held great allure. I was tired of sleep-deprived, stressed-out, too-busy people who shirked downtime in the service of making money so they could buy more stuff; tired of it taking months to see dear friends who lived across town because traffic and overcommitment made it impossible to coordinate a shared meal. It felt like some people stuffed their calendars full so they could seem important, or at least, not have to face themselves during unplanned moments. In Bhutan, I suspected, human connections were more important than how many digital pals you racked up on Facebook. Rather than passively consuming depictions of the world pumped out to them on various screens, the Bhutanese, I imagined, must savor their lives, really live them, thoughtfully and yet spontaneously.

It seemed unlikely that the Bhutanese swirled about busily through the days, never quite triaging their to-do lists, assaulted by the modern scourge known as multitasking. Surely life wasn't marred by such jarring interruptions as call waiting, and the disorientating phenomenon of barely audible cell phone calls made to "check in" with friends and family and give the illusion of connection. Thumbs weren't maniacally text-messaging so the humans they were attached to could "keep in touch" while averting their gaze from others in their paths.

I longed for a way of life in which people made it a priority to look into each other's eyes and communicate, soul-to-soul, uninterrupted, like in that Zulu warrior greeting we'd practiced in happiness class. I yearned for meandering conversations about all things important, all things banal. Bhutan, I imagined, might be as close as you could get on earth to what I'd been craving—a real, live, actual community, where being wired took a backseat to being present, face-to-face, experiencing the here and now.

After more than two decades of reducing even the most complex issues down to a thousand words or less, I was tired of observing life from a distance, of synthesizing and distilling data with little time to process meaning. I'd long considered myself fortunate to have made my way in a cutthroat profession; when I was a kid growing up in Flatbush, Brooklyn, the news business promised glamorous access to a world far different from my own. Being able to ask questions and tell stories, much less getting paid for it, had long felt like a tremendous privilege. And yet, over time, the warping nature of the business was clear: Every experience could be spun as an item, and human relationships existed to serve the demand for news and information. The rushed conversations to facilitate deadlines had left me impatient in normal interactions; why couldn't people get to the point faster? Quick, clipped scripts punctuated by quick, clipped communiqués via email seemed to be impacting my ability to think more deeply, to respond with the slow deliberation necessary for life's bigger decisions. I felt like I was rushing, reacting, all the time.

Most of the jobs in journalism today are like information-factory work—Lucy-on-the-assembly-line style—or eating a steady diet of dim sum. You'd sample many items every day, fast, then gorge on the morsel assigned to you, trying to digest it as quickly as possible. A few hours later, you were expected to spew it out to the world in the form of a "story." And on this particular radio show where I was currently employed, it had to be a very short story: ninety seconds or less, for the most part. Even though you probably couldn't fake your way through a debate on the subject, you were suddenly an authority on it because millions of people had heard you talk about it on their commute home. The aftereffects were the same as an unsatisfying meal. Bloated, hungry—I felt hungry for knowledge, deeper meaning, time to synthesize the world around me.

I also worried about the effects of the news on all who consumed it. For all the good the global village had achieved—exposing us to other cultures we'd never visit, making us aware of strife in other parts of the world, educating us about important issues in our communities—it also was making us info-zombies. Just because the images are constantly beamed into our lines of sight in our living rooms, at the grocery store, while we were pumping gas, we live with the delusion that this virtual ringside seat to the action equals a real understanding of the world at large. Stuffed with factoids about the stock market and electoral college and weather patterns, the general public believes they understand these complex systems, when in fact they can't adequately be boiled down to sound bites.

Context isn't modern media's strong suit, and the broadcast

media in particular; raw data and pictures and sound are. The gray areas, the nuance, rarely get explored. Wars and starving children become images on the screen that you can turn off at will, not real, live complex problems. Bad things happen to other people. Thank God that didn't happen to us, honey. Change the channel, please.

Now, my media malaise wasn't simply a result of my midlife disillusionment. It had been brewing for ages. Since not long after I'd started working, in fact.

When the space shuttle *Challenger* exploded, I was a young copywriter at CNN Headline News. A tape editor and I were locked in a tiny room for the twelve hours afterward, charged with crafting half-hourly updates that incorporated into our report whatever information ticked off the AP news wire. I watched the shuttle blow up so many times that day, I knew in graphic detail how it had broken apart. The impact of seeing that horror play over and over led me to do exactly what you're not supposed to do in a workplace, particularly in a newsroom: break down and cry. I couldn't believe we were repeatedly watching people dissolve before our very eyes without pausing for a second to think about them. (It turned out later to be even worse: They hadn't exploded; they had sunk to the bottom of the ocean.) Thankfully, my colleague was also a friend, and he didn't blow my cover. He put his hand on my shoulder, sent me to the restroom to wash up, and told me to come right back to the edit room to keep working. Afterward, I got promoted for doing such a fine job turning around first-rate updates on deadline.

Years later, during the standoff between cult members and federal agents in Waco, Texas, my dissatisfaction reached a new intensity. I was field producing for another network, and after sitting and staring for weeks at the embattled compound from the safety of the media village a mile away, my colleagues and I watched through high-powered telescopes as federal agents stormed in. Flames shot high, engulfing a building that had people—children—inside. We members of the media diligently trained our cameras on the action, shouting to one another about the logistics of "going live." Reporters in the foreground of the action boasted that their network was "at the scene."

At the end of the day, when a friendly woman knocked on the door of the news truck to tell me she'd been dispatched so I could take a break, the tears flowed yet again. The presence of a new person jolted me back to the reality of the day. There were humans dying yards away as we frantically broadcast the disaster to the world.

September 11, 2001, did me in. Mercifully, I wasn't even working at the time. A month earlier I'd lost my maddening job as "Internet correspondent," which meant reading viewer email aloud on cable TV. I'd been axed in a round of cutbacks after the dot-com bust. As the mayhem of the terrorist attack unfolded several miles south of where I lived, I couldn't bear the thought of watching it on television. The analysts, the experts, the pundits, the din of the speculative commentary were all being doled out before there was actual information to convey. I didn't want to follow along with this packaged-for-TV disaster, as each gruesome detail was revealed. All I wanted to do was be silent, meditate and pray. I wasn't conscious of ever having wanted to do those things much before, but it seemed a more productive course of action than staring zombielike at the television, wallowing in the unfolding chaos with a remote control.

It was then I decided to turn off the news, in every medium, and instead deploy my own Human News Network. For weather reports, I stuck my hand out the window or chatted with neighbors. For hard news, I listened to and asked questions of friends; everyone loved to share opinions about stories they'd read, heard, or seen. If an item piqued my interest, I'd seek out more about it. It was like having my own personal clip service. I studied what I needed in order to write freelance news articles to pay my bills while I looked for full-time employment. There was room now for books, research on topics that interested me, conversations with friends. Downtime to just think. More time to walk and cook and swim. I felt liberated, smarter than ever, genuinely in touch with the world around me. The real world, not the mediated one.

Except, I hadn't really cut the cord, not entirely. Like someone trapped in a bad marriage, I concocted an ironclad excuse for why I wasn't getting out. I needed a job to support myself, and what else was there that I could do after twenty years of little else but the news business? And after being out of work for so long, I considered myself very fortunate when I landed the gig in Los Angeles, in the vaunted medium of public radio.

BESIDES BHUTAN'S UNDEVELOPED media culture, my other attraction to the country was its almost institutionalized resistance to conspicuous consumption. That shopping was a pastime for so many people in the United States distressed me. I was hardly an ascetic, or the type who makes compacts not to buy anything but toilet paper and food. I was simply trying not to suffocate under mounds of belongings: trying to live as simple, uncomplicated, and uncluttered a life as possible. There was enough extraneous junk and chaos waiting for you once you stepped outside.

Finding pleasure in giving things away was a developing habit for me. I'd taken the once-unimaginable step of donating my twenty-years-in-the-making collection of five hundred books to the public library. This occurred after I'd paid several thousand dollars over two years for a storage closet in New York, indecisively letting them collect dust. ("Should I move them West, or should I hedge my bets that I'll move back East?" I mulled each month as I wrote the check.) Until one day I made the call and begged for the cartons to be hauled away, aware that for many educated people this was an action tantamount to suicide. Or, at least, cause for institutionalization. One dissenting alleged friend dubbed my action, simply, "idiotic."

My coveted collection of books really wasn't necessary anymore. I felt secure enough in my intellect not to have to flaunt my impressive personal library in my tiny apartment any longer. I could get most anything I wanted to read, reread, or simply fondle for sentimental reasons in practically an instant at the spectacular public library located two blocks from where I lived in downtown Los Angeles. And I could support a vital (if, to some people, arcane) public institution in the process: With the money I'd saved not buying more books, I started making an annual donation to the Los Angeles Public Library, stoking my middle-age ambitions to be a patroness of worthy causes.

As for my television, I'd hung on to that only to watch the very occasional DVD or videotape. I'd long ago ditched the cable. Until the rare occasions when I wanted to turn it on, I obscured the screen with a painting.

And yet, I continued to be a hypocrite.

Not only did I keep working in the news business, I had just arrived in one of the last places on earth to be corrupted by media and consumer cultures. My mission was to teach them how to "professionalize" this new radio station they'd just begun, which I suspected was code for "make us sound like every other radio station in the world," instead of letting it grow organically to become its own sort of Radio Shangri-la.

EVER SINCE TELEVISION arrived in Bhutan in 1999, more people have been opting out of the agrarian lifestyle that supported their ancestors and is still the mainstay occupation. Now young people flock to Thimphu for their education and a chance at jobs that promise plush benefits (like working behind a desk, with a computer, and not in the fields). No one has officially drawn the connection between the introduction of mass media and the swelling of the population in Bhutan's capital city. But no one can deny it, either. A generation ago, it wouldn't have occurred to young people to leave their families and their villages.

Being wired to the outside world, of course, doesn't make Bhutan any less geographically remote, or any less costly to leave. It still requires days of travel to get in or out. Besides, most people in Bhutan don't have much cash, and credit cards don't exist. No matter how rich you might be, there is just one airline and one airport. Permission to travel in either direction is meted out with great deliberation and is typically granted to the lucky few who win scholarships to colleges and universities outside the country.

But thanks to the wonder of satellites and a vast network of interconnected servers, you can more clearly see what it's like out there in the world without having to go. And that window to the world changes your perspective. As fiercely, traditionally Bhutanese as you might be, as much as you might vow you'll never leave, those other ways of life depicted on TV look mighty tempting. When television beams a window on the world—the possibility of other—right into your home, it's hard not to become enthralled. Or, at least, intrigued. Those images sure get you thinking about what you have, and what you don't.

IN 2006, THE KING allowed media infiltration to reach another milestone. Two private weekly newspapers were licensed to compete with *Kuensel,* the once-government-backed paper that had long been the only game in town. Its founder had been primed for the job with an education at the finest schools. These new rivals, the *Bhutan Observer* and *Bhutan Times,* hired young staffs with no training or experience, and who flirted with the promise of press freedom guaranteed in the not-yet-signed new constitution. But only a bit. Free speech, Bhutan-style, still did not extend to criticism or examination of the monarchy—a line few would dare to cross even if it weren't forbidden. Most stories involving the royal family still had to be run through government censors, no matter how benign. And if they involved His Majesty, it was implicitly understood that they'd receive the most prominent placement, no matter how banal his actions. Nevertheless, the mere existence of competition began to transform *Kuensel* from a polite, deferential organ to a more solid, inquisitive journalistic news organization.

And then came this new entry: Kuzoo FM. Tenzin Dorji was plucked from the ranks of educators to manage the operation. A staff of nine twenty-somethings was hired. Anyone with time and curiosity was encouraged to just show up and volunteer, particularly if they were in high school. Kuzoo was a youth-focused station, after all.

At first, the station broadcast from an old closet in a government building that housed the youth sports department. A few months after its debut, Kuzoo moved to another structure on the property, which long before had served as the residence for the foreign minister. It was a two-story building with a narrow staircase, a warren of rooms, and worn burgundy carpet. The building's two most charming features were a front porch on the second level that offered a lovely view of the grounds (although the floorboards wobbled precariously if too many people stood out there) and the sky-blue-tiled kitchen designated as the studio.

The space wasn't converted as much as it was *adjusted*. Heavy white cardboard was laid over the sink to discourage anyone from turning on the faucets. A plastic tarp taped over a hole in the ceiling kept a flock of cooing pigeons from landing on whoever sat at the mixing board.

Several old computers were set up on battered school desks in the adjoining rooms, and the young staff began waiting their turn to "prepare their shows" (which meant downloading music illegally off the Internet) and adding whatever few CDs they might own or could borrow to add to the library of on-air music. Not that the library could ever grow very large. The average middle-class teenager in the United States had an iPod with a bigger hard drive than the one that engined Kuzoo.

As local radio stations and newspapers in the West down-sized and dissolved in a rapid death-spiral—victims of media consolidation, the Internet, and the bottom line—Bhutan's media landscape was expanding with abandon. Media were seen as a crucial component of the impending democratic elections, and afterward, a force to keep watch over the newly elected government. The king knew that for democracy to take root in this long-standing monarchy, a competitive news landscape was a critical part of the equation.

What he didn't factor in is how much the kids loved their music.

4

BEWARE THE *EMADATSE*

KESANG, THE KUZOO DRIVER, LOOKED CONCERNED; his lips were pursed and he was shaking his head disapprovingly. After driving Ngawang and me to the store, he was now in charge of holding the basket while I stocked my kitchen, courtesy of Kuzoo. He appeared to be unhappy with my selections. Ngawang had taken us to a little grocery on the lower road, across from Changlimithang Stadium, where the coronation celebrations would be held sometime in 2008.

"My auntie owns this place," said Ngawang, waving to the woman behind the counter.

The shop was the size of a small convenience store, but more chaotic in its inventory; floor to ceiling, every shelf was covered with all manner of packaged goods, from shampoo to potato chips to tea, side by side, in varying quantities. Two of these, ten of those, all teetering on top of one another. One abrupt move and it could all come crashing down. Nothing was organized in any particular way; it was as if each item, as it arrived in the store, was shoved into whatever sliver of free space was available. A few of the packages looked familiar, like Lay's Potato Chips (although I had never seen the Spicy Indian Masala flavor in Los Angeles) and, not surprisingly, Coca-Cola. (An attempt to bottle Pepsi in Bhutan had recently gone bust—because of a management issue, the newspaper reported, not a shortage of fans of carbonated beverages.) "Those are from India," said Ngawang, seemingly unaware that the origin of these big brands was, in fact, the United States. Giant next-door neighbor India was the closest and most important source of all things shiny and refined.

At least a handful of items in here were unfamiliar to me, and several dry goods like lentils were unlabeled. No matter who was buying, I preferred to consume food that hadn't traveled from so far away.

It was my second full day in the Kingdom of Bhutan. I was so hepped up on caffeine and adrenaline, I hadn't had the chance to succumb to jet lag. At every turn, one of the Kuzoo staff was offering, "Tea . . . coffee, madam?" "Tea . . . coffee, madam?" (By coffee, they meant Nescafé, which appeared to be the only kind to be had here, and the presumption was that most Westerners preferred that as their hot beverage of choice.) Even after I reached my limit, I kept saying yes—the prospect of a warm mug was so inviting.

The message behind the repeated gesture was clear: I was a lady; I was senior to them; I had come from quite a distance to help; and this was the simplest form of welcome. And I did feel welcomed, despite how nervous most people seemed to be about striking up conversation with this curious visitor who'd dropped into their orbit.

I hadn't been alone for a minute since I'd arrived, except when I slept. The first day had been a blur, a whirl of introductions, new faces, a busy lunch with Sir Tenzin at Plums

Café right across from the traffic circle in town. He knew practically everyone in the restaurant, and they all heartily welcomed his foreign consultant.

Kesang and Ngawang had shown up at my door again early this morning, just as I was getting dressed, to squire me to the studio. I hoped to persuade them that, really, making it the half mile down the hill and around the corner to the station would be a pleasure, not a hardship. As long as I could fend off the stray dogs, I'd love that walk each day.

They seemed to be enjoying the responsibility of taking care of me. On our drive to the store in the late afternoon, Ngawang appeared a bit exasperated, though, by my stream of questions.

"What is it Mr. Phub Dorji does, since he doesn't run Kuzoo?"

"He works in His Majesty's secretariat."

"But what does he *do* there?"

"I'm not sure, really." I didn't want my curiosity to be mistaken for rudeness, so I dropped the topic. I was starting to detect that short, vague answers were typical here.

"Is that marijuana growing over there?" From the window of the van, I'd spotted blankets of pot erupting on either side of the street, an occasional flower peeking through.

"It grows wild all over," Ngawang said, in the same "visitors are so predictable" tone in which she'd decoded the phalluses. "We feed that to the pigs to make them fat."

I hadn't caught sight of any pigs yet, but I sure hoped there were chickens. I could live without meat, but I couldn't live without eggs. As I searched for them in the tiny store, I wondered aloud what was bothering Kesang.

"Is everything okay?" I asked. A nervous look had come

over him after he'd whisked a half-pound bag of rice out of my hands and into the basket. I hoped I hadn't done something to offend. I wasn't accustomed to food shopping with an entourage. Back home, my neighbor Bernie and I would embark on weekly grocery expeditions together, but we typically maintained our own carts.

"Kesang's worried about what you're buying, Lady Jane," Ngawang said.

"Why?"

"You don't have enough rice."

"This is plenty of rice for just one person," I said. I'd picked up rice only because the most prominent appliance in my kitchen was a rice cooker. Besides, it was becoming clear that I'd get plenty of the grain whenever I ate outside the apartment.

"Oh, that wouldn't be enough for us," she said. "We each eat four plates of rice a day. That bag over there"—she pointed to a twenty-five-pound satchel on the floor—"would last my family about a week." For the exact same reason that people in the richest parts of the world chose to eat little starch, people in the poorest ate a lot of it: It filled you up. Only the wealthiest could indulge in a low-carb fest like the Atkins Diet, because they had the luxury of plentiful, lean meat to fill them up instead. That the Bhutanese smothered their unpolished, pink rice in a yak-cheesy, fiery-hot chili stew called *emadatse,* and savored it three times a day, was testament to how they'd ingeniously discovered a way to live off, indeed enjoy, a low-cost food.

"Are there any eggs here, do you think?" I asked. I kept peering under every well-stocked shelf and table, and still hadn't found any.

"Eggs are very hard to find right now. Bird flu. No eggs coming in from India," Ngawang said matter-of-factly. "The eggs that are around are *very* expensive." The prices had shot up to the equivalent of a quarter apiece.

Oh no, I thought, as I grabbed several rolls of crepey pink toilet paper tucked beside some beer. I'd noticed with a measure of defeat that my father had been right; this bathroom essential didn't seem to be provided in the Kuzoo restroom, or any of the places Sir Tenzin had taken me to so far. Best to carry my own.

"If we can find eggs, I'd be happy to pay for them myself," I said, and then I immediately regretted it. I didn't want to sound like some swaggering rich American, but I was beginning to worry a bit about the food situation.

At lunchtime again today, I'd stuck a fork into a bowl of *emadatse* and thought I might die—both from the spicy heat of it and the runny processed cheese of it. Perhaps I'd fall in love with Bhutan and its people, but I was fairly certain I would never become a fan of *emadatse*. Locally grown foods, good; local cuisine, beware. I really needed an egg.

"Nuts. What about nuts?" I asked, ticking through a mental checklist of my staple foods. Then I spotted another necessity, a couple of dusty cans of tuna fish, and grabbed them, greedily, though there wasn't another shopper in the store. The label declared *Thailand*. I figured I could bring that down to Kuzoo for lunch, once Sir Tenzin tired of trotting his new American volunteer/consultant around town during the midday meal.

"Nuts are also *very* expensive," said Ngawang, and then walked over to a package of cashews that looked pale and crusty, like they'd been sitting around for a couple of years. They were even pricier than they'd be back home; $1.50 for what amounted to a large handful. In a country where per capita income was $3 a day, of course no one had indulged.

"Peanut butter?" I asked hopefully, and Ngawang held up

a dusty yellow plastic tub of the stuff, from India, and handed it to Kesang. That would be useful. Then she displayed a loaf of white bread whose simple wrapper announced it was from Norbu Bakery in Thimphu. "You'll need this, too. You Westerners like bread. Nobody eats this stuff here."

"Someone must," I protested, "if they make it."

Ngawang's aunt shouted to her in Dzongkha. "My aunt says the cornflakes are in the back here. She says the Westerners always love cornflakes."

I started to say "I'm not a big cereal person," and in truth I wasn't a big milk fan, either, any more than I was of white bread. But then I found myself savoring the idea of nice, mushy cornflakes. Though I hadn't had any in years, the memory of the familiar comforted me. Having a box on the shelf would probably be a good idea.

Kesang drove us back up the hill to the Rabten Apartments and carried in our purchases. Ngawang immediately began unpacking them all, and while she was organizing the kitchen, managed to turn on the hot water boiler and make us tea.

"Don't worry about the eggs," said Ngawang, putting some rice in the cooker so I could have something to eat later on. "I'll find you some."

And I had a feeling that if anyone could find me anything in all of Bhutan, it was Ngawang.

ALMOST ON CUE, as soon as we'd finished our tea, Sir Tenzin arrived to take me on a promised twilight drive of the city. He'd been enjoying playing tour guide, showing me around and bragging to whomever saw us that he had an American consultant at his disposal. Since we were about the same age, I figured I wasn't obliged to refer to Sir Tenzin as "Sir." But I did so anyway, partly to dispel any notions that Americans were boorish, and equally, perhaps, because of his commanding and intimidating presence. Had he learned this from being a school principal, or was this innate? He was taller than most Bhutanese I'd met so far, about six foot one, and his personality filled up the room. He seemed as quick to anger as he was to laugh or smile, switching from garrulous to silent in an instant and staring into space, as if he'd tuned out you and the world around him so he might collect his thoughts. Except that his demeanor didn't seem meditative as much as distracted.

I wondered if this had anything to do with Sir Tenzin's affinity for *doma,* the Bhutanese equivalent to chewing tobacco. *Doma* was a curious, tacolike packet made by slathering a leaf with lime paste (not the fruit but the acidic residual of boiling limestone) and wrapping it around a small brown nut called an areca. There couldn't possibly be any positive health benefits associated with sucking on this "delicacy." The trio of ingredients emitted a smell worse than the stinkiest cheese. But what magnetized its users was the warming effect it reportedly had on the insides, the way it lightened the head—the same impact as a shot of whiskey, people said. Those who indulged in *doma* insisted the high did not impede their ability to work. They also had convinced themselves that the lime paste wasn't eating away at their guts, even as doctors diagnosed a growing number of cases of stomach cancer and gastritis. (The spicy food was believed to be a culprit in those conditions, as well.)

On the matter of this addictive substance, there seemed to be two types of people: those who refused to touch the stuff, and those who did so with great frequency and gusto. Sir Tenzin was in the latter category. The two camps were easy to identify; the teeth and lips of *doma* users were stained, to various degrees, the color of blood. A light sheen of red seemed to be the mildest of the side effects. This scarlet mark did not deter *doma* users in the slightest; they would congregate the way cigarette smokers might outside an office building in New York, furtively rushing together for a quick hit. The king had banned the sale of tobacco products several years ago, but had he attempted to ban *doma,* his obedient subjects quite likely would have staged a revolt.

Doma wasn't to blame for Sir Tenzin's momentary pause at the first stop on our twilight drive. We were pulling up outside a little place in the center of town when he fell silent. The sign outside the shop was unlike any other I'd seen. In pretty cursive script, it announced, THE ART CAFÉ. It was the first shop I'd seen that looked as if it could have been located in other parts of the world. A couple of cute tables were arranged out front, and at one of them, two young men sat talking, with big colorful mugs in their hands.

"Is anything wrong, sir?"

"No, no, just give me a moment, please," he responded distractedly. I hopped out of the passenger door. After a minute, he stepped out, too, without a word. And as he approached the café, he swept down in a long, elegant bow.

"Your Majesty," Sir Tenzin said to the two young men. They said not a word in response, simply stopped for a moment to receive the greeting, and then kept talking. Unsure what to do, I smiled lamely, curtsied, and followed Sir Tenzin into the store.

Pretty photographs of prayer flags and mountains hung on the walls of the shop, a mini-exhibit. I noticed salad advertised on the menu board, and in the corner by a woodstove sat the first other non-Bhutanese I'd encountered, two women chatting away in German. From a small selection of fresh baked goods, we ordered a couple of cupcakes to go. Sir Tenzin asked for a bottle of Coca-Cola. I was dying to know who those two guys were, but I knew I shouldn't ask until we were alone.

Back in the car, under my questioning, Sir Tenzin explained that one of the men was a prince, the younger brother of His Majesty the king. After spotting him, Sir Tenzin had paused to prepare himself to give a suitably formal greeting. It was clear he didn't want to talk about this encounter very much; he was far more interested in talking about his plans for Kuzoo.

The car radio was tuned to the station. RJ Ngawang introduced a song by Akon, the Senegalese-American hip-hop sensation. It was probably the dozenth time I'd heard "Don't Matter" in the few days I'd been in Bhutan.

"Terrible pronunciation," said Sir Tenzin, shaking his head. He had just a bit of a British lilt in his voice, acquired during his days at a Jesuit school in India.

"Akon, or the radio jockey?" I hadn't exactly expected Kuzoo, in the hands of the first generation of Bhutanese to grow up with television, to be playing a bunch of traditional Bhutanese music and public-service programs, but I was a bit surprised by just how much pop music from my side of the world cascaded over the Kuzoo air. Because of the cost of production, there was little in the way of modern recorded Bhutanese music. Music from neighboring India and Nepal was banned from the airwaves, though it wasn't clear whether that was an official edict issued from on high or a decision made by the radio jockeys themselves.

He laughed. "That radio jockey. All of them. They mumble a lot. That girl in particular. They get nervous."

"We all do," I said. "I can help you with that, sir."

Sir Tenzin's car chugged up a winding road that promised
a sweeping view of Thimphu Valley, and led to the broadcast
transmission towers for both the Bhutan Broadcasting Service
and Kuzoo. The city was cast now in a twilight golden hue,
the same light we'd have this time of day in Los Angeles. The
insistent longing of Akon was a discordant sound track for
this magnificent vista, as discordant as the presence of this city
in such an otherwise starkly undeveloped country. From up
here, the sprawl of the growing capital was evident. Buildings
in various stages of construction emerged in the embryonic
skyline, pushing the boundaries of Thimphu farther out from
the center—a sure sign development had come to this place
where electricity hadn't flowed until a quarter century ago.

Off to the left, the majestic structure known as a *dzong*
gleamed in the light from the setting sun. Each district had a
dzong that served as central administration for government
and clergy; this particular one in Thimphu was called "the for-
tress of glorious religion." A golf course wrapped around the
grounds, and I asked Sir Tenzin how Bhutan came to feature
a game associated with rich people, and which was considered
an environmental blight.

"The third king loved to play golf." Sir Tenzin smiled, as if
that was all there was to say about the matter. "It's not my
game, though. I haven't got time for sports."

He pointed to the spot straight ahead, way across the valley,
where land had been cleared for the construction of what was
to be one of world's largest statues of Buddha—170 feet tall. A
band of light shone down on the area where the giant Buddha
would eventually sit, almost like a spotlight. I squinted to be
sure I wasn't imagining the gleam.

"One day, maybe in my lifetime, Thimphu will have a skyscraper," said Sir Tenzin, and he laughed at his own suggestion, for it seemed so impossible. Buildings were forbidden from reaching higher than six stories, for reasons both practical and aesthetic; nothing could tower over a region's *dzong,* for one thing. For another, modern conveniences that made taller buildings possible, like elevators and escalators, were costly uses of power. Regardless of their size or function, all structures were mandated to be built in traditional Bhutanese style; even the most recently constructed buildings—like the airport terminal—were fringed with ornate, colorful woodwork and sloping roofs. This ensured a fleet of artisans work, and at the same time flaunted the national heritage.

"This is the fastest-growing capital in Asia, after all. I still can't quite believe how big we've become in just the last few years." Sir Tenzin waved his hand at all the construction.

"Imagine the Kuzoo studio in a glass building. Topped with the traditional Bhutanese structure, of course." He laughed again.

Even from high above the city, I could see how unlikely a proposition this was. The thought of modern buildings popping up high above the traditional ones, disturbing the order of the cityscape, was unsettling. Yet if Akon and Christina Aguilera could dominate the airwaves—if cupcakes were being baked and Coca-Cola swigged and a person like me had been allowed in—anything was possible. Just as Bhutan was undergoing a cultural invasion that threatened to erode its unique foundation, its capital city might someday, not very long from now, look like any other.

Watching Bhutan change over time would be like watching a baby grow, I thought. I already felt a little maternal and protective of this unusual country, worried for its future.

Sir Tenzin continued. "You know, I wanted Kuzoo FM 90 to be Kuzoo 108," he said. The number 108 was sacred in Buddhism. It was the number of volumes in the Kanjur, the Buddhist scripture. Sir Tenzin's innate prowess for marketing was admirable, given that he was trained as an educator and raised in a country whose very foundation was anti-materialistic. "The Ministry of Information and Communication wouldn't let me have it, though. The planes use the frequency 107 to communicate. Too close on the dial, too much chance for interference."

He shook his head, then looked out the windshield. "I love the BBS logo," he declared, crumbling bits of his cupcake into his hand so as not to lose a single bite. "The conch shell." He motioned toward the sign near the transmission tower. Little squiggles denoting "transmission" radiated from the sides of the shell. It was at once cute and elegant.

"How did that get to be the symbol of the broadcaster?" A conch shell seemed a peculiar icon for a landlocked country.

"The conch is one of Buddhism's eight lucky signs. It is believed to awaken sentient beings from their sleep, their state of ignorance," Sir Tenzin said, licking his fingers. "Also, back in the villages, the conch was how people used to make announcements."

"Before BBS, and then Kuzoo, of course."

"Yes." Sir Tenzin smiled and washed down his last bite of cupcake with a swig of soda. A combination of the sweets and the excitement of his new mission gave Sir Tenzin's face a look of contentment. It was clear he believed he had the best job in the world.

5

GOD OF THE NIGHT

IF YOU WALKED INTO ANY VILLAGE IN ALL OF BHU-
tan and shouted "Karma," a quarter of the heads would
turn. There are only about fifty names in the whole country. A monk blessed a baby with a duo of them shortly after
birth. There are no familial surnames, and most names are
unisex. So it is entirely possible that a family could be made up
of a mother named Karma Wangdi and a father named Karma
Lhamo, a child named Karma Choden, and another named
Lhamo Wangdi. It is only in the last quarter century that birth
certificates have been kept; many Bhutanese older than that
don't know their exact date or even year of birth, another reminder that even today in the bustling city of Thimphu, a simple, rural life isn't so far away. As Bhutan becomes more
modern, some of the more daring Bhutanese parents break
tradition in order to distinguish themselves, altering the spell-
ing of familiar names or abbreviating them. Or by forgoing
the monk and choosing the names themselves.

Tsheten Denkar was the monk-given moniker of the Kuzoo
radio jockey who'd since adopted a sexier handle: Pink. Her

new name had its roots in her work as a DJ in Thimphu's blossoming party scene. Even as she juggled her ever-changing shifts at the station, she continued to work the booth at Club Destiny on party nights: Wednesday, Friday, and Saturday. Her long hair was permed and highlighted with streaks of brown and blond, her lips perennially glossed and pouty. Pink had carefully crafted her image as a Bhutanese disco kitten. The name was an invisible but key part of her tranformation into a sensation in the club and on the air.

Off air and out of the nightclub, things were not going well for the twenty-five-year-old woman formerly known as Tsheten. After seven years, her marriage was unraveling. Marriage had long been a very casual institution in Bhutan; a couple declared themselves married when they started living together, and unmarried when they stopped. Now, the ways of the West were imposing on this tradition. More elaborate ceremonies were becoming common, as were more acrimonious, complicated divorces. Pink's situation was so strained that her mother had sent for the family's monk for guidance.

The family was also facing another life-changing issue they wanted the monk to address. Pink's sister, Tshering, had prayed and prayed she'd get a job as a flight attendant on Emirates airline. Her fervent appeal had worked. Like Pink, Tshering had one leg in the modern world. But only one. Like many single Bhutanese women, she still slept in the same bed with her mother at their shared apartment. Now she would be moving to Dubai and flying to exotic ports heretofore accessible only in her dreams. No more tediousness of going back and forth, day in and day out, serving on the only flight the Bhutanese airline ran daily: Bangkok to Paro. Paro to Bangkok. As an exotic and costly tourist destination that attracts the famous as well as the rich, Bhutan ensured the staff of Druk Air the occasional celebrity sighting—Matt Damon, Orlando Bloom, Bette Midler, and Demi Moore had been among the recent stars to visit. Better still was the honor of serving members of the royal family who might happen to be on board. Relocating to another country and going to work for a foreign airline would expand Tshering's world, and the idea of living away from family for a while was alluring—even if to do so for anything other than education was considered by many to be very un-Bhutanese. The pay would be exponentially better than what she earned now, more than enough to allow her to save money, which would never be possible at home.

The monk determined that both sisters needed to be cleansed so they could proceed. A series of *puja*s was in order to ready them for the immediate futures they faced. He'd be in town for several weeks to accomplish his plan.

*Puja*s are special prayers performed by holy men to give additional heft to a message you want to transmit to the gods. These holy men have the expertise and wisdom—the divination—to know which gods need to be sought out, which chants are necessary to best help remove whatever obstacles are in the way.

The intensity and length of the *puja*—how many monks are needed, and for how many days—depends on the severity of the situation. Moving into a new home requires *puja*s for the old place and the new. New jobs and the ending of relationships qualify, too. No one in Bhutan questions anyone who misses school or work because they have to attend a *puja*. The ceremonies are considered a normal part of daily life.

How prevalent they are is evident as you walk the streets of Thimphu on most any day. The moan of bagpipelike horns floats in the air, punctuating the throaty chants of monks and mingling with and occasionally drowning out the more mundane sounds of honking cars and barking dogs that comprise the aural cityscape.

Buddhism, I was learning, was far different in this nation where the religion was dominant than it had appeared back home, far more complex than the yoga, meditation, vegetarianism, and fat smiling statues of Buddha that Westerners typically associate with this peaceful and mystical religion. The Buddhas in Bhutan, in fact, are skinny. A life of overindulgence and grandeur was exactly what the original Buddha, a prince who renounced his fortune and set off in search of enlightenment, opted to leave behind. Here, yoga isn't part of the layperson's spiritual practice; rather, it's an exercise class taught three times a week at the hospital by a German doctor eager to help chubby Bhutanese ladies slim down. As for meditation, most young Bhutanese dismiss it as something their parents or grandparents do, but not them. "Too boring," they say.

Culturally, Bhutan-style Buddhism is ubiquitous, embedded in daily life. There is absolutely no separation of church and state in Bhutan; the lower half of the country's flag is orange to represent the religion. The government funds many of the monasteries, and each district's administrative seat, the *dzong,* also houses monks.

Virtually every home features an altar, housed in a room of its own if space allows. A step at the bottom of every doorway trips up unwelcome spirits. Old men and women walk the streets spinning handheld prayer wheels, lost in the murmur of their chants. Even television programming is infused with the religion; every morning at 6:00 a.m., the Bhutan Broadcasting Service kicks off its day with prayers chanted against a backdrop of scenic video clips of the country's spectacular landscape.

New construction—schools, residences, a government-sponsored park—isn't inhabited or put to use until it is consecrated by monks. Religious holidays, such as the First Sermon of Lord Buddha or the Birth of Guru Rinpoche, dot the official calendar. Specially trained monastic astrologers are consulted about virtually every aspect of life—illness, marriage, trouble that befalls a family, major decisions.

Draped across the landscape of Bhutan are endless ribbons of color, bright prayer flags hoisted as protection against certain gods, to coax others forward, and to repel bad spirits. These fluttering squares, in various states of fade and tatter, are almost as plentiful as the trees the king has enacted laws to protect. They're hung in places that seem impossible for a human to reach; it's believed that the closer they're raised to the heavens, the more effective they will be. The flags fly until they disintegrate, which can take years. Their tattered remnants are lingering reminders of the human call to a higher power—and of how this religion pervades the very air.

To the uninitiated, the rules and rituals associated with Buddhism as practiced in Bhutan might seem absurd—elaborate and colorful and rife with inexplicable superstition. Circle a religious structure three times clockwise to accumulate merit. Circle on this auspicious day, and your merit will be doubled. If your family's monk or astrologer advises against travel, but there's no way around making the trip, you pack your suitcase early and leave it outside the door to trick the spirits. You might also carry printed prayers in your pocket or your purse, for extra protection. Animals cannot be slaughtered during

certain holy months, but it's acceptable to purchase and stock-
pile meat in advance to consume during that time. If meat is
consumed, it is preferable to choose cow over chicken, for
chickens feed fewer people, and the bad karma from killing is
lessened when more people benefit.

Most compelling to me were the underlying principles of
the religion: Compassion for all beings, and the interconnectedness of everyone. The ideals of wisdom and knowledge.
Self-reliance. Acceptance and forgiveness. What you possessed
and achieved wasn't what was important. These were the
principles I'd learned in happiness class, writ large. Most reli-
gions espoused similar values, but there was something about
the Buddhist approach to delivering the message that spoke to
me, a decidedly lapsed Catholic.

The holy men and women roaming the streets of Bhutan's
capital city reinforce the messages of the faith. They wear burgundy robes and sport close-cropped hair; they usually travel
in clusters. Some live in the monasteries or the sole nunnery in
the hills above the city. Others come from the outlying areas to
stock up on supplies.

While monks are as common as birds, a special kind of
monk always commands particular attention and respect: a
Rinpoche, which means "precious one," and most with that
name are recognized as reincarnations of lamas. They're distinguished by a ribbon of gold fabric worn around their burgundy robes.

So it created quite a stir when the Rinpoche who'd traveled
to Thimphu to attend to Pink and Tshering walked into the
offices of Kuzoo FM. It was my second week in the office, and
I'd been spending my days talking to staff, helping them with
simple problems like English pronunciations, and answering

questions about my life back in the United States. Rinpoche held himself like a man who had been told from an early age that he was special. But for the robes, he looked like a hipster thirty-year-old, with spiky black hair and a confident strut—a guy from town stopping in to guest host a show, or say hi to his friends.

When I spotted him in the hallway outside the Kuzoo workroom and studio, I waved hello, then immediately hoped I hadn't offended him with my casual gesture. But he waved back, sweetly, undisturbed, as I was obviously an outsider and not schooled in monastic protocol. Beside him was a dumpling of a lady who, judging by her features, had to be Pink's mother. She beamed proudly, delighted to be seen in the company of someone so holy.

The arrival of a person of seniority typically compels Bhutanese to rise and politely but cursorily bow their heads and say, "*Kuzu zampo-la,* sir." But when the gold-fringed Rinpoche stepped into the room, the young Kuzoo FM staff immediately stopped what they were doing, rose, and approached him, single file, heads bowed. Mechanically he reached inside his robes, produced a handful of thin silk cords, and placed them on each head that paraded by, every gesture accented with a little hum of a prayer. It was a simple blessing, as reflexive as genuflecting and crossing before you entered a church pew.

After receiving the blessing, the staff returned to their seats and proceeded to continue whatever they were doing, appearing now completely unaffected. I was rapt. I couldn't take my eyes off Rinpoche. He must have felt my stare, as he soon motioned in my direction, while he addressed Pink in Dzongkha.

"Oh, that's Lady Jane, from California and New York," she

told him in English. People seemed more familiar with my home state than my adopted one, so I'd started answering the question "Where are you from?" with a dual response.

"New York," said Rinpoche. "That is a great country." He paused, as if he was imagining the distance. "My father went to New York once. . . . Come here."

I accepted the summons and rose from my chair. As he'd done with the others, he adorned me with the red silk cord. Mimicking the other Kuzooers, I bowed my head, low. But I'd failed to notice the second half of the ritual—pulling the cord forward and tying it around my neck. Rinpoche laughed kindly as Pink intervened, completing the task.

With barely a move of his arm, Rinpoche then pulled a three-foot fringed white silk scarf from inside his robes and threw it around my neck with a nearly invisible flick of the wrist. A standard greeting for an honored guest. He looked toward Pink and murmured in his native tongue.

"He says that's because you did many good deeds in a former life," Pink translated.

I smoothed out my hair from under the red silk blessing cord and adjusted my scarf. I found myself considering the idea of past lives: I liked this notion that it wasn't only cats who got nine chances. That whatever goodness we might accumulate in one lifetime would influence where we went in the next. But what about the bad things we'd done? Was it possible to transcend them? Were our next lives determined by a median average of this life's actions? Maybe in my next life I'd have a talent for speaking other languages, or a gift for playing guitar. Maybe, in the next life, I would get it right: enter a profession where I did some good for humanity—become a teacher or a scientist or a social worker. Or fall in love with a wonderful man and be a full-time best-mother-in-the-world to our many adopted children. Dangling in this fleeting day-dream about the laments of the past and unknowable future, something occurred to me: This life right now, as a forty-three-year-old woman from Brooklyn, New York, who had moved to Los Angeles for a job in public radio, who was tem-porarily residing in a remote kingdom in the Himalayas, with all the strange, wondrous, and sometimes awful chapters that had led me here, was pretty okay. With each passing day, a little more than okay.

I sat on a rickety chair right next to Rinpoche, hoping that a little of his spectral radiance might wash over me.

Sir Tenzin entered the room and the staff rose to greet him, as if they were addressing the teacher in grade school. "Hello, sir." Sir Tenzin didn't respond, but started speaking to Rinpoche in Dzongkha, as if he'd been expecting him to be there.

Rinpoche didn't engage in formalities, either. "I need some rice," he said in English.

Sir Tenzin rushed back out as quickly as he'd rushed in. In moments he returned with a small bowl of uncooked grains, from which sprouted four sticks of incense. Sir Tenzin pre-sented this offering, formally, with both hands. Rinpoche ac-cepted it and rose. He walked to the other side of the room, lit the incense, and sat down near the transmitter that beamed Kuzoo's signal out to Thimphu Valley, the technical heart of the station.

Some of the Kuzooers who'd been glued to their desks now stood. A few others remained seated but turned away from their computers to watch. Pink's mother giggled a bit, like a teenager, her cheeks flushed red. Sir Tenzin stood proudly next to Rinpoche, who closed his eyes and began to chant, presumably for the station's well-being and success. It was a murmuring hum; it sounded like a longer version of the blessing that accompanied the cord. The incense burned bright and strong, wafting around the room with its powerful, earthy smell. Every few measures, Rinpoche would toss a few grains of rice in one direction, then the next, as if to scatter his prayers evenly around the room.

Though I didn't understand the words, I felt moved by the ritual, by the power of Rinpoche.

The prayers continued for about fifteen minutes. A few of the Kuzooers impatiently stroked their keyboards, eager to get back to work. The station phone rang, and Pema scurried over to answer it in a whisper, lest it keep bleating in interruption. At last Rinpoche gave a final bow, indicating he was through. Grains of rice were strewn across the tattered burgundy floor covering. I had just witnessed my first *puja*.

As everyone resumed their positions at their keyboards and settled back into work, Rinpoche crossed the room and addressed me solemnly.

"Is everything okay?" he asked in perfect English.

What do you say to a holy man when he asks you that question?

Did he want a real answer, or was this the Bhutanese equivalent of the empty American query "How are you?" Could he tell I'd been struggling? Someone with the spiritual powers of a reincarnated lama could likely feel from a distance that I'd had a disastrous few years. I didn't know what to say. We were in a cramped room, surrounded by young people I was supposed to be teaching. How much did I want them to know about me?

To answer Rinpoche honestly, I mustered up something to the effect that I was okay, yes, but "searching." I'd never used that word before—I thought it vague and pretentious—but now it felt honest. What exactly I was searching for I couldn't quite say. A plan for the future? Cleansing? Peace?

For a moment it wasn't clear if Rinpoche had understood me. Then he called out for a piece of paper and a pen.

"Call me if you'd like to talk more," he said. And slowly and deliberately, he scribbled down his cell phone number. In case I forgot whose number it was, he added above it in block letters: *RINPOCHE.*

LATER THAT AFTERNOON, Kuzoo still basked in the glow of the blessing. Pema and I sat in front of our respective computers researching information for a new show that would begin that night. It was to be called *The Doctor Is In.* Sir Tenzin had run into one of Bhutan's two psychiatrists the day before and, visions of CNN in his eyes, had corralled him into visiting the Kuzoo studios to cohost a weekly call-in show.

"We can be like King Larry," Sir Tenzin said brightly.

Or rather, Pema could be. Because she was so diligent and productive and interested in being all over the airwaves, I'd taken to calling her Oprah, even though she couldn't have been more physically opposite than the superstar. Pema stood no more than five feet tall and weighed perhaps ninety pounds. Her cheeks were freckled like a midwestern farm girl's, and her long hair hung down past her shoulders with a slight wave. She frequently fiddled it all into a bun as she stared at the computer. Maven of popular culture that she was, she didn't have to ask who I was referring to. Early yesterday morning,

I'd caught her surfing the Neiman Marcus Web site for Burberry pocketbooks. Even the tiniest cost triple her monthly salary.

"Where did you learn about Burberry, much less Neiman Marcus?"

Pema turned in her chair and looked at me as if I were a clueless idiot.

"Sex and the City," she said. "A friend brought the DVD from India." She didn't believe I'd seen the show only once; she seemed to assume that on the series' native soil, each home would be blessed with a continuous feed of episodes.

In a country where many preferred to be treated with the holistic and spiritual tradition of Bhutanese medicine, psychiatry was an alien concept. Bhutan was still a place where people actually talked to their families and friends about the trials and tribulations of daily life, and trusted that whatever haunted them would somehow work itself out. Saddled by worries or problems, they'd deploy the monks and Rinpoches. Radio was the perfect medium for the psychiatrist to make his services known—to explain how therapy worked and what kinds of issues it addressed. As was the case with all health care in Bhutan, traditional and Western, visits to doctors were free.

"Let's see," said Pema, orderly and matter-of-fact. She'd already chosen the theme music for the show, Michael Jackson's "Heal the World." (Presumably for the title, and not because she saw the pop singer as a paragon of mental health.) Now she was plundering the Web for background information to explain the first topic Dr. Chencho wanted to address: anxiety.

"This says there are five main types of anxiety disorders." She was reading from the Web site of the National Institute of

Mental Health, the first thing to come up on her Google search. "Generalized Anxiety Disorder, Obsessive-Compulsive Disorder, Panic Disorder, Post-Traumatic Stress Disorder, and Social Phobia."

None of these seemed to be an affliction with which Pema could have been personally familiar. She was magnificently confident, the type of confidence that could edge into bossiness.

"Do you know what any of that means?" I asked.

"Yes, it spells it out right here," snipped Pema, who I feared would read on the air the whole list and their descriptions word for word.

Across the room, Pink sat absorbed in a musical otherworld, headphones pressing down on her long wavy hair, scanning tunes for her next show. This didn't keep her from hearing her cell phone chirping, a special ringtone I'd not heard it play before. She answered, then walked over to me.

"It's for you," she said, as if I got calls on her number all the time. I took the phone, surprised.

"Hello?" I said.

"Let's have dinner tonight." The gravelly, accented English of Rinpoche was commanding. "Pink will bring you to my hotel."

The prospect of a private audience with this monk intrigued me. Maybe he'd had a vision he wanted to share that could shape my future. I wasn't sure I even believed in the idea of a vision, or even of healing prayer. I had no idea what I would ask or say or expect. But I figured you should never refuse the attention of a holy man—especially when he calls you.

From the backseat of Pink's little car, I witnessed dusk sweeping over the skies. Ngawang had also come along for the ride. I liked these two women so much, even though I didn't really know them yet. The streets of Thimphu began to bustle as day turned into night, filled with life. Shops were full, and business was particularly brisk at the snooker parlor, where players wagered on their games, eagerly leaning across crowded tables. As we navigated the streets on our way to meet the mystic, I allowed myself a moment of pride for my adventurousness. When I was about the age of my companions, something happened to me that could have convinced me never to venture out again. When I stopped to consider what had happened, it astonished me how far I'd come.

In the summer of 1981, when I was seventeen years old, a chance discussion with a friend on a subway platform tipped me off to the existence of a brand-new cable channel called CNN. The outfit was new and so small-time that simply by making a bold phone call to the number listed in information, I landed myself an internship at the New York bureau. That led to another, and another, and finally, when I got out of college, it was by default the place where I sought full-time employment.

For the princely salary of $11,000 a year, I moved to Atlanta to work at the network's world headquarters. I'd never been to the city, so I relocated there sight unseen, as there wasn't time or money enough in the fledgling network's budget, or mine, to first check the place out. Back in its early days, CNN didn't wield enormous influence on the world stage as it does today; then it was disparagingly referred to as Chicken Noodle News.

Most everyone at work turned out to be just like me—young, ambitious, from somewhere else, not long out of school.

Our jobs and hours were constantly changing, but in spite of the flux, we cobbled together the kind of accelerated support system that develops when you're in an intense and demanding situation. Drinking beer at eight in the morning, after slogging through exhaustion on the overnight shift—both are excellent bonding rituals.

One June night, about a year after I'd started working there, I returned home from a birthday party for my friend Michael. It was after 1:00 a.m., quite late, considering that I had to report to work at 8:00 a.m. for the day shift. Just a few weeks prior, I'd moved across the building's courtyard to my very first apartment without a roommate. The place wasn't fancy in any way, but it was all mine—a sweet little studio with a claw-foot tub and French doors that separated the living area from where I slept. It was cheap and close to work, even if the neighborhood was a bit so-so.

The landlord had yet to unstick the windows, which had been painted just before I moved in, so they were stuck open a few inches. My several attempts to push them down failed, but it was hot enough that I hadn't called again to complain. Those cracks kept me from suffocating in the oppressive summer heat, as a window-unit air conditioner was beyond my means.

Exhausted from a long night, I stripped off my clothes, collapsed naked onto the futon on the floor, tucked my eyeglasses underneath the edge, pulled up the top sheet, and fell right to sleep.

I've never been able to calculate what time it was when I was wakened by a loud thud. At first I was certain the noise was from a picture falling off the wall. I'd hung a framed poster of chili peppers in the kitchen and it had fallen in the middle of the night the week before, too. I hadn't quite gotten the hook in the wall right. So I shifted my position on the futon and figured I'd rehang it in the morning. Then I heard another noise.

In that instant, I became aware of movement across the room. It sounded like a window being forced open. No, that couldn't be. Blind as a bat, I fumbled in the pitch dark under the futon to excavate my eyeglasses so I could confirm that this was my imagination at work. Where had I put those specs? No way, that couldn't be a person. My heart and stomach felt it before my head accepted the fact. An intruder had entered the room and was now headed toward me.

A scream emerged from my throat, so loud, just a pure scream, no words, no "help me." The paralysis of terror took hold. As I write this, I can feel the wave of adrenaline rushing through me, hear that sound I made so long ago. It was more of a reflex, a reaction, than a cry for help. A hand locked over my mouth to silence me. I felt a pointed object against my neck, and the man reinforced this action with words.

"Shut up," he said firmly, quietly, "or I'll kill you."

Even if I'd been bold enough to defy him, I didn't have the capacity to continue making any sound. My nakedness, my impaired sight, the fear that I might die all combined to render me silent, terrified, incapable of movement.

I wished I could be dead, that this man would kill me, so I wouldn't have to live with this memory. The only act of self-preservation I could muster, as he raped me, was to beg him not to ejaculate inside me. To please not make me pregnant. There was no retribution for my daring to speak; he complied with my request. When he was done, he apologized. As he pulled up his pants and zipped them, he said he was sorry we had to meet this way, sorry if he hurt me, hopeful we might see each other again.

Then he left through the front door, as if he'd been an invited guest.

WITHIN A YEAR I'd accepted a position at a television station in central North Carolina. Moving to work in local news in a midsize market wasn't exactly the career trajectory I'd intended. Yet a smaller city, a new city, a city that didn't remind me of that night—all seemed like a good idea. My new job involved producing the eleven o'clock nightly newscast, which meant leaving the studio at just after 11:30 p.m. for the drive home. Perhaps it would kick-start me into making peace with the dark.

It was easy to walk to the parking lot with my coworkers, without seeming needy or explaining why I didn't want to go outside at night by myself. But at midnight as I pulled into the parking space at my apartment building, the stillness, facing the quiet of the night on my own, would make me sweat. I'd dart out of the car, heart beating fast as I sprinted inside. Once I got safely inside, I'd turn on every single light and keep them burning until dawn, as if electricity would shield me. I'd rationalize: Wasn't there a zone of protection offered from above to people who had been through a trauma? Just one trauma per person per lifetime, right? I couldn't fully convince myself that this was the case.

As the months passed, I continued on with my double life. Most people around me saw a confident young woman, even if they couldn't understand why I'd left a national network—

CNN was starting to gain notoriety, by now—to work in this small city in North Carolina. One weekend night, I needed milk from the grocery store. I grabbed the keys, ran down the steps, and got into the car. On the quiet road that connected my street with the one leading to the shopping center, I stopped for a traffic light. At that instant, the magnitude of this simple act occurred to me: *I did it! I left the house! It's dark out, and I left the house!* When the light turned green, I was so happy that I was crying. In the aisles of the grocery store, I didn't even try to conceal my tears. I was reclaiming my life, my confidence, that feeling of normal we take for granted before the unexpected turns us inside out. That night before bed, I gleefully switched off every light in my apartment. I fastened the chain locks, but didn't stick chairs under the doors. As I eased into sleep, I breathed steadily, softly: Now I could get back to life.

And twenty-two years later, here I was in a car in Thimphu on the way to meet a holy man, the Rinpoche. And in some strange way it is because of that night, not despite it, that I could be here.

Pink navigated into the rocky parking area, stopped the car, and we emerged into the darkness of the winter evening.

THE HOTEL TANDIN is a run-down little place at the top of a five-story building, just up the street from the traffic circle in the center of town. We marched up those five flights of stairs, and Pink knocked on a door just outside the bar. The sounds of chanting seeped into the hallway.

"He's meditating," said Pink, shrugging. She quietly cracked open the door and motioned for Ngawang and me to enter.

The room was large and in its center were two single beds, side by side. Rinpoche sat on one of them, legs crossed, continuing his chants, seemingly oblivious to the interruption. It felt as invasive as walking in on someone in the bathroom. I sat down in a chair near the door, far across from him, so as not to disrupt his privacy. A very long five minutes later, he snapped out of his trance. He raised his head and offered a cursory greeting, then snapped his fingers and started demanding help. Though he was speaking Dzongkha, his tone translated perfectly: He was ordering Pink to do something. Flustered, she sifted through a bag of supplies on a little shelf outside the toilet, and dug out a little white bottle. Rinpoche held back his head as if he were an injured pony.

"The pollution," Rinpoche explained, his chin in the air and his gaze fixed upward as Pink dutifully nursed his eyes with droplets. "It's terrible here in Thimphu. Now move over here, and tell me." He motioned that I should come closer, to the twin bed opposite where he sat. As soon as I was in place, he looked at me deeply, intensely. I didn't know what to say. Now that we were here, I didn't want to tell him anything. Whatever mystical air Rinpoche had around him, whatever I had hoped he might imbue me with or chase away, the mood was broken by his demeanor, the surroundings, this sad little room. That finger-snapping incident revealed him as a boor, not the paragon of kindness, compassion, and understanding I'd imagined a monk would be.

Here we were, though, across from each other, his expectation building. I spoke, but not as openly as I had planned.

"It's a very difficult time for me. I feel like everything is up in the air, in transition. Like I'm in transition."

Rinpoche spoke in Dzongkha, and Ngawang interpreted.

"He says it is clear you have many obstacles facing you back home," she said. "Particularly in your work. There is someone there who is working against you. You cannot move forward with the current situation."

"Okay," I said. What he was saying was true. My job and the nature of the industry were wearing on my soul; several coworkers were obstacles, too, and the on-again, off-again overnight hours were physically exhausting. But those weren't the problems. Time hadn't healed all wounds, but it had smoothed them out a bit. It was up to me to do what I'd done all along, just keep moving forward and being open, aware. Kind.

The only thing holding me back was me.

I had answered the call of this holy man, seeking salvation, explanation, or a road map for my life. But as I looked into his eyes, I saw a clear message, even if it wasn't the one he was trying to convey. He wasn't the answer. He didn't have the answers. Ngawang broke the silence. "He says right now there's a *puja* taking place in Sikkim where there are many monks."

The Indian state of Sikkim was hours away. Could a *puja* be conducted remotely? When you needed to be cleansed, didn't the monks come to you—pray and chant in your presence? Or was it simply enough to trust in their power?

Ngawang's voice was tinged with skepticism as she obediently filtered Rinpoche's words.

"He says the intensity of your obstacles requires that you hire seven monks and a lama for three days. You will also have to pay for their meals." She glanced down at her cell phone, which was buzzing with a text message.

Rinpoche scolded her in Dzongkha.

"That sounds pretty expensive," I said. "How much?"

"He says it will be three hundred ngultrum a monk each day, plus eight hundred for the lama." Ngawang seemed to possess a great faculty for numbers, especially when it involved currency conversion. She stopped to calculate, and to glance at Pink. Both girls looked surprised. "Eight thousand seven hundred ngultrum."

I'd just cashed $150 worth of traveler's checks at the Bank of Bhutan in the center of town and had received 6,500 ngultrum. Pink and Ngawang each earned just 5,000 ngultrum every month for the long, erratic hours they logged at Kuzoo. Sir Tenzin counted it out in cash to each employee on the first of the month.

Eighty-seven hundred ngultrum was a lot by any standard, even for salvation. What would this *puja* cost if I were Bhutanese? I wondered.

The girls seemed keyed into this—embarrassed, even. Just because Rinpoche smelled a rich American didn't mean they did. I was their coworker, their friend.

"You can think about it," said Pink sweetly.

"Well, I don't really have to think about it. That's quite expensive."

Rinpoche chattered a response in Dzongkha. Ngawang relayed, "He says if you pay a hundred dollars, that will be okay." Her smile told me she was on to the extortionate monk.

For a split second, I worried this Rinpoche might pray to the wrong deities if I refused. Make my obstacles more intense. Then I remembered that I didn't believe in spells. Superstitions weren't the parts of this religion that made sense to me. What I'd been discovering, ever since that happiness class back home, about self-awareness, self-reliance, and compassion did.

I looked straight into Rinpoche's eyes, and smiled. "Thank

you very much for the consultation," I said politely. "But I'd like to offer you something for your time and just go have dinner now."

Eyes wide, Rinpoche spat out some words in disgust.

"He says he is not a businessman," Ngawang said, looking up from her cell phone as if to punctuate Rinpoche's displeasure. "He doesn't want any money."

The air in the seedy hotel room was thick and tense. I wanted to leave, but out of respect for my friends, I decided to swallow my frustration. I rose tentatively, afraid of seeming too abrupt, and the girls got up, too. Rinpoche collected his cell phone, a sleek Motorola RAZR like the one I had back home. He commanded us to wait for him outside.

At the noodle shop just behind the sole movie theater, in the center of town, Rinpoche slurped at his soup while watching cartoons on the television that bleated in the corner of the restaurant. Like an insolent little boy ignoring the grown-ups at the table, he fiddled with his cell phone. I made small talk with the girls. And when I asked the waitress for the check, Rinpoche waved his hand at me dismissively.

"You pay next time," he said clearly in English, and reached into his robes for his wallet.

A WEEK LATER, Ngawang and I snuck out of the station before the afternoon hip-hop show that she hosted to visit her older sister, a doctor, at the hospital. The biggest workplace problem in Thimphu wasn't yet that people surfed the Net instead of doing their jobs. There weren't enough computers, and online access wasn't reliable enough for that to be an issue. What chomped into the meat of the workday was the inevitable, interminable family visit. All day, every day, mothers, sisters, cousins, and boyfriends would just stream into offices, schools, and shops to say hello, drop off lunch, have a cup of tea, or just hang out. Because of this, I had met more family members of coworkers in Bhutan in a few weeks than I had in three years of working with the crew in Los Angeles.

The fact that one of Ngawang's sisters was practicing medicine didn't mean she was off-limits. Someone would bring us tea in the examining room while she was seeing patients, Ngawang assured me. She did it all the time. There wasn't a sense of modesty or privacy in Bhutan; everything was communal. And there certainly weren't any doctor-patient confidentiality laws.

About three quarters of the way to the hospital, we came to the National Memorial Chorten, at the confluence of the upper road and one leading into town. Every day, hundreds of people flocked here, from dawn till well after dark, to circumambulate this enormous and sacred religious structure—a form of walking prayer that accumulates merit with the gods. Ngawang guided me clockwise around it the requisite three times. Sometimes, she said, she prays simply because she knows it will make her father feel better.

"I don't believe in it," she said. "These things are just part of who we are. It's just what we do. My father asks me to pray to the god of the night, so I do. He believes that the soul leaves the body when you sleep, and if you don't pray, it might not return." She paused as we made our way around for the third circle. "That's what happened to my mother."

I grasped Ngawang's arm.

"Do you miss your mother, Lady Jane?" Ngawang asked.

The screen saver on my laptop was set to a smiling and

gorgeous thirty-year-old image of my mother that my father had dug up and digitized not long ago. Ngawang loved learning that "Jane," my middle name, was also the name of the lady in the photo, the woman who had given birth to me. The original Jane, I told her. Of her mother, she had just one tiny black-and-white shot, only an inch square—smaller than a passport snapshot. Twenty years ago in Bhutan, photographs had been as unusual, and as dear, as electricity and telephone service. The young woman in the picture looked identical to Ngawang. There wasn't any money in her wallet, just her national ID card and this memento.

"She is the same age in this picture as I am now," she said.

I could feel my heart tweak for how much she missed the woman she never got to know.

"I do miss my mother," I said as we made our third round, surrounded by other worshippers. "But I haven't seen her in a long while. I can see her only a couple of times a year."

"What do you mean?"

"Well, she lives three thousand miles away from where I do."

"You don't live with her?" Ngawang sounded very surprised. Though the Bhutanese knew from the movies that many Westerners didn't live with their families, it still surprised them to meet someone in person who was a case study in this curious way of life.

"No, I don't. I haven't lived with my family since I was sixteen years old."

I explained that in the United States, kids often couldn't wait to leave home, and I realized how foolish and sad that must have sounded. Especially to someone who had lost her beloved mother so young.

"You must get very lonely," Ngawang said. "If you ever get

lonely here, you call me and I'll come stay with you, okay? I'll keep you company, my sweet Lady Jane."

I promised I would, even though it would be impossible for me to convey what a triumph it was that I could not only stay alone but actually enjoy it. The god of the night could have captured my soul, but he lost.

Ngawang pointed out a shop I hadn't noticed before, tucked off the street across from the chorten. It was one of the few shops on the upper road, and one of the only places in Thimphu where you could find fresh baked goods—like the ovens they were baked in, a luxury in Bhutan. We darted across the traffic and made our way into the shop to get a snack. A nice-looking cookie for me. An enormous bear claw for Ngawang.

And so, two new friends chomped on sweets. It felt like the right time to ask the question I'd wanted to ask for days now.

"What did you think of that Rinpoche, Ngawang?"

"He was really handsome, wasn't he?" Ngawang said, perking up as if she had a crush.

"Handsome? He's a monk!"

"Some monks can marry, though." Ngawang smiled, and stuck another piece of pastry into her mouth.

"Well, I hope you don't marry that monk. Do you think I made a mistake by not letting him do the *puja* for me?"

"No way," she said, wiping powdered sugar from her mouth with the back of her hand. "You did the right thing. That didn't seem right, what he was asking." She took another bite, and some crumbs fell to the floor. Her phone trilled after being silent for a long while. The James Bond theme song, which meant her father was calling. "You know. You can't trust all the monks just because they're monks."

6

BHUTAN ON THE BORDER,
OR, THE START-UP COUNTRY

A CITY IS AT ITS BEST, ITS PUREST, AT DAWN. EMPTY, raw. You can see the veins of it. Before the rush of the day begins, it seems more Hollywood set than reality.

In the slow pace of morning, Manhattan is almost quaint. Bleary-eyed dog owners, some wearing pajamas, sleepwalk as their charges take care of business. The stillness punctuated by the whine and whir of a steady, slow parade of garbage trucks or the squeal of kneeling buses. Washington, D.C., even at its busiest, is slow by comparison. But its scrubbed-clean, stately charm takes on a special sort of majesty in the early morning light, as if the buildings were preening for admiration. Downtown Los Angeles is more alive at 6:00 a.m. on a weekday than at most other times; cars streaming into parking garages, suited throngs marching to their high-powered jobs in international finance and law. But on weekends, when it's early, the streets are so empty it feels as if there's been an evacuation. At dawn any day of the week, eighteen miles away in Santa Monica, the beach is desolate, too, but for determined joggers and the homeless men still sleeping beside the trees.

As the sun rises in Paris, the scent of freshly baked baguettes fills the streets, although no store is yet open so you can enjoy one. The canals of Amsterdam are still and shimmering in the early hours, and the houseboats rarely look so inviting. Once, as I wandered aimlessly, wired by jet lag, a crazed man chased me through the streets of the Jordaan district, shouting at me in Dutch, the only sign of life I've ever seen in that neighborhood so early. In Greece to attend a very special anniversary party, my mother and I meandered through Athens in search of an early breakfast, the smells from the fishmongers assaulting us as gulls hovered overhead. Bangkok never seems to slow. Even at the airport at 4:00 a.m., the twenty-four-hour massage joint is as busy as a nail salon in New York on Saturday at noon.

And then there is Thimphu, the capital city of Bhutan. A city in a country so remote, so undeveloped, that it isn't quite sure what to make of cities. A city whose population has quadrupled in the past ten years. Even as it grows exponentially, and especially in the early light of morning, Thimphu feels a bit like a gangly village, rather than the bustling hub it becomes once the day is under way.

It is six thirty in the morning, in the dead of winter. It's chilly, but not as cold as this season could be, high in the Himalayas. Six scraggly stray dogs wander aimlessly in a pack, crisscrossing the street, oblivious to what little traffic there is. A lone luxury SUV rumbles past, probably a dignitary being driven to the airport or his office. As part of their compensation, ministers are given these fancy vehicles, which only a handful of private citizens can afford.

A truck barrels by. Twenty Indian men stand close together on the flatbed, being driven to a construction site for the day's labor. A few Nepalese ladies stoop to sweep the street with short-handled brooms made of straw. Their eyes are heavy, as if they've already logged eight hard hours, even though they've just begun the day. A baby strapped to one woman's back somehow manages to doze through the action.

The sidewalks are pockmarked with infinite cracks and holes and splats of bright red spit, remnants of the ubiquitous *domu*. It's a risk to walk almost anywhere in Thimphu and not fix your gaze downward to watch your step. But if you do, you are robbed of the vista of the most lovely Himalayan sky. Clouds hang low like tufts of cotton candy, hugging the mountains and giving the valley the air of a fairy tale.

There are no traffic lights in this city. The starched cop who directs the cars with his tai chi–like moves is not yet on duty. There's no need. This early in the morning, you could walk in the center of this street fearlessly. The snooker parlor, jammed with agitated players well into the evening, is shuttered now, as are the fabric stores, bars-cum-restaurants, beauty "saloons," and the shoe shops all selling the exact same merchandise. In an hour, crossing any of the streets will require patience and skill, like navigating a chase scene in a video game. Children and dogs will clutter the sidewalks then. Weathered ladies peddling bright red chilis and rice will pour them onto the filthy, uneven pavement, an ad hoc display that doesn't seem to deter most buyers.

At this time of day, I'll be lucky to find an open shop. The only place where it might be possible is on the main strip, Norzin Lam. Midway down the block, I see a sign of life. There's an open door at the Zeeling Tshongkhag, a place that's becoming one of my usual stops. I poke my head in.

"Can I come in?" I ask.

I'm always polite to people in stores, but in Bhutan, I am

hyperaware that every place I go I am representing not just Kuzoo FM but the United States.

The proprietor, Pema, welcomes me with a shy smile. "Yes, madam." I have learned I am madam not by virtue of my age but as a sign of respect. People with less experience using their English nervously call me "sir," aware only that it is an honorific, not one that is gender based.

"I need some cookies. To bring to Kuzoo, for the *Early Bird* show," I say, somewhat apologetically because of the early hour. As it would be with most merchants on the planet, why I need what I need isn't as important as the fact that I am here to buy. But I also announce this to remind him that I'm not some random tourist. Not that many tourists are typically on the streets of Thimphu, at any time of day. But here, as in other places around the world, if you look like an outsider, prices can rise quickly.

"Of course, madam."

I've been stopping in nearly every day for weeks now, and usually buy from his sister, who hasn't yet arrived.

There are no fresh baked goods in this store. None of the few venues that do bake are open yet. So I choose a package of peanut-butter-filled cookies from India. The radio jockey hosting the *Early Bird* show today loves those. I need a snack to soothe my stomach, so I grab some plain digestive biscuits. I buy a box of tea bags, black, just in case the studio's supply of tea is locked up. I hand the man a 100 ngultrum note, a little over $2 with the current exchange rate, and get back 40 ngultrum in change.

The streets are coming to life. Some passersby return my smile warmly, if shyly. A few—the minority—don't look so happy that I'm here, and glower a bit. Most children see me as an excuse to practice their English, and they giggle when I respond to their spirited shouts of "hello." After I'd been here a week, a few kids who hang out near this particular store started running after me whenever I walked down the street, shouting "Kuzoo FM, Kuzoo FM."

There is a slight hill up the road a bit, and a steeper one when you turn at the Dutch-sponsored dairy station, the only place in town where you can buy fresh milk—if you bring your own container. Men and women and kids leave clutching Coca-Cola bottles filled chalky white. Dogs roam this side street, as if the gates of the pound have been busted down. (Soon I learn there isn't a pound, and that's part of the problem. Stories abound about people being swarmed or bitten by the strays.)

As I make my way back to the upper road, I'm breathless, both from the altitude and from the steep incline. On the far side of the street, directly across from the Bhutan Chamber of Commerce and Industry, adjacent to the Danish embassy and in front of Bangladesh's, sits the place where I spend my days.

By the time I march up the narrow flight of stairs to the studio, I've had quite a workout, and I've walked only about a mile. With the cookies in hand, I feel suddenly aware of the sensation I'm experiencing. I'm falling in love with Bhutan.

THE BUDDHISTS WOULD SAY that everything you need is right here, within you. There's no need to seek outside yourself for the answers. Nothing—no place, no person—can complete you or make you happy. The longer I live, the more I see and experience, the more certain I am that this is true. And yet, occasionally, a shakeup in location, or in the company you keep, can touch you in just the right way, awaken something inside you. At precisely the moment you need it.

Timing and circumstance collided to ignite this love affair. It didn't hurt that I had a lifelong fascination with anyplace in the throes of evolution. The college I'd attended had been around for only a decade when I first enrolled. The most exciting work experiences I'd had were with start-up ventures, companies where we made it all up as we went along. In many ways, Bhutan was a start-up, too—an ancient, once-secluded kingdom transitioning now at warp speed. A new king, a new democracy about to dawn, a new constitution. The twin cultural influences of technology and media were spreading rapidly, challenging and eroding Bhutan's very foundation. It would need to quickly adjust to interruptions from the world outside its borders, the world that had been blocked out for so long.

Being in Bhutan today felt like taking a ride back in a time machine, to that transformative era that much of the rest of the developed world had experienced a hundred years prior, before trains and cars and electronic communications changed how we were connected to one another, and so, the very rhythm of life. And yet, this moment for Bhutan was entirely different. This never-colonized kingdom was geographically landlocked, but given its skill at isolation, it might have been a remote island; the changes and developments here, now that they were permitted, were accelerating at a frenzied pace.

There was another, more important reason I'd become so enamored. It had to do with the people here: the cadence of their speech, their wry sense of humor, their odd brand of innocence, and their newfound worldliness spurred by the infiltration of their borders. The fierce pride they had in their history, in their kings. The pace of their days. The superstitions and deep spirit of Buddhism that informed everything they did. Everyone here knew everyone, or at least knew how to find the person you were looking for. Each person had a unique role. Karma was the artist and Kinley the newspaper-man and Pema the head of the environmental group. There was a feeling of interconnectedness, a sense of community, a camaraderie I'd experienced only on a college campus.

The non-Bhutanese I'd been meeting were a key factor in my reaction, too. I'd never met such adventurous souls, people so committed to living life outside the sphere of comfort and routine most aspire to have. I'd become friends with a handful of other outsiders: a divorced nurse from Canada who had hit the road once her daughters were grown, volunteering her skills in countries that needed it. A midwestern couple about the same age as she, committed to doing the same. They and the others I met were active participants in the world. People who went out of their way, really out of their way, to meet other humans unlike themselves, and see how they really lived. Not from a hotel or a tour bus, and most certainly not on a screen. No View-Master living for them.

As a member of the demographic majority in the United States, I also appreciated the bizarre, humbling wonder of be-ing a minority in Bhutan. A minority most people here had trouble identifying. I liked it, even in the rare times it was un-comfortable. The better-educated citizens know about the United States, and a subset of those know it well enough to identify specific, obscure locations, often places they'd gone to study. But the majority of the people know only that you look different—that you aren't Bhutanese. Being there put the United States in a completely different perspective, the way staring into the vastness of a natural wonder like the Grand Canyon does. The United States may be the superpower, and the center of your universe, but it isn't the center of everyone else's. More reminders that the world does not revolve around one way of eating, thinking, being.

Loving Bhutan is, like so many love affairs, complicated. It's not like becoming a Francophile, or a fan of Hawaii, or using every vacation to visit all the national parks or Major League Baseball stadiums or NASCAR racetracks in the United States. Bhutan is not a checklist kind of vacation on which you hit the hot spots, not an easy place, not a luxurious place to adore. It has many flaws, and it is rife with contradictions. It doesn't boast the typical assets common to vacation destinations, such as plentiful sunshine twelve months a year, or expert chefs who avail themselves of the bountiful fields (if you happen to be a fan of chanterelles and fiddlehead ferns, time your visit during the short summer season when they are as plentiful as kudzu). Bhutan may be simple and unspoiled, in the way rural America might have been at the turn of the twentieth century. With a tour guide beside you, it may seem like the promised Shangri-la, some sort of fairy tale, with endless miles of untouched land and vistas of mountains and trees so lush it's hard to imagine they're real. But it is poor. It is rough. And the sum total of the good and the bad and the strange combine to render Bhutan captivating and magnificent.

THE APRIL 1914 issue of *National Geographic* magazine is filled with advertisements for modern innovations that herald an era of convenience and speed and eroding boundaries: motorcars and tires, round-the-world steamship vacations, newfangled conveniences such as vacuum cleaners and electricity-powered refrigerators and canned soup. But the eighty-eight-page photo-essay that is central to this particular issue is the Rosetta stone for an odd chapter in Bhutan's history. It offered the magazine's 330,000 subscribers the first-ever introduction to the kingdom, a place only a handful of outsiders had seen with their own eyes and few others had even considered.

The title of the story was dreamily evocative: "Castles in the Air." Its author was a British political officer named John Claude White, commander of the Indian Empire. White had initially been assigned to oversee neighboring Sikkim, and participated in the failed 1903 British invasion of Tibet, euphemistically referred to in the history books as the Younghusband Expedition. It was during that mission that White met Ugyen Wangchuck, a powerful Bhutanese figure who had managed to unite his people after years of internal strife. Wangchuck wanted to ensure his country remained independent of its powerful and enormous neighbors. Keeping the peace with the British agent for India was one way to maintain sovereignty. When Wangchuck was installed as Bhutan's first king in 1907, White was his invited guest dignitary.

In the article, White details how with an entourage of "coolies, elephants, mules, ponies, donkeys, yaks, [and] oxen," he traipsed around the region that India had dismissed as a "tangle of jungle-clad and fever-stricken hills," "a region not sufficiently characteristic to merit special exploration." He found plenty to explore—and document. With a thirteen-by-ten-foot camera rig that took three mules to carry, he exposed dozens of plate-glass images of pristine mountain vistas, as well as of the king and his subjects. Many of these delicate negatives improbably survived the rocky months-long journey around and out of the country.

His descriptions of the untouched land before him read like a dispatch from another universe, as if he were observing another species: "The Bhutanese are fine, tall, well-developed men, with an open, honest cast of face, and the women are comely, clean, and well dressed and excellent housekeepers and managers," he wrote. "It is impossible to find words to express adequately the wonderful beauty and variety of scenery I met with during my journeys, the grandeur of the magnificent snow peaks, and the picturesqueness and charm of the many wonderful jongs, or forts, and other buildings I came across; but I hope my photographs may. . . ."

No doubt his haunting images of frozen waterfalls and water-propelled prayer wheels; of a smiling, barefoot, *gho*-clad king; and of an odd, rare goat-antelope called a takin captivated many an imagination. They certainly caught the eye of a *National Geographic* reader in El Paso, Texas, a woman named Kathleen Worrell. And they might have languished collecting dust on her bookshelf had the Texas State School of Mines and Metallurgy not burned down a few years later.

Mrs. Worrell, wife of the school's dean, had noted a resemblance in the photos between the landscape of her city and this country called Bhutan. And so in the aftermath of the school's destruction, she convinced her husband that the college should be rebuilt to reflect the style of the kingdom's unique structures.

Now, in modern times, no one could possibly mistake the Franklin Mountains for the Himalayas. The rugged rockiness of the El Paso landscape and the lush Kingdom of Bhutan bear almost no resemblance to each other—except for the fact that each shares borders with an enormous neighbor. The mountains that cut through El Paso are grayish brown, rough like elephant skin, and rarely see snow. They're tiny in scope—just twenty-three miles long, with an elevation at its very highest of just around eight thousand feet. The majestic white peaks of the Himalayas tower to twenty-nine thousand feet and span six countries—nearly fifteen hundred miles. Not to mention they also play a critical role in nature: They feed three major water sources that support more than a billion people.

But in the year 1914, with black-and-white still photographs the only window on the world, large-scale commercial air flight but a dream, and no cameras perched on satellites providing vistas accessible from your laptop computer, it is possible to see why Mrs. Worrell saw a connection between these two places. Why she felt compelled to encourage the re-creation of a land she had never seen and would never get to is another matter, a mystery that can never be answered, since little else is known about her, and no heirs exist to convey any legends.

The commissioned architects took their cues from the only source they had, all that existed in the world at the time: Mr. White's photographs of the landscape and his accompanying descriptions in "Castles in the Air": "This view gives a very good idea of the sloping architecture of the walls and the projecting roofs made of split pine," he wrote, never realizing this detail would later help when blueprints for replicas would be drawn. "All the walls have a distinct camber, and . . . the windows are of a peculiar form, with the sides sloping inwards. Each building is two stories high and is painted . . . a dull light gray on the lower story, with a broad band of madder red above."

The drawings rendered for the creation of the buildings in El Paso look very much like the real thing; they were likely also the first of their kind ever drafted. The Bhutanese themselves, to this day, work from memory, not blueprints. Another major difference in the El Paso construction was the use of nails. No such hardware was used in Bhutan at the time; roofs were kept in place with rocks, doors hung on sturdy wooden hinges. Traditional Bhutanese structures didn't have glass in the windows, either.

The reconstructed Texas State School of Mines and Metallurgy debuted in 1917, with sixty students and perhaps the most unusual architecture of any school in the United States. Over the past century, the name of the university has changed twice, and its size has ballooned, but its looks have become increasingly Bhutanese, except for one brief period: After a new building emerged from the wraps of construction in the late sixties to reveal its discordantly modern style, one local wrote to the paper expressing concern about the departure. It was so out of place that in 1971 it was "Bhutanized" to better fit the landscape and ease critics. Never again would the university's administrators allow such a deviation to occur.

As a result, the school now known as the University of Texas at El Paso is an acid-trippy agglomeration of ninety buildings spread across a 366-acre campus, each building a slightly different interpretation of Bhutan's architecture. Even the 1,600-car parking garage and the guard shacks at the entryways to campus are housed in Bhutanese-style sloping-orange-roofed structures. So are the automatic teller machines—an unintentional bit of irony, since only a handful of ATMs exist in Bhutan, and most people don't use them. A Hilton Garden Inn built on the edge of campus continues the theme.

This modern Bhutan is punctuated by occasional flourishes of authenticity. A twenty-foot imported altar and a twelve-by-sixteen-foot religious scroll known as a *thangka* provide a colorful display behind the espresso bar that greets you in the lobby of the libary. Bhutanese prayer flags flutter behind the campus's Centennial Museum; the front of the building is flanked by enormous urns styled to resemble Bhutanese prayer wheels. Right across the street, on off-campus soil, the suburban-strip-mall style that dominates so much of the American landscape resumes.

For the most part, if you stop someone in and around the campus and ask why UTEP looks the way it does, they'll look at you as if that's the most spectacularly odd question. As far as they know, it just does, that's all. Some are aware of the university's connection to Bhutan, but most have no idea, really, where that is—or why a tiny Asian kingdom they've never heard of happened to influence and infiltrate the school's architecture.

Decades after the death of Mrs. Worrell, one curious member of the university's administration took it upon himself to delve into the aesthetic roots of the campus. It was the sixties, a time when Bhutan was still shuttered to the outside world. Before Internet connections allowed speedy research, this man, Dale Walker, obsessively sleuthed addresses, packed up photographs of the university buildings, and sent them along with queries to people around the world who might authenticate the look of the school. His most important correspondent was the queen to the third king. Her response arrived on stationery as fine as tissue paper, a year after Mr. Walker had first sent his letter.

"Dear Mr. Walker," she wrote, in her letter dated December 4, 1967. "It is thrilling and deeply moving to see a great new university built in faraway America inspired by Bhutanese architecture. Only the topmost windows are unlike Bhutanese windows, as here they are made entirely of carved, painted wood. I think your new university buildings are beautiful, combining modern design so harmoniously with ancient

Bhutanese architecture. I wish our new buildings in Bhutan could be so finely built."

In later correspondence, the queen expressed hope that Bhutan might someday work more closely with the university. She even asked if they might enroll a student. The answer was yes. Jigme Dorji, nicknamed Jimmy by his classmates, became the first student from Bhutan sent to study in the United States. He graduated with an engineering degree in 1978.

Mr. Walker also solicited validation from the few other Westerners who had traveled to the country. Burt Todd was the first American to visit Bhutan, in 1949, after befriending the soon-to-be queen while they were students at Oxford. He confirmed for Mr. Walker that the forts of Bhutan were "almost identical" to the buildings in El Paso. In 1959, journalist Desmond Doig was the first allowed to report from the country. He told Mr. Walker he had believed the pictures he'd received were of new construction in Thimphu: "When I was told they were American campus buildings, I was genuinely amazed."

John Claude White most likely never knew what he inspired, for he passed away in 1918—just one year after the first Bhutanese-themed buildings opened in El Paso. Kathleen Worrell could never have imagined just how much she did make her corner of Texas resemble the Himalayan kingdom she admired but never got to see. But because of them both, and the power of the press that invisibly united them, Bhutan and El Paso are forever, indelibly, linked.

THE LINKS GROW ever stronger. Over the past twenty years, the university's president, Dr. Diana Natalicio, has cultivated the school's relationship with the kingdom, welcoming more students from Bhutan each year. UTEP has even started to market its unique identity with brochures that proclaim it "Bhutan on the Border." The kingdom's own borders have been penetrated by a growing number of characters, and among this diverse constituency, one thing is certain: Anyone who comes close to the kingdom falls under its spell.

Some of those who have become enthralled have gone on to play a critical role in Bhutan's history. A Jesuit priest named Father William Mackey created the first high school in Bhutan in the sixties, and began a long friendship and study exchange between Bhutan and his native Canada. The late Michael Aris, who as a young man tutored members of the royal family, published several important books on Bhutanese history at the behest of the third king. Controversial insights into Bhutan were revealed by Nari Rustomji, an Indian advisor to Sikkim. His book was long banned in the kingdom for its controversial frankness about a dark aspect of Bhutan's history: the plot by the mistress of the third king to claim royal power for the children he'd fathered with her. The mystically inclined actress Shirley MacLaine made a trip to Bhutan as a guest of the starstruck acting prime minister in 1968, and wrote about her spirit-seeking adventures in *Don't Fall Off the Mountain,* another work long prohibited in the kingdom.

Since Bhutan opened its borders, stories have abounded about alliances great and small, between outsiders who befriended the powerful of Bhutan and those who connected with regular people. Bhutanese love to tell stories about single, careerist Western women who visit on vacation and fall for their tour guides—suggesting that they couldn't find men back home and couldn't help being swept off their feet by the chivalrous Bhutanese. This kind of forbidden love affair is the basis of a book by a Canadian woman named Jamie Zeppa, who worked twenty years ago as a teacher in eastern Bhutan and fell in love—and had a child—with one of her students. After a stint as a golf pro at the Royal Thimphu Golf Course, Rick Lipsey returned home to create the Bhutan Youth Golf Association, which for years dispatched two pros a year to the kingdom to teach kids—and adults—the game. So inspired was digital photography expert Michael Hawley by the visual splendor of the country, he published a book of photographs about it that's also the world's largest, at five feet by seven feet and 133 pounds, and costs $10,000 a copy.

Among many of the modern fans of Bhutan there is something of a competitive spirit to prove one's devotion to the place—and one's power to access members of the royal family and other VIPs. A kind of "My Bhutan is bigger than your Bhutan, my attachment greater." These boasts have to do with not just the desire to help the Bhutanese but the fierce need to stay connected to the land and its people after leaving it, wanting to attach somehow to Bhutan rather than just love it purely and wholly—allowing that love alone to be enough. Bhutan gives you so much, makes you aware of all you have, that it inspires you to somehow mark the territory, claim it as your own.

With each incursion, each friendship, each exchange, though, a tiny bit of the old Bhutan melts away, and a new and different one emerges. Each of us who loves it—no matter how that love is manifested—permanently changes it.

7

THE SYMPHONY OF LOVE

Ngawang, Pema, and Pink were bickering and giggling conspiratorially in the center of the Kuzoo work area. Each had a piece of paper in hand; it looked as if they were working on a script. Their idea of sophisticated audio production was to divvy up the text and record tag-team, one line each.

"Herpa-tett-ez B," said Pink, struggling with the words in front of her. "Herps."

Word was out that Kuzoo would run free ads to show potential advertisers the power of radio, in the hope of one day attracting paying customers. The initial funding from the sale of the king's BMW gave the station a cushion of security, so making more cash to pay the bills wasn't yet an urgent necessity. Which was a good thing because the bulk of the "ads" on the station still came from the government ministries, with announcements about holiday closures and requests for bids on projects. None of the businesses in town were used to advertising, nor did they have the budget. Just putting a sign in front of the store was considered a frivolous investment, and even those signs that were installed were more about function than about competition. Proprietors hoped people stopped in, but if they didn't, no problem. Such was life in a Buddhist kingdom where Gross National Happiness, and not a grab for cash, was the guiding principle.

A messenger appeared at lunchtime from the Health Ministry to deliver the script for the new ad. Valentine's Day was looming and schools were out on their two-month winter break. This meant extra nights of parties for kids with time on their hands, and the potential for hormones gone awry.

" 'Sexually transmitted diseases exist among us,' " Pink read slowly, deliberately.

"Herps," struggled Pink. "Herpah-tet-ahs B. 'Sexually transmitted diseases exist among us.' "

"So romantic!" cackled Pema.

"CONE-dom," Ngawang intoned. " 'These infections are all passed through sex without a CONE-dom.' "

"No, no, no, CAHN-dom," insisted Pema. Her love of reading, or perhaps it was her encyclopedic knowledge of *Sex and the City,* made her proficient with the script: " 'Gonorrhea, syphilis, and HIV/AIDS are all around us.' "

A cell phone rang. The tune was "Summer Nights" from *Grease.*

" 'These infections are all passed through sex without a CONE-dom,' " Ngawang tried again, her voice tentative. Her struggle with the word made rubbers sound very formal.

"CAHN-dom," shouted Pema, even though the girls were sitting right next to one other. She was impatient, and a much quicker study than just about anyone else at Kuzoo.

"How do you say this word?" Ngawang asked me, pointing to the script.

"Pema's right," I said. "Cahn-dom."

"Herps," repeated Pink.

I walked over and peered over her shoulder. "Okay, no, it's HERP-ees," I said. "And that other word is hep-a-ti-tis." No one asked what these afflictions were, which might have been because they knew, but could also have been mere disinterest.

"'You cannot tell whether someone has an STD by looking at them. That is why you have to use a condom EVERY TIME,'" proclaimed Pema, her tone that of the smartest girl in the class. "'Happy Valentine's Day!'"

"'Happy Valentine's Day,'" Pink and Ngawang echoed the last line of the script, which they would all read in unison. The three of them burst into laughter again. Then they shut the door and shushed me so they could record.

It doesn't take much to create a radio program: a micro-phone or two, a mixing board, a transmitter, and a relatively quiet room. That was about all Kuzoo had, along with a cou-ple of faded Backstreet Boys and Spice Girls posters taped up on the walls, and an on-air sign mounted outside the studio. Its lighting mechanism worked about half the time, but almost everyone ignored it anyway. They'd just barrel into the studio regardless of whether someone was transmitting live.

Kuzoo FM was what most radio stations in the United States hadn't been for a very long time, an anything-goes bullhorn to the people. A core staff of paid radio jockeys kept the station going, but anyone who was interested could just show up and contribute, however they wished. You could bring in music. You could hang out in the studio with whoever was hosting the show (though eventually there were rules prohibiting *that*). You could answer phones. Volunteers weren't just welcome; they were encouraged. Even the typical college station in the United States had long ago ceased to be so egalitarian.

A highfalutin promotional campaign hadn't been necessary to clue everyone in on the existence of Kuzoo. People started stopping by the compound that housed the station as soon as it launched, hanging out to see how things worked, answering phones or otherwise inserting themselves into the free-for-all. What might have been transmitted around the town or the country by word-of-mouth just six months earlier could now be communicated instantaneously, thanks to the magic powers of broadcasting. And just as the citizens of Thimphu or any village in Bhutan helped out one another, without question, the people of Kuzoo unfailingly broadcast whatever messages came their way.

"Folder with important papers lost by the Hong Kong market," read the message submitted by a worried-looking man who showed up on the grounds one day. "Reward. Call 17-27-15-98."

"Floodwaters rising near the *dzong,*" said the Ministry of Home and Cultural Affairs. "Please leave the area immediately until further notice."

"Little boy lost by Changlimithang Stadium," the police called to report. "Please claim him at the satellite police office in town." Twenty minutes later came word that the child had been picked up, and a follow-up on-air announcement ensued. Being comfortable with writing copy quickly wasn't a bad skill to have around here.

Doing quick bits of rewriting, helping with the pronunciation of English words, and sharing midday meals with Sir

Tenzin were shaping up to be the mainstays of my contribution to Kuzoo. As each day passed, it became more apparent that I was little more than an accessory, not expected to do much in particular, really, besides be exactly who I was: the experienced volunteer consultant from afar. Any hope I might have had of inspiring these young broadcasters to use their new radio station as a tool to prepare for their impending democracy was folly. Of far greater interest to them was where to download Destiny's Child and Alicia Keys on the Internet, especially given the slow connection speeds and dearth of computers.

To give myself a mission, I'd assumed what I saw as an equally important role: Kuzoo den mother. Lacking any formal duties, I'd sit around the station from very early morning till early evening, observing, offering suggestions, reading what came in over the fax, and making sure everyone ate, even though what I was feeding them was hardly food. Apart from spicy yak-meat pizza and cookies or chips, there wasn't much in the way of take-out, not to mention common culinary ground—the pizza was only a slightly older and less exotic presence in Thimphu than I. I could educate by osmosis. Most of the staff—indeed, many Bhutanese—hadn't interacted much with anyone from so far away.

My lunchtime discussions with Sir Tenzin about copyright violation, music royalties, and licensing fees proved futile. He was convinced, no matter what I said, that international laws could not possibly apply to Kuzoo.

"Who would bother coming after us here in Bhutan, anyway?" he'd counter dismissively.

While I suspected he was right, and that only a chance luxury vacation by a music industry executive who happened to turn on a radio might bust Kuzoo's illegal goings-on, I felt it my obligation to point out the importance of respecting intellectual property.

Kuzoo's desire to become more professional and its decision to import an outsider to help make that transition was understandable. It wasn't uncommon for the radio jockeys, none of whom had appeared live on the air before, to forget the basics, such as turning on the microphone. A few, racked by nerves, compensated on the air by sounding a bit comatose when they spoke—a strange contrast to the bright bits of music they loved to play.

These kinds of mistakes could be easily solved with a little adult supervision and cheerleading. And in addition to providing both in person, I convinced Pema to ration a piece of printer paper from her Fort Knox of a supply cabinet, typed out in giant, bold forty-eight-point type a list of recommendations to get them started, then posted my rules inside the studio:

Before you go on the air, please remember to:

- **Take a deep breath**
- **CHECK that the microphone is on**
- **Remind listeners that they're tuned in to Kuzoo FM 90**
- **Encourage listeners to email us or call in or come volunteer—it's THEIR station**
- **Have fun! Enjoy yourself while on the air!**
  (After all, this IS fun, isn't it?)

All of these were reminders I often needed myself back home, as did my beleaguered colleagues there. But at work in

Los Angeles, we didn't get the pleasure of playing Foo Fighters and Jay-Z.

ONE OF THE GOALS on the list sent to me before my arrival, to inspire staff and volunteers alike to be interested in reporting news, seemed simple enough. Given the impending democratic elections, it also made sense; the intent of this station was to give the youth of Bhutan the tools to examine and monitor their government-to-be. So far, that had translated into a five-minute "newscast" each evening, which amounted to nothing more than the rewriting of items from the newspapers and the Bhutan Broadcasting Service. With Sir Tenzin wrangling everyone he could find into the conference room, I conducted my first—and last—formal workshop at Kuzoo.

"WHAT IS NEWS?" I scrawled on the giant whiteboard I'd asked Sir Tenzin to buy for the workroom. It was there to encourage people to share their ideas. (To date, I seemed to be the only person using it.) Twenty participants were dutifully in attendance. Perhaps fearful there might be a quiz later, they wrote down every word I uttered about the Five Ws and H that were the foundation of journalism.

"Who. What. When. Where. Why. And How," I explained. "These are the elements of every story. Your job is to ask the questions and find out the answers."

No one said a word, and even when assigned the task of telling a story, the only person who seemed to understand, or be interested in, the exercise was Sir Pema, Kuzoo's second in command.

He was a shy man with a round face and glasses; his bookish demeanor, not his looks, made him seem older than thirty-five.

Sir Pema had come from a remote village in the far east of Bhutan, and had been chosen to attend a Jesuit school in India where the best and brightest of Bhutan got sent for their educations. He had gone on to earn a master's degree in education in Canada. His curiosity had been aided and abetted by new technologies that fueled his quest for news and information. He'd wax poetic about James Bond, the X-Men, or Johnny Depp and seemed shocked when I couldn't converse about the latest Hollywood blockbusters. First thing every morning at the office, as soon as he could get online, he read the *New York Times;* at home at night he was glued to CNN with near-religious fervor. (The fact that I'd worked at both places upped my street cred with him.) He'd quote Maureen Dowd and "King Larry" as if he'd been hanging around at a bar with them the night before.

"*Who?* Stray dogs. *What?* How many of them there are. *When?* Right now. *Where?* Thimphu. *Why?* No family planning. *How?* That's the problem," he said. Sir Pema appeared to possess the keen powers of cultural observation necessary to succeed in the news business, powers that were otherwise lacking among the Kuzoo staff. Daily life was something they took for granted; the ongoing battle with strays wasn't really an issue to them. It was just the way things were. This had to do a bit with the Buddhist belief that things simply are the way they are, and a lot to do with the unwavering Bhutanese devotion to authority. Reverence for that seemed embedded in them genetically, just like the adoration of spicy hot food.

It was also, I was learning, considered rude to ask too many questions. Other than Sir Pema, my pupils appeared utterly disinterested in the idea of taking out a microphone and questioning the world around them. It was clear they were present only because they were told to be. My news session wrapped up with a thud. I decided that during the rest of my days here, I'd resort to subtler teaching methods than the classroom.

The next afternoon, the utility of the radio station for something other than the transmission of pop music became very clear to all. Sir Tenzin walked into the station with a thick document tucked under his arm.

"Class Ten results," he announced, and he dropped the document in front of the female Pema with a hot-off-the-presses flourish. "Announce on the air that they're here." The day the scores were released was one of the most important of the year, even if it did fall square in the middle of winter recess.

Pema, aka Oprah, obediently stepped into the studio, faded out the music that was playing, and, in her best "breaking news" voice, informed the people of Thimphu that the all-important test scores had been released. And that Kuzoo would be happy to give callers their results.

Class Ten grades determined whether a student could continue high school for free. Those who failed had to pony up close to $1,000 a year to finish their degrees at one of the handful of private schools in Bhutan, or had to study across the border in India, a more common fate. Given that the average midcareer civil servant took home a salary of $350 a month, coming up with the cash to pay for an education was simply out of the question. Failing Class Ten could decide your fate forever. Those who couldn't complete two more years of education could never hope to get a modern job, behind a desk. Perhaps they'd even have to stay in the village to work in the fields. And with a population of children that swelled each year, competition for slots in schools as well as for employment was intensifying. The sweet Kuzoo driver, Kesang, must be from a particularly poor family, I deduced; since he didn't speak English, he must have had to drop out of school very young to work.

Instantly, the phones lit up. Students—spared the trek to their schools to find out their scores—jammed the lines. Tiny voices identified themselves and asked to learn their fate: "We-sel Wangmo, *la*. Motithang High School. Did I pass?"

For two days, the staff and volunteers of Kuzoo fielded nervous requests for results. Kids even started calling in from outside the broadcast area; word had spread that Kuzoo had a copy of this important document.

But that wasn't the only thing keeping Kuzoo busy.

As IN SO many places, February is a dreary time of year in Bhutan. The difference is that the skies, when the gray does melt away, are perfectly blue and framed by snowcapped Himalayan peaks that make you feel as if you're in a heavenly dream sequence. Assuming heaven also features tooting horns and foul emissions from the cars that jam the streets below. And thousands of those scruffy, barking stray dogs.

One thing bolstering winter spirits in Thimphu this particular February—aside from the first measurable snowfall in the city in two years—was Kuzoo FM's Valentine's Day contest. The young volunteers behind the effort had dubbed it grandly: the Symphony of Love. Two free dinners for two at the only hamburger joint in town were offered as a prize. Listeners were asked to call in and sing love songs on the air, then vote on their favorites. The meals would be awarded to the two most popular singers. It was the first time a contest of this kind had been held anywhere in the kingdom.

To build excitement, a taped announcement, recorded by Pema in the supply closet, ran a dozen times a day.

This goes out to all the LOVE-birds who are planning to go out on Valentine's Day. Boy, do we have a treat for you! All expense paid for two couples at the Zone. You heard it right! Show your love how much you care. The person who gets voted the most wins. Call us. Text in your votes. Or express in words by writing a poem to us—we will be waiting!

Every night at 7:30 p.m. for the three weeks leading up to February 14, listeners transformed Kuzoo into a public karaoke bar, crooning and croaking their renditions of love songs over the airwaves. The irony of a bunch of Buddhists celebrating a holiday that started in honor of a Christian saint was completely lost on the city. Listeners didn't seem to care, either, that each evening's serenade was generally more cacophonous than symphonic. Kuzoo's two phone lines jammed up immediately with singers and voters alike.

A ratty old notebook, pages shy of being completely covered in ink, was used for the tabulation. Whoever was hanging around would answer the phone and strike a tally beside the number assigned to each contestant. The question of accuracy wasn't an issue. Everyone trusted their system—and one another. PricewaterhouseCoopers would never have approved.

The idea for all this was, of course, firmly rooted in that

fine import called *American Idol*. Bhutan was not immune to the fever for *Idol* that was consuming the rest of the world. People rushed home each night to see the latest installment, beamed into Bhutan on a time delay via satellite on an Indian TV channel. In this country where television was still a relatively new phenomenon, any show that even appeared to be a live broadcast whipped the public into a frenzy. And when it had to do with the glitz of a Hollywood so far away, allowing for discussions over people with very un-Bhutanese names, such as LaKisha Jones and Jordin Sparks, all the better.

No less popular this February was the subject of who had sung on Kuzoo. In shops and offices and on the main street in town, everyone buzzed about it, bragged in the morning if someone they knew had been heard on the air the night before. As a representative of Kuzoo, I'd be offered unsolicited commentary on the previous evening's callers anywhere I went. "The man from last night, not very good. The girl, excellent," one man told me. "And that fellow who dedicated his song to *both* his girlfriends—very funny!"

The Symphony of Love ratcheted up to another level the already feverish adoration of Kuzoo.

THE CONTEST, PREDICTABLY, had its scolding detractors—chief among them one of the elder advisors to the station. Madame Carolyn was a sixty-something-year-old woman from Britain who had been imported decades earlier to tutor members of the royal family. She was one of a handful of outsiders on whom Bhutanese citizenship had been bestowed—an honor of which she was understandably proud, and which she flaunted to each newcomer she encountered. Madame Carolyn

declared modestly that she didn't understand why "HM"—
cheeky, irreverent shorthand tossed into conversation by those
privileged few who had personal access to His Majesty—had
asked her, an "old hag," to have anything to do with the station. In fact, she took quickly to the microphone, zealously
taping segments about classical music, and little educational
bits about English grammar and vocabulary. "Word of the
day: unreconstructed," her voice would trill, and then she
would go on to recite the dictionary definition. Hers was the
"eat your vegetables" portion of Kuzoo. Well-intentioned, definitely; necessary, perhaps; but nowhere near as fun as the
Pussycat Dolls and Jack Johnson.

When visitors to the station assumed I must be the Madame
Carolyn they heard on the air, I was surprised and a bit disturbed to be mistaken for this legend. It wasn't so much that
she was twenty years older than me; I didn't want to be associated with such prim behavior. What the confusion of identity
underscored was the fact that to many Bhutanese, Brits and
Americans are indistinguishable—no matter how different
we think we sound.

The idea that Kuzoo resources were being dedicated to
something other than the celebration of Bhutan disturbed Madame Carolyn.

"We should be doing a call-in show to honor His Majesty's
birthday," she scolded, lips pursed, to no one in particular.
This February 21 would be the first time the nation would celebrate the new king's date of birth. "Or to mark Losar." Losar
was the Bhutanese New Year, which this year landed just
before the royal birthday. Both merited national holidays
that would shut down the country for days. Madame Carolyn
insisted she could not understand how young people could

prefer serenading one another with silly love songs over hon-
oring their king and their national heritage.

TWO NIGHTS BEFORE Valentine's Day, the Kuzoo volunteers
gathered in the room adjacent to the kitchen-studio to prepare
for the finale. They'd taken to shortening the contest's name:
"SOL" they called it, unaware of the decidedly unromantic
usual meaning of the acronym. A giant bag of Lay's Spicy Indian Masala potato chips was passed like a football around the
room. Several people flipped through the notepad, filled to the
edges now with strike marks. Close to two hundred people
had sung on the air. Scores of text messages carried votes to
staffers' personal cell phones—everyone in town knew someone who worked at Kuzoo. Their choices had dutifully been
recorded on the pad.

This was also the time of day when the newscast got prepared. Since it was a Monday, a day when none of the newspapers published, Ngawang had to rely on the BBS as her sole
source of information. This involved transcribing, by hand,
what had made the news that evening; the margin for error
here was high. I had tried to convince Sir Pema, Sir Tenzin's
deputy, that if all we were going to do was crib from other media, the way broadcasters back home plucked the majority of
the stories *they* reported from newspapers, we should just halt
the effort entirely. This was not a Western convention we
should emulate, I said. But the fact that this was how it was
done in the West made it all the more enticing. Sir Pema was
dedicated to the idea that there needed to be at least the es-
sence of news on Kuzoo. In his mind, it somehow offset the
pop music and gave the station at least the illusion of serious-

ness. But he stopped short of pushing the Kuzooers to go out and report for themselves.

The items that Ngawang had transcribed from the BBS newscast at the top of the hour included: a forest fire; the naming of a panel of government officials to oversee next year's elections; a hike in the price of Indian cars to twelve thousand ngultrums—about $250 each—and the revelation that the availability of low interest auto loans had swelled the number of vehicles in the kingdom to thirty thousand. After Ngawang had transcribed and then reworded these stories, I helped her comb through the copy and do a practice read. Like anyone just starting out in radio, she was self-conscious on the air. Especially since everyone you know becomes your biggest critic when they listen in. One of her uncles had ranted about her recent past performances, saying that her English was poor, while a friend had complained she was sounding "too American." I'd hoped that wasn't a dig at her affection for me.

A public service message had been faxed in, too, from the Ministry of Home and Cultural Affairs. It tied into the car stories we had to report. We changed its dreary bureaucratic-speak into zippier language:

> If you're listening to Kuzoo in your car . . . hear this:
>
> Starting next Tuesday, you might get stopped for a random emissions test. The police want to crack down on people who are not getting their cars tested for emissions. So they're going to randomly stop drivers as of February 20. Air pollution is on the rise here in Thimphu. So we hope you'll get your car tested for the sake of our air . . . and also to avoid having to pay hefty fines. This has been a public service announcement from Kuzoo FM 90.

A pretty sixteen-year-old volunteer named Lhaki piped up as she heard Ngawang rehearse.

"So glad about that," she said. She was sitting on the floor with her legs crossed, holding a guitar, long hair hanging past her shoulders, bangs brushing into her almond eyes—a Bhutanese Joni Mitchell. "My parents both bribed the emissions inspector to lie about their cars so they could pass. So selfish."

Disaffected teenage angst oozed from Lhaki's every pore. The week before she'd shown off a few sketches in her tattered notebook, each as intricate and bizarre as one of the omnipresent religious scrolls—the sacred *thangka* paintings depicting various Buddhas that hung in virtually every room in Bhutan, not far from the requisite photo of the king. Each had a Hieronymus Bosch–like quality to it, complex and colorful, playful with a tinge of sinister. One of Lhaki's drawings depicted her interpretation of Hell, accompanied by a simple declarative caption in cursive writing: *Life sucks.* On another page, in the same style, was a happy valley of love, filled with flowers and rainbows and suns, and dozens of tiny babies floating gaily around the landscape like cherubic angels floating in an Italian Renaissance painting. I wondered if she'd ever seen one or if she'd simply pulled the images from the recesses of her dark, complicated teenage brain.

"I don't want to get married or have my own kids," she said with such conviction that I wanted to fast-forward into the future to see what Lhaki did, in fact, do with her life. "Just take them in when they have no parents."

Lhaki and her constant companion, TT, were the nightly hosts of SOL. TT was a gawky, sweet boy who'd collapsed his Bhutanese name, Tshewang Toshi, into the much hipper moniker. He and Lhaki made quite a duo. Without a hint of guile, together on the air they embodied a bizarre fusion of the sweet funniness of George Burns and Gracie Allen, the edgy familiarity of a PG-rated Howard Stern and Robin Quivers, and the goofy sarcasm of Beavis and Butt-Head.

"So," I asked, "who is winning SOL at this point?" I hadn't been paying very close attention to the competition. Usually by the time it started, I'd been at the station for a dozen hours and was leaving to have a beer or dinner with one of my other ex-pat volunteer friends. People I'd met literally on the street, simply because we looked the same. We were thrown together by fate in the same strange land at the same time. These new friends gave me a sense of what was going on in the rest of Thimphu. We all faced similar challenges, and it helped to hear that Mark the physical therapist from Nebraska and his wife, Penny, an English tutor; Pam the nurse from Toronto; Ed the golf pro from Nova Scotia; and Mayumi the Web designer from Queensland, Australia, were experiencing their own workplace challenges. We also provided an excellent support system for one another regarding an equally important matter: where to find palatable, chili-free food, which we often consumed with one another. Mostly we talked about how we felt we were taking more from Bhutan than we could ever possibly give.

Lhaki was nonchalant as she ran through the front-runners in the Symphony of Love contest. "Well, there's me, there's TT, and there's a little girl."

"Wait," I said. "Run that by me again?"

"TT got the most votes, I got second most, and a little girl from Motithang got the third most. So we go on tomorrow night to play again and see who the top two winners are. I'm taking TT out if I win, and if TT wins, he's promised to take me. And if we win first and second prize, we've promised to take Thujee and Khandu along."

I had to stop for a second to make sure I'd understood Lhaki correctly.

"So you and TT have actually been *competing* in SOL? While you've been hosting it every night?"

"Yes," said Lhaki, strumming on her guitar, oblivious to my tone of voice. "Well, the other night Thujee hosted, but mostly it's been me and TT. People seem to like the live guitar."

"Does that seem right to you? That you're hosting the show and can play the guitar while you sing? You're on the air all through the evening . . ."

Lhaki looked up at me now, her eyes widening with confusion. It was clear she didn't understand my inquisition. "Well, sure. We've worked hardest on the contest, so it is only fair that we get the hamburgers."

This had the makings of a public-relations disaster. Sir Tenzin had convinced the newspapers to cover the overwhelming success of SOL, including the grand finale. When the reporters found out that the winner and runner-up of the contest actually worked at the station, the credibility Kuzoo was establishing would go down the tubes. Or maybe I was projecting. Maybe no one would notice or care. That possibility was even more distressing.

My already queasy stomach interrupted this stream of worried thoughts by announcing its distress with a loud burble. This had been a "bad food day." What I needed right now was the comfort of my home bathroom, not the closet-size commode at Kuzoo with the toilet that rarely flushed.

Ngawang asked Kesang to give me a ride home in the Kuzoo van. As we drove, I frantically dialed Sir Tenzin's mobile number with the cell phone she had scrounged up to lend me. No answer. There is no voice mail in Bhutan, so leaving a message wasn't possible. Just moments after Kesang dropped me off, Sir Tenzin materialized at the door of my apartment, entering the room with his swirl of urgency and drama.

"They tell me you're sick. What do you need? Do you need to go to hospital?" I wondered if news of a sick person had traveled as quickly here before the mobile phone. Most likely, yes. A sick person was always cause for concern, particularly when it was a guest from afar.

"Thank you, sir. Really, I don't need anything. But that's not what I was calling you about. There's a problem with the Symphony of Love . . ."

"I'm very busy now, Jane," Sir Tenzin said as he carefully began to wrap up an afternoon hit of *doma*. I braced myself for the awful smell that was inevitable once he started sucking on it; I wasn't sure my stomach could stand it just now. "Can't you just take care of it?"

Sir Tenzin was like a lot of men I'd met over the course of my career, one of those "big picture" thinkers. Details were not his strong suit; ideas were. So was tossing out those ideas and commanding the staff to execute them. He loved the buzz the Symphony of Love was getting, loved the kudos around town, but had little interest in or worry about its execution. Unless he happened to tune in and hear someone say something he didn't like—at which point he would roar into the station, yelling, correcting someone's grammar or on-air performance.

"No, I'm worried about something and I need your help. I just found out that two of the three people in the finals for SOL . . . work for Kuzoo."

It didn't immediately register for Sir Tenzin that this posed any sort of problem. He looked like he was about to shrug and say "So what?" But my demeanor forced him to pause. He nodded for me to go on.

I reminded him of the series of anticorruption spots the government had been running in the newspapers and on the BBS, encouraging citizens to report any cronyism or swindling that appeared to be taking place.

"Sir Tenzin, they could make an example out of Kuzoo. Maybe the stakes aren't as big, but the principle's the same. And we're going to look awfully stupid if the *Bhutan Times* takes issue with our own people winning the contest."

The Symphony of Love, to no one else but me, was a living metaphor for the upcoming parliamentary election. (Whose exact date, like the king's coronation, was still under review by royal astrologers.) A time to teach the youth not just about self-expression—creative and democratic—but also about right and wrong. If they thought it was okay to stack the deck in a contest involving love songs and hamburgers, well, who knew what would happen when they went to the voting booth?

Sir Tenzin understood. "Okay, okay, let's have a meeting. You can explain."

"But I need you to be there and back me up, sir." As a volunteer and not their real boss, my reprimand might not hold

as much weight. As soon as Sir Tenzin agreed, I excused myself so I could run down the stairs to the bathroom.

LATER THAT EVENING, the SOL team was shuttled into the
conference room that had long ago served as a living area.
That this building had once housed the foreign minister might
suggest that it was once grand. There was, however, no indica-
tion that this was true. It was hard to imagine this was ever
anything but a rumpus room for a youth-oriented radio station. Taped onto the wood paneling, opposite the portrait of
the king, hung a giant yellow poster declaring Kuzoo's mission statement. Its hand lettering added to the dorm-room
feel:

> *We, the youth, must keep ourselves informed.*
> *We should arm ourselves with the knowledge to make our*
> *   own futures brighter.*
> *Youth is temporary and fleeting but the foundations we*
> *   build today will decide how bright the prospects will*
> *   be for the rest of our lives.*
> *Kuzoo aspires to be the voice of the youth of Bhutan.*
> *Kuzoo aspires to inform the youth of Bhutan.*
> *Kuzoo is the youth of Bhutan.*
> *Kuzoo is ours; the future is ours.*

A taped recording of that message, read by a sampling of
Kuzoo's most youthful volunteers, ran at the start of each
broadcast day. No one seemed to be able to name the author
of those words. I suspected it was the handiwork of Madame

Carolyn. It didn't seem likely that anyone else, particularly a young person, could possibly have written it.

"Okay, okay, everyone, thank you for coming," Sir Tenzin said, standing before the group. Fearful of his notorious temper, everyone quickly quieted down. "I need your attention to an urgent matter."

Watching him work the crowd, I wondered whether he would get the political bug and run for office when the time came for elections. Sir Tenzin was at his most charming when groups of visitors toured the studio. If he could sit still long enough, he'd have made an effusive on-air personality.

"Madam Jane here is going to make an important announcement."

I stayed seated on one of the frayed upholstered benches in the room, to appear casual, to defuse my message. The room was so silent that when my stomach gurgled loudly, I wondered if everyone in the room could hear it.

"First of all, I wanted to say how great it's been to see all of Thimphu get so excited about SOL. The whole town's been talking about it, as you know, and that's a great sign of how successful you've made Kuzoo. So congratulations for that."

Thujee led everyone in a cheer: "S-O-L! S-O-L!"

He'd just graduated from high school and was anxiously waiting to see what kind of scholarship he might get for college, his sights set on the United States or Europe. It was becoming vogue for young Bhutanese to save up so they could sit for the Test of English as a Foreign Language, administered in India, and then hope to find a scholarship or private sponsor so they could be educated in the West. For each student who got to study abroad, five more got the fever. To pass the time, Thujee had been hanging around the station a lot lately, picking up slots as a volunteer deejay. With his cheerful demeanor and sense of confidence, he was a born leader as well as radio announcer—more poised and eager than most of the paid staff. Beside TT and Lhaki, he was the most popular of the volunteers—on the air, and off.

"Quiet, please," Sir Tenzin shouted over the din. Years of being a high school administrator made him deft at teenage crowd control. He nodded for me to continue.

"You've all heard me talk about what a huge responsibility it is being on the air. You probably know that Sir Tenzin used to be a principal." I paused for dramatic effect, looking out at the group so they could nod their yeses. "Now, what if he told you that his daughter was going to win a big prize at his school, simply because she was his daughter? Would that seem fair to you?"

I knew no one would answer. Bhutanese didn't like to call attention to themselves in a crowd. So I called on Lhaki, who was sitting on the floor up front. She was still clutching her guitar, suppressing her strum.

"Umm, well, I guess not."

"Right. Even if she was really, really, really great, and really deserved the prize, that wouldn't seem right, would it?"

Thujee spoke up. "No, it would seem corrupt."

"Exactly, Thujee. And it would be hard for you to trust Sir Tenzin if he told you his daughter had to win, even if he truly believed that she *deserved* to win." A few heads timidly bobbed in agreement. "Well, that's what I wanted to call your attention to today. You have all worked incredibly hard for the past few weeks on this contest, and you're the reason why it's been such a huge success. But you've also worked hard to gain the trust of the audience. And how do you think they'd react if the people who won the contest also *ran* the contest?"

"But we deserve the hamburgers," chirped Khandu from the back of the room. "It doesn't seem right that we don't get to win. We've worked so hard on SOL."

"But don't you see? You *do* win. You get to be on the radio. You got to make up the contest. That's the most important part about this station, you know. You have this amazing way to communicate with the entire city—soon the entire country. People depend on you for information and entertainment. That's your reward."

Remorse washed over the faces of the Kuzoo youth. Lhaki, TT, Thujee and some of the others looked as if they were about to cry.

"So, knowing all that, what do you think we should do?" I continued.

Lhaki shifted her guitar and sat up straight. "I think we have to take ourselves out of the competition. It wouldn't look right if one of us won."

Sir Tenzin stood to the side, fidgeting. I was pleasantly surprised I hadn't needed him to back me up.

"That's great, Lhaki," he said, and I was even more surprised that he'd been listening closely. "Really great. Thujee, do you have the list so we can call the new finalists?"

"Yes, Sir Tenzin," Thujee said, "I've got it. We'll start calling now."

The crowd dispersed, launching into action. The evening's Symphony of Love was to begin in just fifteen minutes. Lhaki stood up, smiling to no one in particular, and strummed her way around the room, as if nothing had happened, as if this was the way it was supposed to turn out all along. A few minutes ago she'd been upset at the mere suggestion she shouldn't win the contest, yet now she was fine with having lost her chance at victory and hamburgers.

As I watched her, I considered Valentine's Day and loss. The mysteries of the brain and emotion, of letting go, of moving on. Maybe it was her short lifetime of Buddhist education that allowed Lhaki to snap back so quickly. The topic of the last episode of the Buddhist-themed *Dharma Bites* show had been "impermanence," one of the fundamental beliefs of the religion. I'd listened intently as the hosts explained the concept: Everything is always in a state of flux. Nothing lasts forever—no triumph, love, no happy feeling, no state of sadness. Clinging to a person or place or moment in time was futile and unwise and led to suffering; so did wanting things to be different than they were.

Maybe it was, in fact, simple teenage rebound and not her religious upbringing that was making the outcome of the contest sit well with Lhaki. Still, I liked considering this concept of impermanence. "Youth is temporary and fleeting," the Kuzoo manifesto declared. Babies didn't stay babies forever. Our bodies changed and grew old. Feelings morphed over time.

Impermanence wasn't a word you'd ever want to associate with Valentine's Day, as silly a Hallmark holiday as it was. Love was supposed to last forever. And yet, anyone slightly older than the typical Kuzoo volunteer knew that was a fairy tale. So why did we insist on pretending that it did, and that it should? It seemed to cause us nothing but misery, in exchange for a momentary feeling of pleasure, comfort, the illusion of safety.

Once, I'd been proposed to on Valentine's Day by a man I

adored; a year later he'd run away, with no explanation. Four years after that, the improbable occurred: As I meandered alone through Central Park on a snowy Valentine's Day, I spotted him on a romantic walk with a beautiful red-haired woman, who I later learned was his new bride. Thrown into turmoil by the emotion of the coincidence, I found myself settling into acceptance, even feeling pleasure for him, over his new life. Right now, as another Valentine's Day approached, I could acknowledge that it was okay that my fiancé had left, fine that he had—maybe, in fact, even better that he had. All these years I had believed that everyone else commanded stability, while I floundered about. That was ridiculous. How many loveless marriages had I witnessed, complicated relationships including children and tangled finances that made it difficult to escape? How many unhappy single people did I know who were waiting around to be rescued by someone, anyone before they allowed themselves to start living? Who did I know who had anything without compromise? Existing involved compromise. Life, particularly a love life, was far richer and more complicated than a fairy tale. Sometimes— more often than not—love came to you in a short fit of wonder, warmed you, enthused you, and then vanished as suddenly as it had arrived. And that was okay, too. Sitting here in this faraway radio station, where I'd just won a small victory, I could see now that I had it good in my own unique way. I was living a rich, full life. What more was there, really?

Kuzoo's devoted listeners had a soft spot for the youngest contestants in the Symphony of Love. With Lhaki and TT disqualified, two little girls emerged as the top vote-getters: a ten-year-old named Kiba Yangzom captured first prize, and an eleven-year-old named Kinley Choki Dorji placed second. Kinley said she'd bring a friend to the Zone as her "date." Kiba brought her big sister. The *Bhutan Times* headline that week proclaimed "Two Little Kuzoo Idols Are Here!"

Sir Tenzin decided that, under the circumstances, a celebratory party for all of the Kuzoo staff and SOL volunteers was in order. He cut a deal with the owner of the Zone to serve up Cokes and snacks to all Kuzoo volunteers who stopped in on the evening of Valentine's Day. In the end, everyone did win.

A culture of dining out was uncommon in Bhutan, particularly among young people, who rarely had much pocket money. The Zone was a treat for all, and it was the only place in town where you could get a real hamburger, with fries. (The Swiss Bakery sold small, spicy meat patties on rolls and called those hamburgers, but that was a Bhutanese interpretation.) At night, the owners of the Zone dimmed the lights and illuminated the disco ball for those who might be inspired to dance. The establishment's crowning feature was its karaoke machine, one of only two in Thimphu.

Thujee emceed the evening as if it were a live broadcast on Kuzoo, working the room and sounding a bit like Phil Donahue, though he'd have had no idea who that was. He had the hyperbolic phrasing of broadcast down cold. "Let's give a hand to our generous sponsors here at the Zone," he announced. "The Grammy this year shouldn't go to anyone from Hollywood. It has to go to the young ladies who are singing here today. Give them a big hand!"

The disco ball sparkled; hoots and hollers and clapping hands egged Thujee on.

"And now, everyone, give a warm Kuzoo welcome to Kiba Yangzom, winner of the grand prize of the Symphony of Love. She's going to entertain us with the hit 'Where Is the Love' by the Black Eyed Peas! Take it away, Kiba!"

Thujee handed her the microphone. The karaoke machine clicked into gear, and the tiny girl shrank into her chair, over-whelmed at having an audience. Someone behind the bar trained a spotlight on her. Once she started singing, her confi-dence grew, her voice becoming a bit louder. Soon, everyone at the Zone joined in. From the corner of my eye, I spotted one of my expat friends, Ed, the golf pro from Nova Scotia, searching the darkened room to find me. I waved him over to join me at my table and as I did, as the whole room swayed to the music, my heart swelled.

I might never see any of these people again after I left Bhu-tan and I wasn't likely to accomplish anything grand during my time here. Or anywhere else, for that matter. I might not ever find the big love that had eluded me, and by now, it was pretty clear I wouldn't have kids of my own; raising a child alone was out of the question, financially and logistically. But here, all around me, was love. Nothing mattered more. Not the romantic kind—that was nice, but it wasn't forever. What was important, and abundant, was the love that filled the room right now. No Valentine's Day I'd experienced had been as wondrous as this, so full and beautiful.

In a corner, Pema, Ngawang, and Pink sat sipping sugary wine coolers. They'd gone to Pink's apartment to change after work, and were heading next to Club Destiny, the nightclub where Pink moonlit as a deejay. This was the first time I'd seen them out of their national garb, dressed up for "party night." They looked like pretty twenty-something gals anywhere who were ready to hit the town: tight T-shirts embellished with bling, low-rise jeans, smears of unnecessary makeup on their pristine skin.

Despite their festive getups, they radiated glumness. I knew the syndrome: on this couple-crazy holiday, neither Pema nor Ngawang had boyfriends, and Pink was going through a divorce. The last time they'd gone out dancing, they complained the next day at work that there weren't even boys they wanted to flirt with at the bar.

I considered giving them a big-sisterly lecture about how Valentine's Day was just a silly marketing conspiracy to convince you that without a "special someone" you were inferior, incomplete. I thought of doing the "girl power" thing, telling them how lucky they were to be beautiful and young and employed in a profession people clambered to work in back where I was from. How they were lucky to be alive at a time when their country was opening up in new and exciting ways. To please not make the mistake I'd seen so many women make, delaying life while waiting for a man to ride into the picture so they could be half of a couple and not need to find themselves. I even contemplated telling them my own Valentine's Day stories.

But all of this was talk, and talk they didn't really want to hear. I myself couldn't have appreciated this when I was their age. You had to suffer through a few Valentine's Days before you could understand what really mattered, anyway. So I ordered the girls up another round of wine coolers, got myself a shot of Bhutan Highland whiskey and Ed a Coca-Cola. Together we swayed to the music of the karaoke machine. A little while later, we would all head over to Club Destiny to go dancing.

8

MY BEST FRIENDS IN THE
WORLD RIGHT NOW

THERE ARE A FEW VERY IMPORTANT THINGS TO
know about the Bhutanese New Year, in addition to the
fact that shops, schools, offices—almost everything except Kuzoo FM—shuts down for three days in celebration.
For one thing, slaughtering of animals is prohibited. By government decree, the butchers remain closed throughout the
first calendar month. Killing is never good for one's karma,
but it is seen as a particularly inauspicious way to launch a new
year. That doesn't mean *eating* meat is forbidden; merely the
act of slaughter and the *sale* of meat are illegal.

For another: Drinking as much alcohol as possible is considered an essential part of the celebration. The drunker you
are, the thinking goes, the happier you are, and the likelier you
are to remain that way for the rest of the year. Thankfully, this
holiday is traditionally marked at home with the family, so the
roads in town aren't necessarily glutted with "happy" drivers.
In fact, on this particular New Year, the streets seemed emp-
tier than I'd seen them yet. Even the five or six stray dogs that
escorted me down the hill to Kuzoo each day appeared to be

taking a holiday. Perhaps the fact that it arrived just before the first-ever celebration of the new king's birthday in February was contributing to the serenity in the streets.

The salient points about this holiday called Losar were conveyed to me by Tenzin Choden, the radio jockey at Kuzoo with whom I'd had the least interaction. She was the quietest of the bunch, so soft-spoken that in person as well as on the air she was barely audible; she also had a husband, so she felt less compelled to hang around the studio before and after work. She'd show up at the appointed time to host whatever slot she was responsible for and then leave. Strictly business.

Then there was her general suspicion of me, a foreign interloper. This had much to do, I inferred from her comments, with the way I dressed. Since I had been told that it wasn't disrespectful for a Westerner to wear Western clothing, I opted not to outfit myself in the Bhutanese national dress. As a newbie and an outsider, I felt like a clumsy poseur in the beautiful, brightly colored ensemble. Plus, it was nearly impossible to put it on properly without the aid of a fleet of assistants. The national garb consisted of layers of *wangju* (shirt), *kira* (dress), and *tego* (jacket) cinched with a stiff, wide fringed belt, and with a simple broach at the breastbone. Like an old Bhutanese house, it seemed to be held together magically, with nary a nail or screw. Struggling to assemble this outfit, neatly, I thought, must be what it's like for a man the first hundred times he ties a necktie, only far worse because the entire body is involved. The day I'd tried my hand at draping my body Bhutan-style, total strangers, male and female, rushed up to me on the street to smooth me out. "You look beautiful in *kira,*" they'd say disingenuously, their tones making it clear that I *might* look beautiful in *kira* if I'd only learn to put it on correctly. Then they'd tug and pull and adjust to restore my honor. I was surprised my regular pack of stray-dog escorts hadn't chimed in with their opinions, too.

Tenzin Choden was always meticulously attired in the national dress, including perfectly matched, dainty three-inch heels, which Bhutanese city women wore as evidence they'd successfully moved beyond the farm. The limousine shoes did not stop her from jauntily making her way up the steep hill and narrow staircase to the kitchen studio as casually as if she donned flip-flops. It was hard to imagine the starched twenty-four-year-old Tenzin ever dressing down. I imagined she must have a special *kira,* even, to sleep in.

"When you want to wear Bhutanese, you tell me," she said disapprovingly, as she gave my all-black getup of turtleneck, stretchy pants, and clunky walking shoes a once-over. "I'll come over to Rabten Apartments, and help you get dressed. You will look very nice."

For all the self-assuredness I'd detected in the Bhutanese ladies I'd met, Tenzin in particular seemed to possess confidence in abundance. Her family was in the construction business, several Kuzooers had whispered, which was polite shorthand to disclose that she was wealthier than most of the others. This explained the fact that she owned her own personal laptop, a luxury everyone at the station coveted most (having an iPod ranked second). Because of this possession, she had the freedom to work on her reports from home.

Given all this, I was surprised when Tenzin asked for help on a special project she'd assigned herself, a taped report on the meaning of the Bhutanese New Year, Losar. Why Tenzin chose to sink her teeth into an additional bit of work wasn't clear; in the back of my head, I allowed myself the fantasy that my failed workshop and ongoing casual talks in the workroom each day might actually have sunk in, but I knew in my heart that that probably wasn't the case. Whatever it was that had inspired Tenzin, I was happy to help.

To begin gathering interviews for the report, we walked down to the row of meat shops near the vegetable market, below the lower road where the bloody carcasses that hung in the windows would make even the most devoted carnivore commit to tofu and kale forever. They looked like Upton Sinclair's nightmare incarnate, flesh dangling, flies swarming, the occasional stray dog panting and drooling nearby. Tenzin whipped out a little minidisc recorder that she'd borrowed from the Kuzoo supply closet and interviewed a handful of shoppers (in Dzongkha) and butchers (in Nepali) as if she'd been wielding a microphone for years. Since most Bhutanese didn't want the job of slaughtering animals at any time of year—very bad for the karma—Tenzin explained that the majority of the meat proprietors were immigrants. When she was done, she announced, "Okay, we can go now," and marched us back up the half-mile hill through the center of town to the studio.

Now it was midway through the holiday, and Tenzin was finally ready for feedback on her edited segment.

The only other person in the studio was RJ Kinzang, a sweet, eager young man of twenty-three who came from more modest means than his colleague. He was the eldest of nine children; his family ran a tiny general shop off one of the rattier side streets, and they all lived above it. He was there hosting the country music show. What better way to ring in the Bhutanese New Year than with a little twang? More than anyone, Kinzang loved working at Kuzoo, and loved being on the air. He was the guy everyone asked to cover for them when they didn't want to come to work, which usually had something to do with their staying out too late the night before—or being slotted to host the country show. Kinzang didn't drink, couldn't afford to party, and never complained about doing the country show, the early bird show at 6:00 a.m., or anything else, for that matter. He was the only one of the radio jockeys who had any sense of Kuzoo mania or his growing (and polarizing) celebrity in the community. The audience either loved the way he spoke English, or they mocked it wickedly, but they all knew who he was.

Tenzin turned down the Garth Brooks playing on the workroom monitor so I could hear her opus free of distraction. I wobbled in the rickety desk chair, and braced myself.

The piece began with a short burst of traditional Bhutanese music, and after a few seconds, Tenzin's voice mixed in underneath. Her read was clear and deliberate; I'd never heard her speak that way.

"Losar, the Bhutanese New Year, is considered a very auspicious time, marking the beginning of a very happy and prosperous new year. People believe with the starting of the new year, all things will go well and prosper. So to celebrate the special occasion, government offices are closed, shops are closed, and people stay home from work to be with their families."

I reckoned I was one of five people who'd tune in who didn't already know everything Tenzin was reporting.

"To know more about Losar and the change in the year, which is the Hog year, I interviewed Sir Lugtaen Gyatso, principal of the Institute for Language and Cultural Studies at the Royal University of Bhutan, which is located in Semtokha, Thimphu."

Informing listeners that Semtokha was in Thimphu was the Bhutanese version of "Who's buried in Grant's Tomb?" The music swelled a bit, and Tenzin posed a question:

"What is the significance of Losar, and could you explain about the origin of Losar, *la*?"

The *la* was the most charming of the Bhutanese verbal tics. It was frequently tacked to the end of a sentence, usually a question, to soften it. Often, it was deployed deferentially, by younger people talking to elders, or anyone to an authority, as a sign of respect.

Sir Gyatso responded:

"Well, Losar is New Year. Its significance is very straight-forward, because it's the beginning of a new calendar, the beginning of a new time that everybody wishes to see unfold. So many wonders. We Bhutanese, being religious, we believe in spiritual power, and therefore we Bhutanese strongly believe that a good beginning is a sign of a good conclusion. I think the significance of Losar is to begin with a good start that will last until the last day of the year."

From there, Sir Gyatso got a bit more technical. This New Year, it seemed, wasn't the only one in Bhutan. There were actually nine different starting points to the year. Each had a different name. After letting him ramble on for a few minutes, Tenzin asked what was in store for this year of the Female Fire Hog.

Sir Gyatso sounded apologetic, as if it were his fault that the heavens were delivering a clunker:

"This is not going to be a great year. After every nine years comes a year that's considered to be a bad year. And every tenth year is supposed to be the worst year of that decade."

Whether this was the ninth or tenth year in the cycle, I

couldn't quite glean from his comments, but the underlying message was clear: Things were not going to be good, not for a while. I understood why the coronation of the newly anointed king and the democratic elections had to wait until 2008.

Tenzin asked what could be done given the dire astrological predictions.

Sir Gyatso's response was very Buddhist, very wise. Big tasks would have to be tabled out of respect for misaligned stars, but life had to go on, despite the astral challenges.

"I think there is no timing for good things. We can always try to be good human beings, do a little bit of soul searching, ask ourselves, 'How good a human being am I?' We can still try to do something good, and avoid doing something bad."

Now Tenzin introduced an interview with the proprietor of the Wong Meat Shop, who said he'd been mobbed with customers in the last few days before the meat ban took effect. Excerpts of Tenzin's interviews with the shoppers followed, and she translated that they were saying, basically, they couldn't live without meat. After all, eating well and plentifully at the beginning of the year was another way to ensure it would be a good one.

Sounds of a giant vat of liquid sloshing about for a few seconds mixed together with her next narration:

"Drinking is part of our celebration for any occasion. As the celebration nears, Karma—name changed—is busy helping her mother make *ara*."

Ara is a clear wine, distilled from rice. A Bhutanese friend plied me with several large glasses one night. It left my head thick and cloudy. It was delicious, but it wasn't something you'd drink if you were hoping to do anything productive the next day.

In this place with so few names, and where everyone could identify a person with only the vaguest description, I loved that "Karma" had felt compelled to conceal her identity. Whatever her real name, she sounded as sweet as Goldilocks making porridge.

"I'm making *ara* for Losar celebration, *la*. People should be very happy, and in order to make my family intoxicated and happy, I'm making *ara*."

"Can you consume all you are making, *la?*"

From the background audio, one suspected that Karma either had an enormous family, or was running a distillery. She responded, matter-of-factly:

"Somehow we have to make money. We will sell half of what we make."

The Bhutanese music mixed in again, and our intrepid reporter returned for the finale:

"All will be busy preparing for their Losar. Some will be frying snacks, some will be decorating their altar, some will be practicing for the archery tournament, and so on. That is all for now. I hope you enjoyed listening to the Losar program. Until then, on behalf of Kuzoo FM 90, it's Tenzin Choden. For now it's bye and Happy Losar."

As the Bhutanese music trailed to a close, Tenzin looked at me, her eyes wide. It was clear that she was pleased with herself. I wanted to say so many things, helpful suggestions and edits to make it a "better program," at least to my ears. Had she shown me a script beforehand, I would have felt freer to contribute them then. Of the many editorial tweaks I might have suggested, though, none mattered quite so much as the fact that she'd taken the initiative to prepare the report in the first place.

Back home, a story tied to a holiday would have been prepared weeks in advance and aired the day before. Though the piece wasn't terribly illuminating, it was perfectly fine. In fact, by the standards of Kuzoo, it was quite an achievement. She had collected sound and edited it, and mixed in music and recorded a narration. So I resisted the urge to criticize, and said, sincerely, "Good job, Tenzin"—praise she didn't seem a bit surprised to hear. She flashed a big smile and scurried into action, copying the audio onto her thumb drive, marching into the studio without knocking, leaning over Kinzang, and uploading it onto the playback computer. When she was ready, she hit Play, and her Losar segment was beamed out to all of Thimphu, probably halfway through a nice fresh batch of *ara* now, anyway.

A FEW MINUTES LATER, the Kuzoo phone rang. Madam Kunzang Choden (no relation to Tenzin) was calling to tell me that her husband was on his way over to pick me up. I'd almost forgotten I had a Losar lunch date with Bhutan's first female novelist, who also happened to be, along with Madame Carolyn, the other half of the king appointed Kuzoo board.

Madam Choden was a tall woman with a sweet, round face, her thick hair pulled back into a bun. She looked like a cross between an earth mother and a kindly, youthful grandma; there was an air of formality about her that was almost regal. The Kuzoo staffers told me she was a descendent of a prominent religious family from central Bhutan. She was held in such high regard that most people called her "Ashi," an honorific usually reserved for the queens. I myself called her Madam, and she didn't correct me.

Long before she started writing, Madam Choden had lived a life that read like fiction. Like a handful of Bhutanese of her generation—though most of them male—she had traveled at age nine to next-door India to get a proper education that could not be had at home. Schools were scarce in Bhutan in the 1960s, mostly reserved for monks, and construction of the roads was just getting under way. To get to the convent school where she'd been enrolled, Madam Choden had ridden on horseback for twelve days with an entourage of attendants.

She went on to earn two bachelor's degrees, one in India, the other in Nebraska, and, for a time, had been a teacher. Now she was one of a handful of authors to have emerged in the kingdom. She had published several books of Bhutanese folktales, as well as a novel, which happened to be about a girl from a remote part of Bhutan who, premodernization in the sixties, yearns to explore the world.

Madam Choden had just returned from a visit to the United States to see her children, who were studying there, and had brought home a fever for American public radio. When I told her I worked in radio, I could feel her brightening. And that's when I'd been invited to lunch.

Promptly at noon, a little white car sped up the hilly drive-way to the Kuzoo studios. Since I'd arrived in Bhutan, it was the first time anyone had shown up at the exact moment they said they would. A gray-haired European gentleman emerged, strode to the other side of the car, and opened the passenger door, all with a flourish of chauffeuresque formality. He intro-duced himself as Walter, stuck out his hand to shake mine, motioned for me to get in, got back in the car himself, and sped down the hill and onto the road, as efficient as a Swiss timepiece. Madam Choden was so quintessentially Bhutanese that I had forgotten she was married to a native of Switzerland. He was a handsome complement to the good looks of Madam Choden. Several of the more erudite Bhutanese had spouses from outside the country, a fact I'd observed with curiosity.

Around a few corners, past my apartment, and left, right, left along a winding road, up a driveway to a house hidden on a hill. We stopped in front of a little country cottage I never would have found on my own. The branches of the barren trees blew in the wind; the air felt empty and quiet, as if the whole city were inside today. It wasn't as cold as a February day might be in New York, but it definitely felt like winter.

A yapping little white dog served as welcome committee— a house pet as opposed to a stray—followed by an elegant Madam Choden, who accepted the box of cookies I handed her. The bakeries had been closed and I'd had to resort to Indian imports. She announced that Rinchen, her maid, had just pulled the pesto pasta off the stove.

"Pesto from my trip to the United States. Trader Joe's," she said proudly. "I also have crackers and anchovy spread from Paris."

My stomach danced with pleasure at the prospect of such delicious food.

"And since it's a holiday, we must have some of this wine, too," Walter said, pulling a bottle from a cabinet. I squinted to read the label on the sly, as if I were looking at a mirage in the desert. Wine was very hard to come by in Thimphu, except for *ara;* at the watering hole in town frequented by expats you had to order an entire bottle, because demand for imported wine was so low that it wasn't cost-effective to open one to sell by the glass. Since the local microbrew called Red Panda was available for only twenty-five cents a glass in most bars, spending $15 for a bottle of whatever wine was in stock seemed not just decadent but wasteful.

Walter caught me staring and kindly indulged my curiosity by holding up the bottle so I could get a better look. It was my favorite, Shiraz, from Australia. "We get it at the duty-free shop. It's the best they send us here."

As he poured three glasses, I heard noise at the door, and Madam Choden left the room to tend to it. She reemerged into the dining area moments later, followed by a very tall, distinguished-looking Western man, fortyish. Her introduction was as formal as if she were debuting him at court.

"Presenting Martin Gallatin, Thimphu's newest and most eligible bachelor," she said, though she finished with a giggle.

Dear God, am I being fixed up? I wondered as I savored the spiciness of my wine. Was he widowed, divorced; was she a Bhutanese lady; were there kids? Half the generous glass Walter had poured for me was already warming my insides.

Martin, whose name isn't really Martin, looked my way and said a lukewarm hello. Perhaps I was as much a surprise to him as he was to me. He handed over a pot of jam to Madam Choden.

"Here's all that's left of Claudine," he said, smiling, and I supposed this Claudine must not be deceased. If she were, this Martin was pretty crass.

Walter led us out to a beautifully set table on a glass-enclosed patio filled with plants. A cat lay wrapped around a lamp, her stomach rising and falling peacefully with each breath. We could have been in the French countryside, or in a cabin in North Carolina, or in a thousand other charming places on a quiet day. But where we happened to be was in a pretty cottage in the capital city of Bhutan at the dawn of twin holidays.

"I can't place your accent," I said to Martin, as Walter poured him a glass of wine and refilled mine. I felt a bit greedy, but it was delicious.

"You can't? Well, guess." I was trying to be charming, but Martin didn't seem to bite.

"Well, hmm, are you German?" Swiss-German, I figured. Maybe that's how he knew Walter.

"German, *la*." He looked at Walter. "Dear God, no. I'll try not to be insulted. Germans, *la*."

I couldn't tell if Martin was trying to be funny in mimicking the Bhutanese way of talking. I was getting a bit drunk, and I feared I'd made an ugly American mistake by remarking that someone who was likely trilingual had an accent. Unilingual me was the one with an accent. I wished I were back at the station drinking watery instant coffee and listening to the music, helping RJ Kinzang line up country songs.

Casting about for a way to save face, I said, "Okay, I think I've got it. Thai! You're from Thailand, that's it!" Walter and Madam Choden were generous enough to laugh at my effort.

Martin looked my way and smiled; I hadn't offended him terribly, after all. "Yes, *la*! That's it!" He sipped some wine and patted the little white dog. "Actually, I am Norwegian, by way of Switzerland."

With that settled, the conversation somehow turned to potatoes. The United Nations had announced that the next year would be "the year of the spud." The tuber was so abundant in central Bhutan that there was talk of opening a potato chip factory. Both Walter and Martin were integrally involved in agricultural development in Bhutan, and they extolled the virtues of the vegetable as an important cash crop for Bhutanese farmers. I shared my anecdotal market research about the preference among the Kuzooers for imported chips in flashy packages over my preference: the tastier, fresher homemade kind.

"Packaged goods," chimed in Madam Choden. "There's a fascination here for packaged goods, because people never had access to them before. They're seen as a sign of affluence, worldliness. That's why we have so much litter. No one knows what to do with the wrapping, because few food items before ever came in wrappers."

Circuitously, we moved to a discussion of Martin's time in another part of Asia, where Walter and Madam Choden had lived for a while, too. He related a lengthy tale about an American girl with whom he had become smitten. She later published a story in a prestigious literary journal about the circumstances of their meeting. Martin found this very impressive, but it also left him with a measure of defeat. He had written his own interpretation of the events and hadn't managed to get his into print.

I shifted uncomfortably. Martin was dominating our Losar lunch, when I'd been hoping to learn more about Madam Choden and her writing, and about the library in town where she was a volunteer, the museum she was building on her ancestral land, what her home district of Bumthang was like, and whether Bhutan was ready for its first democratic elections next year. Not about a strange man with a crush on some younger woman he'd never see again.

Eventually, under my persistent questioning, Walter and Madam Choden pulled out pictures of their kids. We feasted on the crackers and anchovy paste, and the pesto pasta was served up. When the requisite pot of *emadatse* arrived, I quickly passed it on without taking any. Another bottle of wine was opened. Martin grabbed my camera and snapped some photos of us all.

All of a sudden it was 3:00 p.m. and Martin had to go wrap up some things before the holidays continued with time off to honor the king's birthday. Everyone insisted he must drive me down the hill, even though what I really wanted to do was walk down and breathe in the quiet of the new year, work off some of the wine, savor the most delicious meal I'd had since I'd arrived. But Walter and Madam Choden were emphatic, and they waved gaily as we pulled out of the driveway.

In the privacy of his car, one on one, Martin dropped the annoying theatrics, and his vulnerable side emerged. He suddenly became a more enjoyable companion. As the car chugged down Norzin Lam and approached the studio, I popped the question I'd been dying to ask.

"So what exactly happened to Claudine? And when?"

"She left, with our kids. Seven months ago."

"Where did she go?"

"To Switzerland. She's at her family's place."

"How old are the kids?"

"Eleven and nine."

"How long have you been here?"

"Six years."

I imagined, in my limited experience of Bhutan, and without knowing a thing about Claudine, that it might be a particular

challenge for outsiders to raise a family in Thimphu. There
appeared to be a small community of expats who were here
through various nongovernmental agencies, and they were
said to be fairly tight-knit. But it must have been hard to be so
far away from familiar territory and the creature comforts of
home, especially when you had kids. There had to have been
other factors contributing to Claudine's departure, though.
Marriages didn't just dissolve like that—particularly when
there were children involved.

"Have you looked up that writer woman you keep talking
about? You still seem kind of obsessed with her. . . ."

"I'm not obsessed with her."

"But she's about all you talked about at lunch. Besides potatoes."

Martin pulled up in front of the old foreign minister's
house-turned–radio station and stopped the car.

"Probably because you remind me a bit of her, *la*." He
laughed nervously, as if he knew what he was saying could get
him into trouble. "But yes, yes, I have looked her up, and she's
married. They both are rather well-heeled, if you know what
I mean."

"Ah. It helps to be if you're going to be a writer. Maybe she
really loves you and is waiting for you to confess." I looked
him in the eye and smiled, to make sure he could see I was
teasing. "Send me the story. I'm curious."

I found myself flattered that Martin had made a comparison between me and this literary prodigy he admired and, suddenly, irrationally jealous that this invisible woman had
captivated him.

"Her story? Or mine?"

"Well, I'm more interested in yours. But sure. Send both."

"I will. Let's have dinner this week?"

"Yes," I said without hesitation.

THAT NIGHT, I sat in the quiet of my little apartment, tethered online with the dial-up connection and listening to the Bhutan Broadcasting Service news on TV. It was rare for me to be on my own in the evening here, and I found myself liking this self-contained multimedia bubble. It felt different in the Himalayas than it would have back in Los Angeles, less like a lonely way of killing time; television, in particular, was a fun curiosity here rather than a droning nuisance. But why? In the end, news was news and commercials were commercials, weren't they? Even the Indian channels piped in on cable were screeching dreck; the only difference from home was the looks and the names. The BBS still had a rough, homespun edge to it, more utilitarian than glitz, which somehow made it more palatable.

"We'll bring you the international news after this short break," announced the *kira*-clad anchorwoman from behind the news desk, which looked like any other news desk except that it was adorned with the signature Bhutanese woodwork. She had just shown pictures of a roadblock due to a landslide on the highway near Bumthang that had stranded hundreds of people. One road being shut down could immobilize much of the country.

An animated clock with a second hand that was rapidly flying around the dial flashed on the screen, and an announcer declared: "Time to file your PIT. Time to file your PIT. Time to file your PIT. Time is running short! File your personal income tax now."

Beauty shots of flowers and birds, set to lovely music, flashed on the screen, and after a few seconds, a woman read in Bhutanese-accented English, as if she were reciting poetry: "Wherever you are, whatever you do, when you think of refreshment, think of ice-cold Coca-Cola."

A static shot of a shop downtown, crammed with merchandise: "Kidsy, your exclusive kids store, announces Losar sales. . . ."

Photos of a newly relocated gym: "Sakten Health Club and Saloon are pleased to announce Relax and Recover and Rejuvenate. . . ."

Commercial break over, and back to the studio, where the anchorwoman informed the people of Bhutan about a stone-throwing mob attacking the deposed Nepalese king as he embarked on a pilgrimage. Of a court in southern India sentencing three members of a regional political party to death for killing three female students in 2000. Of the death-by-remote-control bomb blast of a key Pakistani health official, who was leading a polio immunization drive. In comparison to the outside world, little Bhutan lived up to its reputation as the last Shangri-la, peaceful and serene—its reward for being long sequestered. What would a villager in the remote reaches of the country think of these reports? News of a world beyond in strife, bracketed by simple commercials offering consumer goods. It was a good thing the government was committed to Gross National Happiness, because that philosophy seemed a crucial necessity to offset the effects of a few hours in front of the television. "Happiness with what you have" wasn't exactly the backbone philosophy of advertising and media and news.

An email from Martin popped into my inbox, inviting me to dinner. "I have fresh greens here," he wrote, knowing how enticing that would be to a nutrition-starved visitor; good-looking fresh vegetables were hard to come by in winter in Thimphu. His story was attached, and he insisted I didn't have to read it.

I opened it immediately. It was beautiful, and funny, and long—an account of running into this woman and her friends as they toured a village. In the story, Martin confessed to what I suspected might be true: He turned on the sarcasm in the face of attractive women to mask his insecurity. An introspective scientist whose third language was English and who could write very well. This Martin was intriguing.

TUESDAY AROUND 5:30 P.M. I heard a chugging noise in the driveway outside my apartment. Martin had arrived to pick me up. When I got in the car, I noticed he was more relaxed, and more handsome, than I remembered.

I didn't usually leave Kuzoo so early, but everything was so quiet, what with the holidays, which would keep schools and offices shut a few more days. The ride to Martin's was comically short, just a quarter of a mile. *All this time I've been here,* I thought, *this man has been around the corner and I had no idea.*

The side door of the house opened into a lovely, homey kitchen. A dozen pairs of shoes of various sizes sat neatly lined up just inside the entryway. Martin offered me a pair of floppy women's slippers in exchange for my boots; Claudine lived on. Blue glass bottles of filtered water and colorful Bhutanese thermoses, used to carry food on picnics or to work, lined the windowsills. A shopping list lay on the table: *prayer flags, TP, salt.* Martin motioned for me to sit and offered me a choice of a Red Panda or a bottle of the same wine we'd had with Walter

and Madam Choden; I opted for the latter, since the taste of
the red we'd enjoyed was still fresh in my memory. Besides,
the birth anniversary of the king seemed to merit a more formal beverage. A cork was popped, two glasses poured, and
Martin started cooking.

While he fixed the meal, he asked with a keen interest
about my work and my life. He refilled our glasses, lit a candle, and served us, never interrupting the flow of questioning
or my responses. This was how I'd often prepare dinner for a
friend back home, and I was enjoying being the guest. The
wine was a truth serum, and I felt comfortable giving in to the
gently somber mood of this house and of the holiday. I could
tell this man everything, and he wouldn't care or judge me; we
were strangers thrown together in an odd place at an interesting moment in time, and we weren't likely to ever cross paths
again beyond the borders of Bhutan. And so I poured out the
highlights of my life as if I were in a confessional—the good,
the bad, the ugly, scenes from my life I hadn't shared even with
people I considered good friends. I ended with how now, in
my forties, I couldn't help wondering "if" about everything.

Martin looked straight at me, the glow of the candle all that
was lighting the room. The only light outside the kitchen window came from the waxing moon; everything around us was
perfectly still. Every once in a while, one of the house dogs dutifully guarding the front door would yawn, as if to remind us
we weren't alone. I had this hunch Martin would understand
the notion of loss, since he'd experienced such a profound one
himself. He had on his face an expression of pure empathy,
and I wasn't ashamed of anything I'd said. Or anything that
had happened in my life.

"I think everyone, if they're paying attention, asks the 'if' question," Martin said, breaking the silence. "Sounds like we're both in a state."

"Well, I'm in a different state, of course, than you." My losses were ephemeral. He had a longtime partner and children somewhere else in the world.

"Yes. It never occurred to me this might happen."

"It must be very hard not to see your kids."

"Eight thousand four hundred and seventy miles," he said without a second of calculation. The light from the candle flickered in his eyes; I could feel his sadness and the purity of his emotion. "It is very difficult."

I breathed deep and steady. I wanted to thank Sebastian or karma or whoever it was who'd led me here to Bhutan, to this place where the people, the conversations, everyday life was what I hoped it could be. I felt better here, freer than I ever had, more *me* than ever before.

Abruptly, he stood up and cleared the dinner plates, poured two glasses of port, and said, "Let's go to the living room."

To do that, you had to walk through a formal dining area; I squinted to see if in the darkness I could make out a picture of his family, but I couldn't. Walking into the living room was like landing in Narnia—a magical, dictionary definition of a family room, hidden, beautiful, warm. I wondered: What had happened here in those six years? The life that had unfolded in this house was still so present. A child's drum set in one corner; several plush couches inviting you to sink in; enough books, CDs, DVDs to stock a small public library—fiction, science, Asian themed, Euro themed—kid's stuff everywhere. The moon shone in from one of the windows, and the stars were bright; I was drunk from the wine and getting drunker just smelling the port. Here I was in Bhutan in this beautiful space with this complicated man, and I never wanted to leave.

But of course, I had to. At some point—some point very soon, in fact. The clock was ticking toward the end of my stay. And that was okay. It was more than okay; it was perfect, actually. The Himalayan air, the very notion of Gross National Happiness, and the exercise of the three good things—the cocktail of them had convinced me to embrace the moment before me, now, to appreciate it for what it was, but not to hold it so tight that I never let it go. For another moment would occur, and then another.

As content as I felt right now, I felt heartbroken, too. Imagining the loss and sadness and confusion of Martin's situation conjured up all the loss and sadness I had ever felt; Martin had managed to have a family, and even though it had fractured, it was sacred. I tried to manage this realization as we relaxed into the room. He positioned some pillows so he could lay out on the floor, and I chose a particularly inviting chair across from him. Using his computer as a jukebox, he played songs for me as we talked—unusual music: ballads and vocalists I'd never heard before.

On the occasion of His Majesty the king's twenty-seventh birthday, I was about to be seduced by a tall, recently separated, clearly heartbroken scientist in the home it seemed his family had evacuated in an instant and which he preserved as if they were coming back the next day. I wanted to know everything that had happened for Martin, everything about him; I wanted to understand everything about Claudine and the children. Even though I couldn't possibly. And then, as he worked his way through his musical collection, Martin said the words that broke the spell, that he had to have known would break the spell.

"My French lover adores this song."

It hadn't disturbed me to be on the brink of an embrace with a married-but-separated man whose estranged wife's slippers I was wearing while I lounged on Thai silk pillows they'd probably bought together in a fit of long-forgotten domestic bliss. Well, it didn't bother me that much; I had taken it on faith that I wasn't interfering in an active marriage, but you never really know, do you, what's happening beyond what someone reveals? They themselves might not really know. But this casual mention of the "lover" changed things. Was this lover the reason Claudine left? Did she live here in Thimphu? If she didn't, where could they have met and how could they possibly carry on an affair? I tried not to act surprised at Martin's revelation, as ham-handed as it was.

"French lover. Obviously she has good taste. Someone in Bhutan?"

"No, no, French lover in France."

"Where did you meet?"

"I met her in Europe. She's very young."

By now I had determined that Martin was a year older than me, forty-four.

"How young is very young?"

"Twenty-four."

"Ah. Ridiculously young. But not quite fifty-fifty young."

"What's that?"

"Literally half your age."

Martin smiled.

"You'd better be careful," I said, trying on the role of advisor. "Someone that age is bound to want to have children. Eventually. "

"I wouldn't mind having more children. But I don't think this will come to that. I don't know why she has anything to do with an old man like me."

"Well, I do. Men are tedious until they hit forty."

Some sense overtook the wine and the port and the exhaustion and the dashed desire to get closer. Martin had revealed that there was a woman in his life; I had misunderstood the cues. Even though I was unlikely to see him again, I couldn't be a part of this. It was time to go back to my little place in Rabten.

"You know, I'm really exhausted. It's probably a good time for me to head home."

Now Martin was the one trying to mask surprise, and he started to stand up, as if he were expecting this. "I'll drive you down the hill, of course."

"No need to."

"Yes, if the dogs don't get you, the rats might. I insist."

Small talk was punctuated by dog howls as we wended our way out of the driveway. Had someone pushed the car, he wouldn't have needed to turn the ignition on to get me home just down the hill. None of the houses we passed showed any sign of life. As we entered my driveway, the two resident chubby Rabten dogs hovered anxiously around Martin's car. We sat and talked for so long that Martin finally turned off the engine so as not to disturb my neighbors. Without the heat of the engine, I got so cold I folded my coat around my knees, but we just kept on talking.

Finally, I said, wow, it's really freezing, and it's late, and thank you for a wonderful meal—God, real green things, delicious, how wonderful—and thanks for all the music. And I leaned over to give him a good-night kiss on the cheek, because I meant it. It had been an amazing night in what had been a month of gorgeous days and evenings halfway around the world from any world I knew. And my attempt at a sweet, polite thank-you morphed into an embrace, and all the tension of the evening was poured into a very long, very beautiful kiss.

Morning arrives and I walk into town; the streets are as empty today as they'd been the night before. The ridge that juts out from the mountain, where a line of cypress trees are perched on the edge, grabs me every time. Just the right distance between them, as if nature had intentionally yard-sticked the arrangement. Their simple beauty looms high above the city; just looking at them makes me happy. They would make my list of three good things almost every day.

Except I haven't done a list in weeks now. I've been so caught up in the richness and fullness of every minute here, I haven't even remembered to make lists. I haven't felt the need. It's become second nature just to look at each day, even when it was ordinary or even when something was going wrong, and find the goodness.

Today, in honor of the twin holidays, three of my expat friends are celebrating with a special lunch. Today's gathering will be much different from our usual appointments to drink Red Panda beer in my apartment or grab enormous plates of fried rice for $1 at the restaurant Chopstix in town. Instead we are heading up to the fancy resort, the Aman.

I spot Ed near the long line of prayer wheels on the square.

He's all spiffed up today, wearing a sports jacket. The attire seems perfect on him, but out of context given the surroundings. Too country club. Several Bhutanese stand around him, smiling, grinning. They are wearing woven triangular hats, hats I haven't seen before.

"Nomadic yak herders," he explains, gesturing toward them, clearly confused about what to say. "They don't speak any English, but I think they want money. I gave them some. . . ."

They also want to stare at him. Likely they've never seen a tall, light-haired Caucasian man dressed in casual business clothing. I step into sight, and they want to examine me, too, a short lady covered in black clothing. I wish more than I have the entire time I've been here that I could speak their language, so I can ask what they're thinking. I'd heard stories from Bhutanese who were my age and had grown up in the villages, without seeing paper—paper!—or wristwatches until they were teenagers. As much as I think I comprehend the magnitude of the changes here in recent years, as compassionate a student as I may be of the impact media will have on the people, I am aware that I don't really have any idea what it's like to be Bhutanese.

Pam arrives. She'd come from the hospital, where she's preparing medical equipment to take to the remotest reaches of the country. Ever since her divorce, she's been running around the world to volunteer as a nurse in different countries. Most of the villages here in Bhutan that she'll visit have never seen Western medicine of any kind.

"Good day." She nods, even though she knows they don't understand. "Have a good day," she says, and moves us toward the road, politely and firmly. Ed and I obediently trot along behind her.

Yet I find myself magnetized and looking back. I don't have a nursing degree like Pam, but there must be something useful I can contribute out here in the world, out from behind the desk to which I'd long been tethered. Face-to-face with the most traditional Bhutanese I've met, I want to know more. Not just about Bhutan, although there's no question I haven't had enough time here. These nomads inspire me to want to see more of the world, experience more of it. To become a bit more nomadic myself. To help the world somehow, instead of chronicling its demise from a journalist's perch and a news-room. I believe I have just made a Losar resolution of a sort.

Our friend Mayumi rushes up from the street with a wave. My three companions peel me away and into the taxi, and we start the drive out of the center of town and up, up the wind-ing road. The resort is built on land owned by one of the queens and attracts the kind of tourist any country would love: The price for a room is a thousand dollars a night. And it's as beautiful as it should be for that much money, a Westerner's fantasy interpretation of Bhutan. It evokes the kingdom, but it is nothing like it, with sophisticated muted tones, instead of the local brightness; plush furniture, instead of the hard-backed utilitarian fare in most places. Giant picture windows to showcase the view. We are enjoying lunch here at a reduced price, the local's discount no real local can afford, $50 a head. As nice as it is to eat a lovely meal in luxurious surroundings with good company, I wish we'd given the nomadic people this money and gone to my place, where I'd have made us spa-ghetti from the Swiss Bakery.

"Here's to the new year," we say, hoisting our glasses. "Here's to the king and a long, healthy reign. Here's to all of us in Bhutan."

Ed's face twists with tears; he doesn't even try to conceal his emotion. Mayumi is leaving in a week, and that's when Pam is going on the road. And I will be gone not long after. Our shared meals and confidences will soon be history. We are like four whirlpools that have run together for a while, Ed declares poetically; these weeks we've had together have felt like years. When time is limited and the environment is so different from your own, relationships skip the "how do you do" phase and go straight to the heart of friendship.

He's right, I think, as we toast again, but surely not just any environment could conjure these feelings. There's something about Bhutan, even in the language. *Kuzu zampo* means hello in Dzongkha, but there isn't a word for good-bye.

9

THE THUNDERBOLT,

PART TWO

ON THE MIDDLE FINGER OF MY LEFT HAND IS A circle of hammered gold, topped with a large, tear-shaped oval of turquoise. I got it at the shop across from the bank on Norzin Lam. There are five or six such stores up and down the main strip that sell the few items you can take home to remind you of your visit, as if *things* could possibly do justice to an experience here. The stores sell beautiful handwoven textiles, many of them purported to be relics from the shopkeepers' family trees; in an age of inexpensive machine-woven copies imported from India, it's better to turn grandmother's handiwork into cash. Little statuettes of various Buddhas, jewel-adorned prayer wheels. Prayer flags that couldn't possibly look the same when displayed in one lonely string anywhere other than in the magnificent open landscape of these mountains.

The only souvenir I wanted was this ring. The yellowness and the heft of its matte gold, and the simple, brilliant blue of the stone, drew my eye when I'd seen it on the hands of men and women around town. The question was where to buy one for myself.

A tiny, hunched old lady guarded the entrance to one particular shop. Day in, day out, she stood out front with a cat curled by her feet, its stomach rising and falling softly with each breath, the two of them a still and quiet duo. Occasionally the lady's face would brighten into a smile in response to a passerby's *"Kuzu zampo-la."* But this wasn't tourist season, so buyers were scarce.

After careful consideration, I decided this would be the place where I would spend my money. The shop was a bit run-down, and might not have had the selection of the others, but I preferred it to the shinier outfits on the other side of the traffic circle, over near the tourist hotels.

The lady seemed surprised as I made my way through the door. She'd probably long ago given up hope that I might make a purchase, for I passed by the shop at least a few times each day. She motioned for me to stay by the counter as she walked to the back, I supposed, to fetch someone. A woman about my age, who identified herself as the lady's daughter, emerged. She could help me, she said, since she could speak English. She asked where I was from, what had brought me to Bhutan, and when I was leaving. I told her that I was headed home tomorrow.

"So sad that you have to go. Will you come back to Bhutan?"

"Oh," I answered, "I hope so. I hope so." Her mother returned to the counter and handed me a cup of tea. As I often did in Thimphu, I felt like an honored guest, and not in this case simply because I held the promise of a sale. A visitor from so far away was still a special occasion.

"May I see that ring, please?" I pointed to one of three similar rings in the jewelry case, the smallest among them. The lady complied, and slipped it onto my hand without effort. It fit perfectly. I held out my arm, wrist pointed up, and admired the adornment. It looked as pretty as I'd hoped.

"So sixty-five hundred ngultrum today is about . . ." I tried to calculate out loud, looking at the tiny white label of a price tag. The exchange rate changed daily and the ngultrum, pegged to the Indian rupee, had been rising in value lately.

There was no need to be approximate. The lady whipped out a calculator from under the counter and started pressing the keys.

"A hundred forty dollars."

"Hmm. I'll have to go get some money across the street . . ."

I didn't even bother to ask about credit cards; only one shop accepted them, and with a steep surcharge, to boot. Plastic was still the domain of visitors. Most Bhutanese used only cash, though printed currency had been introduced only forty-odd years ago. The couple of automatic teller machines at the bank weren't designed to work with anything but a local account.

"Traveler's check? We can take a traveler's check." First I'd heard of that here. As I pulled out some checks and endorsed them, I joked that I was "getting married to myself." The old lady smiled broadly, wanting to be agreeable, but not understanding. Her daughter took my words literally.

"Yes." She smiled, and then she told me what I already knew. "That is a wedding ring here in Bhutan."

THE NEXT DAY, I admire my Bhutanese jewel while I wait to check in at the Paro Airport ticket counter. I love this portable souvenir, and I love the significance I've ascribed to it, too. I am married to myself. Who else do I really need? It has taken me forty-three years to feel whole, to believe that nothing, really, is missing. Now is what matters; I have all I need. What's important isn't some promised future event, relationship, or achievement. The world is smaller now, and larger, filled with possibilities. Every time I catch a glimpse of my hand, I have a tangible reminder to celebrate. And to thank Bhutan for having cinched my feelings tight.

Right this moment, I am exhausted with the emotion of leaving and the prospect of going back to my job and to Los Angeles. Sir Phub Dorji stopped by in the afternoon to bid me farewell; it was the first time I'd seen him since the day I arrived in the kingdom. After our tea together, I stayed up all night dancing at Club Destiny with the Kuzoo gang, and then at Benez, a bar near the traffic circle. There, a Bhutanese patron told me in his drunken haze how, after finishing graduate school in journalism in the United States ten years ago, he came back to Bhutan and quit his job at the newspaper not long after. "Everything about the job—and me—was different," he said. I already suspected that my reaction to home would be the same. The question was whether I'd allow myself to do something rash.

Once we closed down the bar, Andy, one of my younger expat friends, walked me through the empty town and up the hill to Rabten. I wasn't afraid of the dark, desolate streets as much as I was worried about going back into the apartment. Earlier in the week, I'd spotted a rat while I was getting dressed in the morning and couldn't handle the idea of coming face-to-face with this new roommate. "So, you have a Bhutanese boyfriend," Sir Tenzin had joked after I'd rushed into

Kuzoo in a panic. Rats, indoors and out, are a part of life there and no one fears them.

It was around two in the morning. Since I didn't have an actual alarm clock, Andy said he'd be my human one—the idea being we'd stay up until dawn, when I had to leave for the airport.

For the next four hours we drank tea, trying to work off the beer we'd been guzzling. The colorful silliness of a Bollywood movie flickered in the background as we talked about the future. After he got back to the United States, Andy planned to pack up and move to Montana to go to vet school. He'd been adrift since dropping out of college the year before. He had that sweet brand of earnestness men often grow out of as they get older and goals get dashed. As for my intentions, I knew better than to plot them out. This whole Bhutan experience had dropped in my lap; how could you ever force a plan? Life just evolves around you, presents opportunities for you to reject or seize.

By 6:00 a.m., we were sprawled across the couch and chairs in the living room, fighting drunken exhaustion. I turned on the television to get one last glimpse of the morning prayers that kicked off the broadcasting day. The throaty chants of the monks had soothed me each morning, even though I never learned what they were saying. I would miss them. Now they were being drowned out by the sound of the car that had arrived in the driveway to take me to the airport. I said good-bye to Andy and left him to get some rest.

Blinking back sleep on that scary drive to the airport in Paro, I marvelled at the sky as it turned from black to gray to blue in the sunrise; I didn't want to miss a sight or a sound in my last few hours in the kingdom. I needed to sear as much of this landscape as I could into memory. There would be plenty of time to rest on the seventeen-hour flight home from Bangkok.

There's a tall blond woman ahead of me in the line at the ticket counter. Draped over her right shoulder is one of those tote bags you get when you give money to a public television station. Hers says KCET, which happens to be in Los Angeles. A fair-haired person alone would have caught my eye, much less one carrying a bag with a logo from back home. Friendly chitchat follows, the "where do you live" niceties that happen when you find something in common with a fellow traveler, far away from home. She points to a cluster of people across the ticketing area and tells me she's been here on vacation with her husband's family for the last two weeks. Seven of them, staying at the swanky Aman where I'd had lunch on the king's birthday. I fire up my mental calculator: Four rooms at a thousand dollars each, times fourteen days . . . $56,000 would construct an entire village.

It wasn't till I learned about this family that it occurred to me—really hit me—just how different the experience of being a tourist in Bhutan would be from mine. Particularly if you traveled deluxe. Just to get there you have to be moderately well off. The plane ticket from Bangkok to Paro alone isn't cheap—around $800 round-trip. Of course, you have to get to Bangkok, too, although flying in through India might shave off a couple of hundred bucks. The $200-a-day minimum "tourist tax" on each person is the kingdom's way of deterring an onslaught of budget tourists and backpackers on spiritual quests, like the people who swarm to neighboring Nepal and India. Bhutan doesn't mind spiritual seekers; it just wants to attract a higher grade, and discourage them from staying too long.

The blond woman's sister-in-law winds up sitting across the aisle from me on the plane and she's excited to show off her pictures. She's a good photographer and has a serious professional camera, not one of those point-and-shoot pocket-size digital things I own. For the past two weeks, she'd been squired around to splendid sights, and pulls up evidence of her travels on her state-of-the-art Mac laptop. Monasteries gleaming in the sun, portraits of stately *dzong*s set against spectacular mountain vistas that I'd gone nowhere near. Gorgeous portraits of smiling Bhutanese of all ages; exotic flowers captured close-up in supersaturated colors. The promised Shangri-la has been served up to this group on a beautiful, hand-carved platter. The pièce de résistance is the family portrait: all seven handsome adults, wrapped up in the finest and brightest hand-woven *kira* and *gho*, purchased on the trip—not a tuck of fabric or belt fringe out of place. The lady whispers to me that that was the day they met His Majesty. I wonder to myself: When someone drops that kind of money in Bhutan, is a royal welcome part of the deal?

When she finishes, she asks to see my photos. I warn her: My Bhutan is very different from your Bhutan. Yes, please, she says eagerly: I want to see. She has Bhutan fever, that mesmerized glow. She also possesses the breezy self-confidence of a person who has lived a privileged life and who is not used to being told no.

Taking pictures has never really been my thing. But I had to take photographs during my time in Bhutan—how often would I travel across the world? Though I carried my little camera with me every day, I had to constantly remind myself to remove it from my purse and use it. Once, while I was in college in western Massachusetts, a friend and I stopped to admire a gorgeous sunset, an enormous orange circle descending across the valley. At age seventeen, having hardly been out of New York City, I'd never seen anything like it. I wished out loud that we could preserve it on film for future enjoyment. My friend admonished me. "Just enjoy this moment, the light. Don't feel like you have to take it home with you. You can't." From then on, anytime I saw something beautiful, I resisted the urge to look at it through a lens, challenged myself to just enjoy it. Let the camera in my brain make a record, if need be, and enjoy the feeling what I was seeing evoked.

Fighting back the fatigue of my sleepless night, I decide to indulge my travel companion's request. I lean over the aisle, cradling my laptop, so she can get a good look at my impromptu slide show. Every once in a while, Pink's sister the flight attendant—days away from leaving for her new job on Emirates—interrupts us to make her way up and down the aisle.

This is the first time I've looked at my snapshots. Here is the Kuzoo studio, I narrate, perhaps the only radio station in the world that broadcasts from an old kitchen. Here is my apartment, and under that chair in the living room is where I saw the rat I suspected all along was sharing my space. He was this big, so huge, like a cat.

Here are the kids at the golf course, I say. I explain to my seat mate that, no, you wouldn't necessarily associate golf with a poor Buddhist kingdom, but an Indian military officer convinced the third king to build the course behind the Thimphu *dzong,* and a generation of players was born. Only nine holes, though, and the canteen at the course serves up pretty good Chinese-style fried rice.

Here's Pema and Ngawang of Kuzoo recording sound with a minidisc player. They were taping Ed's demonstration of a game he made up called gol-chery, which fuses golf with archery. Clever, no? The kids loved it.

This is Pema getting her hair curled and Pink getting her eyebrows threaded at a beauty "saloon" before a night on the town. That flight attendant who keeps passing us? She's the sister of this girl in the picture.

This is our boss at Kuzoo, Sir Tenzin, up by the BBS broadcast tower. This is Sir Pema, the second in command at Kuzoo. What he really wants is to be a philosopher. That's the Kuzoo van. And Kesang, he's the driver.

Here's a group shot from our trek up to Takshang, Tiger's Nest. It was right before a naked young Rinpoche ran down the trail. Yes, it's magical there, isn't it?

The collective effect of my little slide show is like seeing this latest chapter of my life flash before my eyes. My heart is swelling. Had I really been living in this place that these people spent thousands of dollars to see? Me?

No matter how dear you are to them, there are two things your friends are unlikely to do for you in Los Angeles. Helping you move is far and away number one. But an easy number two is picking you up at the airport. Which is why the various offers to drop me at LAX when I left, and to fetch me on the evening of my return, surprised and flattered me. They also made me feel a bit ashamed. I hadn't missed a thing about home, with the slight possible exception of the grocery store. And my swimming pool. The sole swimming pool in Thimphu had been under repair for several years, with no opening date in sight. If it would open back up, and if I could avoid the Bhutanese cuisine, I believed I could live in Bhutan very happily for a long time.

The person I chose to welcome me back from this adventure was my friend Sarah, a world traveler who lived in the neighborhood next to mine. Of her many good qualities, her greatest is that she is always game for just about anything. Almost more than anyone I knew, Sarah loved that I had made this trip. She had lived in almost as many exotic places as she had visited, and I knew she would be sympathetic to the jolt experienced by a returning traveler.

My suitcase had literally fallen apart as I pulled it off the baggage carousel, so I was wheeling it carefully to keep it from disintegrating before I found her. I considered just leaving the whole mess right there and rushing back upstairs to departures to board the next flight back to Asia. As a testament to the magnitude of this journey I'd just completed, Sarah had actually parked her car and come into the terminal, so she was waiting for me as I spilled out in the exodus from the baggage-claim area. Action-oriented person that she is, and knowing how exhausted I must have been, she insisted on hauling the enormous bag all the way out to the parking lot and hoisting it into her trunk. Then she produced a bottle of water and an apple. "You probably need this," she said. How fortunate I was to come home to the care of such a kind person.

A wise older friend had warned me that most people wouldn't know how to ask about my journey. "People will say,

'How was Bhutan?' but they won't really want to know," he had said. "They won't know what kinds of questions to ask." I knew that worldly Sarah wouldn't fall into this category; instead she posed almost too-specific queries about the service on Thai Air and Druk Air and currency exchange and the layout of the new airport in Bangkok. About the food I'd been eating, and the people I'd met. We agreed there'd be plenty of time, after jet lag wore off, to get into that.

She wrestled the mangled suitcase out of the car and upstairs, without my help. We sat and drank some tea, and I was thankful not to have to come home to an empty apartment. It was a Sunday night, and we both had to go to work the next day. I'd booked the return ticket with as little time as possible between my arrival in Los Angeles and my return to work. My instincts must have told me that if I'd given myself a minute to consider it, I might have thought better of it and not gone back.

EVERYTHING AT WORK was exactly the same as I'd left it. There was little to no fanfare at the office. It's not that I expected or wanted any, but I also didn't expect the utter indifference. "You're back already?" asked one of my more harried colleagues, a woman slightly older than me who ended nearly every conversation we had with, "Well, of course you can do that. You're *single*." Most of the others were too busy to notice I'd been gone, much less returned, with the exception of the few dear people I considered friends. Maybe, I suspected, nobody wanted to hear about an adventure they didn't get to have.

The scramble of the day felt even more hurried than usual.

I was constantly on the phone, all in the service of getting the sound bite. Everything moved like clockwork, on schedule, not a moment left to chance. Inside the office and out, it all was too fast, too large. The streets were too busy, the pavement too smooth. As grateful as I was to have more plentiful choices of food, the enormous grocery store overwhelmed me. Everyone took the shiny comforts, the ease of everything around them, for granted. Didn't they know how charmed their lives were? Even that magnificent view out my apartment window that I used to treasure—now I just wished those San Gabriel Mountains would morph into the snowcapped Himalayas, and that a pack of stray dogs would crowd my ankles every time I stepped out the front door to walk to work each morning.

It's not that I suddenly hated Los Angeles. I could see more clearly than ever that my life was good, really good. There was an endless parade of guests through my apartment. I'd built a fine community over the years by hosting a party every Friday night. The enormous pool behind the building was huge and beautiful and just the right temperature, and every day I got to see my fellow swimmers there. Two blocks away was the gorgeous, well-stocked public library that had been my ultimate inspiration to part with my books for good. A couple of farmers' markets set up downtown each week and allowed me to enjoy California's abundance of fresh produce without getting in the car.

The only easier commute than mine would be to work in my living room; I didn't even have to fight traffic to get over to the office, thanks to a pedestrian walkway that connected both sides of the street. I got to sit in climate-controlled splendor all day, in front of a computer, and interview leaders in their fields. My stories got beamed out on a show that was heard by millions of devoted listeners. The rotating overnight hours were like living in a constant state of jet lag, but nothing about my days was very exacting. In fact, life was very pleasant.

And that was the problem. It was all *too easy*. Too civilized. Too flat, colorless. I couldn't just go back to a world of work, leisure, and consumption. That would feel like going back in time, living on the obvious, predictable path.

The reactionary thing to do would have been to renounce it all, to pack it all up and just leave for somewhere, anywhere— to change my landscape before my mangled suitcase cooled. But my return was my endurance test of all I'd been learning. I fought the tendency to think another location, other people, another world, would be better and yet to accept that the way I'd been living wasn't right for me anymore. There was no better place. There were no better people. All I really needed was here inside me. The answers would follow in due time.

And so I settled into my routine. I chatted with my neighbors at the pool. I gritted my teeth at the office. I spread the word that the Friday-night parties would resume, and each week, I cooked up the usual big pot of soup to serve. I visited friends in various parts of town and shared meals. My wise mentor had predicted correctly. "How was Bhutan?" most would ask in an obligatory, cursory way. The "How was your day?" of travel. I taught myself to smile and simply say, "Great, just great," until and unless a follow-up question demanded more of an embellishment.

The pictures I showed the lady on the airplane came in handy. They were like having a secret friend. They jogged my memory as the vividness of Bhutan began to fade. I had some

of the better shots blown up and posted them on the wall at
work, in my line of sight. Right on the edge of my cubicle, I
hung a giant picture of the king, attached to a calendar from
the Bhutan National Bank. My coworkers would walk by and
say, laughing, "Wow, is that the Thai Elvis?" And I would
laugh back, and then answer, defensively, protectively, as if he
were mine, "No, no, that's His Majesty, the king of Bhutan.
The youngest monarch in the world. He presides over a land
that's going through a sea change, a transformation."

What I didn't add was: so had I.

The driveway to Sebastian's off-the-grid cabin in western
New England goes on forever. It's rocky and, remarkably,
even bumpier than that terrifying Bhutanese highway. After a
while, there isn't a pretense of pavement. Dense woods in every direction obscure the sky. Sebastian had promised that
when we got to the end, there'd be deer and turtles and a lake.
This property has been in his family for decades, so this similarity to Bhutan, this roughness, couldn't be by design. Now I
got a hint, though, of how he could feel so at home in the wilds
there.

There were supposed to be four of us here for the weekend,
but the patron saint of our friendship, Harris, along with his
new girlfriend, bowed out at the last minute—too busy, he
said, to get out of the city. It was all very natural and ordinary,
as if my going to Sebastian's, much less alone, was no big deal,
as if we saw each other all the time. When I'd laid eyes on this
man only once before.

Since before I'd gone to Bhutan, we had kept in touch by

email. Each time we'd communicate, once a week or so, he'd invite me to his cabin, as if he forgot I lived clear across the country. "You're welcome, anytime," he'd say. A visit east for a family reunion meant I'd finally be close enough to take him up on the offer.

In the hours before he picked me up in the Upper West Side of Manhattan for the drive north, I felt a strange sense of anticipation and nerves, as if I were a girl with a movie-star crush about to meet her idol. Who was this man, really? What was he like? What would it be like to see him again? There was no way this second meeting could match the intensity of the first. Imagination in these matters could get you into trouble, I knew well from experience. Charming, witty emails and phone calls were not accurate measures of how you would get along face-to-face. I was about to get an intensive crash course in the reality of Sebastian.

FOR HOURS WE TALKED and cooked and laughed and ate and drank, starting with tea and graduating to wine and then a special whiskey he'd been given as a present. We moved from the kitchen to the porch to the kitchen and back outside again. We covered everything and nothing in particular, like old friends who'd been reunited after a long separation.

Bhutan was a part of the conversation, of course, but it wasn't the only topic. We got done with that at the beginning. He explained the little mystery I'd been unable to solve, that his ties to the kingdom were through an old friend who helped him to become a guide many years ago. After he'd led trips for several years, Bhutan had become something of an addiction.

The connections continued back in the New York area, particularly with the handful of Bhutanese dignitaries and students who traveled through and temporarily resided there. He felt a deep love for the country and its people, and an attendant sense of obligation to help however possible.

I told him about my visits with the friends whose names he'd given me, and how they'd welcomed me warmly. And how every time I gave him credit for connecting me to Bhutan, I was corrected that it wasn't Sebastian, but rather my karma that had united us.

We discussed his business at length, for it was at a crossroads, and my own personal crossroads with my work. I teased him that since he'd hooked me up with Kuzoo, perhaps he could come up with what it was I should do next. He teased back, wondering how it was possible for an East Coast person to love Los Angeles. We stared at the lumbering turtles, and even spotted a deer, and as the sun began to set, a chill infused the night air. I excused myself to get a sweater from inside the cabin. And as I stood up, Sebastian reached over and grabbed me, kissed me hard and long, and held me tight.

FOR MANY PEOPLE, the happiest end to this part of the story would be to tell you that this magical weekend never ended. That I eloped with Sebastian to Bhutan in a fit of passion, where a venerable lama presided over a ceremony uniting us forever. That we returned to New England and I helped run his business, eventually growing it into a mighty empire as our love deepened and matured. How, with all these riches, we eventually adopted several Bhutanese children and sent piles of money back to build schools for the kids we couldn't take in. A fairy-tale romance that swept across international borders, born out of a single chance encounter. Cue the music; get Hollywood on the line.

What actually happened was this:

On Sunday afternoon, Sebastian drove me back to a town just outside New York City, where he was scheduled to deliver a lecture on tea. My childhood friend Liz, who lived right nearby, picked me up so I could spend the night with her family. When we got to her house a few minutes later, she said I seemed a bit out of it. "I feel dazed," I explained. "I'm not quite sure what just happened." Sebastian had, on second inspection, been as wonderful as I'd imagined he would be. We had gotten along famously. What I knew for certain was that Sebastian and I would be friends, always, that we'd forever be connected because of Bhutan. But in those forty-eight hours, I had also learned enough to know that this time we were spending together could never be anything more. Shouldn't be.

Now I had new photographs to add to my collection. One is a shot of a bale of hay on a dairy farm we visited that belonged to Sebastian's friends. It resembled one of those oversize Claes Oldenburg sculptures, like a giant piece of shredded wheat, the gold of the sunset shining brightly in the corner. That magic hour of light in the early summer as it starts to dim, the temperature readjusting to cool.

The other picture is of Sebastian, a few minutes later, sleeves rolled up, a big grin on his face, mugging for the camera, eyes wide, the gray flecks in his hair catching the sun, the sky bright blue behind him. Reveling in the beauty of the twilight. I knew I couldn't freeze the clock right at that instant, and even if I could have, it would have been futile. But my resistance to forward motion was for good reason: When this

weekend was over, a piece of who I used to be would be finished, too. Now I understood what that thunderbolt I'd experienced when we first spotted each other was all about. I had
mistaken it for romance—true love, even. But in Bhutan, the
Land of the Thunder Dragon, a thunderbolt literally signals a
roar of power. A moment of enlightenment.

10

DAWN OF DEMOCRACY

THE PEOPLE OF BHUTAN WERE NOT SORRY TO SEE
the year of the Female Fire Hog come to a close. It had
been an astrologically sour one. Arbiters of the skies
had warned that it would be a bad time to do just about any
thing: get married, have a child, start a job or project, begin
new construction. Judging from the nests of bamboo scaffolding rising above the streets of the capital city, and the numbers
of babies slung over the backs of women as they trundled
around doing their chores, activity in the capital had hardly
come to a screeching halt. Life had proceeded—but with many
extra prayers and cautions. To combat the misaligned stars,
the official astrological calendar of Bhutan had recommended
"appropriate preventive religious ceremonies." Maybe you
went ahead and moved a few things into the home of the person you intended to marry, but delayed the complete union of
possessions until 2008. In the meantime, you were well-advised
to deploy a bunch of monks to make things right with the gods.

Leaving the year of the Female Fire Hog behind didn't
mean the Bhutanese were any less wary of the coming one.

The dawn of the year of the Male Earth Mouse also meant the dawn of democracy in Bhutan—and with that, the formal diminishment of the all-powerful monarchy that had reigned for a century. Bhutan's king would continue to lead, but no longer would he possess absolute power. A year into the king's tenure, Bhutan was still adjusting to this new, young monarch, and the absence of his beloved father on the throne. No one was terribly keen to elect the parliament he'd insisted they create, or to see him give up power.

Getting citizens to the polls on December 31 posed a challenge, and not because the date marked the Western New Year's Eve. It had to do with a higher power. In the weeks in advance of the election, official notices had been placed in the newspapers:

REQUEST TO TEMPORARILY POSTPONE ANY PILGRIMAGE PLANS
Bhutan is a Buddhist country, and annually around this time in winter, everyone wishes to pay homage to holy places in the neighbouring countries. Nevertheless it is essential for every citizen to be present in the country and be able to serve our homeland when such a historic event is taking place. At this time, National Council and National Parliament elections are in progress. Therefore, we suggest that every citizen should by way of voting contribute toward the country's prosperity. When this is done we will have enough opportunity in the future to pay homage to holy places.

Nothing less than a royal edict would convince the devout Bhutanese to give up their sacred annual treks. Though voting was not compulsory, the official Bhutan Voter Guide did declare it the moral responsibility of the people to cast ballots. If they did not, it continued, they ran the risk of being "guilty of letting a less competent political party or candidate come to power." If the menace of moral failure didn't compel a proud citizen to the polls, what would?

Lest the people be overwhelmed with too many decisions and campaigns at once, the election board had decided to split the daunting responsibility of choosing a parliament into two dates. In the first round, this New Year's Eve, ballots would be cast for a National Council, with each district (or *dzongkhag*) electing a single representative. A few months later, at a date still to be determined by astrologers, the Bhutanese would be asked to vote for a slate of candidates affiliated with one of two newly formed political parties.

On December 31, 2007, voting commenced across the tiny kingdom.

IT HAD BEEN just under a year since my first trip to the kingdom, and time had done nothing but intensify my curiosity about the place, my craving for more—the landscape, the people, the feeling of calm that had swept over me while I was there. The serenity had mercifully remained, but I wanted a booster shot. I needed to see this place again. I knew I'd never completely solve the riddle of Bhutan, never really "get" it. I also knew the way I felt during my first visit, the richness of experience, could never be duplicated. All I was sure of was that I needed to return.

Back in Los Angeles, I'd entertained any Bhutanese visitors I could and met anyone with even a remote connection to the place. A local couple who had collected photographs of Bhutan by the explorer John Claude White and published a book of them? Let's have tea. The labor minister's wife and children, whom I'd met through our mutual friend Sebastian? You are welcome to stay with me. A friend of a friend who'd returned from a trip? Let's drink some wine so you can show off your photos. My friend's daughter had heard me talk so much about the country, she'd written a report about it for her fourth-grade class. ("Bhutan is the happiest country on the face of the earth . . .")

In the spring, just weeks after I'd arrived back in Los Angeles from that first trip, a twenty-five-member Bhutanese trade delegation mining California for business opportunities jammed into my tiny apartment for a pizza party. (To make the slices more spicy-palatable, the ladies in the group discreetly pulled hot chili sauce from their purses.) I gave them a tour of the studio where I worked, encouraged them to help themselves to the stacks of free books we always had on the shelves to give away, and helped mitigate disappointment over their lack of sales. Their intricate handwoven items just couldn't be mass-produced on the necessary scale for the U.S. market

The trade visit had unintended consequences: Because of it, I met the small but close-knit community of Bhutanese living in Southern California. (One of them became the recipient of my dusty old television set, which I was delighted to finally give away.) And my connection to the group motivated them to offer me a visitor visa for a return trip to Bhutan. After I'd put in for vacation time, I had bought my plane tickets and stuffed my suitcase with Gold Toe socks and a hand-me-down Burberry purse for Pema, courtesy of my stylish friend Barbara, and the royal astrologers made my return an even more auspicious one. My arrival would coincide with the first stage of the election.

KUZOO WAS PREPARING to perform its most important community service yet: beaming out the results to the people as soon as the votes had been tabulated. The news would be revealed simply, by reading a fax from the election board on the air as soon as it chugged over the line to the well-worn machine in the workroom. News coverage had been suspended at Kuzoo not long after I'd left. Someone in His Majesty's secretariat had reportedly yanked the puny daily news report off the air when a newly hired radio jockey had committed a transgression; she chose to lead a newscast with a story about taxi fares, rather than a routine item about the king visiting one of the *dzongkhag*s. Even though her news judgment was correct by journalistic standards, her respect for the monarchy as a Bhutanese citizen was in question. So much for the freedom of the press guaranteed in the as-yet-to-be-ratified constitution. I wondered if the kindly, generous king himself would have interpreted her action as a slight.

In the fourteen months since the station had launched, there had been other, more sweeping changes for Kuzoo. Sir Tenzin traversed Bhutan's rocky terrain with an engineer, rigging up repeaters so that the signal could reach beyond Thimphu Valley. Now all but five of the remotest districts in Bhutan could tune in. Second in command Sir Pema stepped in to run day-to-day operations.

There had been another, formative development: Kuzoo's transmission frequency had been moved, and alongside it, a new one had been added, this one broadcasting in Dzongkha. So passionate and devoted was this new crop of listeners that they decided to throw a party to thank the staff. Perhaps for the first time ever in the history of radio, a fan-appreciation day was orchestrated not by a radio station itself but by its listeners. They proudly called themselves the "Kuzoo family." From hours away, from every direction, several dozen of the most ardent audience members trekked to the modest Kuzoo studios, decked out in their finest *kira* and *gho*—with their similarly attired children and colorful thermoses of tea and food in tow. The first to arrive, at 6:30 a.m., was the man who'd appointed himself "Kuzoo *gup*," Dzonghkha for mayor. He proudly greeted partygoers who descended on the grounds as if he owned the place.

A crowd of more than a hundred people assembled; it was a chilly winter day, my first back in the country. Sir Pema and I stood on the front steps with Ngawang, marveling at the "family" members who squealed with delight upon meeting one another in person for the first time. Word was a marriage had even occurred as a result of two frequent callers taken with the sound of each other's voice on the air.

"I had no idea how many people loved Kuzoo," Ngawang said, shaking her head. One of the fans passed a basket of cookies, and we all each grabbed one.

"I knew they were enjoying Kuzoo," said Sir Pema, "but I had no idea this much!"

The main radio jockey for the new Dzongkha station emerged to make some announcements to the crowd, which obediently hushed at the sight of him. In his native language, he began to speak. Several lines in, I made out my name and felt all eyes turn in my direction. "Madam Jane," he said, followed by the words "United States." Having traveled farther than any of even the most geographically remote of the Kuzoo fans, I ranked as the most honored guest and received the first shout-out. I felt a bit embarrassed at being singled out.

With a growing awareness of their own impact on their tiny country, the staff of Kuzoo settled in on election night, ready to relay the winners as soon as the electronic voting machines had finished tabulating. No chance for hanging chads here; even in communities not yet wired for electricity, the voting machines that had been deployed had touch screens and were battery powered, imported from India and reputed to be impenetrable. To fill the time, those on duty played a merry stream of New Year's Eve party music.

I was torn over where to spend this historic election/New Year's Eve. Despite my allegiance to Kuzoo, I knew my friends at the station would understand why I chose to accept another invitation, one that required my being across town.

THE PAIR OF pimply faced military guards who man the entrance to Villa Italia look barely old enough to carry the machine guns they have strapped to their sides. The property they are securing is an oasis just blocks from the center of Thimphu, but it's one particular resident who warrants their presence.

Carefully trained vines soften the concrete walls that separate the property from the noise and imposition of the busy, narrow street just outside. Apricot and apple trees dot the yard. Despite its name, Villa Italia's exterior architecture is typically Bhutanese, trimmed with the colorfully painted, ornately stacked wooden edging that adorns every building across the land. The interior of this apartment building, though, lives up to its title; richly tiled bathrooms and terrazzo floors lend an air of understated European elegance. Modern Italian fixtures and appliances distinguish the villa from the handful of other fine homes in Thimphu that are also inhabited by VIPs.

The gathering I have decided to attend is on the topmost floor; during this trip, I was staying at a borrowed apartment on the ground level. About half the guests focused on the fact that 2008 was about to begin, their sights set on the clubs they'd visit after a fusion meal of breaded chicken cutlets and *emadatse*. The other half was more concerned with election coverage—including the host himself, for he was to be a candidate in the second, as-yet-unscheduled phase of the election.

Lyonpo Ugyen Tshering—*lyonpo* being the Dzongkha word for minister—had ably served Bhutan in a number of roles. He and seven other king-appointed ministers had resigned their posts earlier in the year in order to form a political party and run for office. Leaving one's job was a prerequisite for tossing one's hat in the ring, to avoid any conflicts of interest and allow the candidates to focus on this important election. This group dubbed their coalition Druk Phuensum Tshogpa, or DPT, which translates loosely to mean Party of Blissful Harmony. The campaign slogan they crafted wisely incorporated an important piece of Bhutan's national identity: "In Pursuit of Gross National Happiness" proclaimed their campaign literature.

It almost didn't matter that the rival People's Democratic Party (PDP) had chosen as its theme a phrase that smacked of a high school campaign promise: "Service with Humility. Walk the Talk." Their decided advantage was that the uncle of the king was at the helm. A citizenry that revered its monarch seemed quite likely to choose a person close to him for the crucial job of leading the first democratic government.

Each party published manifestos that promised lofty improvements for their countrymen: help for the poorest, installation of roads and electricity for the remote areas still unconnected, access to education for all, continued protection of natural resources. Each offered only vague suggestions about how these formidable goals would be accomplished. And each promised, first and foremost, to uphold and further promote the beloved monarchy, ignoring the reality that by their very existence, they would be undermining it. There weren't any major philosophical differences between the two groups, and neither touched on any subject that could be construed as controversial, most notably the refugee camps over the Nepalese border, filled with a hundred thousand people with disputed Bhutanese citizenship. (The refugees claimed to have been tossed out because they weren't ethnically pure; the Bhutanese government maintained they had illegally immigrated.) But issues weren't really the point in this election. In the end, the deciding factor would be the popularity of each party's members, and their tenacity in campaigning. Though the PDP had an edge because of its royal connection, no one presumed that meant they had a lock on a win.

For the DPT to boast important civil servants like Lyonpo Ugyen among its roster of stars was a tremendous asset. He was descendent of a family that had served the king honorably and he himself had given his career to his country, including nine years as Bhutan's ambassador to the United Nations. Lyonpo Ugyen's personality was as much an asset as was his résumé; he radiated a calm, quiet demeanor, a commanding presence. "Lyonpo Ugyen—he's like a Buddha," said one of our mutual acquaintances. In Western clothing he looked like a handsome college professor, with dark, thick hair that was graying just enough to give him a further sense of gravitas, while his friendly, bright eyes shone with a youthful gleam. A serene sliver of a smile graced his face almost always, and he was quick with a joke or turn of phrase. Outfitted in his Bhutanese *gho,* he was a man you'd comfortably entrust with a giant sack of cash or a newborn baby.

Like most of the elite citizens of Bhutan, Lyonpo Ugyen had begun his studies with the Jesuits in India and had gone on to attend fine universities in the United States. He enjoyed a long marriage to a formidable Italian beauty, and the magnificent Villa Italia was her creation. It was a testament to Lyonpo Ugyen's standing in Bhutan, where cultural preservation and ethnic homogeneity are highly regarded, that this "mixed marriage" hadn't become a political liability.

As would-be politicians go, Lynopo Ugyen was as Teflon as Reagan, as charming as Clinton, and as wise as Carter. To the people of Bhutan, he posessed the quintessential qualities of a modern steward: humility, worldliness, and reverence of the homeland. And because of this, he could very likely be Bhutan's first elected foreign minister.

The decor of the Tshering family living room was, like the evening's menu, a museum to the merged cultures of its owners: At its center sat a large, brightly decorated Christmas tree, its colorful lights reflecting in the glass covering the prominently placed portrait of His Majesty the king. The living room also boasted several more personal photographs of the revered monarch at various stages of his life, posed with Lyonpo, his wife, and their children. As a young man, His Majesty had been educated in the United States, which had coincided with Lyonpo's service as UN ambassador in New York City.

Guests crunched on Bumthang-made potato chips, and the Bhutan Broadcasting Service played in the background. The BBS was doing its best impersonation of CNN, even if it had neither the budget nor the worldly reach.

"This is a historic evening for Bhutan," declared the anchorman, Tshewang Dendhup. "You are watching history being made." Such a declaration was very un-Bhutanese, but if ever there was a time for drama, this was it. And Tshewang was the perfect person to utter it. He was perhaps Bhutan's best-known export, having appeared as the star of the film *Travellers and Magicians,* and as the real-life love interest in a book by the young Canadian teacher who had, for a time, become his wife.

The coanchor, Dawa Sonam, was Bhutan's answer to Anderson Cooper, his demeanor the perfect broadcast blend of serious and convivial. He chatted with reporters stationed at various polling places across the country, as slides with their pictures and the names of the districts they were calling from appeared on the screen. Only one live video shot was possible, since the BBS owned only a single microwave truck—a donation from Japan. That was parked at national election headquarters, just about a mile up the street from the BBS studio. Even if there had been more trucks available, the ability to beam live pictures across the rocky Bhutanese terrain would have posed a challenge for the most experienced engineers, for mountains would have obstructed the signal.

Although the simple phoned-in reports didn't exactly make for lively imagery, viewers were ably regaled with tales of their fellow citizens who had dutifully made their way to the polls. Despite educational initiatives in advance of election day, not everyone understood how the voting machines worked. A seventy-eight-year-old woman confessed, "I pressed the first. Did I vote for the right candidate?"

A forty-four-year-old yak herder trekked four hours from his village to his local polling station, and declared that he'd cast his vote for the eldest candidate in his district. "The old are always wise," he said. "Elderly people will know the difficulties and problems we face and be able to raise these issues in meetings."

National law prohibited knives in polling places, which caused confusion among men in the remotest regions, who were not accustomed to leaving home without them. "We didn't mean to be disrespectful," one man said after having his machete temporarily confiscated. "The knives are just something we men carry with us always."

The ballots featured thumbnail photographs of the candidates. This served two purposes: to assist the half of the population that was illiterate, and to help distinguish among contenders with identical names. In one of the races, for instance, four people were vying for the area's National Council seat: Jambay Dorji, Sherab Dorji, and two Ugyen Tsherings— neither the one whose living room I was sitting in.

"Look, I won *and* lost in Paro," joked Lyonpo Ugyen as the results flicked up on the screen. One Ugyen Tandin had received 2,886 votes. The other got 1,883. Sir Dorji and Sir Dorji trailed behind.

Of the four female candidates in various races across the country, three had claimed victory—a fact both news anchors mentioned several times, clearly impressed that their fellow citizens were willing to allow the fairer sex to govern. By 10:00 p.m., all victories had been announced. Attention and the television set were then turned to the real CNN, so that the guests could witness fireworks displays and other celebrations that marked the arrival of 2008 around the world.

ACROSS TOWN AT KUZOO, the radio jockeys performed their national duty, reading the names of the winners before resuming the music and their on-air party. A little before midnight, exhausted from the twin forces of a long journey and a week of overnight shifts back home, I turned the electric heater in the bedroom of my borrowed apartment on full blast, quickly stripped off my clothes, jumped into my pajamas, and crawled into bed with my little portable radio.

Three of Kuzoo's new radio jockeys were leading the on-air party in the kitchen studio: Namgay (female), Namgay (male), and Choki.

"The phones are jammed with callers," announced Choki. "Who's this on the line, please?"

"Hi, guys," the voice said. I recognized it immediately as Ngawang.

"Hey, it's Kuzoo RJ Ngawang. Wow, great, how are you?" her colleagues responded.

Ngawang sounded as if she was a combination of glum and tired and was a bit hard to believe when she said, "Actually, I feel great, because my friend Lady Jane is here in town and that's so good. I've missed you, Lady Jane, and I'm glad you're back."

The three radio jockeys sounded, in contrast, a bit *too* happy. I wondered if they were tipsy.

"Yes, yes, Lady Jane! Welcome back to Bhutan. Yes, yes, Ngawang! Happy New Year, everyone! You are listening to Kuzoo! Is there any other message, Ngawang?"

"Umm, well, I hope to see you more in this new year, Lady Jane. And I hope my dreams come true this year. Best wishes to everyone." Ngawang sounded as if she might fall asleep.

"What song would you like us to play?" the female Namgay asked.

"Your choice," said Ngawang.

And without the radio jockeys saying another word—thus a quicker return to their bubbly—the music started. The song they'd chosen was "Complicated" by Carolyn Dawn Johnson, a Kuzoo staple. It had to be the twentieth time it had aired that day.

Shortly after midnight, the Kuzoo radio jockeys took a break to run what they described as a very important New Year's announcement. It had been recorded by the shy Sir Pema. The staff adored having him at the helm; he was studious and quiet, the temperamental opposite of Sir Tenzin, as well as a kindly, paternal advocate who listened to their hopes and aspirations. Sir Pema's own long-term dream had just come true: He'd not only been accepted to a philosophy course in Bangkok but he'd been awarded a scholarship from the king's office to subsidize it. Perhaps because of his imminent departure, he was willing to boldly transmit his voice across the land.

"After the partying and drinking," he said in a quiet, noble voice, "Kuzoo would like to wish you a happy New Year with a poem by Alfred, Lord Tennyson. Ring out the old, ring in the new.

Ring, happy bells, across the snow:
The year is going, let him go;
Ring out the false, ring in the true.

He continued with a slight modification.

Ring out the grief that saps the mind,
For those that here we see no more,
Ring out the feud of rich and poor,
Ring in redress to all mankind. . . .

Ring out false pride in place and blood,
The civic slander and the spite;
Ring in the love of truth and right,
Ring in the common love of good. . . .

Ring in the valiant man and free,
The larger heart, the kindlier hand;
Ring out the darkness of the land,
And ring in Gross National Happiness.

With only the slightest wink in his voice to his having modified this great poet's work for the youthful Bhutanese audience, Sir Pema concluded his greeting:

"Kuzoo's New Year's mantra: 'Let bygones be bygones.' The year 2007 is behind us, and 2008 beckons us. Warm wishes to all our listeners. May you have a really bright and prosperous New Year."

With one election down and one to go sometime this coming spring, soon the new constitution would be adopted and the new king officially installed. For Bhutan, the year of the Male Earth Mouse would indeed be a historic one.

THE NEXT DAY, I do something I haven't done much of yet in Bhutan: play tourist. I'm going on a field trip to a place all tourists go, about an hour outside Thimphu. It's called Dochula Pass. It is the site of a memorial built for Bhutanese who died in a conflict with Indian separatists in 2003. It's also a perfect vista for one of the most magnificent confluences of mountain ranges on the planet.

My companions are a fresh crop of Bhutanese tour guides who I am tutoring in English. It's sure to be an informative trip, with one visitor (me) and forty accomplices trained to explain the landscape. As a thank-you to the trade department for inviting me here, I offered to help out however I could, and I'd been assigned to help the guides practice talking to foreigners. They are undergoing a special hospitality training course in preparation for the king's coronation.

Sitting in a room and asking these shy young Bhutanese to speak English in front of their friends hadn't worked very well. I'd sliced paper into strips and written topics on them I knew tourists, particularly American tourists, would be most likely to ask about. I'd call up a guide and ask him to choose one, and have him riff on it with me: "Why are there penises painted on the houses?" "How come the king has four queens?" "What will the new democracy mean for Bhutan?" "Why is Bhutanese food so spicy hot?"

The pupils clammed up under pressure to speak to a chatty foreigner in front of a group. The best way to warm these guys up, I figured—and most of them were guys—was to get them out of the dank, dark conference room. I asked the course leader if we could take a short field trip, to Kuzoo, a long two-block walk on the upper road. They all knew where it was, of course; everyone knew where everything was in Thimphu. They'd all just been too shy to go in for a visit—these same hardy young people who can set up and break down elegant campsites with ease in hours, and deftly navigate the bamboo woods and ancient trails of the most remote locations in their country simply by looking at the sky.

"Who wants to go to Kuzoo?" I asked. All hands flew up, and the enthusiasm wasn't just because it meant getting outside. Our mob moved as a unit out to the street, and as we walked I made a couple of cell phone calls to be sure arriving en masse would be okay. "Five at a time," I said, and I took them in, in small groups, doing my own best impersonation of tour guide. "You're about to see the world's only radio station in a kitchen." I'd still not confirmed this to be true, but my pride in Kuzoo allowed for this reasonable conjecture.

Ngawang happened to be behind the board in the blue-tiled studio, and before I opened the door, I told the guys who we were going to see. "RJ Ngawang? That's Radio Jockey Ngawang?" they exclaimed. And as they crouched against the tile in the studio while she introduced a song, they were all gaping like awestruck teenagers. Ngawang was just as shy as they were. She deferred to me to explain how the studio worked.

"Are you really here at the station all night long, *la*?" one of the guides asked shyly. Ngawang giggled; no one at Kuzoo liked to admit that the station ran 24/7 thanks to a computer. It seemed duplicitous somehow, inauthentic.

"Virtually," I said, pointing to the computer, and we left it at that.

The trip was so successful, I suggested another. "Let's go somewhere in the area, so you can show *me* something," I said. The course leader saw my point. There was a tour bus out back and a driver at the ready.

It's a beautiful, cloudless winter day. The guides are bursting with energy, thrilled to be out of the conference room again. We drive into the parking area at Dochula, and they all gasp in unison. We have hit the equivalent of the view jackpot; it's one of those days when all the mountain ranges are perfectly visible from this spot. In the foreground is the Punakha Valley, and off in the distance at various points are spiky, soaring snowcapped peaks. There isn't a sign of man-made life as far as the eye can see.

Everyone rushes off the bus. Suddenly, I'm a schoolteacher with a classful of star pupils.

"Madam, that's Gangchenta, the Tiger Mountain."

"And that there is the highest peak in Bhutan."

"Madam, look over there. That is China, there. Can you see?"

"In that direction, see? You can see Gasa, the only district in Bhutan with no motor roads. It takes five days trekking and you can get to the most beautiful hot springs. . . ."

Now my guides insist we walk to the maze of 108 religious structures, chortens, that form the memorial portion of this stop. Again I am bombarded with factoids.

"The number 108 is symbolic, madam, for it is the number of volumes in the Kanjur. That is the Buddhist scripture. And that is why there are 108 chortens here."

"They were built thanks to Her Majesty the queen Ashi Dorji Wangmo. This is a memorial for fallen soldiers."

"Yes, *la,* the soldiers died in 2003. . . . "

"Up there, over there. See, Her Majesty is giving us a sacred temple. See? Over there? It will be opened soon, madam."

A few of us stroll among the statues. They're at different heights, and as beautiful and impressive as they are, as sacred as they may be, they've got nothing on the view, the endless ridges of mountains. The afternoon wind is picking up now and most people aren't wearing overcoats on top of their national dress. Soon we are gathering near the bus, where the coldest of the group are huddled together, a few of them grabbing a smoke, a few others continuing their discussion of the spectacular view. A transistor radio has materialized; it must be Kuzoo playing.

The group is being corralled for a picture, and they insist I must stand in the center. Several cameras are passed down to the front. *"Emadatse,"* shouts the photographer, the Bhutanese equivalent of "Say cheese." And as we smile and pose for the shot, some of the guys are singing along, and I make out the song that's wafting out around the country, and entertaining us here on this fine winter afternoon. It's the old hit by R.E.M. "Losing My Religion."

WHEN I HAD only a couple of days left in Bhutan, at the station, Ngawang asked for a favor.

"Would you call me there?" she asked. "To the United States?"

"What does that mean, exactly? To call you? What do you need to be able to visit?" I had learned from this trip that Bhutanese citizens could only "call" foreign visitors if they could explain to immigration authorities the favor that had been performed for them, or establish the existence of a long friendship. This was to avoid skirting the payment of the tourist visa. The challenges of "calling" a visitor to the United States were different, of course.

"I think you just have to write a letter."

"What about? Work?"

"Sir Pema would let me take leave. Especially if I was going to come to work with you. I could do an internship!"

I tempered my natural instinct to automatically say yes and considered the proposition. I loved having houseguests; even though my apartment was tiny, people crashed in my living room all the time. I wished I could afford a bigger space so I could offer a bit more comfort and privacy, but for most visitors, the blow-up Aerobed was perfectly suitable for a visit of just a couple of nights. An appearance by Ngawang felt heftier, though; it introduced larger concerns than my usual worries about the size of my bathroom or the lack of a private space in which guests would sleep. The trip would be long and expensive. Could I offer to subsidize it without offending, or would I be expected to subsidize it, which would be offensive to me? Ngawang would be more of a responsibility than a typical visitor, and I'd be working and not able to squire her much. And yet the prospect of showing her around Los Angeles and where I worked was exciting. It was bound to be educational and eye-opening, and for Ngawang, maybe even life-changing—the way visiting Bhutan had been for me.

I couldn't stay in Bhutan, I rationalized, so I might as well at least bring a bit of Bhutan to me.

So I said yes. And as soon as I got back to Los Angeles, I grabbed a piece of letterhead at the office and composed an official invitation.

11

AMERICA 101: "THAT'S COOL"

THE INTERNATIONAL TERMINAL AT LOS ANGELES International Airport is the winged, modern version of Ellis Island. Of course, the mode of transportation is plane, not boat. And there are just as many people leaving as there are arriving. Here the stew of nationalities that comprise the United States is starkly evident: People of every imaginable skin color, mingling, hopefulness in their eyes, some carting boxes and bulging suitcases of items they're transporting to make *there* a bit more like *here,* and to replicate *here* what they've left behind *there.* For every five pieces of luggage, there is one box containing a flat-panel TV.

The Friday night Ngawang was to land in Los Angeles, I was so excited that I got to the airport an hour and a half before her plane was due. This was one guest I would, without hesitation, not refer to a taxi or shuttle. I didn't expect her plane to arrive early, but I did want to ensure a prominent place in the receiving line of eager friends and family and bored-looking car-service drivers. On my way, I stopped at the supermarket to buy something I'd never bought before: a corny welcome balloon, visual reenforcement of my excitement over this important visitor.

It seemed the least I could do. The trip Ngawang had just made was numbingly long. To shave off a bit of the cost, she had traveled a more arduous route than would a typical visitor to Bhutan: seven hours in a car out of Thimphu, three days on a train across India to Delhi, then nights of bunking at the Bhutanese embassy to wait for a call from the American authorities to see if she'd even be granted a visa. My personal invitation was no guarantee. U.S. customs agents are wary of allowing in another inevitable nanny.

"This will be a kind of mini-internship," I had told Ngawang after sending the letter, "for you to see how media companies work here. But it's a closed invitation. You can't stay forever." Because my apartment was small, my job and hours ever-changing, I explained, I couldn't house her for more than a few weeks. While it felt rude to emphasize, I knew it was necessary to be clear. As far as the Bhutanese were concerned, it was your obligation, if someone came to visit, to put them up for as long as they needed or wanted to stay. Bhutanese living rooms were lined with couches, bumped up arm-to-arm and pressed against the walls, at the ready for whoever needed to sleep on them. Ngawang assured me that she understood, that she didn't want to leave her family or her country permanently.

The day the phone rang with news from Delhi, Ngawang's excitement practically pulsed through the lines: "They said yes! I can come there!" Now the travel details had to be arranged. A day and a half later, another call came through informing me that she would arrive on Friday night. I felt a tiny bit like prospective parents I'd known, waiting for the fateful, life-altering call from the adoption agency. Of course, this was very different. But having Ngawang in my orbit turned out to be more like having a child around than I'd imagined.

THE GIANT ELECTRONIC signboard announced arrivals from all kinds of exotic places: Manzanillo. Singapore. Manila. Ngawang's plane from India by way of Frankfurt, the board said, was delayed. Just like my first visit to Bhutan, I thought, as I surveyed the waiting area. Everyone here was expecting someone who had journeyed from another land; most likely none had ventured all the way from Thimphu.

More than three hours elapsed before my friend emerged from the bowels of the airport. She looked so much less formal than she would in her Bhutanese dress, more like a typical college student: a sweatshirt, an orange backpack, faux Crocs to match, hair pulled back in a ponytail. Behind her, she dragged a small suitcase. She looked tired but not depleted. The forgiveness of youth, this representative of the modern Bhutan. Ngawang now could count herself among the elite few from her country to have actually seen a plane, been on one, much less flown halfway around the world.

"How was it, how was it?" I asked, hugging her tight, aware that I was completely incapable of imagining what it would be like to land in the United States for the first time. During college a friend from Switzerland had come home to Brooklyn with me for Thanksgiving, her first trip to the New York metropolitan area. When she caught a look at the lower Manhattan skyline, she'd gasped, loudly, at the live vision of a vista she'd seen a thousand times in the movies. From her, I learned the wonder of seeing for real a place you'd long imagined, and how perceptions rarely matched reality.

"Okay," said Ngawang, who wasn't nearly as demonstrative. "Long. What day is it?"

"It's Friday evening."

"I left on Friday evening. Wow. That's cool."

The elasticity of time as it relates to world travel was just the beginning of a series of events that would elicit that exclamation. The next phenomenon was the five-story parking garage, crammed with cars of all shapes and colors and sizes, far more varieties than the five types of vehicles that roam the streets of Bhutan. Despite the cool, nighttime desert air, I flipped down the top of my dusty old two-seater convertible; Ngawang had never been in, much less seen, one before. Out of the airport and onto the eight-lane freeway we went, weaving through the balletic tangle of traffic. Cruising sixty-five miles an hour on a straight open road was as much a thrill for her as riding the Cyclone at Coney Island would be. Especially when we ascended the long arc of a ramp to exit the 105 so we could spill out on the even wider 110. I could feel Ngawang gasping for breath with the speed, motion, and height.

We were surrounded, in every direction, by twinkling lights.

"There aren't this many people in all of Bhutan." Ngawang sighed.

She was right. If you drew a circle on a map around downtown Los Angeles, it was likely to contain the equivalent of the kingdom's population—around 650,000 people. The Los Angeles school system had more students in it than her entire country had citizens. Ngawang's sensory overload reached a new dimension as we neared the towering buildings of down-town, shimmering in the distance. As we got closer and closer, they commanded the sky, stern and intimidating. The mod-ern, manufactured version of that spectacular range of moun-tains I'd visited with the tour guides.

We drove inside another parking garage, this one with a remote-controlled electric gate. An elevator transported us to the eighteenth floor, a height she'd never experienced from in-side a building. The floor-to-ceiling glass windows in my apartment offered Ngawang a panoramic view of twinkling lights flickering in every direction. The centerpiece was the stainless-steel Disney Concert Hall, a structure that resembles a silvery spaceship and dazzles even those who haven't trav-eled from a place where every building is the same general shape and color. It dazzled me, and I had been gazing at it ev-ery day for years now.

Ngawang planted the welcome balloon in the bamboo vase that sat where the television I'd given away used to be. Then she slumped onto the sofa, conceding defeat to exhaustion. She had arrived, and soon she would conquer America. After a sip of tea and a glass of water and oohs and aahs at the UFO-like building and the magic of the blow-up mattress unfolding into a comfy bed at the press of a button, she fell off to sleep—ex-hausted by the jet lag and travel and the overstimulation of the sights and sounds of the country she had longed to see. And she hadn't even seen it yet in the cold light of day.

BEFORE HEADING WEST on the freeway the next morning to go to the beach, I detoured to a nearby Jack in the Box. Every young Bhutanese was intrigued by the idea of take-out food.

They thought Americans ate McDonald's three times a day, the way they ate three plates of rice and chilies and cheese.

"Ngawang, what looks good on this menu?"

The number of options on the enormous board at the drive-through was too much for her.

"Egg kind of thing, or sweet kind of thing?" The only food I'd seen Ngawang eat besides *emadatse* and mounds of rice was the occasional slice from a pie I'd picked up at Druk Pizza. And sweets.

"Umm, sweet?"

Her brow furrowed, and I could see she was studying the prices, deploying her internal currency converter to calculate dollar to ngultrum.

"This is my treat," I said. "Everything is my treat, okay? You are my guest, and it's my pleasure." I pulled up to the ordering station, and a voice squawked through the display.

"Thank you for choosing Jack in the Box. May I take your order, please?"

Ngawang burst out laughing. "Who is that? Where is he?" She craned her neck out my window. This had to be a practical joke.

"You'll see in just a minute. Two coffees, please, large, cream and sugar, and an order of French toast sticks."

The box talked back. "Thank you. Please drive around."

The young guy at the window took my cash, and I explained that my friend here had never been to a drive-through before.

"She's from Bhutan," I said, forgetting that that wouldn't really mean a thing, since most people I encountered seemed not to have a clue *what* Bhutan was, much less *where* it was.

Ngawang snapped a photo with my digital camera with the aplomb of a budding paparazzo.

"Bhutan, wow. Where's that?" The guy's lip was pierced, and both his arms were covered with sleeves of angry-looking tattoos. His friendly demeanor offset the menacing body art.

Ngawang was too shy to respond to this illustrated man.

"It's a tiny kingdom between China and India," I said, playing spokeswoman. "My friend is a famous DJ on the radio there."

The guy smiled. "Wow, that's so cool! No drive-throughs there?"

"No *fast food* there." Surely an even more preposterous concept for this guy.

As was this entire transaction for Ngawang. The taste in the tiny container of syrup and the breeze in her hair on the open road soon replaced the oddity of it with sweeter sensations.

THE CLOSEST STRETCH of beach accessible to downtown Los Angeles is just north of the famous Santa Monica Pier. The misty, cool early morning didn't deter Ngawang. The second I stopped the car she jumped out onto the sand, dug in her toes, then, without a word, rushed over to the ocean to wet her hands. This citizen of a landlocked country could now say she'd touched the Pacific.

"Ahh, the beach!" she shouted, and I'd never heard her sound so happy.

"Does it look like you imagined?" Although she hadn't had to imagine it. She'd seen it a thousand times, just not in person.

That made her completely different from her father, who was exactly my age. Growing up in an electricity- and television-free Bhutan, not long after formal education in the country had begun, he probably had no idea what a beach looked like when he was the age his daughter was now. TV had provided my friend a glimpse of all manner of places and people that her older family members hadn't seen until much later in life. By the time she was a teenager, with the introduction of broadcasting into the kingdom, the need for imagining almost anything had vanished. This fact seemed to tantalize me far more than it did Ngawang, who was caught up in the vast expanse of ocean before her.

"It's even bigger than it seems on television!" Ngawang picked up some sand, gently, as if she were handling a precious flower. "Is this where *Baywatch* happened? Every teenager in Bhutan knows Pamela Anderson!"

This was almost as good for Ngawang as an actual celebrity sighting. She spun around in a circle, soaking it all in.

Across the Pacific Coast Highway, she spotted something else, a sleek modern structure, all glass, windows tinted dark. "Up there, look!" she said. "That's my first black house. I've never seen a house that was black before."

It was 1:00 a.m. Monday, time to report for work. Though these overnight hours were punishing, they had their advantages: They kept me out of the politics and manic deadlines that were the hallmark of working dayside. An added bonus was the occasional turnaround day off to adjust to the new schedule. Working the graveyard shift meant a different sort

of rush, putting together and then delivering three seven-
minute live newscasts, with several hours' break in between
each one. It was pleasant enough, and fun, too, though the
dulling effect of the inverted hours was a bit like having a
straitjacket on your brain. Whenever my head really hurt from
the flip-flopping schedule, I imagined what it was like for my
grandmother, who'd logged overnight shifts at the Brooklyn
Navy Yard while raising nine kids in a three-bedroom apartment. That put nuisance into perspective.

Taking Ngawang to the studio in the dark of night made
sense; this way she could ride out her jet lag, the office was less
busy and therefore less intimidating, and with fewer people
around, there was less chance she'd get in the way. There
wasn't really anything for her to do but observe. Just seeing
how we worked, the pace, the intensity, the fixed deadlines,
would be shocking, and unlike Kuzoo FM in every way.

We entered the back door using the special after-hours
code, and snaked around the maze of cubes to my show's area
of the building. She thrilled when the automatic lights popped
on as they sensed our presence. Imagining it through Ngawang's eyes, I felt embarrassed by the largesse, the plushness of
it all. Even the oldest computers were three years newer than
anything in Thimphu, and there was one on every desk. Without people behind them at this hour they seemed like even
more of a luxury, machines standing by, just in case.

There were other, even more wondrous visions: the office
kitchen, with its dueling microwaves, toaster oven, dishwasher, and a cabinet stuffed full with mugs. The plentiful
supply of tea and coffee and sugar and little coffee creamers in
different flavors. Milk was far too dear back in Bhutan to

waste in tea; instead, caffeine was whitened with milk powder. And at Kuzoo, the small stash of beverages was kept under lock and key, reserved for special guests.

"Free?" she asked, amazed, and then she saw the pharmacy cabinet, which momentarily trumped the drinks supply. "Free meds, too?"

The five coworkers who shared these miserable hours welcomed Ngawang warmly, and sleepily volunteered to help explain their particular jobs on the show. While I went about putting together the first newscast of the evening, Ngawang meandered around the office, snooping at the colorful pictures and artifacts that decorated each cubicle. That each person had his own dedicated desk was another curious luxury.

As we walked to the studio to go live, Ngawang asked, very loudly, the name of one of my coworkers who she'd been talking with earlier. "That fat girl," she explained. She was having as hard a time with our names as I had, at first, in Bhutan. I told her she must not, under any circumstances, refer to that woman that way within earshot of anyone else.

"But why not? She *is* fat." Ngawang wasn't being rude. She was just being descriptive.

"Well, I understand that she's, well, overweight. But . . . it's just not polite. It would hurt her feelings."

"Back in Bhutan, they call me Bunny." Ngawang smiled and pointed to the gap between her teeth. "Look, just like a rabbit. It doesn't bother me that people say that, because I do look like one!" Then she patted her belly. "Plus people make fun of my weight, too. I'm not exactly skinny. Doesn't—how do you say her name again?—doesn't she know she's fat?"

"No, I get the honesty of it," I said. "I appreciate the honesty. It's just that here, that kind of honesty can hurt a person's feelings. It's just not cool."

By dawn, Ngawang had bonded with the woman whose name she couldn't remember, and with Jeff, the friendly, patient engineer, who generously offered to mix taped promos for Kuzoo that Ngawang could take home. Another engineer, Erin, invited Ngawang to speak at an audio production class she taught at a community college. When the IT crew arrived in that morning, I asked them to show Ngawang their work area, since she loved computers so much. She charmed them, too. Everyone seemed to want to be friends with the woman from the exotic place they knew only from the pictures on my desk.

WHILE MUCH ABOUT life and work in Los Angeles dazzled Ngawang, there were many things she didn't like or understand. How I could not have a television set, for one. The self-flushing toilet in the office bathroom "freaked her out." So did the size of my apartment. Though I had shown her pictures of my lovely but compact one-bedroom, it didn't compute that I had so little space, and no lawn. She'd imagined, she said, that everyone lived surrounded by the flora seen in one of her favorite movies, *Edward Scissorhands,* with a grand, sprawling house alongside lush, plentiful greenery. We had discussed at length the fact that I didn't live with my family, yet Ngawang kept wondering where they were. That the other cities where I'd told her they lived were in other states and the states were on the other side of the country confounded her; a young Bhutanese woman could no better comprehend the distance between California and Florida any more than I could have understood how far Haa was from Trongsa. Showing her on a map hadn't helped.

While Ngawang absolutely loved the dishwasher, she was disturbed that I didn't have a live person to load it, or to cook and clean for me, as she and most of her friends did. Why didn't we rich Americans have at least the same—or better? As for the absence of a television, I explained that was a life-style choice, but why I would want to make that choice made no sense to her.

The idea that we had to call friends before showing up at their houses was also unsettling. "In Bhutan, you would just stop by," she said, "and if they weren't there, the maid would give you tea while you waited."

Over the years, I had entertained dozens of guests of different ages and nationalities, but never like this, a visitor bewildered and enthralled by the simplest experiences. Her very frame of reference was fundamentally different. With every step and around every corner, I felt Ngawang exclaiming, pulsing with surprise, even if she didn't say a word. Often, she didn't; but almost every waking minute, she wore on her face an expression of pure astonishment, a combination of over-whelmed and startled and thrilled. And it was different from the startling exhaustion for me of processing Bhutan for the first time—exactly the opposite, in fact. There, you react to the absence of development, the quiet of the landscape. In the United States, you are assaulted by how everything is enor-mous and paved and polished. The culture shock I'd experi-enced when I returned from Bhutan was dwarfed by watching Ngawang react to the overdeveloped world for the first time. I felt a larger sense of investment in her exposure to the world beyond her own, a responsibility, even. A collision of sensations, the big sisterly and maternal, overwhelmed me. I didn't have a sister, and I wasn't likely to have a child, but I had this woman in my life now who filled those roles in her own way. She just happened to be a young woman who happened to be Bhutanese.

OF ALL THE good and bad and strange and wonderful things Ngawang was observing, it was a knock at the door one afternoon that undid her. There stood the uniformed UPS man, wielding a package and a wireless tracking device. After I signed my name and closed the door, Ngawang literally fell to the floor in the hallway in astonishment, shaking her head. There are no street addresses in Bhutan. Mail, if you get it, is delivered to a central postbox in town. To have a package appear at your door—that was pure magic.

"In my home village, I am modern and learned because I now work in the city," she said. "I can explain technology to them that they don't understand. Here, I am seeing so many things I did not know about. Here in America, I am a dumbo."

"You are not a dumbo," I said, crouching down to hug her. "You're from a different world."

"But you have so much more," she parried, accusingly. "You're all rich!"

I couldn't dispute that, on balance, most Americans had more stuff or more money than the average Bhutanese. But beyond the material, were any of us richer, really? Everything we owned, the way we lived, came with a price.

"Okay, Ngawang, so I have more cash, and don't forget, I'm twenty years older than you. But look at what you have, at your age. Your family owns a house, and several plots of land, free and clear. You are all close by and help each other out. My family lives across the country, and my parents still have a mortgage. It costs half of what I earn every month to pay my rent, and then there's everything else." I picked up the pile of that month's bills: home phone, cell phone, Internet access, YMCA. My car, I explained, was older, and owned by me outright, so I had no car payments, but then there was the cost of gas and insurance.

"And medical care. If I get really sick or have an accident, I could go broke. And I'm luckier than most people, since I have some health coverage." Ngawang's eyes widened as I explained our medical system. Health care in Bhutan was free, and so were medications. And because of that, Bhutanese in Thimphu went to the hospital for the slightest cough or bruise.

My standard of living, I explained, was far better than that of many of my family members, of many Americans. That had something to do with the job I had, with being cautious with money, and with not spending what I didn't have. It also, I said, had to do with the fact that I didn't have kids.

"Do you get it, Ngawang? Yes, we make more money than you do, but as you can see, we spend almost all of it, too. And everything costs more, too."

Ngawang patiently listened, but I knew she wasn't hearing most of what I said. She was intoxicated by the land of plenty, even if the land of plenty had proven to be more complicated and confusing than she'd anticipated. For my young friend, the view from the eighteenth floor, and that snazzy little car, was pretty enthralling. We shared a craving for worldliness; our birthplace and generation altered our vision of it.

I COULD SEE subtle signs that homesickness was encroaching on her spectacular odyssey. "The next time I come to the United States, I want to bring my family," she declared as we meandered around downtown's Broadway after work one day. Mine was a household more subdued than any she'd inhabited; absent a crowd of people. And she missed her cell phone trilling twenty-four hours a day. Not that she was without callers here. They included a young Indian-American student at UCLA named Milloni, who had stayed with Ngawang's family in Thimphu the year before while she did field research. A young Bhutanese woman living with her aunt in Queens, New York, who had married one of the American golf pros and found marriage and the United States not to her liking. And a Bhutanese man who was finishing his master's degree at a university just outside Tokyo. He'd never met Ngawang in person; they were virtual friends, from Kuzoo .net. He liked her enough that he called her almost every day in Bhutan, where the cost was a steep fifty cents a minute. With the per-minute charge to the United States far cheaper, he'd been calling twice a day.

"Mr. Japan is on the line for you," I would announce before handing over the phone. Each time they talked, I'd tease her about her boyfriend.

"He's not my boyfriend. I'm not even sure I'll ever meet him in person," Ngawang would protest.

"Aren't you curious, after talking to him all this time?"

"We'll see if he *deserves* to meet me," she'd tease back.

The one person who wasn't calling was Ngawang's sister

in Nebraska. Which was where she was supposed to be headed next.

FRIDAY ARRIVED, and our week of overnights was through. To celebrate, we headed to the hot tub behind the apartment building, hoping to beat the intense sun before it broke through in earnest. Ngawang sat perched on the edge, too modest to wear even the one-piece bathing suit I'd loaned her; her feet dangled in the water, her pants legs rolled up modestly to mid-calf.

"So, Ngawang, I heard you tell someone at the office last night that your visa lasts for three months." It was curious that she hadn't mentioned that to me. "What are we going to do about your sister in Nebraska, and your going to see her?"

"She hasn't gotten back in touch with me." Ngawang looked down at her toes in the tub.

"She knows for sure that you're here?"

"Yes, I wrote to her. And I sent her your phone numbers."

"I don't get why she hasn't been back in touch. Wasn't she expecting you?"

"She must be very busy."

Bhutanese often explained away a lack of communication with "I am very busy." But what could this lady be so busy do-ing that she was avoiding her sister?

"So let's talk about what you want to do. Remember I said it was great for you to visit me here for two weeks."

"Well," Ngawang said, splashing her feet in the water, try-ing to play down what she was about to say. "I was thinking I would get a job."

For a second I thought the splashing had mangled her

words. But I could tell by the look on Ngawang's face that I'd heard absolutely correctly.

"Ngawang, getting a job in radio is hard for people who have lived in this country forever."

"Not in radio. I was thinking maybe at a hotel or something."

"You're going to give up working at the radio station, and leave your family, so you can clean rooms at a hotel?" The tone of my voice was the same as a mother whose fifteen-year-old daughter had just come home with a tattoo.

"Not clean rooms. I don't want to do that. I figured I could work in accounting or something."

A blinding glimpse of what should have been obvious struck me. When Ngawang said I'd made her dreams come true, I thought she was talking about her dream of *visiting* America. Now I understood that she had meant her dream of *stowing away* in America. How naive she sounded. How naive I had been to issue the invitation for her to come here.

She continued. "I know some Bhutanese girls in New York are babysitters, but I don't want to be a nanny. I want my own kids, but I don't want to take care of someone else's."

I took a deep breath. "Ngawang. Do you understand why they're nannies? It's not because they *want* to do that. It's because *they can't get other jobs.*" My voice was very loud, and I stopped to compose myself, even though no one else was around. It was, after all, only ten in the morning, and most normal people were at work. "You can't just walk into a hotel in Los Angeles and get a job as a bookkeeper. You have to get a work permit before you can even think of trying to get a job, and that's incredibly hard. Not to mention expensive. Maybe even harder than if I was to try to stay in Bhutan and get a job." Assuming I'd have the temerity to overstay my visa there, I could live very nicely for half a year on just a few thousand dollars. Ngawang had three hundred bucks in her wallet. And, like most Bhutanese, no credit card.

"What about that man at the airport when I got here? I spoke English better than he did."

"What man at the airport?

"The guy who asked me questions when I got here. He was Chinese, an old guy. I spoke English better than him! He can't be American. How did he get that job? And that guy in your office, David; he's Chinese. What about Milloni? She's Indian, isn't she?"

The fundamentals of the melting pot that make up these United States had completely eluded Ngawang. That kind of information didn't get transmitted on *Baywatch,* or *Sex and the City,* or *Friends.*

"I don't know anything about the Chinese guy at the airport, but trust me, if he was working in customs, he's a U.S. citizen. David is Korean, not Chinese—and he's Korean-American. He happens to have been born in Texas. That's in this country! And Milloni, I'm not sure where she was born, but she was raised here, too. America is made up of people from all different places."

"That's not how it is in Bhutan. I thought everyone in America would look like you," she said, eyes glued to her feet, the splashes intensifying. During all those years Bhutan had sealed itself off, people from virtually every other part of the globe had been migrating from their hometowns, establishing roots in new places that promised greater potential, intermarrying. In Bhutan, a mixed marriage was when someone from the east of the country married someone from the west, a fairly new phenomenon given that for years few had even left their villages. Cross-cultural unions like the few I'd encountered in Thimphu were rarer still.

"I know it's not like that in Bhutan. I'm very aware of that. The United States is a very different place than Bhutan."

Bhutan wasn't perfect, any more than any human was perfect. It was greatly imperfect. And it had produced legions of young people like Ngawang, modern Bhutanese who loved their country but, unlike their parents before them, yearned for more. Bhutan's pride and joy, its unadulterated culture, was in danger. The connection to the world beyond was to blame. The minute tourists came in and students went out and television took hold of the people's brains, there went the Buddhist precepts and the cultural tradition and the status quo. Everything in Ngawang's line of sight conspired to make her feel that if you could only get your feet onto American soil, piles and piles of money could be excavated from the streets or would fall from the heavens. And that money would buy things, items that were the keys to happiness. That message was conveyed in television shows and movies, which Ngawang watched in a near-continual feed at home. And it was enhanced by the tales of the few Bhutanese who made their way to the United States and sent back stacks of cash. Somehow, they managed not to explain how hard they had to work to earn that money, what kinds of jobs they had to do, the cramped dorm-room-style living conditions they had to endure to be able to save even the few dollars a month they wired back home. How they lived with the constant fear of being found out and deported. Then there were those lucky, super-smart people who won scholarships. They lived under the nurturing gaze of an academic institution, and while life might

not have been cushy, it was rarely the grind of an illegal im-
migrant. (Economics were not the only category warped by
the media. At that training session I'd done for the tour guides
over the winter in Thimphu, one of the young men had whispered to me: "Are the women in your country really as, umm,
sexy as they are in the movies?")

There was another enormous problem: Most of the foreign
tourists Bhutanese do come into contact with, if they come into
contact with any, are fantastically rich. They're spending thousands of dollars to get to Bhutan, and at least several thousand
once they're there. Everyone had a story about some guide
who'd been "adopted" by a wealthy Western visitor who'd
"sponsored" him for a trip or even through college. Or a visitor who'd fallen in love with Bhutan and decided to, oh, subsidize the building of a school or a dormitory or to help support
an entire family. The families for which Bhutanese served as
nannies in New York or elsewhere in the world, well, they
were wealthy enough to have nannies!

And I was part of the problem. Breezing into Thimphu,
twice over the course of a year. It was not that much different
from wearing enormous diamonds and chartering a helicopter
into a famine-stricken area. I might think I lived simply, with
my one-bedroom apartment and six-year-old car, but the very
idea that I had taken the planes to get there, that I possessed
what I did and had paid for it by myself, was utterly amazing
and lavish—even if it was also a little bizarre. What Bhutanese
saw as evidence of the outside world was not representative of
the day-to-day life of the average American citizen. Much less
a stowaway.

A plane flew overhead, and appeared to skim the fifty-five-
story Bank of America office building two blocks away. When

I'd first moved to Los Angeles, I'd sat in this very spot and worried about the flight pattern before I realized it was an optical illusion. I wondered where this jet was going, and wished I could packNgawang and me on the next flight out, so I could march her safely back to Bhutan, where she belonged. Where she could flourish, if she put her mind to it. Where she could be surrounded by her loving family, always.

"So have I made it clear how it's not going to be possible to get a job here, or at least the kind of job you think you'd want? How living here is not what you think? And how if you take one of those other jobs, and work illegally, how much trouble you can get into?"

Ngawang looked right at me, steely, and didn't say a word as I continued. This is what I'd been spared in not having children, I thought: denying a person you loved something they wanted dearly but that you knew wasn't in their best interest.

"Let's discuss what we're going to do. I'm not sure I understand why your sister hasn't written back to you. Why don't we try calling her?"

Upstairs on the eighteenth floor, Ngawang's virtual entourage came calling—her girlfriend in New York on the cell phone, Mr. Japan on the house phone. When both conversations ended, Ngawang tried reaching Nebraska again, with no luck. We agreed that who she really needed to talk to now was her family back in Bhutan. With the fifteen-hour time difference and the absence of voice mail, it took us two days to reach them. Though the conversation was conducted entirely in Dzongkha, I didn't have to understand the language to grok that the discussion was contentious. She revealed no details except that her family was angry with her.

But she said, conceding defeat, "Okay. I will go home."

THE TICKET ON Air India was confirmed. Since I had to be at work, Ngawang's friend Milloni agreed to transport my charge to the airport the next day. I had met her and felt I could trust her. She appeared at the appointed time in my driveway in a late-model Audi, a far fancier car than mine. We loaded Ngawang's luggage into the back; with all the presents she'd been given on her visits to my friends' various newsrooms, her luggage had doubled to two bags. We said our good-byes quickly, because we were blocking traffic. I felt relieved as much as I did sad to send her on her way.

The next morning, Ngawang called me from Milloni's cell phone to wish me well. By that night, I assumed she was in the friendly skies, well on her way home. By Monday night, I figured, she'd at least be back in Delhi.

It was only about three weeks later, when I hadn't heard from her online, and no one at Kuzoo had reported seeing her, that I started to worry.

12

BABY WATCH

A MONTH AFTER NGAWANG WENT MISSING, THE Druk Phuensum Tshogpa (DPT) swept the National Assembly election with a landslide victory. Even the founding members of the DPT party were surprised. Just days before ballots were cast, polls showed it to be running neck and neck with the People's Democratic Party, the coalition led by the king's uncle. Because of that royal association, it was assumed the PDP would easily emerge victorious. In the end, though, with 80 percent of the population voting, the DPT swept forty-four of the forty-seven seats.

This was not in any way interpreted as a condemnation of the beloved monarchy. It was seen as a rejection of the king's *family*. Since His Majesty had insisted that democratic rule was the best form of government, armchair political analysts interpreted the landslide in favor of the DPT as evidence his subjects understood the importance of electing a slate of candidates who were less tied to him.

The members would serve for five years. The DPT chief Jigme Thinley was appointed prime minister, and my Villa

Italia host Lyonpo Ugyen was indeed installed as foreign minister. Immediately, the new lawmakers got down to work. Viewers who tuned into the BBS in the middle of the day no longer saw a placeholder camera trained on Thimphu Valley; they could witness the nation's first-ever parliamentary proceedings, live as they happened. The democracy that had been foisted upon them was to be as transparent as possible, and there was no better way to do that than to telecast the governmental sessions each day.

One of the first acts of business of the new parliament was the ratification of the years-in-the-making constitution. Monks chanted as Bhutan's fifth Dragon King signed three copies of the historic document—one in English, two in Dzongkha, one of those inscribed in gold—to enact it officially. The forty-seven National Assembly members and twenty-five representatives of the National Council then each solemnly approached the throne and added their signatures, a long process broadcast to the people to remind them that they now had a voice in their governance. (Even if it was a responsibility they hadn't requested.) The sacred documents were immediately put on display for the people to behold. All who visited were given bound copies to take home, as well as little juice boxes and a coin as tokens of appreciation. Heavy rain and a flood marked the day, which some interpreted as a sign that even nature was shaken up by the occasion.

This unprecedented document spelled out equality for all; the rights to vote, to life, liberty, and security; and to freedom of speech and religion—although Buddhism was still classified as the official religion, and criticism of the royal family was still verboten. The majority of the assembled citizens who braved the rain to attend the ceremony were actually there for another reason: to gaze at an enormous, sacred, century-old religious scroll called a *thongdrel,* unfurled in commemoration of the historic event for a rare public display. It is believed that those who stand in the presence of this tapestry will accumulate much merit. One woman said she had trekked for hours from a faraway village in order to see it and soak up the karma it offered. She hadn't been aware—until a reporter told her—that the reason it was being exhibited was because of the new constitution. Another woman, a farmer, had asked her husband to accompany her into Thimphu to see the king because she had heard that his powers had been diffused. She was very sad about this development, and wanted the chance to see her beloved monarch in person.

In that summer of 2008, constitutional freedoms were still less important to many Bhutanese than their devotion to Buddhism and their king.

IN THE MIDST of these changes in Bhutan, which I followed online from afar, Ngawang resurfaced. For months I'd been unsuccessfully looking for clues to her whereabouts. I felt a combination of guilt and annoyance and intrigue by her disappearance. No one at Kuzoo FM back in Thimphu had seen her or heard from her. There was no activity on her Facebook page. Calls to her friend Milloni went unreturned. No one on the other end of the numbers she'd dialed in New York returned my calls, either, nor had the mythic sister in Nebraska ever materialized. I had no number for the faraway Mr. Japan. I considered calling Ngawang's father, since his number was recorded in my Skype, but decided against it. After all, Ngawang was a grown woman—checking in with her friends was one thing, but calling her parents was another. My instinct told me she was somewhere that was safe; the mystery was *where* she was.

And then one day, her name appeared in my inbox:

hey hi sweet lady jane

well am fine n am with my cousins out here at new york

sorry i didnt check my mails

will be going home may be after two weeks

how is everything going out wit you

keep in touch

"New York?" I wrote back. "What the hell are you doing in New York? How did you get there? What's your phone number so I can call you? Would you please call me? Does your family know where you are? Do Sir Pema or Pema?" They had both just written again that she still hadn't been seen.

My mind started racing: Just how long did Ngawang intend to stay in the United States? Forever, or till the expiration of her visa? Where was she staying? What was she doing all day? Had she planned this all along?

Frantic, I considered hopping a plane and scouring Jackson Heights, Queens, the neighborhood with the largest population of Bhutanese in the United States, but wrote that off as folly. I didn't hear back from her.

The month of May arrived and went. By now, Ngawang's

visa would have expired. I had succeeded in liberating myself from my job in Los Angeles and was making plans to go back to Kuzoo to volunteer for the summer. But before that, I'd visit Washington, D.C., as a volunteer at the Smithsonian Folklife Festival, where a faux Bhutan was being raised. The largest delegation of Bhutanese ever to leave the country at one time, 144 people, were headed to the American nation's capital to set up a living museum exhibit about their culture. Monks would bless visitors in an authentic Bhutanese temple that had been constructed on the National Mall; archers, including the king's brother Prince Jigyel, were to demonstrate the national sport; a weaver would sit at a loom creating a colorful cloth and wrapping those who wished in *kira* and *gho*.

One afternoon in the days before the festival began, I spotted Madam Kunzang Choden, the writer and Kuzoo advisor, over near the Metro with her husband, Walter. (I wondered if they knew about my dinner with Martin, who had emailed me earlier in the year to report that his work had relocated him to Thailand.) Madam Choden was to be one of the main speakers in the foodways tent, to discuss the curious culinary customs of her people, including and especially their devotion and addiction to fiery hot chilies. She had just published a book on the subject.

We said our *Kuzu zampo*s, and commented on the magnificent location and the weather, and Madam Choden then said, quietly, as if she'd been waiting to clue me in, "I hear you sponsored Ngawang to come to the United States. She's always been dying to go. I thought you knew she'd been trying to get here for a long time. . . ." And then she shook her head, disapprovingly, too polite to say another word. She didn't need to.

Later, another Bhutanese friend revealed more details. He

said Ngawang had boasted that she was working in New York in a shop belonging to some friend. Right after he started spilling the story, he clamped himself down and refused to say any more. And then Sir Pema let slip in an email that he had known all along Ngawang was in New York. He'd been sworn to secrecy, but eventually caved to my persistent concern.

Now, I thought darkly, I had another dubious connection to the Kingdom of Bhutan, besides going to help start a radio station whose mainstay turned out to be illegally downloaded Western pop music. I'd been an unwitting accomplice to the illicit plan of a young Bhutanese to explore her American dream.

It wasn't until the end of June that word came from my wayward friend, via email, informing me that she had finally returned home. I was relieved to hear it. She refused to discuss the who, what, when, where, why, and how of the whole New York adventure, but before she'd returned home, she had consented to meet in person the man we'd taken to calling Mr. Japan. He'd just wrapped up his graduate studies outside Tokyo and was himself returning to Thimphu. Once they were back on Bhutanese soil, their yearlong phone friendship morphed quickly into romance. Both families had blessed the union. They were waiting for the monks to give the go-ahead about which day was most auspicious so they might officially move in together and consider themselves married.

And when I read that, I knew she must be pregnant.

I knew what it was like to have a whirlwind courtship that led to marriage after a life-altering experience. Mine had happened exactly twenty years earlier, back when I was Ngawang's age, in fact. My husband-to-be and I had met when he came to work at the television station in North Carolina. Not long after, I'd had that epiphany on the way to the grocery store. This liberation from my fear of the dark, I assumed, meant I was now healed and ready to join with this wonderful man. United from a point of strength, not weakness. Running off and getting married in a fit of passion, after just several months, felt like my way of declaring to the world, "That rapist didn't ruin me. See?" It was the first impetuous act of my short life thus far.

And then, my new husband lost his job at the station in a management shakeup. He got an even better one—in, of all places, Atlanta. The scene of the crime was the last place I ever would have chosen to move, but in the media business, you went where the work took you. I rationalized: It wasn't Atlanta's fault that I was attacked; it could have happened anywhere. If I could survive returning there, I believed, I'd be demonstrating my capacity to adapt to anything, to show how unflappable I was. It would be an illustration of my boundless ability to forgive—to transcend geography. People who refused to leave a certain location or go to another were histrionic, inflexible, oversensitive. I was not going to be one of those people who let history get in the way of progress.

Even the best intentions can be fraught with delusion. I had greatly underestimated how hard it would be to settle into the place where this horrible thing had happened, perhaps even more than I'd underestimated how complicated it was to be married. Within a year, another job offer rescued us, and back we went to North Carolina. I found myself felled by a mysterious lethargy that I first attributed to moving. In the course of trying to determine what was wrong, the doctor I visited of-fered a prescription: counseling.

Everything is fine, I insisted. That's all in the past. Still, I obeyed and found a therapist. I was tired of being tired all the time. As we talked, a diagnosis emerged. It wasn't fatigue; it was depression. I was consumed with doubt and anger. Here I was, barely a quarter of a century old, connected to this man, moving around for his work, depending on him for financial and personal security. How did I get here? This wasn't how I imagined my life to be. I believed I loved him, but what did love mean, exactly? My problem was this sinking feeling that I was ill-equipped and unprepared to be a wife.

Almost as if to prove that I wasn't really an adult, I found myself stymied in how to confess my misgivings to my poor, sweet husband. To say "I've made a mistake, there is something wrong, I don't quite understand, please forgive me. Would you mind, please, if I exile myself to a room, and let some time pass, so that when I emerge I'll be healed, recalibrated—and then we could just skip happily forward into the future?" If I had had the courage to ask, he would likely have said yes.

But instead of speaking my doubts, I shared my deepest fears with a notebook. I wrote down every bit of it. How I felt trapped, how much I doubted it all, how I hated everything, including my poor husband, how I wished we both were dead. I didn't mean it. I didn't know what I meant, how I felt. I put my confessional notebook in a drawer in my desk and left town for a few days for work. And when I'd returned, my husband was waiting for me at the door, his face washed with devastation. In his search for clues to my distress, he'd read what I had written.

Not long after, my whirlwind marriage was through.

〜✌︎〜

IT WASN'T UNTIL I was forty—thirteen years after the split, in the throes of my life review—that I began considering what a mistake it had been to let that marriage go. Over the years, I'd rarely discussed it, even with people who knew me back then. The whys and particulars of how it came to be and how it came apart were easier not to reveal to newer people in my life. To say, "I got married in reaction to having been raped," required the disclosure of layers of personal history, and now I wasn't even sure if the way I'd interpreted my history was true. What a good and patient partner he was; what an excellent father he would have been. I was wiser than I'd realized in having chosen him.

But I understood now the youthful haze of mistaking desire for love and the foundations of a lasting partnership. That eagerness to move on with life, to rush into the future, lock things down, the false sense of feeling that by moving quickly, you're taking control of your destiny.

And so I understood as I watched Ngawang rush into marriage. She'd gotten her American adventure out of her system; it hadn't quite worked out the way she'd planned. Perhaps in uniting with Mr. Japan, she was reacting to the disappointment of not having achieved one of her dreams. Now she was ready for the next thing. I hoped her impetuousness would yield a different outcome than mine had.

NGAWANG HAS COMMANDEERED her fellow radio jockey Kencho to pick me up at the airport in Paro. Kesang the Kuzoo driver is busy, and Mr. Japan is at work. I know I must be an honored guest because Kencho and Ngawang hate each other, so I'm flattered that they've made peace long enough to take this drive together, all because of me. Arriving in Bhutan for the third time in a year and a half now seems ridiculously normal. I remind myself not to mistake the familiarity for true understanding. I have a much better sense now of Bhutan, but I still know better than to presume I really understand this place. The mystery keeps me coming back.

Kencho's happy I'm here to help out again with Kuzoo, because he doesn't care for the new boss who has replaced Sir Pema, now that he's gone off to his studies in Thailand. Ngawang doesn't like the new lady, either, but she's preoccupied with the details of moving into Mr. Japan's house. The monks have given the okay for this to take place later in the week. It's all very matter-of-fact. Ngawang getting married after disappearing for a while. Me breezing in from halfway around the globe, resolved not to demand answers about the past. I'm more concerned with what is happening with her right now; I ask Ngawang point-blank as we start to drive.

"Are you expecting a baby?"

Her response is calm and measured. "Maybe," she says, as if it's no big deal. "We're going to the doctor tomorrow."

On the ride from Paro back to Thimphu, my two friends compete like little kids for my attention, talking over each other with their stories, but I can't help tuning them both out. The roadwork is complete, the drive shorter and far less death-defying than before. Or is it just that I'm more comfortable here? It's mid-July, and monsoon season, and it's just started to rain. Kencho could have a new career as a New York City taxi driver; he's barreling down the highway at great speed, navigating past the other traffic and the cows and crouching humans. The magnificent palette of green on view in the summertime distracts me, and Kencho interrupts his monologue to turn Kuzoo on full-blast. A taped report he prepared about Gross National Happiness is about to air. To help quantify the concept to the outside world, an index has been released that aims to allow other nations to measure the happiness of their citizenry. Who needs such a scale? I think. By now, I've learned that the ingredients for happiness are simple: giving, loving, and contentment with who you are.

IT ISN'T UNTIL the next day that I meet the mysterious Mr. Japan, whose monk-given name is Sonam Penjor. He's a tall man, big, with a sweet, solid personality; he greets me as if I am a long-lost relation. My immediate reaction is to like him. He and Ngawang have come by Kuzoo after having visited the doctor, who confirmed the news I suspected. I offer congratulations and hug them both.

Ngawang has in her hands proof of their baby, a snapshot from the ultrasound. A tiny little sprout of new life inside my young friend. Her excitement feels almost childlike, while Mr. Japan has the demeanor of a mature father-to-be, not shocked by the immediacy of the prospect at all. He says, with confidence, that he is very ready to start a family. One day, maybe I'll get the details on Ngawang's New York adventures from him—assuming he even knows.

"I hope it's twins," Ngawang says hopefully, the way you might say you wished for snow.

"I hope it's *not* twins," I say, remembering the time I was in the delivery room to assist a single friend, almost forty years

old, who'd visited the sperm bank. Just seeing two babies delivered at one time gives you a glimpse into what caring for
them each day might be like. One baby at a time is all a girl
Ngawang's age should have to handle.

"Well, I hope it's a boy," she says.

"As long as the baby's healthy," says Mr. Japan, patiently.
"That's what matters." This guy is all right by me. For a minute, I try to imagine how different my life would have played
out had I stayed married. Would we have had children?
Would we have lasted these twenty years? The only thing
that's certain is that I would not have had the experiences I've
had, and most definitely not this connection to Bhutan. In my
forties, I understand how each decision has consequences. I
also see the preposterousness of thinking you can have it all,
much less trying to.

WHEN NGAWANG ASKED if I would be her baby's godmother,
I didn't hesitate to say yes. I understood my being so anointed
had nothing to do with my perceived competence to care for
this impending child should anything terrible befall her or the
baby's father. After all, between their extended families, there
are enough guardians to care for all the students in a small
school. And as much time as I'd spent in Bhutan over the last
two years, I still technically lived too far away to do much
practical good.

Besides the love that propelled this gesture, I knew this
honor had been bestowed on me for two other reasons, reasons
that were inextricably linked: I was American, and because of
that, I offered access in the future to opportunities the baby's
blood relatives could never provide.

Charged with the responsibility of godmotherhood, I could one day invite Ngawang's child to the United States. I'd feel invested enough to pay, perhaps, for his education. In a modern Bhutan, it was simply better for a new baby and his family to know they had a friend on the other side of the world. Even without the formality, I'd be happy to be there for this child, to help however I could. By the time he was old enough to travel by himself, maybe I'd have more than a blow-up mattress in the living room to offer. But in giving me a title, Ngawang knew she was giving me a responsibility—and she knew me well enough to know I wouldn't take that responsibility lightly.

As many pregnant friends and new babies as I'd been around, I'd never been offered an official role. (I'd mercifully never even been a bridesmaid.) The closest I'd come was that time I'd witnessed the birth of those twins born to my single friend. But that was more about attending to her than to the babies. I liked the idea of being a godmother. Even if, in Bhutan, virtually any woman who comes into contact with a child is called "auntie." It filled me with delight to know that across the planet, in this country I loved, there would be a little Bhutanese baby who would grow up learning he could count on me.

Is IT POSSIBLE that the royal astrologers in Bhutan knew, when they had divined November 6 as the most auspicious day for the coronation of the fifth king, how important a week it would be for the rest of the world? Astrologers may not possess crystal balls, but perhaps a scan of the heavens foretold a volatile time of unprecedented change. Or perhaps it was all a happy accident that the world's most envied and reviled democracy and the world's newest happened to close out 2008 with back-to-back milestones. And that at the helm of those two democracies were two men who, while they had had vastly different upbringings, shared oddly similar philosophies.

King Jigme Khesar Namgyel Wangchuck was formally coronated as king of Bhutan just hours after the landslide election of Barack Obama, America's new president-elect. Though King Jigme had attained his position purely by dint of birth, he was, in his own way, a living symbol of global interconnectedness. He'd attended prep school (Phillips and Cushing) and college (Wheaton) in the United States, then studied for a master's in England (Oxford), and preferred basketball to the national sport of archery. (Teams of tall strapping players would be summoned to the court in Thimphu when His Majesty wanted a game.) The fifth king of Bhutan might not achieve the greatness of his father and grandfather and great-grandfather before him, for history would show they had brought their country into the modern age. But the mandate before this king, during a time of unprecedented change, was no less critical. While Obama's election was still dominating world headlines, Bhutan's fifth king addressed a crowd at the Changlimithang Stadium, where thousands had waited in line all night to ensure they got inside:

> Ultimately, without peace, security and happiness, we have nothing. My deepest concern is that as the world changes, we may lose these fundamental values on which rest our character as a nation and people. The Bhutan we see is vastly different—unrecognizable, even—when compared to the Bhutan in the time of our first king. As long as we continue to pursue the simple and timeless goal of being

good human beings, and as long as we strive to build a nation that stands for everything that is good, we can ensure that our future generations for hundreds of years will live in happiness and peace.

THREE MONTHS LATER, we are on baby watch in Thimphu, awaiting the arrival of one of the next generation of Bhutanese. The ultrasound long ago revealed the baby would be a boy. To bide the time, Ngawang visits monks, drinks vanilla milkshakes from Karma Café, overdoes it on the chilies because once the baby comes she'll have to dial down the culinary heat for a while. Uncomfortably large and hoping to move things along, she takes long walks over bridges, which the Bhutanese believe will induce labor. She and Pema and I ride into town to the fabric store to buy a petticoat for the delivery, a garment designed to protect her modesty given the inevitable crowd of family who will gather when the baby debuts. In the altar room of her in-laws' house, right next to the bedroom where Mr. Japan and Ngawang sleep, monks are on duty, chanting prayers for a healthy baby. Out back, a special tub has been constructed where the new mother will soak off the pain daily in a hot stone bath. After tea one morning, Ngawang's mother-in-law fills it up and tests it out herself.

One Saturday we sit for hours in the hospital waiting for the only one of the three gynecologists in the city who Ngawang trusts to examine her. He sends her home to wait some more. As the due date comes and goes, and Ngawang becomes larger and more impatient and uncomfortable, I invite her over for a sneak peek at the baby gifts I've brought; Ngawang's not allowed to take them into her home until a healthy baby has arrived. No showers in this culture, at least not yet; purchasing items in advance is seen as a jinx. Ngawang particularly loves the stuffed bear sent by friends of mine she'd met in Santa Monica. "This is for me," she says, and I know she isn't kidding. She oohs and aahs at the little hats and bibs and onesies, all from the Gap, a very exotic American brand, though much of their stuff was made in factories closer to here than to the United States. I've brought along a stack of kiddie books, too, about things this baby isn't likely to see much of until he leaves his homeland: One's about trains, another about boats, another astronauts, none of which exist in Bhutan. Maybe Ngawang is done with adventure, but that doesn't mean her baby has to be.

While we wait for his arrival, I fill the time by stopping by Kuzoo; Radio Jockey Kinzang loves having guest hosts with foreign accents, and by now the listening audience has heard me yap on the air on many occasions over the past two years. I also find myself enjoying long lunches with friends, where other friends happen by and hours elapse, filled with meandering conversation. Thimphu is changing, but the rhythm of life here for me is still a delight.

One afternoon my dining companion is Phuntsho, a woman about my age who is divorced with three children, two studying in India and one at the Bhutan on the Border, the University of Texas at El Paso. We are discussing how, in the second half of our lives, we want to change professions. Phuntsho says she's thinking about becoming a nurse. I reveal my recent, very peculiar recurring dream.

"It is a gigantic room, filled with babies. There is a long line of bassinets, all in a row. It is up to me to take care of all of them, just me. And I work my way down the line, pick up each baby, and kiss him on the head. And all of a sudden they are all cooing and crying, and I am falling asleep. . . ."

Phuntsho smiles slyly. She knows how outrageous a fantasy this is, and I do, too. I take this dream as a sign of my morphing ambitions, to figure out how to help children who have no one else.

To do this in Bhutan would be impossible; there are no orphanages here. There isn't even a formal adoption policy. The maternity nurse at the hospital keeps a list of prospective parents, and calls them when a mother wants to give up her child. There just aren't that many unwanted babies, Phuntsho says. After spending time here, I wonder if this is denial speaking, or a matter of resources and culture.

Close to 40 percent of the population is under fourteen years old. And a growing problem is that kids born "without fathers" are lost in the system. Without proof of both parents' citizenship, the child is forever in limbo, denied the rights of a full-fledged Bhutanese—meaning, most notably, that the child can't enroll in school. Many of these children—no one knows just how many there are—are the result of a long-standing village ritual called "night hunting," where a man crawls through a window into a woman's bedroom and sleeps with her. When I first heard about the custom, I was startled by its similarity to my own experience. Only now is anyone in Bhutan openly beginning to call this rape, but it happens with enough frequency that the parliament has been grappling with a law to ban it.

When a "fatherless" baby was born on the farm in the days before modernization, the additional hands were welcome; but as subsistence farming becomes less common, a whole new class of children is growing up who have no prospects for the future. One of the four queens of the fourth king has been an active proponent of family planning, but it's believed that only 30 percent of Bhutanese use birth control. Among young Bhutanese, the issues are becoming the same as anyplace else: a growing demand for the morning-after pill, available over the counter for a little over $1.50; a spate of botched abortions in clinics across the southern border in India; paternity tests to determine the father of the child. The ways of the Western world encroach.

Like it or not, perhaps an orphanage in Bhutan is inevitable.

The day after we share this discussion, Phuntsho calls me on the phone.

"Actually, I thought about it and there is something here that is close to an orphanage, where they could really use your help. You will find it interesting," she says. "We leave tomorrow at ten a.m. Prepare to fall in love."

She picks me up near the traffic circle in the center of town, and we make the trek toward Paro on the upgraded highway. After an hour or so of driving from city to city, we turn onto a rough unpaved road that climbs high up the mountain. Up we go through a small community of a dozen or so houses called Shaba. Monkeys are swinging in the trees, and our vehicle kicks up dust as it rumbles over the rocky terrain. It feels a bit like an Asian safari.

"This is much improved since Rinpoche," says my friend reverently, as if we were driving on smooth glass. I'm happy to have missed what it was like before. This particular Rinpoche, she explains, is the ninth reincarnation of a manifestation of the mighty Guru Rinpoche, the saint credited with introducing Buddhism in Bhutan. Just twenty-eight years old, Rinpoche is revered for his tremendous compassion. For three years now, this good holy man has been taking in boys whose families can't care for them, or who have no families at all, providing them food and shelter, and educating them in the monastic tradition.

After the last hairpin turn we emerge at a magnificent spot. The crystal silence of isolation; an unseasonably warm winter day in the age of global warming. Right next to where we park sits a small chorten, a row of tall prayer flags, and the Neyphug Monastery, a large structure built in 1550 that has seen better days. Its exterior is literally crumbling. Phuntsho points to two hermitages that can be reached only by walking through the forest, a three-hour trek from here.

Off to the side, a dozen tiny boys wash themselves in a makeshift outdoor shower. A few larger kids are tending to chores; the rest are crowded in a small room to watch a cartoon—thanks to the one evident luxury: satellite TV. Forty children clad in red monks' robes gaze intently at an old television set. Absent neighbors, this is their lifeline to the world.

If I hadn't just been told they were orphans, I probably could have guessed. These kids may be lucky to be here, but these are hardly deluxe accomodations. Filthy, threadbare bedding lines the floors of several packed sleeping rooms, shabby posters of handwritten ABCs are taped up for decoration and instruction. A fraction of the belongings in the average American kid's room would go very far here.

"You can come teach the boys English," says Phuntsho. "They don't learn much of it, for their monastic studies are in Dzongkha, but these days, everyone needs English." A more immediate and urgent need is for futons, pillows, blankets, so the kids get more cushioned sleep. I make a mental note to investigate how to send them some.

Rinpoche is away, trying to raise money from supporters in Taiwan to build a dormitory for the kids. His eighty-year-old father, Lopen, greets us warmly. He wears the red robes of a lay monk, a *gomchen,* and he's as round as a teddy bear. A sweet boy with a slightly crossed eye smiles at us as he serves us tea and lunch; it's an honor to be so close to the visitors. I eat my red rice, politely, and pass my bowl of *emadatse* to Lopen, who appears only a bit surprised that I won't eat it. Then he digs in himself. Afterward, he gives us a tour.

We walk the dark, dusty, cold rooms of the monastery. All the religious relics have been restored, Phuntsho says, but the building, like the living quarters, direly needs attention. A life-size statue of Guru Rinpoche fills one shrine; an enormous Buddha sits in another. There are wall paintings by a revered lama, images of a thousand Buddhas; the largest of them is believed to once have spoken. There's also a sacred eighth-century statue of the guru that we don't see. It's opened to the public just once a year. All these relics, Phuntsho tells me, possess great power and many blessings. At each stop, she prostrates herself three times, and we tuck money on each altar as offerings. I say a silent prayer for a healthy and happy life for Ngawang, Mr. Japan, and their baby.

Back inside the small residence we have another round of tea; Lopen doesn't want us to go just yet. He fumbles for his reading glasses and settles in to study the thick, bound astrological calendars Phuntsho has brought. The start of the Female Earth Ox year is a week away. Phuntsho pulls up her purse from the floor and takes out a four-inch-thick stack of cash. It's money that's been sent for a series of cleansing prayers, a *puja,* to be conducted for a boy back in the United States who is ill. After consulting the astrological tables for information about the boy's birth year, Lopen asks when I was born. Squinting through his lopsided spectacles, he nearly presses the forecast book to his face.

Phuntsho relays his prediction in a serious tone: "It is not going to be a good year for you. Watch your health. Wear red every day, preferably under your clothes." I take a mental inventory of my closet at home, scanning for red clothing. "They really need to do a wind horse *puja* for you. You have to be very careful," she says. This *puja* will rebalance my energy and ward off illness.

In my purse, I happen to have a crisp $100 bill. A friend in Thimphu has repaid me for books I'd brought from the States. I fish out the other cash I have on hand, dollars and ngultrum. All told, the sum that other Rinpoche wanted from me two years ago. I press the money into Lopen's hands.

"It's for the boys," I tell Phuntsho. "For the orphanage."

"They will say prayers," she says, and she translates after he begins to speak. "Lopen says they will do a *puja*."

I don't argue. If they feel the need to do a *puja,* so be it. The mental power of sixty young monks, with Lopen at the helm, can't be a bad idea. I'm happy to accept the prayers. Yet happier still not to be looking for answers anymore.

TEN DAYS LATER, Ngawang gives birth to a healthy baby boy. Eight pounds, eight ounces. Right out of the womb, he resembles a tiny version of Mr. Japan, with the same sweet face and a generous pile of hair. His entrance into this world is thirteen days after his due date, which happens to be a year to the day after Ngawang arrived in Los Angeles, and two days into the year of the Female Earth Ox.

The monks anoint him with a beautiful name. Kinga Norbu: precious jewel, loved by all.

The astrological forecast for the new year is terrible in almost all regards. Rain will be scarce, food in short supply—economically difficult, all the way around. There's one exception. They say it's a particularly lucky year in which to be born.

POSTSCRIPT

Not long after I returned from my initial trip to the happiest place on earth, I had lunch with an acquaintance who posed a question I'd never asked myself, much less another person.

"What would you like to be doing five years from now?" she said, leaning in, Oprah-style, across the basket of breadsticks.

My God, I thought. *Who knows?*

Five years. Five years ago I could never have imagined jetting off to a Himalayan kingdom and finding my entire perspective of the world, and myself, turned upside down. Why would anyone want to imagine the future, much less plan it? I didn't say that, though. I didn't want to make her feel bad, since she seemed to be one of those people who liked plotting her life. I just knew you couldn't do that.

So I gave her as vague an answer as possible: "I really have no idea."

"But," she insisted, "do you want to be married? Do you want to move out of Los Angeles? Do you want to keep doing the work you're doing?" There was a sense of urgency to her line of questioning, as if my entire future rested on the words I now uttered.

"I really, honestly have no idea," I said. "All I know for sure is this: In five years, I would love to feel as great as I do, as strong as I do, right this minute."

My lunch companion looked at me expectantly. She seized on the word "great," and she wanted to know more, the specific things that were causing me to feel so good. I told her there wasn't anything specific to add. That was the triumph, I told her. I didn't feel good because I had a new romance, or a new job that paid tons of money, or anything visible or measurable. None of those things that usually set people to the "Yes" gauge on the happiness scale had happened to me. I didn't feel good because I expected nothing bad ever to befall me again; instead, I trusted that I could handle whatever came my way.

Best of all, I told my dining companion, was that what I wanted from life had changed. I wasn't waiting for something to fall into place so that life could get started. Life was brimming all around me. And now I understood that what I gave was more important than what I got.

It was Bhutan and the three good things that helped me arrive at these conclusions, I told her, and I explained how the exercise worked. I could see the skepticism in her eyes.

"Try it, if you'd like," I said. "Maybe then you'll see."

MY PERSONAL PERSPECTIVE isn't all that's changed since my first trip to Bhutan in the winter of 2007; so has much in the kingdom.

In advance of the coronation in November 2008, a dog pound was temporarily erected and a new sterilization program launched. Of the estimated 1,200 strays in the city, 360 were spayed or neutered. As a consequence, the canine population has been seriously reduced, and it is now possible to walk the street without being mobbed. Although at night it's still common to be serenaded by the howls of both strays and house pets.

Despite the cries of the existing papers that there was not enough advertising to go around, three new papers were granted licenses to operate. The kingdom's first daily, *Bhutan Today*, began publishing in time for the coronation in November 2008. One eight-page issue in early 2009 was crammed full of reports that illustrated the impact of Bhutan's association with the outside world. A cover story, in English, lamented the continuing demise of the main language, Dzongkha. One student was quoted as saying the influence of Western movies and fashion and the "coolness" of speaking English leads people to be uninterested in speaking the native Bhutanese tongue. On page two, an editorial lamented the same concern raised by the Kuzoo advisor Madame Carolyn the year before, that more Bhutanese celebrate Valentine's Day than Losar. The same piece railed against the hypocrisy of the national ban on the sale of tobacco and how it made smoking seem even more alluring. In an editorial titled "Professional Fools," the writer deemed "weird" the recent announcement by the government that there was room for only 40 percent of the Class Ten students to continue their studies, and wondered, "Where will the rest go?"

In 2008, an enterprising Nepali tailor began an alteration service to make it easier for foreigners to wear the Bhutanese national dress without an army of assistants. For about three dollars, she'll custom alter a half *kira* so that it wraps easily around the middle and is fastened with Velcro and hooks that adjust to your inevitably changing waistline. It falls exactly like a half *kira* would if you put it on the traditional way.

There are now infinitely more karaoke machines in the capital city than the two that existed in early 2007. The most interesting is at the Tiger Bar on Norzin Lam, for it allows you to sing along in Dzongkha.

Toilet paper is now a far more common amenity in various public restrooms than it was during my first visit.

Evidence of a growing leisure class abounds. Shades of Starbucks are evident in coffee shops that debuted on opposite sides of Thimphu in the fall of 2009 and have created a market for what had once been a rare find in the capital city: brewed, takeaway caffeine. There's also now a wine shop, which features a small selection of French, Australian, and even a couple of California vintages in addition to several from India. The first fast food to come to the city is also an import from Bhutan's giant neighbor; it's a franchise called Hot Dog. (Which happens to have been launched by Pema from Kuzoo, along with her entrepreneurial Indian boyfriend.) A second, called Tsab Tsab, Dzongkha for "fast fast," is modelled after McDonald's.

Not long after the two-lane Thunder Bowl opened for business in a subterranean location in the center of Thimphu, a second movie theater debuted in a rapidly growing area at the edge of the city. This one boasts a state-of-the-art sound system. (The run-down theater in the center of town is still mobbed, despite the fact that it hasn't been cleaned in thirty years.) Each theater plays only Bhutanese films. The number of movies being produced is declining, though, as filmmakers encounter the difficulties of recouping their investments.

The grand $450-a-night Taj Tashi hotel debuted in the center of town in the spring of 2008, and though it mirrors the Bhutanese-style architecture around it, its stateliness is a bizarre contrast to the rest of the buildings nearby. It caters mostly to visiting dignitaries and, at mealtime, an occasional sampling of the city's small expat crowd. It features a spa, a pricey bar called Ara where you can order martinis, and a swank Sunday brunch buffet, not unlike any other elegant tourist hotel in the world. Critics have wondered if it is sacrilegious for the hotel to have used common Buddhist religious artifacts as hardware throughout the grounds, such as horns for door handles.

Sometime in 2010, the Bhutan Post intended to begin delivering mail residentially, after assigning the city's first-ever street addresses. A postal code was also in the works; the absence of one can make sending packages from outside the country a challenge. FedEx now delivers to Bhutan, but posts a long list of restricted items.

There continues to be some confusion over how to refer to the four queens now that their husband is no longer king. Specifically, should the honorific Queen Mother be used for all four wives, or should that be reserved only for Ashi Tshering Yangdon Wangchuck, since she is the one who actually gave birth to the man who now reigns over Bhutan?

Rumors that the new king ordered the removal of painted phalluses from the sides of buildings throughout the country because some tourists found them offensive turned out to be unfounded. The phalluses remain.

And the authentic Bhutanese temple built on the National Mall in Washington, D.C., in the summer of 2008 for the Smithsonian Folklife Festival was acquired by the University of Texas at El Paso. UTEP's president has been advised to check with astrologers about the most appropriate location on the grounds, as well as the most prudent date for the work to begin.

As for Bhutan's new democracy: Their first session saw heated internal debate about sitting fees for members, what they should be paid over and above their salaries for the days they must appear in session. After criticism in the media, the idea of the fees was dropped, but the elected officials awarded themselves a car allowance, as well as a subsidy to pay for a driver.

A year into the first term, the National Assembly banned television cameras from covering their deliberations live. They argued that the complexity of the discussions confused the citizens. One critic said the parliamentary members' real concern was that they themselves don't really understand the issues and didn't want their constituents to see. The National Council immediately reversed course and said they would continue to allow live coverage of their proceedings. Even in its infancy, democratic governance appears to be disappointing, if not polarizing, the people. "I didn't expect they'd do anything except look out for themselves," one young man said to me in the winter of 2009. "Only His Majesty has our best interest in mind."

EPILOGUE: LOOSE MOTION

T HE BRIGHT SUN DOESN'T QUITE OFFSET THE CHILL
in the air, but the incline of the walk up to the giant
Buddha statue makes it feel a bit more temperate. It is a
few weeks before Kinga Norbu's first birthday. He's home
with Ngawang, sick with a ferocious cold; Pema and I decide
to take this Saturday jaunt anyway, even though they can't
come along. She's wearing sweats and carrying a backpack,
and we're both wearing sunglasses and jabbering our way up
the hill like the two old friends we are by now. We discuss
Pema's new job at an organic products manufacturer, men, the
state of the world, and gossip involving our various mutual
friends. Pema's thrilled with the latest gift I've brought, a little
Louis Vuitton purse. It's another hand-me-down from my
friend Barbara. Pema can't believe how kind this woman she's
never met has been to her. I can't believe I keep aiding and
abetting Pema's brand-goods addiction, even if all it involves is
being a Sherpa.

A group of boys passes us; they make a disparaging remark
about the two *chilips,* which is rude slang for foreigners. Pema

is flattered to be so incognito that she's unidentifiable as a Bhutanese, but also wants to put the boys in their place, so she starts
nonchalantly speaking to them in their native tongue about
the weather and where they're going. Turns out they're headed
to the Buddha, too.

Though they climb up through the woods and we stay on
the paved road, built in anticipation of the carloads of visitors
who will one day make this voyage, we arrive at the construction site at about the same time. A caretaker allows us in,
breaking the rules since there's no work taking place today.
When I was here last year, there was just a clearing; now the
Buddha has begun to take shape, and the distinct gleam of the
140-foot structure peeks dramatically through the mask of
scaffolding. I wonder if when it's complete it'll look majestic
or Vegasesque or a bit of both. The boys are taking pictures.
We do, too.

"I love you, Lisa Jane," shouts Pema, as she snaps away at
the Buddha; then she trains her point-and-shoot camera on
the ever-widening footprint of the Thimphu Valley below.
There are so many cranes and construction sites mirroring the
one before us that it looks like a giant game of SimCity. "I love
you back, Pema Lhamo," I say, and for a minute I forget how
odd it is that I have this lovely friend, all these lovely friends
on the other side of the world from my home. It feels less odd,
really, than it does lucky.

IN THE WINTER of 2010, three big things were occupying the
minds of the people in Thimphu. The first was the premier
occupant of a new six-story structure next to the clock tower.

As weary Indian laborers frantically tacked on the roof, curious customers packed the ground floor of Druk Punjab, Bhutan's first commercial bank, sipping the free tea and eagerly signing up for new accounts. The bank was an outpost of an Indian concern, and it promised a critical link to the outside world that neither the established government-owned banks, the television, nor the Internet could: ATM cards that would work in India and in Bhutan, making it possible to travel for business or pilgrimage without wads of cash. There were other enticements, too: lower interest rates on loans that made it easier to build a new house or to buy one of the new cars from the fancy showrooms cropping up on the outskirts of the city. All this was big news in a place where just forty years ago there wasn't any cash money and where the idea of institutional lending to the masses was still a cutting-edge concept. The pièce de résistance was the bank's promise to introduce in a few months the ultimate trapping of capitalism: credit cards.

As if to tamp down the encroaching acquisitive spirit just a bit, and remind the Bhutanese of their Buddhist roots, a series of meetings was being held by educators during the annual winter break to discuss exactly how to introduce the fundamentals of Gross National Happiness into the school curriculum. Lately the Bhutanese elite had begun to feel that outsiders were doing a better job of examining and practicing the national philosophy than they were themselves. A lama was deployed to teach meditation skills to the assembled principals of the schools; by taming their minds, the thinking went, they'd be better equipped to help their students tame theirs. The prime minister graced one of the sessions with a four-hour speech that summed up his concerns:

Our challenge is that schools [should] not produce selfish economic animals who are only motivated to succeed at the cost of relationships, environment, and family. We have to convince the children that what parents have has nothing to do with who they are. Our little country, once so blissfully isolated in a remote corner of the Himalayas, seemingly protected by high mountain peaks, wisely and peacefully governed by a lineage of great enlightened monarchs, is now buffeted by powerful forces we could not have imagined or conceived just a generation ago. Though some have brought benefit, those powerful forces are not always benign, and some of them threaten not only our profound heritage but even our lives and land.

What the prime minister *didn't* mention was that the latest powerful force to ruffle Bhutanese prayer flags had come at his invitation, in the guise of the international consulting firm McKinsey & Company. This merry band of bright-eyed young MBAs, dispatched from McKinsey's offices in next-door India, had been hired for $9.1 million. Their mission was to evaluate the nation's inner workings and mine them for greater efficiencies and value. After a months-long inquisition at each of the ministries, the McKinseyites had handed down a wide-ranging series of observations and recommendations about how to better "brand" Bhutan. Chief among them was a push to monetize the GNH thing, for GNH was seen as Bhutan's most alluring (and therefore its most marketable) asset. To achieve this, the McKinsey team proposed nixing the tourist tariff and allowing guests to book directly with hotels; there would be no more wiring thousands of dollars to tour operators you'd never met in order to secure your visa, guides, drivers, and Druk Air tickets. The idea was to make it as easy as possible for tourists to enter Bhutan and ramp up the number of annual visitors to the country from 27,000—the high to date—to 100,000 a year.

Those in the travel industry expressed fear that by eliminating the barriers to entry, the mystique of Bhutan as an exclusive, elite destination would be damaged. What they really feared was that the government was trying to put all but the best-established travel professionals out of business. Others worried that Bhutan might someday soon resemble Nepal, jammed with spiritual-seeking backpackers. Still others snarked that what McKinsey was recommending was simply not possible: If filled to capacity for 365 days, the two jets owned by Druk Air would hold only 93,000 humans. It seemed delusional at best and irresponsible at worst to imagine that a place that had worked feverishly for so long to keep the world out could possibly consider allowing so many people in. And more practically, they lacked the infrastructure to accommodate them all. Besides, how would those who did venture to Bhutan deal with the cult of spicy hot chilies? Bhutan was on the brink of yet more change, this time at the hands of highly paid advisors who wouldn't have to live with the consequences of their recommendations.

I'M NOT SURE I've ever been so cold; I don't remember it being this frigid here in the winter. I'm in bed under the covers in a not-shabby hotel, far better than the guesthouse where my hosts first stuck me when I arrived last week, where the only thing covering the window in the bathroom was a sheet of newspaper and fleas danced off my suitcase. This room's a suite, and boasts a modern convenience not widely available in Bhutan: a wall-mounted electric heater. Not that it chugs out any measurable warmth—the room's too big, and the draft seeping in from the half-inch crack in the patio door is too ferocious. Central heat and insulation are inventions that haven't quite made their way here, much less the luxury of a warm bathroom. Even locals grit their teeth through their wintertime ablutions.

All the clothing I've got on isn't offering much protection. Two layers on the bottom, four on top, a huge scarf from Bumthang that Ngawang gave me when I arrived, and a Yankees World Championship 2009 skullcap covering my head and ears. Oh, and fluffy pink chenille socks. I just took my hands out from under the three blankets to grab my cell phone and text in my vote for singer number 6 in the Druk Star contest the Bhutan Broadcasting Service has been running. Her shy smile and sweet trill captured my attention. From my woefully inadequate understanding of Dzongkha, I deduced that she's from a tiny district in the eastern part of the country, and that made me root for her all the more. For twenty seconds, number 6 diverted my distress over my frozen nose; plus she drowned out the cacophony of howling dogs—soprano, alto, and baritone—outside my window. At least this time, by overdosing on Cipro and carefully policing what I eat, I've managed to stave off that awful affliction of the stomach, euphemistically known as "loose motion." Which is, come to think of it, the best way I can think of to describe the changes that are unfolding so rapidly here in the so-called last Shangri-la.

What I'm wondering at this moment (besides how I'm going to scurry to the toilet in this cold for the inevitable middle-of-the-night pee) is what to make of this McKinsey recommendation. My predisposition was to mistrust the suits. But maybe something positive would emerge from this odd marriage. For one thing, what purpose was that long-standing $200-a-day charge for all outsiders serving, really? The government took $65 off the top; the leftover $135 had given a generation of Bhutanese the illusion that they could become rich as tour operators, even if they had no interest in that kind of work. Even without the tariff, because of Bhutan's size and location, it would be difficult for it to become as jammed with visitors as Nepal or India. Wouldn't it? Besides, the Bhutanese were doing a fine job of polluting and littering the landscape themselves. An animated commercial on TV implored youngsters to stop tossing trash on the streets, and a recent report showed ten new cars a day entering Bhutan's roads. Just the other day I spotted a woman drinking from the first disposable cup I'd ever seen here.

The government argued that expanded tourism would lead to more jobs, which were necessary to employ the growing population. Sixty percent of the residents were under the age of twenty-nine. They were better educated than the generations before them and had been watching TV for a decade, acquiring sophisticated wants and desires that could no longer be fulfilled on the farms and in the villages. Every day I heard another tale of another nanny crammed into a New York City apartment and supporting four Bhutanese back home. These incomes funded the purchase of apartments, cars, and siblings' educations back on the other side of the world, and fueled the aspirations of an alarming number of young people in Bhutan, too. Buddha, schmudda: In the front window of the public library hang children's drawings of Santa Claus. "I wish we had Christmas in Bhutan," reads a caption, "so we could get presents." Bhutan is facing a dilemma that belies the premise of Buddhism and of Gross National Happiness: It's human nature to want an easier way of life. And more stuff.

Maybe the MBAs from McKinsey could impose some order on the chaos of Bhutan. Case study: The circumstances under which I'd come here this time would make even the most junior of strategic consultants' heads spin. The woman who invited me to make this trip, a high-level official at the Tourism Council—arguably the most powerful agency in Bhutan given that it brings in tens of millions of dollars to the country each year, which is second only to the revenue from hydropower exports to India—has gone missing. A friend of hers had told her I was looking for another volunteer gig, and she had written to say she urgently needed my help, for six months if possible. To my surprise, I found myself balking at that kind of commitment but agreeing to a two-week trip so that we might at least get acquainted. I confirmed the dates of my stay with her, and her assistant arranged the visa and local travel. When I arrived after my long journey—familiar, but no easier now that I've done it five times—my hostess was mysteriously absent. And no one who works for her quite knew what to do with me.

Almost a week after I arrived in the country, the mystery was solved. A friend in the States wrote to tell me of a report he heard on public radio that mentioned that the queen of Bhutan (the reporter didn't get into the minutiae of how this particular queen was actually one of four) was appearing at the renowned Jaipur Literature Festival in India to promote her book. My would-be hostess, a woman charged with helping revamp the entire nation's future, is also expected to attend to her queen; when the queen goes on a trip, this woman is expected to accompany her. No one considers that her two roles might create a conflict. No one thinks it strange that I schlepped around the world, at my own expense, to find no instructions have been left for me. (I wonder what the McKinseyites, who preach the language of efficiency, must think of the idea that the royal family still takes precedence in this democracy. I also wonder how long it is before anyone—at the newspapers, in the private sector—openly starts investigating the finances of the royal family. Even in the burgeoning age of investigative journalism, that would still be unthinkable now.)

Royalty has back-burnered my purportedly urgent mission. I know better by now than to be surprised by this. And yet, this time it annoys me. A lot. I don't want to be here, a *chilip* in the land of chilies. I want to go home. I love this city, even if it is becoming ever grittier and more congested; the streetscape of Thimphu has infiltrated my dreams. For so much, I owe Bhutan an enormous debt of gratitude. But this is not where I belong.

The view of the valley out my hotel room window is the same angle as that of the live shot on the BBS after-hours filler. I squint and wish I could transform the twinkling lights of the city before me into what I can see from my apartment window in Los Angeles.

It occurs to me that if I shift the bed away from the wall and in front of the heater, I might soak up a bit more of its warmth.

FOR A FEW days now—without much else to do and after hanging out with the staff of the new weekly newspaper, *Business Bhutan,* and running into old friends—I've been trading text messages and emails with the opposition leader, Tshering Tobgay. He's statesmanlike in an Obamaesque way, super-smart, direct, striking, and accessible to the people through various channels: his blog, Facebook, Twitter. I met him briefly two summers ago in a shop in Thimphu, where I was buying a cell phone recharge voucher and potato chips on my way back to Kuzoo, and he breezed in to pick up a snack for his daughter, who was waiting in the car.

"Hey, I just saw you on TV," I said. This was before the National Council voted to prohibit televised proceedings of its debates.

"Yes." He smiled. "And who are you?" I explained that I'd been volunteering at Kuzoo. It turned out he'd heard my reports from the Smithsonian Folklife Festival and was a fan of public radio from his time at Harvard. That radio job may have driven me a bit batty, but it sure offered street cred.

Now, a couple of years later, here we are on a windy winter afternoon at Karma's Coffee, sitting with our dueling Mac-Books over a series of hot brewed coffees, commiserating about Bhutan's future like two old friends. I share what I've managed to glean about the McKinsey plans, how the MBAs are making lists of sacred sites and landmarks around the country and figuring out how to rank them as "products." The various districts of the country are being broken down into "circuits." "The Eastern circuit," as the young, smiling McKinsey lady describes it, will be where meditation centers are developed for Westerners who wish to travel to the "spiritual heartland" of Bhutan, as if there is such an actual location, and pay thousands of dollars to live authentically through homestays with the locals. Meditation centers in the last Buddhist kingdom? Isn't that like building igloos for Eskimos? Land is currently being claimed under rules of eminent domain and regional airports are being developed so that future visitors won't have to suffer through the rocky, undulating, death-defying twenty-four-hour drive across the country on the national "highway." Soon the previously underexplored side of Shangri-la, home to unspoiled natural wonders and simple farm people, will be more easily accessible to the outside world. How simple and unspoiled would they remain as a consequence?

Tshering Tobgay is worried. He also knows that the widely held belief by Bhutanese about how rich outsiders are is a myth. "People here think you all have weeks and weeks of vacation time, too," he says. "As if you can just dash around the world for a few weeks with kids." Another thing that disgusts him is the business of "teaching" GNH in the schools.

"Not everything is demand and supply," Tshering Tobgay says, lifting his fourth cup of coffee. "You can't teach Gross National Happiness and inner peace. Next thing you know, McKinsey will be recommending that we buy an ad in the Super Bowl, like we're Coca-Cola."

With that, he lifts up the lid of his MacBook and whips out his cell phone. "Have you been reading the blogs? People are so angry about all of this," he says. "Now, if you will please excuse me for a few minutes while I conduct a little business."

I rise to leave, and he motions for me to sit down. First, he calls his webmaster, and then makes a series of calls to the media outlets to alert them to a press release that has just this moment been posted to his blog. In between, he directs me with a grin to his site, where he says what practically everyone I've been talking to, including my tourism department hostess, has been saying—but won't say publicly. The new constitution offers freedom of speech, but that document doesn't trump the hidebound tradition of loyalty to the state:

> The Opposition Leader called on the Minister of Economic Affairs . . . yesterday to express the Opposition Party's concerns on the Royal Government's recent policy decisions on tourism. . . . Liberalizing the tourist tariff will undermine the positive brand image that our country has carefully cultivated and enjoyed over the last three decades. . . . A target of 100,000 tourists per year by 2012 may be unsustainable and undesirable, given the country's existing absorptive capacity and small population base of barely 600,000 people, most of who still live in scattered communities.

The opposition leader takes his title very seriously. As he works the phones to drum up a little media attention, I savor my ringside seat to the new democracy in action. Maybe next time I see Tshering Tobgay he'll be Bhutan's second elected prime minister.

THE NEXT DAY, I'm waiting outside the offices of the Tourism Council of Bhutan for a friend to pick me up for lunch. A man passes by and asks where I'm from; even in Thimphu, it's still not common to see foreigners, especially at this time of year. "Los Angeles," I say. "California. United States. And you?"

"Luentse," he says wearily. It's a remote district in Bhutan's untrafficked northeastern corner. I had just read about this corner of the country in the travel materials last night; there are hardly any roads there, the residents are unfettered by modernization, and few outsiders have trod the pristine, un-developed terrain, which offers spectacular flowers and natu-ral beauty. Just the kind of place the McKinseyites are working to commoditize.

"I would love to see that," I said solicitously, although I wonder how my stomach would handle the food. "I hear it's very beautiful."

"To you it may sound beautiful." He smiles as he gets into a Toyota Land Cruiser. "To us it is backward."

ON THE LAST NIGHT of my stay, Ngawang and Mr. Japan stop in to say good-bye. They are coming from the hospital; the baby is better, home with the mother-in-law, but now it's his father's turn to be ill. He's availed himself of the free health care, as many people do, to make sure his flu is really just a flu. No wonder the McKinsey report has declared this system fi-nancially untenable in the long term.

As we sip ginger tea made by Pema's new organic-products employer, we discuss the frustrations of my visit, Ngawang's displeasure at the ratty guesthouse where I was first housed, and how upset she is that while I volunteer and pay my way here, $700-a-day consultants are deployed for events like the GNH conference, which she'd covered for her new weekly show on the topic. I shrug and say it's okay, really.

"Money is important, especially now, so I can buy things for Kinga Norbu," Ngawang says, "because if he's happy, I'm happy."

I tsk-tsk as Mr. Japan looks at her sideways. He smiles his thoughtful smile, amused by his wife but not annoyed by her.

"I used to think money mattered more than GNH," he says. "But now I'm not so sure. I see those poor African people on television, and they seem very happy, even if they don't have much."

He looks weary; I know it's far colder in their house than it is here in my hotel room. No wonder they've all been sick. I ask him if he'd like my Yankees cap, and as he takes it, he gives me a warm hug. So does Ngawang, apologizing that we've not been able to spend more time together on this trip. They both remind me of their standing offer to visit their family in the countryside. After they head out into the darkness, I turn on the BBS and slip under the covers. I want to fall asleep to the sound of my friend Namgay reading the newscast, and wake up in the morning with the chanting monk who begins each broadcasting day.

THREE WEEKS LATER, I'm back in Los Angeles, recovered from the jet lag and the bone-chilling cold, and I happen to check Facebook in the middle of the day. There's a recent posting by Aby, one of the editors at *Business Bhutan: Tourist tariff to be $250 a day 365/7 as of 2011.*

The simplicity of the sentence urgently conveys "breaking

news." I start searching the Net for more information but can't find any. Then I call up the opposition leader's blog. At about the same time as Aby's post, Tshering Tobgay has tweeted this: *Travelling back to Thimphu. Heard the good news that govt has decided to scrap its plans to liberalize tourist tariff.*

It isn't until the next day that I get more information from another Bhutanese friend, in the form of an email. He tells me that the buzz of dissatisfaction on the streets led the prime minister to sit down with members of the tourism industry; as a result of the talks, the tourism tariff liberalization has been declared dead. Indeed, the government decided it shall be raised. That doesn't mean the hope of attracting more tourists is diminished; that goal remains the same, but a commitment to tourism that also preserves Bhutan has been made. A victory for free speech and public outcry.

In the same batch of email, I receive two other Bhutan-related messages. One is from the friend of a friend of a friend, a retired high school principal in Canada who wants to "step out of her comfort zone" and volunteer in the kingdom, a dream she's long had. Can I help her find a way? The other is from a Bhutanese friend's eighteen-year-old daughter, who has been granted a scholarship to a college I've never heard of in remote Minnesota and needs to come up with $12,000 in boarding fees. Can I help her get a job? "An old-age home, a nanny, anywhere," she implores, and I know she really doesn't understand what Anywhere, USA, means or how hard it is to make and save that kind of money.

I find myself inclined to help the first lady and to question and lecture the girl. But first I decide to go for a walk outside in the California sunshine.

ACKNOWLEDGMENTS

LIFE IS A SERIES of random events that thread together in ways that lead to sometimes sweet, often spectacular, perhaps transformative, experiences. This book could not have come to be were it not for myriad fortuitous meetings over the course of my decades, several of which collided over the last several years to lead me to Bhutan.

To that end, I must first thank my old dear friend Harris Salat, who introduced me to my new dear friend Sebastian Beckwith, who introduced me to the country that captured my heart. (That chain of connections traces back to when I was a teenager, when our family friend Adam Cohen introduced me to Hampshire College, where I met Mary Batts, who later insisted I meet Harris.)

Jeffrey Tuchman introduced me to Barbara Osborn, who told me about her husband, John Drimmer, who led the happiness class that helped me begin to see the world more positively even before I ventured to Bhutan.

Had Merrill Brown not gotten me hired at MSNBC a decade ago, I might not have met Bob Sullivan there, who introduced me to Jill Schwartzman at Random House, who then connected me to Dan Conaway at Writers House, who prodded my unformed musings about Bhutan into this book and became a dear and trusted advisor and friend, whom I can never adequately thank. Dan's assistant, Stephen Barr, is the epitome of a positively wired human with whom it is a delight to interact.

Tina Constable, Kristin Kiser, and Heather Jackson at Crown invested in the project, and in me, for which I am eternally grateful; Lucinda Bartley, and ultimately, Sydny Miner, deftly shepherded the project to its end state and out into the world. Thanks to the entire Crown team for their enthusiasm and support.

To the many people who make me feel welcome in Thimphu, among them: Ngawang Pem and Sonam Penjor; Pema Lhamo; Phub Dorji; Sherab Tenzin; and the original staff of Kuzoo FM, particularly Sir Pema and RJ Kinzang; Choki Wangchuk; Ian Alexander-Bell; Patrizia Franceschinis and Lyonpo Ugyen Tshering; Choeki and Ugyen at Rabten Apartments.

Hans Keller, Penny Siekfer, Mark, Kat and Andy Schiffler; Ed Hanzcaryck; Pam Maruoka; Mayumi Futamura; Kunzang Choden and Walter Roder; Peter Hansen. Sandee at Seasons fed me when David Havens wasn't hosting meat night at his apartment behind Villa Italia. Ugen Choden, Kuenga Gyaltsen, Dawa Sherpa, and Bruce Bunting at the Bhutan Foundation, along with Preston Scott and everyone involved in and around the Smithsonian Folklife Festival.

A special thanks to KB Lama for being such a dear and frank friend.

In the United States, I am grateful for Rev. Kusala Bhikshu

at the IBMC, all my teachers at the Ketchum YMCA, and to the Bunker Hill swimming pool (in particular, my neighbor and fellow swimmer George Moore). And for my friends and former colleagues at the public radio show *Marketplace*. A special hug to Bill Slemering for his support.

The resources and support of the Library of Congress (in particular the Asian Reading Room), the University of Texas at El Paso (Special Collections Library), and the Los Angeles Public Library proved invaluable. Willie Quinn, thank you, and the same to Dr. Diana Natalicio. Pam and Kurt Meyer clued me in to the very existence of UTEP.

I am blessed with an abundance of dear friends, but there are several in particular who slogged alongside me patiently during these last several years: Matthew Mirapaul, Bernie Woodall, Liz Dubelman, Paul Slansky and Grace Slansky, Alistrone Berger, Katherine Stern, Preston Wiles, Elizabeth Kaplan, Brian Averna, Jimmy Suskin, Barbara Rybka, and Maggie Curran. Joe Hutsko has long been my chief writing cheerleader.

And to all my family, including and especially my parents, Vince and Jane, Aunt Kay, and my dear brother, James.

Last, thanks to everyone who has ever graced my home on a Friday night, particularly the regulars . . . but especially to the greatest surprise, who appeared at just the right moment, namely Ted Habte-Gabr, and the Wagner family conspiracy to connect us.

Speaking of which, here's to believing that the next person you meet could very well be a source of adventure, if not an agent of change.

SELECTED BIBLIOGRAPHY:
IF YOU ARE INTERESTED IN
LEARNING MORE ABOUT BHUTAN . . .

THIS IS A SELECTION of books, articles, and Web sites about
Bhutan. On the list, I've included an indispensible volume
about Buddhism written by a Bhutanese, along with a movie
made by that book's author that was filmed in the kingdom.

It is by no means an exhaustive bibliography of all that
has been written about Bhutan—there are certainly others in
the relatively small collection of published material about the
place. And over the last two years, in conjunction with the
centennial of the monarchy, many photographic and illustrated books have been released by small presses.

What is listed here, however, would provide the curious
student of Bhutan as much as he or she could possibly learn
without moving there. Links to these materials can also be
found on my personal Web site, www.lisanapoli.com.

Aris, Michael. *Bhutan: The Early History of a Himalayan Kingdom.* Warminster, England: Aris & Phillips, 1979.
————. *The Raven Crown: The Origins of Buddhist Monarchy
in Bhutan.* London: Serindia Publications, 1994.

Choden, Kunzang. *Bhutanese Tales of the Yeti.* Bangkok, Thailand: White Lotus Press, 1997.

———. *Chilli and Cheese: Food and Society in Bhutan.* Bangkok, Thailand: White Lotus Press, 2008.

———. *The Circle of Karma.* New York: Penguin Group, 2005.

———. *Folktales of Bhutan.* Bangkok, Thailand: White Lotus Press, 1994.

Collister, Peter. *Bhutan and the British.* London: Serindia Publications with Belitha Press, 1987.

Davis, Samuel. *Views of Medieval Bhutan: The Diary and Drawings of Samuel Davis, 1783.* London: Serindia Publications; Washington, D.C.: Smithsonian Institution Press, 1982.

Doig, Desmond. "Bhutan: The Mountain Kingdom," *National Geographic* 120, no. 3 (September 1961).

Dorji, Kinley. *Within the Realm of Happiness.* Thimphu, Bhutan: Produced by Siok Sian Pek Dorjee, 2008.

Dowman, Keith, and Sonam Paljor, trans. *The Divine Madman: The Sublime Life and Songs of Drukpa Kinley.* 2nd ed. Middletown, CA: Dawn Horse Press, 1998.

Khyentse, Dzongsar Jamyang. *What Makes You Not a Buddhist.* Boston: Shambhala, 2007.

Lipsey, Rick. *Golfing on the Roof of the World: In Pursuit of Gross National Happiness.* New York: Bloomsbury, 2007.

MacLaine, Shirley. *Don't Fall Off the Mountain.* New York: Norton, 1970.

Meyer, Kurt, and Pamela Deuel Meyer. *In the Shadow of the Himalayas: Tibet, Bhutan, Nepal, Sikkim; A Photographic Record by John Claude White 1883–1908.* Ocean City, NJ: Grantha Corporation, 2003.

Pommaret, Françoise. *Bhutan: Himalayan Mountain Kingdom.*

5th ed. Translated by Elizabeth B. Booz and Howard Solverson. Hong Kong: Odyssey Books & Guides, 2005.

Rustomji, Nari. *Bhutan: The Dragon Kingdom in Crisis*. Delhi; New York: Oxford University Press, 1978.

————. *Enchanted Frontiers: Sikkim, Bhutan, and India's Northeastern Borderlands*. Bombay: Oxford University Press, 1971.

Scofield, John. "Bhutan Crowns a Dragon King," *National Geographic* 146, no. 1 (October 1974).

Solverson, Howard. *The Jesuit and the Dragon: The Life of Father William Mackey in the Himalayan Kingdom of Bhutan*. Montreal, Canada: R. Davies Pub., 1995.

Todd, Burt Kerr. "Bhutan: Land of the Thunder Dragon," *National Geographic* 102, no. 6 (December 1952).

Travellers and Magicians. Directed by Khyentse Norbu. New York: Zeitgeist Films, 2005.

Wangchuck, Ashi Dorji Wangmo. *Treasures of the Thunder Dragon: A Portrait of Bhutan*. New Delhi; New York: Viking, 2006.

White, John Claude. "Castles in the Air," *National Geographic* 25, no. 9 (April 1914).

————. *Sikhim and Bhutan: Twenty-one Years on the North-East Frontier, 1887–1908*. London: E. Arnold, 1909.

Williamson, Margaret D. *Memoirs of a Political Officer's Wife in Tibet, Sikkim, Bhutan*. London: Wisdom, 1987.

Yadav, Lal Babu. *Indo-Bhutan Relations and China Interventions*. New Delhi, India: Anmol Publications, 1996.

Zeppa, Jamie. *Beyond the Sky and the Earth: A Journey into Bhutan*. New York: Riverhead Books, 1999.

NOT ONLY HAS Bhutan never been colonized but Christian missionaries have not had much luck there, either. In the seventeenth century, two Jesuits made their way in. The account of their interactions with Bhutan's then leader, the Shabdrung Ngawang Namgyal, is on the Web, here:

Baillie, Luiza Maria. "Father Estevao Cacella's Report on Bhutan in 1627." *Journal of Bhutan Studies* 1, no. 1 (Autumn 1999). http://www.digitalhimalaya.com/collections/journals/jbs.

WEB SITES

Media

KUZOO FM
WWW.KUZOO.NET

CENTENNIAL RADIO
WWW.THIMPHU101.BLOGSPOT.COM

BHUTAN BROADCASTING SERVICE
WWW.BBS.COM/BT

KUENSEL
WWW.KUENSELONLINE.COM

BUSINESS BHUTAN
WWW.BUSINESSBHUTAN.BT

BHUTAN OBSERVER
WWW.BHUTANOBSERVER.BT

BHUTAN TIMES
WWW.BHUTANTIMES.COM

BHUTAN TODAY
WWW.BHUTANTODAY.BT

Nonprofit Organizations

BHUTAN CENTRE FOR MEDIA AND DEMOCRACY
WWW.BHUTANCMD.ORG.BT

BHUTAN FOUNDATION
WWW.BHUTANFOUND.ORG

CENTRE FOR BHUTAN STUDIES
WWW.BHUTANSTUDIES.ORG.BT

TÂRÂYANA FOUNDATION
WWW.TARAYANAFOUNDATION.ORG

VAST: VOLUNTARY ARTISTS' STUDIO, THIMPHU
WWW.VAST-BHUTAN.ORG

Government

NATIONAL PORTAL OF BHUTAN
(OFFICIAL GOVERNMENT SITE)
WWW.BHUTAN.GOV.BT

THE CONSTITUTION OF THE KINGDOM OF BHUTAN
WWW.CONSTITUTION.BT

TOURISM COUNCIL OF BHUTAN
WWW.TOURISM.GOV.BT

About the Author

Before Lisa Napoli fell in love with Bhutan, she chronicled the dawn of the Internet era as a reporter and columnist for the first Web site of the *New York Times,* and later as a correspondent and columnist for MSNBC. She most recently worked as a reporter and fill-in host for the public-radio show *Marketplace.*

Earlier in her career, Napoli directed two short documentaries about southern culture and field produced coverage of the 1992 Clinton presidential campaign and the Waco standoffs.

A native of Brooklyn, she is a graduate of Hampshire College in Amherst, Massachusetts. You can learn more about Bhutan and the author at www.lisanapoli.com.